LUXURY AND THE RULING ELITE IN SOCIALIST HUNGARY

STUDIES IN HUNGARIAN HISTORY
László Borhi, editor

LUXURY AND THE RULING ELITE IN SOCIALIST HUNGARY

VILLAS, HUNTS, AND SOCCER GAMES

―⦵―

GYÖRGY MAJTÉNYI

Translated by Thomas Cooper

INDIANA UNIVERSITY PRESS

This book is a publication of

Indiana University Press
Office of Scholarly Publishing
Herman B Wells Library 350
1320 East 10th Street
Bloomington, Indiana 47405 USA

iupress.org

© 2021 by György Majtényi

Photos © György Majtényi, Dr. Sándor Tóth, Hungarian National Archives, Institute of Political History

All rights reserved
No part of this book may be reproduced or utilized in any form or by any means, electronic or mechanical, including photocopying and recording, or by any information storage and retrieval system, without permission in writing from the publisher. The paper used in this publication meets the minimum requirements of the American National Standard for Information Sciences—Permanence of Paper for Printed Library Materials, ANSI Z39.48-1992.

Translation funded by the László Tetmajer Fund of the Hungarian Studies Program, Department of Central Eurasian Studies, Indiana University-Bloomington.

Manufactured in the United States of America

First printing 2021

Library of Congress Cataloging-in-Publication Data

Names: Majtényi, György, author.
Title: Luxury and the ruling elite in socialist Hungary : villas, hunts, and soccer games / György Majtényi ; translated by Thomas Cooper.
Other titles: K-vonal. English
Description: Bloomington, Indiana : Indiana University Press, [2021] | Series: Studies in Hungarian history | Includes bibliographical references and index.
Identifiers: LCCN 2020030754 (print) | LCCN 2020030755 (ebook) | ISBN 9780253055910 (hardback ; alk. paper) | ISBN 9780253055927 (paperback ; alk. paper) | ISBN 9780253055934 (ebook)
Subjects: LCSH: Elite (Social sciences)—Hungary. | Power (Social sciences)—Hungary. | Wealth—Hungary. | Hungary—Politics and government—1945–1989. | Hungary—Social conditions—1945–1989.
Classification: LCC HN420.5.Z9 E45513 2021 (print) | LCC HN420.5.Z9 (ebook) | DDC 305.5/209439—dc23
LC record available at https://lccn.loc.gov/2020030754

LC ebook record available at https://lccn.loc.gov/2020030755

To Kata and Márton

CONTENTS

Introduction *1*
1. In the Manor House: A New Elite Is Born *13*
2. The C(adre) Line: Consumer Habits *30*
3. Tradition and Innovation: The Hunt for Concordance *114*
4. Meetings between the System and Its People *173*
5. Luxury: Public and Semipublic Spaces *220*
6. Stain on the Blue Sofa: Luxury and the Elite *287*

Afterword 305

Bibliography 307

Index 331

Index of Names 344

LUXURY AND THE RULING ELITE IN SOCIALIST HUNGARY

INTRODUCTION

INITIALLY, I DID NOT WANT to write a book. First, I wrote an essay in which I pieced together a few mosaics from the life of the party elite in Hungary in the 1950s,[1] but I kept stumbling upon new information on the subject. Friends and colleagues called my attention to texts and data with which I had not been familiar or about which I had simply forgotten. A few ideas began to take shape in my mind—ideas that seemed worth further research—and the subject began to interest me more and more. The horizon of the question itself broadened. From the perspective of chronology, the frame of reference expanded both forward and backward. I was curious to acquire a subtler understanding of the group of communist politicians who comprised the elite in Hungary in the postwar period, and I was increasingly eager to know more about the customs, internal rules, and traditions that this elite inherited, created, and passed on. I began to consider an ever more diverse and extensive array of sources, the individual sections grew into chapters, and the chapters coalesced into a book.

The book was published in Hungarian in 2009 with a print run of ten thousand, which in Hungary is an impressive figure. The first edition sold out, which suggests that the subject aroused the interest of a reasonably broad readership.[2] When the possibility arose of having the book translated into English, I took the manuscript in hand again and made both revisions and additions that, I very sincerely hope, will be of interest and use to the international English-reading audience. The paternalistic style of politics that prevails at the moment in Hungary made some of the details of my original inquiry exciting, relevant, and almost palpable for me, and it unquestionably offers new parallels for further comparative analyses.

The most interesting part of research for the historian is the process of gathering sources and data—that is, the investigation stage of a project, which, for this study, proved remarkably difficult. The archives contain documents from offices and bureaus that functioned at the time, and, quite understandably, the themes of the files did not include the lifestyles of the leaders of the communist regime. Even when this issue did make it onto the agenda at meetings of the highest bodies of the party, characteristically euphemistic language was used. For instance, the villas of the party leaders on Béla király Avenue (a street in a wooded neighborhood in the hills of Buda) were in an area referred to as *szabadság-hegyi* (freedom hill). The prominent hill was given this name by the regime after the Second World War, and the name lasted until 1991. At that point, the name was changed back to the historic name, Swabian Hill (Svábhegy). The parking garage where the party leaders parked their luxury cars was called the Transportation and Technical Enterprise of the Party Administration and Management Division of the Central Committee of the Hungarian Socialist Workers' Party. Only a few party leaders wrote memoirs, and those who did primarily offered explanations of their own historical roles. Thus, the conversations that I had with people who had been part of the milieus of the former elites (for instance, hunters and waiters) were indispensable to my inquiry.

The structure of the book begs some explanation. For methodological reasons—and also because of the nature (or, more precisely, the dearth) of sources—I do not approach the object of my study from a single direction. Rather, I consider the perspectives of many contemporary observers as an acknowledgment of the plurality of viewpoints and interpretations. The events follow various threads, and from chapter to chapter I switch subjects and perspectives. In a given subsection, I might focus on the story of an important figure, and then in a subsequent section, I examine the roles of a different set of players. Sometimes these figures cross paths as the various plots of the narrative intertwine, and sometimes they part ways. The protagonists of the story did not differ from one another simply in their backgrounds or the contexts in which they lived, of course, but I would not have been able to have provided detailed character delineations. A diverse array of other walk-on actors pops up in the course of the drama (if I can be permitted to continue to use this metaphor from theater life). In the end, the various threads of the drama, including the repetitions and revisited sites, actors who return again and again to the stage, bring the reader back to a setting similar to the one where the story begins.

The conclusion of the tale is the beginning of a new historical era—the regime change of 1989–1990—which can be understood as a period in which the country labored to recover from socialism, or at least so it seemed for a long time. The historian, however, must be sensitive not simply to the passing of time—that is, the past (in Hungarian as in English, one can draw a distinction between the "past" and the "passed")—but also to continuities and the present. In other words, in addition to scrutinizing so-called historical processes, the historian must give due attention to permanencies that endure across the historical eras that are so often mapped according to the simplest linear understanding of time and defined from political perspectives. Thus, as I note on several occasions in the book, the historical narrative has bearings on the present, and I make concerted efforts to call attention to the interconnections and overlaps.

In terms of its genre, this book would perhaps be most appropriately characterized as a historical essay. Indeed, it is something of a blend of various kinds of texts—including the essay, the scholarly treatise, and even works of belle lettres—and various relationships take form between these different kinds of texts. One of the virtues of the essay is that it permits one to cross the borders between genres. The writer can move freely between everyday description and conceptual and even abstract representation. The essay is a genre in which, more often than not, critical opinion plays the primary role, not some notion of timeless knowledge beyond appeal.[3] Mikhail Epstein has called attention to the virtue of the essay as a democratic genre. Whereas the logic of other "mythologies"—for instance, the logic of totalitarianism—is founded on authority, the mythology of the essay—a mythology of private ownership—derives from authorship. As Epstein writes, "[Essayism] is an attempt at leaving intact, in the heart of a new, non-totalitarian totality, the experience of insecurity and the sphere of possibility, the sacred Montaignesque 'I cannot' and 'I do not know how,' which is all that remains of the sacred in the face of the pseudo-sacralizations of mass mythology."[4] Thus, the essay is an appropriate genre with which to begin to deconstruct the unified pictures (portrayals of power and society) crafted first in the spirit of totalitarian (state socialist) ideologies and later as denunciations of these ideologies. The essay is a subjective genre. It permits articulation of the divergent stances of various (historical) figures and even the most personal form of writing: the expression of one's own opinion. It also offers greater freedom in writing and style. We refer to this as *essayism*, borrowing the term suggested by Robert Musil in his novel *The Man without Qualities*.[5] My book was conceived in the spirit of essayism, and I make no secret of this. This is how I explain, or, more precisely, justify the at times personal tone, which, of course, is fundamentally always the decision of the author (like the choice of genre itself).

One of the fundamental tasks of the historian is to shape our relationship to the past, and this relationship cannot rest simply on understanding who did what and why and who accepted what and why. For this reason, I have striven to adopt an active, analytical (creative) stance toward the texts on which my inquiry is based and the context in which they were created. As postmodern theory reminds us, the writing of history is a profession, with its own recognized and recognizable rules. *Metahistory*, Hayden White's seminal work, has inspired many historians.[6] His essential thesis statement is that the critical perspectives used in narratology can be applied to the writings of the historian specifically because these writings are texts with authors (whether they are well written or poorly written, and whether the author is aware of their underlying narrative structures or not). In the subsequent paragraphs, I would like to outline the narrative strategies I have used in this book, both deliberately and, given the topic, inevitably.

One can also analyze historical texts on the basis of their emplotment, their argument, and their ideology. If one approaches them from the perspective of their emplotment, then historical texts can be characterized as romantic, tragic, comic, or satirical. If one approaches them from the point of view of their argument, then they are formist, mechanicist, organicist, or contextualist. If one considers them from the perspective of their ideology, then they are anarchist, radical, conservative, or liberal. Thus, since there are four versions of each of the approaches a historian might adopt and sixty-four ways of fashioning a historical narrative. Indeed, there are significantly more, since the historian (and more generally the various authors) do not choose poetical tools in the purest form, but rather mix these tools to create new narrative implements. (And one can imagine far more categories than those identified and used by Hayden White.)

In terms of its emplotment, this book perhaps most resembles a satire, and it has the ironic tone of a satire. The stories about the elites of the time betray the complete relativism of the prevailing value system.⁷ The everyday life of the communist party leaders was characterized by the utter disharmony between a vision of the desired world based on ideological standpoints and real life. One can decipher the individual explanations for this pattern of life, but one can also discern the points of interconnection between them as well as the external points of reference that also gave common meanings to the everyday lives of these elites. The study of the lifestyles and daily lives of the elite can also shed new light on the power relations and the functioning of "high politics" in a dictatorship.⁸ I primarily use irony as a stylistic tool to distance myself from the subject. In general, the use of irony has both aesthetic and moral underpinnings. It offers a rich interpretive experience, but it also constitutes a moral position, since it is a tool with which one establishes distance, and it does not permit unconditional identification with the past or with the actors of history.⁹

My argument rests very much on an understanding of context (in this sense, it is contextualist),¹⁰ since the texts I draw on can only be interpreted if placed in their proper context. Naturally, the phenomenon itself—that is, the life of luxury of the elite of the socialist era—could also be presented through a comparative analysis of the similarities among the socialist systems. I limit myself, however, to a depiction of the phenomenon first and foremost in the context of Hungarian society. This context largely determined the interpretations that could be associated with the lifestyles of the ruling elite in Hungary under the state socialist regime. If we draw sharp distinctions between eras of history, then we notice peculiar relationships between them as well as various forms of mechanical inevitability. In my inquiry, I touch on several eras in the political history of Hungary in the twentieth century. For readers less familiar with this period of Hungary's history, I offer a brief overview here.

In the interwar period, Miklós Horthy, who had once served as an admiral in the Austro-Hungarian navy, ruled Hungary as regent from March 1, 1920, until October 16, 1944. Hungary was formally a (restricted) parliamentary democracy, but autocratic tendencies gradually strengthened as a result of Nazi influence and the Great Depression. Hungary joined the Axis powers in the Second World War and took part in the war on their side. However, on March 19, 1944, German troops occupied Hungary, and on October 15, 1944, the regent was replaced by a puppet Nazi government. Following the fall of Nazi Germany, Soviet troops occupied Hungary, and after a short democratic period, the country became a socialist state, adopting the totalitarian state model of the Soviet Union. This was the beginning of a socialist dictatorship that would rule for more than four decades, from 1948 to 1990. From the perspective of political history, these forty-plus years can be divided into two distinct periods named after the party leaders: the Rákosi era (1949–1956) and the Kádár era, which began with the suppression of the 1956 revolution (1957–1989). Mátyás Rákosi was the general secretary of the Hungarian Workers' Party from 1948 to 1953, and János Kádár ruled the country as first secretary and later as general secretary of the Hungarian Socialist Workers' Party from 1956 to 1988. State socialism ended with Hungary's peaceful revolution of 1989—that is, with the regime change. These periods can be characterized differently on the basis of the political systems and the ruling elites. However, there were important overlaps and continuities between them as well.

If one interprets history from White's organicist approach and regards the past as a single, continuous process, one might well ponder (in the striving to ascribe some independent meaning to the passing of time) the question of how the antidemocratic traditions of the Hungarian elites shape the present, or, more generally, one might simply reflect on the power of these traditions. Why is it that even today both politicians and everyday people in Hungary often see the example for the future in the dictatorial leaders of bygone eras?[11] The fundamental questions are whether to study the various historical eras in isolation from or in comparison with one another, and the perspectives to adopt when studying them.

Historians who adopt a contextualist or formist analytical strategy—investigating the historical phenomenon in its own context or in the linguistic reality of its texts as something unique and independent—reject the imaginative idea that different historical eras are phenomena essentially identical in type and essentially accessible to interpretation on the basis of a uniform and consistent approach. They also reject the notion of a mechanical regularity that determines historical changes. In doing so, they disrupt the coherence of a retrospective overview. That is, in essence, they upset the notion of a coherently unified history. History can be understood as a kind of delicate "embroidery."[12] We can only unstitch the fabric if we are able to follow the individual threads and the underlying design, and it is only worth unraveling if we examine how things are intertwined. Thus, a given era can only be understood if we grasp its interconnections—in other words, if we examine its texts, looking back, emphatically, from the present. No writing is unbiased, and the perspectives and hopes of the historian fundamentally shape her message. However genuinely she may strive to see the past from the perspective of the past, the historian's decisions remain decisions of her present, and her choices are choices of her present. However, the explanation for why events went the way they did often follows from the logic of the process through which the events are brought to light. In the end, a great deal depends on the emplotment of the narrative.

In terms of its ideology, the horizon of my analysis is liberal—and in some cases, radical. I do not endeavor to offer a dispassionate description. I examine the world of the state socialist system in comparison with the recognized values of liberal democracies. I do not think that an analysis of the lifestyles of the ruling elite of state socialism in Hungary provides a general characterization of the conduct of any prevailing elite, the continuities that emerge in the lifestyles of the elites notwithstanding. My study is a personal reflection on the workings of the system, including the society in which it functioned (and which it shaped) and the heritage it left. Thus, from the perspective of both its structure and tone, my text bears affinities with the genre of the essay and the aforementioned mix of styles.

This book, however, naturally is not first and foremost about itself or the intentions of its author, but rather about the object it seeks, in an array of manners, to depict. It is my hope that in the following chapters, while always considering the potentials and limitations of cognition, I have taken strides toward saying something substantial about the lifestyles of the ruling elite in socialist Hungary. I endeavor to do this through a reflective, critical presentation and analysis of the sources, which enable me to examine the object of inquiry from various viewpoints and in various spaces and moments of history.

As I conclude this introduction, I would like to make a few explanatory remarks about the book and the ways in which it might be read and used. Though precise use of terminology is always important, I consider stylistic considerations equally significant. I was not overly concerned with dogmatic consistency in my use of terms such as *socialism, communism,* or *state socialism.* These words always take on different connotations in different texts anyway, and their meanings cannot be clearly and indisputably circumscribed. I did take care, however, to take different shades of meaning into consideration. For instance, under socialism, *communism* was considered an unattainable utopia. *State socialism*, in contrast, was considered more of a scientific term. This very difference in the connotations and functions of the two terms vividly illustrates the gulf between the original Marxist ideal and the actual systems that were created in its name. In the text, I vary their use according to the context. The historian can never allow the question of chronological distance to slip her mind. If she happens to make a pronouncement in the nonsense language of the functionaries of the socialist era, she inevitably takes a step in the direction of the ideological view of the world from which she seeks to maintain her distance. I hope that I have not fallen into this trap. At the same time, I use certain terms in my narrative, such as *objektum* (or "object"; the word in Hungarian has a decidedly mannered tone, as if uttered by an ideologue insistent on ignoring the chasm between socialist discourse and socialist reality), which were very much a part of the discursive world of the socialist system. I have also mentioned certain figures (for instance, Comrade Zamushkin, who made pronouncements concerning the ideological implications of fashion) who, similarly, were instrumental in the crafting of this world.

Finally, I take this occasion to express sincere thanks to the many people whose assistance and encouragement were invaluable to me in my work. I am grateful to all the people who read the manuscript and made deletions and additions. Their critical remarks helped me weed out redundancies, imprecisions, inconsistencies, and other blunders in the text. Furthermore, they called my attention to additional sources and relevant information. I am particularly grateful to Zsombor Bódy, Tamás Csáki, István Csízi, Sándor Horváth, Magdolna Kárpáti, Anna S. Kosztricz, József Ö. Kovács, Arthur Kulcsár, Balázs Majtényi, Judit Anna Majtényi, László Majtényi, Balázs Mészáros, Péter Móczán, Péter Rostás, István Papp, István Simon, András Sipos, Eszter Zsófia Tóth, Sándor Tóth, Tibor Valuch, Valéria Enikő Varga, and the first and last person to read the manuscript, Bea Majtényi. I am also grateful to the people who helped me in my work by unselfishly sharing memories, documents, and photographs: János Aracs, Mrs. Kálmán Berényi, Ottó Feiszt, László Földes, Nándor Hajba, Károly Hetényi, György Kalmár-Maron, Károly Marton, Tibor Meskál, Mrs. Katalin Endre Beretz Nagy, Antal Rácz, Béla Rakeczky Jr., Pál Rosenberger, László Sándorfalvi, László Somogyi, György Tollner, Sándor Tóth, Tibor Vadnai, and Jenő Váncsa. I also owe thanks to the László Tetmajer fund for supporting the translation and particularly to László Borhi, who managed this project, and to Herbert Sophia and Lesley Bolton, who also assisted the publication of this book. I would like to express my gratitude to Thomas Cooper, who translated the book into English, and to Carol McGillivray, who oversaw the copyediting of the English manuscript; they also provided me with advice and suggestions. Their contributions greatly enriched this book, the failings of which, whatever they may be, are mine and mine alone.

NOTES

1. Majtényi 2007.
2. Majtényi 2009.
3. Epstein 1999. Other writers and philosophers, including Musil 1995 and Adorno 2003, have praised the essay for its expressive power. Works that offer overviews include Butrym 1989 and Klaus and Stuckey-French 2012. György Lukács 2010 considered the essay a genre that was still taking form.
4. Epstein 1999, 156.
5. Musil 1996. Musil writes in his "On the Essay," "For me ethics and aesthetics are associated with the word essay," since "it is the strictest form available in an area where one *cannot* work precisely." Musil (1914) 1995, 48.
6. Hayden White 1973.
7. As Sheila Fitzpatrick argues, "As a historian's strategy, studying the everyday is a good way of subverting assumptions made on the basis of formal political and social structures and codified ideologies." Fitzpatrick 2014, 390.
8. Cavender 2014, 37; Fitzpatrick 2014, 396.
9. The work of the historian is founded on imagery and figures of speech, which, according to White, can be reduced to four master tropes: metaphor, metonym, synecdoche, and irony. These tropes, White suggests, determine the various styles of works of historical inquiry. Metaphor and metonymy are tropes that dominated in earlier eras of traditional history writing (the Renaissance and the Classical period), while synecdoche is characteristic of the modern era, and irony is characteristic of the postmodern era. Quite clearly, for White, irony is the most appealing approach to the past. Hayden White 1973.

10. The organicist seeks general principles and regards history as a natural process. The mechanicist, in contrast, works from the precept that there are laws that determine the course of history. The contextualist examines phenomena in their particular contexts and in the historical circumstances in which they took place. In other words, the contextualist seeks to understand a phenomenon in the networks of relationships of the given moment. The formalist, in contrast, offers what is first and foremost a poetical analysis. Ibid.

11. In Hungary, debates between so-called left-wing and right-wing intellectuals often culminate in disagreements over assessments of the Kádár and Horthy regimes. Majtényi 2013.

12. See Hayden White 1973, introduction.

ONE

IN THE MANOR HOUSE
A New Elite Is Born

"THE VILLA WAS LIT WITH lanterns and decorated with colorful silk paper. To the right, in front of the entrance, stood hunters in full attire, to the left the youth of the party, garbed in blue shirts and red scarves. For the man of the day was not only a party man, but also, naturally, a hunter. To the side in the parking lot there were some American limousines, two Soviet military vehicles, several motorbikes, and some coaches. There was also a police car."[1] In his memoir, Fülöp Merán, the scion of a family of counts, reports on an emblematic event of 1946, the birthday of the Csákberény party secretary. "On a long table there was roasted pork, caviar, turkey. And also wild boar, roasted pheasant, and stuffed goose. From crystal pitchers they pour the strong Merán wine that had been confiscated from our Csókakő and Orond vineyards. There are ladies present, some attractive and dressed according to the new fashion. The hostess is also elegant and beautiful." Merán's description of the party also mentions the host: "The party leader turned 40 today. He is in high spirits, and he is a rather likable character."[2]

The above snapshot, which offers a rather idyllic depiction, demonstrates that there were interactions between the old and new elites in post–Second World War Hungary. Obviously, one can also envision the meeting of their two ways of life in the dynamics of cultural and social processes through which elements of a new lifestyle flow into the old one, transforming, absorbing, and overwriting old patterns of behavior. Presumably, much as some of the customs and habits of given individuals did not disappear with the change of regime and the rise of the socialist system, the customs and habits of whole social groups also did not simply vanish without a trace. Lifestyles changed only slowly. People's habits and mentalities cannot be transformed from one day to the next. Just to mention one example, according to the recollections of one of their late descendants, members of the Zsolnay family—a traditional bourgeois family that owned and ran a ceramics factory of worldwide fame—would never have stooped to serving a meal out of a saucepan at the dinner table, even when out of necessity the head of the family was forced to work at the Nagytétény rubber factory making condoms.[3]

While the old social circles cultivated their traditions, new people and new groups were tending to follow or adopt the old consumer habits. Fülöp Merán does not fail to mention, in his memoir, the accordionist at the Csákberény birthday reception, who played a revisionist song titled "Prague Is Not Far from the Border." The song tells of promises to reclaim the Hungarian territories lost after the First World War according to the terms of the Treaty of Trianon: "Although Andy [the accordionist] seemed to be on good terms with many of the people in power, on the inside he may have been 'reactionary.'" In the discourse of the time, the term *reactionary* referred to adherents of the Horthy regime. Naturally, the historian cannot profess to know how Andy felt on the inside, only that he performed as a virtuoso accordionist under both regimes. He first played for József Mindszenty, archbishop of Esztergom and the Catholic prelate of Hungary, and later for Mátyás Rákosi, secretary general of the communist party—much to the delight of both.[4]

One of my intentions in this inquiry is to examine dissimilarity and analogy, new directions and continuity, the habits of the new elite that emerged after the Second World War and the perpetuation and dissolution of the lifestyle of the traditional aristocracy. I use the term *ruling elite* to denote a particular group distinguished by its privileges and its ruling position—a group whose lifestyle was characterized by the exploitation, to the greatest extent possible, of the prevailing power relations.[5] In this chapter, I endeavor to gaze through the windows of the imaginary manor house in which Hungarian party leaders first learned traditional patterns of behavior and then created new ones. I also consider potential parallels and analogies to this Hungarian story and the interpretive perspectives they offer.

I examine the group of communist leaders who rose to power in the postwar era and their lifestyles through the notion of the ruling elite. Whenever a term from the social sciences is used, the point of departure of the analysis is always determined by how the category is interpreted; and vice versa, the term that is chosen determines the approach. In other words, our attitudes toward the object of our research determine this object, and the object determines our attitudes. The social science term I have chosen—the category of the *elite*—is rich with ambiguity from the outset. To address this ambiguity, I will begin by offering a detailed explanation of how I use this category, how my use of the term relates to other texts and interpretations, and how the object of my study is tied to these texts and interpretations by referential associations.

There are two classic works on the ruling class and the elite: Gaetano Mosca's *The Ruling Class* and Vilfredo Pareto's *The Rise and Fall of Elites*.[6] Neo-elitist writers, such as Harold Lasswell, moved away from the concept of the so-called natural elite (distinguished by their personal characteristics) and connected the category to the notion of power, explaining the legitimacy of elites through the concentration of power.[7] Accordingly, members of the elite group secure their dominance over other social groups through their power status and their use of power tactics. Therefore, the circle of the political or power elite can at least in principle be identified as those who possess the most important positions in a given society. Initially (and often later), the use of the term *elite* constituted a strong criticism of democracy, because it implied that in parliamentary democracies, institutions of democratic political representation and participation do not function effectively.

Historical sociological analyses classify the group coming to power not only as a ruling elite but also as a ruling class. According to Marxist class theory, the ruling class is the representative of power; several neo-Marxist authors therefore identify this class with the dominant group of modern societies: the elite.[8] In the Marxist meaning of the concept, the ruling elite of an era cannot be described as a new ruling class with a strong class consciousness. It was, at most, a "privileged class" or social group on the basis of its way of life.[9] I therefore do not use the term *class* to refer to the ruling elite of the postwar socialist era.

Several writers use the terms *elite* and *ruling class* with a critical edge when analyzing socialist systems. The mere use of the term *elite* and the acknowledgment of the power of the elite indicate that state socialism failed to create a socialist society based on the just distribution of goods and property and, in fact, created little more than a dictatorial regime.[10] The application of the two terms implies that communist leaders deviated from the ideology on which the system allegedly rested not only in their exercise of power but also in their lifestyles. The emergence of an elite within a society is closely related to the prevailing forms of political participation. Naturally, these forms of participation are different in democracies and totalitarian dictatorships. Due to the nature of the state socialist system, the elite of the time can be studied on the basis of the operational logic of party-state institutions—in other words, control of the most fundamental positions.[11] Under the Soviet regime, the party headquarters theoretically supervised the channels of selection directly. They founded bureaucratic institutions such as the various local chapters of the communist party, youth organizations, trade unions, and women's federations, which—although they seemingly represented group interests—were state-controlled establishments. Through these organizations, representatives of power selected future leaders, who also acquired most of their knowledge and experience in these groups. This is how party leaders determined their competency and tenacity.

The leading body of the party-state reserved the right to appoint candidates directly to the most important positions. This system of appointment was called the nomenclature system, and appointees on the nomenclature lists were dubbed the *nomenklatura*, or "nomenclature." Based on census data, Michael Voslensky estimates that in 1959 the nomenclature included approximately 750,000 people in the Soviet Union (and the figures did not change radically between 1959 and 1970). Roughly one-third of these appointees, the apparatchik, may have been affiliated with the political leadership. The rest held important positions in the economic, academic, and cultural spheres.[12]

The most important positions were decided on by a rather narrow circle of the ruling elite. These were members of the highest political bodies: the Politburo (Political Committee) or the Central Committee and the people affiliated with them. Initially, the Politburo included only members of the most exclusive party leadership. In 1919, for example, it included Vladimir Lenin, Lev Kamenev, Nikolay Krestinsky, Joseph Stalin, and Leon Trotsky as well as Nikolai Bukharin, Grigory Zinoviev, and Mikhail Kalinin as candidate members. At the Twenty-Third Party Convention in 1966, the decision was made to limit membership in the Politburo to exactly fifteen members and six to eight candidate members. (The number of top leaders was deliberately restricted to preserve the value of these positions.) It is impossible, however, to determine exclusively by the formal hierarchy who belonged to the ruling elite at any given time. Actual decisions on several occasions were made informally (and not only on questions of personnel). In other words, decisions were made by the secretary general at the time or party leaders affiliated with him. In the Soviet Union and in other socialist countries, higher-level political bodies were formal organizations or, at best, advisory bodies of actual leaders rather than real decision-making forums.[13] Like other communist countries, state socialist Hungary also adopted this nomenclature system.

The organization of the nomenclature, however, was unquestionably a matter of significance in the socialist countries; indeed, some people even attribute a vital role to it in sustaining the regime. According to Stephen Kotkin, the societies of state socialism were uncivil societies, since the nomenclature was the single configuration that functioned as an organized unit (in contrast with other, nonorganized groups).[14] Consequently, through the organization and positions of the contemporary bureaucracy, its interests determined the dynamics of the systems of social distribution. Uncivil logic—that is, the lack of autonomy and solidarity (the practice of exerting clout and serving the interests of a particular group)—was characteristic not only of the establishment (in that it did not simply function from the top down) but rather permeated all of society (in that almost everyone had something to lose or fear). In the end, "paternalistic" policy proved successful, and, until the 1980s, there were few mass protests against the socialist regimes because of social injustices or for any other reasons (with the exception of the uprisings of 1956 and 1968).

Changes of regime (political and social transitions) in the postsocialist countries have been examined from the perspectives of the elites as well. In studies of how the Soviet elite was transforming and changing from a plan-command economy to market capitalism, several authors have noted the important role of the nomenclature's privileges and positions in society.[15] As a consequence of the reforms that were introduced, beginning in the 1980s, the privileges that were enjoyed by the elites gradually underwent a transformation. In the course of the economic changes that took place, these privileges to some extent were placed on free-market foundations, or the benefits enjoyed by the elites were legalized. Previously, the privileges had essentially been goods or properties that had been acquired through the exploitation of position or, in many cases, illegally. Accordingly, the entire economic reform was conducted under the control of the elite and to its financial benefit.[16] East Central European regime changes have been similarly scrutinized from this perspective, as certain groups of the elite of the socialist era tried to transform their political power to economic power at the time of the change.[17] This approach implies that the regime changes can be characterized as transformations that took place against the interest of the communist elite but also—contradictorily but not inaccurately—as a shift that was guided by the communist elite.

According to this interpretation, the regime can be described as one in which an exclusive elite group seizes power by force. Because its power seems implacable to society, it is accepted, and the elite can maintain its hold on power and on the system through which power is exerted as long as this system supports its interests. However, the context in which power is used is obviously more complex than this. Studies in sociology and the social sciences consider *dominance* a more accurate term than *power*. The secondary literature uses the terms *power* and *ruling elite*, but with different meanings. The difference lies in the conceptual definition offered by Max Weber, according to which power is the unqualified realization of central goals in opposition to the goals of others, while authority is legitimate rule accepted from some viewpoint.[18] I use the term *ruling elite* because it indicates that the exercise of power was not unlimited, even in totalitarian regimes. Rule is a social practice; within society, those in power are not entirely independent of other agents, even if they exert more power than other members of society.[19] One of the main issues I examine in this book is the extent to which (and manner in which) social interactions shaped the lives of the elite and how their ways of life could be interpreted in the context of contemporary everyday life—that is, what social practices were associated with the acquisition and possession of positions among the elite.

The social sciences have traditionally attributed to the elites of a given era a significant role in the formation of social phenomena. Recognition of the importance of this role may deepen our understanding of the everyday lives of socialist elites. However, this role derives not from the inventive, cultivated, or distinguished nature of the group but from its dominant position—or from the fact that it controls the majority of the resources. Due to their privileged positions, the elites of any era set an example for society as a whole through the distinctive customs and lifestyles they adopt. Social scientists have offered various theories explaining how the customs of the elite spread across society. Many see the spread of these customs as a process that can be likened to the rise and fall of waves that break and then smooth over, becoming one with the waters again but also transforming the shore. Gabriel Tarde contends that waves of change always begin with the elite.[20] According to the so-called trickle-down theory, when higher social groups establish new patterns, they "pass down" (as it were) the old patterns to the "lower classes." Georg Simmel, for example, used this metaphor to describe the dynamics of society when observing phenomena in the field of fashion. From a different perspective, the cause-and-effect relation is reversed; if other social groups follow the traditions of the elite, then the elite is compelled to introduce new changes in order to distinguish itself from the majority.[21] The behavioral patterns and traditions set by the elite thus gradually diffuse. As soon as these patterns and traditions become a palpable part of the spheres inhabited by other social groups, the elite creates new patterns in order to preserve its territory as elite. Herbert Spencer characterized this as a kind of race, an "imitation in pursuit," in which social domination is at stake.[22]

According to this explanation, various social groups conform, directly or indirectly, to the consumer patterns created by the elite. This approach, which examines social change from the viewpoint of the elite, suggests that individuals adopt bottom-up consumer patterns, meaning that in their everyday lives people look to the customs and lifestyles of the upper classes for their models.[23] However, in the study of social history, it might prove more useful not to mystify the social role of the elite but rather to consider the luxury consumption patterns characteristic of this group from its perspective. From this viewpoint, these consumption patterns appear primarily as acts of social demarcation, or symbols of the striving of the elite to separate themselves from the rest of society. Because every individual and every social class attempts to acquire the most crucial symbols of social status and belonging, it is not the possession or distribution of property that matters so much as the meanings attributed to property.[24]

In the symbolic spaces of society, consumption serves as a means of separation and self-distinction. In their everyday practices, people can differentiate themselves from other individuals and groups.[25] Within the elite, the individual's capacity to authenticate group membership is at stake, as is the importance of emphasis on the elite as a unique community, differentiated from other social groups.[26] Setting the example to be followed or envied is a daily struggle for the symbolic strengthening of vital social positions and the social legitimization of authority. In everyday life, however, consumption naturally means more than this for individuals: It implies the realization of dreams and illusions, where the material goal is of less importance than the striving to attain the images and fantasy worlds associated with it. From the perspective of my inquiry, this striving can also be perceived as the effort to create or justify social positions.[27]

Luxury consumption is a tool with which members of the elite distinguish themselves and establish a seemingly safe distance from others. According to Norbert Elias, as part of the culture of consumption, luxury originated among the aristocracy of royal courts.[28] With the impoverishment of this class, the aristocratic lifestyle and aristocratic habits became representative, to use Jürgen Habermas's term,[29] since this class was only able to fashion its prestige through luxury consumption. This lifestyle, which seemed impossible to imitate, was a way of indicating social differences, and this gave rise to a system of symbols. Interior design, fashion, and even eating habits can all bear symbolic meanings. Luxury means consumption "beyond the necessary,"[30] but, of course, everyone understands necessity differently. Luxury not only refers to the accumulation and conspicuous use of consumer goods but also indicates the possession of "sophisticated goods" that are not available to everyone.

Although we tend to see luxury, by definition, as superfluous, the consumption of luxury items is hardly without a function,[31] even if it was initially seen by most people as a phenomenon of its own. Max Weber contended that the rejection of luxury was one of the reasons why nations at the dawn of capitalism were able to accrue goods and wealth.[32] Others, however, examined luxury from the perspective of consumer habits and found that it functioned as a motivating force both for social groups and individuals. Indeed, the strivings of individual social groups to express their status and outline their contours gave rise to the desire for considerations of quality to dominate and shape patterns of consumption. During the era of embourgeoisement, many people tried to imitate the sophistication of the aristocracy and adopt the customs characteristic of its alluring lifestyle. Richard Sennett deemed narcissism "the protestant ethics of modern times."[33]

In the West, under market capitalism, individuals were able to choose from a wide range of goods according to their circumstances, and thus they were able to establish a particular pattern and lifestyle and convey affinities, demarcate identities, and express desires. In contrast, in the socialist regimes, the possession of goods was determined primarily by the centralized system according to which these goods were distributed. The organs of power bestowed consumer goods and also permitted their production or purchase. From the perspective of the legitimation of the socialist regime, the ability to shape consumer habits and the images associated with the prevailing power by the average person was of particular importance.[34]

These regimes sought to assert their legitimacy not only through means of oppression but also by shaping everyday life.[35] Like states in the West, socialist states also made it possible for their citizens to break away from the everyday world and the impacts of socialist ideology. For instance, in their leisure-time activities, people were often able to move beyond the borders of everyday life, and they created spaces where they were free to move and behave at least to some extent as they pleased.[36] These spaces provided a relative and temporary autonomy from the norms and ideological expectations of the regime. The communist authorities sometimes allowed these manifestations of freedom and sometimes attempted to limit them, thus indicating the presence of power in everyday life.[37]

Luxury consumer customs and goods in which party leaders indulged could also represent the power differences within the socialist society. The question arises, however, how luxury and the consumer ambitions to which it gave rise could find expression in an ideological and political environment that was hostile, at least in principle, to the very notion of luxury.[38] In all likelihood, the answer lies in individuals' inclinations toward narcissism. As Sennett observes, "Narcissism sets up the illusion that once one has a feeling, it must be manifest—because, after all, 'inside' is an absolute reality."[39] This "feeling" presumably included personal experiences of power and positions of rule. Individuals could thus express that they belonged to the ruling elite. If someone indicated through his lifestyle that he met the expectations of the community, he justified his position in his own eyes and strengthened it in the eyes of others.

Memoirs have been written on the special privileges and distinct lifestyles of the Soviet elite.[40] Michael Voslensky contends that they essentially lived in a different country—which he calls Nomenclaturia—whose borders separated the elite from the mundane world of everyday people. Memoirs include detailed descriptions of the lives and privileges of the elites residing in the Kremlin,[41] and a few historical and popular volumes have been written on the distinctive features of their lifestyles.[42] The daily conduct of party leaders and their attitude toward power bore affinities with the lifestyles of the elite in czarist Russia.[43] One observes a similar phenomenon in the various East Central European socialist countries, where elites were attached in some way to earlier traditions, and this defined their attitude toward the societies in which they lived.

The history of the ruling elite in the Soviet Union and other socialist countries offers a context for interpreting the lifestyles and habits of the Hungarian party leaders. It is not immediately obvious that the patterns that were dictated by the Soviet elites actually prevailed in Hungary, but there were unquestionably clear parallels. I am not referring to direct influences, but rather to similarities in opportunity. The historical and sociological secondary literature in Hungary prefers terms such as *cadre, cadre class,* or *nomenclature* to *elite*.[44] Many authors do not consider the term *elite* applicable to the socialist era because of the meanings associated with the traditional social functions of the elite. As Hungarian social scientist István Bibó contends, "The primary duty of the elite is to set patterns and provide examples of how to *live* life, how to *behave ethically* in human situations, and how to deepen, refine, and enrich human wants, in other words, to make culture."[45] I do not use the term *elite* to refer to the alleged historical role of a community that creates and sustains values. Rather, I use it as a descriptive-analytical category to denote a group that separated itself (and can be distinctly perceived) within society. It is worth emphasizing that the position of dominance entails the possibility and function of setting norms, even if there are no accepted values attached to it, since the social standing and distinguished position of the elite mean that its code of conduct affects every member of society. At the beginning of this story, at the birth of the new regime, the most essential question was how the group seizing power related to the traditions of the old elite and which examples it would follow and present to the other groups in the society over which it sought to rule.

In 1946, there was concord in the Csákberény chateau. Guests were singing exclusively "reactionary" songs in unison, to the music played by the accordionist, Andy. The accordion sounded the jubilant chords of the "Radetzky March" (a military march composed by Johann Strauss Sr. that had always been popular among Austrian and Hungarian aristocratic circles) and then "The Blue Danube" (a waltz composed by Johann Strauss Jr. that was an essential part of the balls held by the Viennese and Budapest aristocracy). As people began to feel increasingly festive, they stuck pengő notes to Andy's forehead with saliva. Andy left the building and handed the money over to the drivers. The memoir does not mention whether he complained to them about the unusual behavior of the manor's new guests. When bidding farewell, the regional party secretary, the Soviet officers, and the host (Gyuszka, a miller, rented the chateau at the time) saw the Merán brothers out.[46] Upon leaving, the counts threw a last glance at the old building: "In the dark, the manor house looks like it did in the old days."[47]

NOTES

1. Merán 2000, 53.
2. Merán adds a few remarks expressive of some bias: "Later we learn that the chubbier ones are the nouveau riche and the people who have come with the party members, while the slender beauties are descendants of the old classes. There is even a colonel among them, whose behavior shows refinement." Ibid., 54.

3. Jávor 2000, 272.

4. Merán 2000, 53–54. "He played for Rákosi, he knew Mihály Farkas's favorite song, and on several occasions, he participated in the feasts following religious celebrations, where he met Bishops Mindszenty, Shvoy, and Czapik. He enjoyed unbelievable freedom as he openly played even the most reactionary, 'blacklisted' songs. And my God, how he played them!" Merán 2006, 71.

5. On the concept of the elite and the evolution of this concept, see Bottomore 1993; Kovács 2005, Takács 1998. On the relationship of elite and local elite in Hungary, see Tibor Takács 2008, 27–45.

6. Mosca 1939; Pareto 1991.

7. Lasswell 1934, 1948.

8. Bibó 1986, 226.

9. Fitzpatrick 2005, 86.

10. Voslensky 1984; Easter 2000; Fitzpatrick 1979b; Keller 1963.

11. Marger 1981. On the dynamics of the nomenclature system, see Voslensky 1984. Contemporary and historical studies describing the operation of Soviet authority through the centralization of power include Getty 1985, 1999; Djilas 1966; Gill 1988; Trotsky 1972.

12. Voslensky 1984. On the functioning of this "patrimonial" system, see Getty 2013, 96–146.

13. With regard to the dynamics of the Central Committee of the Romanian Communist Party, Aurel Pițurcă, for example, points out that it functioned more as a consulting unit than a decision-making one. Over time, the organization radically expanded: It had 35 members in 1945, 57 in 1948, and 497 by 1989. Pițurcă 2012, 12.

14. Kotkin 2009.

15. Kryshtanovskaya and White 1996.

16. Suny 1998; de Tinguy 1997.

17. On the transformation of the Czech elite, see Mateju and Lim 1995. Jadwiga Staniszkis describes the beneficiaries of the Polish regime change in a process of "political capitalism." Staniszkis 1991a, 1991b. The Hungarian change is delineated in Róna-Tas 1994; Böröcz and Róna-Tas 1995.

18. Weber 1978, 53.

19. Lüdtke 1991; Lindenberger 1999a.

20. Tarde 1903.

21. Simmel 1904, 136.

22. Spencer 1982, 33–34.

23. Veblen 1994, 52; Simmel 1904, 136. For a criticism of the spiral or trickle-down theory of Simmel and his followers, see King 1963.

24. On competition within socialist societies, see Miklóssy 2014.

25. Concerning the "socialist" middle classes, Krisztina Fehérváry emphasizes that they also defined themselves by their lifestyle and consumption patterns. Fehérváry 2013, 24. On consumption in socialist East Central Europe and Hungary, see Tomka 2020, 147–202, Valuch 2018.

26. In Simmel's view, fashion, for example, is also an instrument that one can use to declare being different from others. Simmel 1904, 479.

27. Campbell 1987.

28. Elias 2005, 53–55.

29. On the concept of representative publicity, see Habermas 2011, 5–14.

30. According to the classic definition of luxury, luxury goods are not essential, but they are high-priced (as is their production), and they are available only to a limited few. De Laveleye 1891, 3.

31. Sombart 1998, 30.

32. Weber 1992.

33. Sennett 2002, 356–360.

34. After the regime change, the German Democratic Republic (GDR) seemed to be a suppressed, homogeneous society, even in the eyes of the mainly "Western" social historians, but later research revealed significant differences in the lifestyles of various social groups. Kocka 1994; Meuschel 1992. (However, Meuschel also mentions a shifting interplay between undifferentiation and redifferentiation, "Wechselspiels zwischen Entdifferenzierung und Redifferenzierung." Ibid., 47.) On everyday life in the GDR, see Lindenberger 1999b, 2011. Some claim that socialist regimes established an alternative consumer pattern compared to the pattern that prevailed in the states of the West. Merkel 1996. Others, in contrast, emphasize that consumption in the socialist states bore similar and perhaps greater significance in the separation of social groups than it did in Western societies. For a summary of the relevant literature, see Bódy 2008.

35. Fehérváry 2009. For example, on the role of "socialist" food in the legitimacy of the regime, see Osokina 2001; Gronow 2003.

36. On socialist consumer cultures, see Crowley and Reid 2012; Bren 2010; Bren and Neuburger 2012.

37. Giustino, Plum, and Vari 2013.

38. Luxury might also be key to a more nuanced understanding of the Soviet systems. Jukka Gronow describes the dynamics of the Stalinist regime through the attitudes of the elite to luxury goods. In his view, the

Stalinist regime of the 1930s attempted to establish a consumption culture that would at least be able to compete with the West. The state sent ministers on research trips to the United States, and, as a result, mass production of certain luxury items, such as chocolate, caviar, champagne, and perfume, began. Gronow views Soviet luxury items as kitsch made in imitation of the West and the traditions of the old Russian elite, because they were mass-produced, cheaper replicas of more expensive goods. Through the mass production of these items, members of the elite attempted to legitimize the system for the people. With patterns of consumption, however, they achieved only symbolic results at best. For example, according to Gronow, in the 1930s an American factory worker would have rarely consumed caviar or champagne, whereas a Soviet worker theoretically could have afforded to do so. Gronow 2003, 33, 145–152.

39. Sennett 2002, 335.

40. Lovell 2002.

41. Alliluyeva 1967, 1969; Khrushchev 1970, 1974. Ilya Zbarski, for a time, worked as the head of the Lenin mausoleum. In his memoirs, Zbarski included references to the habits of the first- and second-generation Soviet nomenclature. Zbarski and Hutchinson 1998.

42. Gorlizki and Khlevniuk 2004 and Montefiore 2004 direct attention more to politics than private lives.

43. Burant 1987.

44. The concept of the elite did not exist in Hungary in the postwar era. Studies on elite groups were no longer pursued after 1945. This essentially meant the elimination of the concept and the exile of the category from the social sciences, but not the elimination of power inequalities. Criticism of the Hungarian state and society of the time was disguised as class theory. Debates on the role and constitution of the elite or the middle class before the Second World War were immediately silenced with the emergence of the single-party system. Opportunities for research in the social sciences and studies involving statistics were limited after the rise of state socialism. (In the so-called people's democracies, the study of social stratification was of key importance. Because it influenced the legitimacy of the regime, this research field was long reserved exclusively for ideologists and propagandists.) According to the "Stalinist model" of social stratification, in socialist societies, two classes and one stratum could be distinguished on the basis of their relationship to the means of production. The two classes were the working class, which was structured around state-owned property, and the peasantry, which depended on cooperatively owned

property. Thus, there were two kinds of workers: those in the state industry and those in the cooperative industry. The stratum was the intelligentsia, which in principle was allied to the two classes. The theoretical model of the unified working class, cooperative peasantry, and intelligentsia (the idea of "two classes, one stratum") essentially made any deeper analysis of social stratification impossible. Most studies of 1950s Hungarian society were based on the conceptual "holy Trinity" of workers-peasantry-intelligentsia. Obviously, such studies must be regarded as products of the dominant discourse.

45. Bibó 1986.
46. Merán 2000, 54–56.
47. Ibid., 56.

TWO

THE C(ADRE) LINE
Consumer Habits

CADRE RIDGE

Budapest, the capital of Hungary, came into being with the merger of three cities (Buda, Pest, and Óbuda, or "Old Buda") in 1873. Most of Pest was built on plains, while Buda was built in the hills on the west bank of the Danube River. Even today, Buda is considered an upscale neighborhood of predominantly freestanding homes and villas. After the war, the lifestyle of the new elite evolved on the spacious estates of Buda, in the shade of old, majestic trees, pleasantly secluded from the urban hubbub and largely concealed from the public eye. In the vernacular of the 1950s, Rózsadomb (Rose Hill) and Pasarét (Pasha Meadow), the two most elegant districts of Buda, were referred to as Cadre Ridge.

It was initially the bourgeoisie who, having wearied of the din of the city, started building vacation homes in the Buda hills in the second half of the nineteenth century.[1] The first people to settle on Rózsadomb were members of the lower middle class. Teachers, postal and railway officials, engineers, and architects built houses on the slopes of the Buda hills.[2] The early houses were modest apartments with two or three rooms, a kitchen, and a pantry, and they did not have running water or bathrooms.[3] In time, the area gained prestige as a residential neighborhood. By the turn of the century, three-, four-, and five-room villas were being built with modern conveniences. New residents moved into the old buildings as well, and they remodeled the buildings to fit their needs. The vacation homes were patched up, and this trend continued later under the socialist regime. Sometimes additional buildings were constructed to complement the existing houses, and occasionally attics were converted to rooms.[4]

At the turn of the twentieth century, the villa district in and around Andrássy Avenue in Pest symbolized wealth, but by the 1930s, builders and buyers started targeting Buda—more precisely Rózsadomb and Pasarét.[5] By this time, the elite and the middle class sought to create an urban environment that was comfortable and luxurious. The issue of representation—that is, expressions of social status and wealth—was of secondary importance. Meanwhile, construction in the area surged. In the 1920s, new residents had exquisite villas built in the historicist style in neighborhoods offering the best views. Some of these villas were constructed on the slopes of Gellért Hill (a hill overlooking the Danube River) and Naphegy (a hill overlooking Buda Castle), along the lower section of Istenhegyi Street (which winds into the wooded hills of Buda), at the beginning of Németvölgyi Street (which also winds into the hills from the area around the base of Buda Castle), and on the eastern slopes of Rózsadomb. Rózsadomb became the "fashionable villa district for the upper middle class, and also for the old aristocracy of descent and the new aristocracy of wealth."[6] Several wealthy entrepreneurs had houses built on Rózsadomb, adding to the neighborhood's prestige. A small villa called Pheasant Garden, which was surrounded by a park, was frequented by the Horthy brothers (the sons of the regent) when they sought rest and entertainment.[7]

At the end of the Second World War, the Nazis also recognized the potential of these hillside villas. In 1944, when Hungary was under German occupation, Adolf Eichmann made his Budapest residence at 13 Apostol Street, in the villa owned by the Neuschlosz brothers (wealthy timber and construction entrepreneurs), which had been designed by the famous Hungarian architect Ignác Alpár.[8] By the 1930s and 1940s, the Buda hills had acquired as much prestige as Andrássy Avenue and the villa district in the vicinity of Városliget (Budapest City Park).

The real breakthrough came after the end of the war, when the ruling elite moved to the Buda hills. Functionaries took possession of both prominent villa districts in Budapest: Andrássy Avenue (including the area around the Budapest City Park) and the hillside neighborhoods of Buda (Rózsadomb, Svábhegy, Zugliget, and Pasarét).[9] Eventually, the latter became the final residence of the new elite. Party and state leaders exchanged their apartments for luxury villas that had been abandoned or that, later, had been confiscated by the state from members of the prewar upper and middle classes. In the heyday of this process of villa occupation, families would occasionally take a horse-drawn carriage to select the building they wanted. The State Commission for Unclaimed Property offered them various types of assistance.[10] Damage from gunfire was plastered over, walls were repaired, and the domiciles were furnished in no time. All the new residents had to do was move in and work for the party. Such work allowed them to maintain their standard of living and keep their new villa dwellings.[11] Traces of the previous owners' lifestyles were not swept away completely. The buildings and the furnishings (which often had been acquired from many different places) reflected their tastes and defined the environment in which the functionaries lived. A similar process took place outside Budapest. In the larger cities, the State Commission for Unclaimed Property also seized real estate and personal properties and then distributed them among cadres who, very often, had been ordered to move to the given city from the capital.[12]

Finally, the Hungarian State Security (Államvédelmi Hatóság, or ÁVH, Hungary's secret police) took possession of the villas.

The ÁVH was under the supervision and control of Zoltán Vas, a top official of the party (who is discussed later). The Hungarian State Security thus assumed the position of the representative realtor of the era as it obtained and allotted the buildings. Families who had been driven out of their homes and forced to flee could purchase passports for 250,000–800,000 forints from the state security officers, and they had to surrender their apartments, villas, furniture, and other properties to the state in exchange for their freedom.[13] Top officials of the Hungarian State Security obtained apartments for their girlfriends as well. The department under Andor Csapó maintained several vacant villas and apartments all over the city for "conspiracy purposes," and some of them were given to the leaders' lovers.[14]

Holding a position in the regime that was gradually emerging after the Second World War meant a distinctive lifestyle and, accordingly, an exceptional standard of living. Cadres received substantial financial allowances,[15] although the allowances varied according to rank, of course. Being issued a house was the primary privilege. In the formation of elite groups, control of institutional and informal positions is always a crucial factor. A more exclusive, informal group existed within the contemporary elite: an inner circle that supervised and controlled the distribution of positions and the system for selecting those who would become part of the party apparatus. There was a similar circle (of forty to sixty members) to which certain privileges were available. For instance, they were given villas or were permitted to hunt in the best hunting grounds.[16] In the 1950s, only the narrowest body of the Hungarian communist party (the Hungarian Workers' Party), members of the Politburo, and certain ministers got villas in Buda. For a simple party member in the central leadership (i.e., a functionary in the wider circles of the party), obtaining a villa remained little more than a dream. Several artists and sportsmen, however, were allowed to move into Buda villas in close proximity to the elite. Party leaders made such decisions at their discretion. In general, artists and sportsmen had a better chance than mere members of the state apparatus of meeting and befriending members of the ruling elite. For instance, poet Lajos Kónya, who was president of the Hungarian Writers' Association, lived next to Mátyás Rákosi. After having won an Olympic gold medal, boxer László Papp asked for Rákosi's help in obtaining permission to build on an estate he had purchased in District 12. The secretary general pulled some strings. Papp was told to discuss the details of obtaining a construction permit with Minister János Szabó.[17]

It is symbolic that Mátyás Rákosi first lived in a villa in Zugló (the official name of District 14) at 25 Szabó József Street and from here moved to Lóránt Street in the Buda hills in 1949.[18] The Szabó József Street villa seemingly met the party leader's needs: It was spacious and had a hall suitable for official receptions. One of the prewar proprietors had even had a garage and a driver's room added in the basement.[19] But at Szabó József Street, Rákosi's life was too visible to the public eye. Passersby could see him when he left or came home, not to mention the black cars in which he was chauffeured and the guards who protected him.

Social distinction is expressed not only by the residences of the elites but also by the ways in which they use space. Beginning in the 1950s, the utilization of space by party leaders was limited almost entirely to public appearances at formal events and prominent sites. Due to their central locations, Andrássy Avenue (which, under socialism, was called Avenue of the People's Republic) and Heroes' Square thus became the theater for the representation and staging of power. As is fairly common knowledge, 60 Andrássy Avenue served as the headquarters of the much-feared Hungarian State Security forces. The elite drew visible and invisible boundaries around themselves. The areas blocked off for processions and parades under arms were the visible ones, and they were used to present what members of the elite wanted the public to see. There was another, invisible world that constituted the sphere of the elite's private life and informal relationships. The decline in the prestige of the Pest villa district is indicated by the fact that, after Rákosi moved out of his postwar residence, the elegant, spired building in Szabó József Street became home to a small-scale enterprise, Delta Electronic and Mechanical Ltd. The once elegant halls, which had served as expressions of state power and clout, suddenly were loud with the clatter of lathing and planing machines.[20]

In 1950, a plan was devised to build separate villas for party functionaries on what had once been the estate of a count on Szabadság Hill. Allegedly, the mastermind was the aforementioned Zoltán Vas, president of the National Planning Office, who was endeavoring to get closer to the "foursome" that ran the party: Mátyás Rákosi, Ernő Gerő, Mihály Farkas, and József Révai. Vas himself was planning to move into one of the new villas.[21] József Körner, an acclaimed architect, was commissioned to draft plans for the Szabadság Hill villas, since he had already designed several elegant houses and vacation homes in the 1930s and 1940s. The buildings bear the stylistic features of socialist realism, but the layouts resemble Mediterranean villas with atriums and pergolas.[22] As András Hegedüs recalls, the buildings contained "real luxury apartments."[23]

However, in the end, the villas did not become permanent residences for party elites of the time. Rather, beginning in 1953, they served as guest houses and weekend homes for members of the Politburo.[24] On the Béla király Avenue lot, a four-story government hotel was built in 1985. After the change of the regime, the area became a virtual "public law village museum," since the president of Hungary, the speaker of the national assembly, and, as of 1998, the prime minister of Hungary all resided in these 1950s buildings of ill repute (the fourth building was used by staff members).[25] Other construction work was underway on the slopes of the Buda hills in the early 1950s. For example, Gábor Péter, leader of the Hungarian State Security, had a new villa built for himself and his lover.

Given the ideology of the regime, which theoretically did not allow private construction, no unified tradition in the construction of villas emerged in the 1950s.[26] It is nonetheless revealing to examine which houses were chosen by the people in power who were eligible to make such decisions,[27] since there was an array of choices from among the properties that had been nationalized.[28] Many modern villas had been built in the 1930s next to the old, classicist, romanticist, or Swiss chalet–style edifices.[29] The new constructions bore the stylistic marks of contemporary European architecture, but another trend simultaneously gaining ground was similar to the German Heimatstil, which was considered Hungarian and nationally distinctive.[30] Interestingly, in contrast with functionalist and modern tendencies in architecture, in the postwar era, the historicist style maintained its popularity. Historicist buildings—with porticos resting on Doric, Ionic, and Corinthian capitals and featuring spires and wooden pediments—must have seemed more appealing to party leaders who were not particularly receptive to modern art. Some party members still chose to move into modern buildings. The Havas villa, located in Hankóczy Street on Rózsadomb and designed by the famous modernist architect Lajos Kozma,[31] became the residence of the president of the National Planning Office Zoltán Vas. He was hardly a committed follower of modern architecture, however. After the editorial board of *Új Építészet* (Modern architecture) published a special issue to commemorate Kozma in 1949, Vas canceled the journal, and, similarly, with the stroke of a pen he eliminated the Modern Architecture Club, which had been founded by Kozma (among others).

In 1949, communist politician Imre Nagy and his family moved into the six-room building at 43 Orsó Street, which also had been designed by Kozma. Nagy would become the prime minister of the revolutionary government in 1956 and the emblematic martyr of the revolution.[32] Family legend has it that it was the street noise (which would have been from the nearby tram line, because there was no automobile traffic in the street at the time) that motivated Nagy to exchange the middle-class apartment (which had several rooms) located at 13–15 Kossuth Lajos Square in the building that today is called the Élysée Palace in the center of Budapest, which he had been given as the minister of agriculture, for a villa in Pasarét.[33] The Nagy family added antique furniture to the original, modernist furnishings of the building.[34]

The villas, however, were not simply stages on which the lifestyles of the new elite could be performed. The traditions embodied by the ancient walls also exerted an influence on the customs and habits adopted by the families of the functionaries. As president of Hungary, Árpád Szakasits, who originally had been a social democrat, set up his residence in Leányfalu, a riverside village in the Budapest metropolitan area. As had been the case in the manor houses of the nobility in earlier times, the rooms and the elegantly furnished parlors were distinguished by color.[35] The estates of aristocrats and members of the upper middle class had not served simply as residences of the illustrious families; they were also spheres for social interaction. The spacious rooms, which also functioned as symbols of status and wealth, were designed to host receptions and gatherings.[36]

In the 1950s, the parlors continued to serve as meeting places for circles of friends and politicians. Families regularly gathered, and decisions concerning issues of power and often the personal fates of cadres were made at these gatherings. The everyday lives of cadre families, however, remained invisible. The villas, which were fully equipped with modern conveniences and surrounded by old parks, offered numerous possibilities for leisure activities. Families met in the parks on weekends. Photographs taken by Erich Lessing in 1956 show Imre Nagy playing with his grandchildren in the park of the Kozma villa that he received—as mentioned above—during the Rákosi era, in

1949. The residence of party leader and minister of defense Mihály Farkas was famous among the functionaries. Their memoirs note that the house included a movie room and a billiards room and that the staff also maintained playgrounds and tennis courts in the park.[37] Of course, the villas also served symbolic functions. Members of the ruling elite could use them to demonstrate their power and influence. Farkas once held a reception for generals of the Hungarian People's Army in order to show them his residence.[38]

The majority of the houses were built on hillsides, so the cellars, the servants' quarters, and the caretakers' apartments were located in the basements. If there was no basement, a separate house was built for the staff toward the back of the plot. To house the person who took care of the vast park, several properties included a dwelling for the gardener.[39] These rooms and buildings were also used by the staff under the new regime. In 1957, Imre Nagy's estate was mapped for the purpose of proposed perquisition (it was referred to as the "object"—*objektum*—an example of one of the mannerisms of the functionary discourse of the regime). According to Ministry of Interior documents, the main entrance of the six-room villa faced the gate, and the side door led to the caretaker's apartment. Behind the villa was a smaller building with a two-room flat equipped with all the modern conveniences. Presumably, it had originally been built for the staff or groundskeepers, but it later served as the residence of Nagy's mother.[40] The Hungarian State Security forces surrounded the property with a tall wire fence, the garden gate was constantly locked, and, naturally, the house and its residents were protected by guards.[41]

The homes of the new elite were always protected by armed guards. This excessive caution sometimes had regrettable results. For instance, when the father of poet Lajos Kónya (who, as noted before, lived next door to Mátyás Rákosi) paid his son a visit, the old man, who was hard of hearing, was shot in the leg by the guards because he did not stop when they warned him. In a letter addressed to Rákosi's secretariat, the president complained: "I was at the Association when my wife called me and told me to come home immediately. By the time I arrived, he [Kónya's father] had already been put in a car to be taken to the hospital. They did not tell me where they were taking him precisely, and no one was allowed to accompany him. I told the guards they had been reprehensible in their treatment of an old man."[42]

The lifestyles of cadres living in luxury were reminiscent of the lives of lords in feudal societies. The domestic staff of Gábor Péter (as noted earlier, leader of the Hungarian State Security) "knew him to be a man who did not appreciate their work and did not particularly like to be around them. He lived a sumptuous life, had more than 40 suits . . . and did not allow his employees to greet him with 'liberty.'"[43] The Hungarian State Security left no stone unturned in Hungary in its search for a cook for Péter, after he had specified the height, hair color, and figure of the woman he wanted to see in the job.[44]

But some of the abuses committed by potentates were thwarted. In 1950, for example, following an accusation and subsequent investigation by the Central Board of Inquiry (Központi Ellenőrző Bizottság), the minister of finance had to resign from his post and was stripped of his membership in the Politburo.[45] Eventually, he was expelled from the central leadership, because members of the Politburo (under pressure from Rákosi) believed "his private and sexual life were unbecoming of a Communist leader."[46] With cases like this one, the Hungarian State Security and the Central Board of Inquiry managed to demonstrate that the lifestyles of the people who had been called to account did not conform to the ideology of the communist system. Communist politician Géza Losonczy, in general not one of the functionaries who extended ideological dogmatism to the sphere of personal life, wrote in a party seminar notebook (using the turgid bureaucratese of the age), "The great communist revolutionaries lived a pure family life, and with Lenin at the vanguard, they condemned those who in their love lives and family lives proved lacking in perseverance, unstable, superficial, or hungry for adventure. Such behavior distracts communists from fighting with all their might in the struggle for the triumph of communism."[47] However, the highest circles of the party leadership sought to supervise and control the private lives of the cadres not for abstract, ideological reasons, but rather simply because they wanted to supervise and control the functionaries themselves. A statement attributed to Tamás Major, director of the National Theater, became something of a mantra in the higher circles of the regime under socialism: "Our dicks are all in the hands of the Central Board of Inquiry."[48]

Functionaries viewed people working for them as their entourage, so the fates of these people were intertwined with the fates of their leaders. In 1951, for example, when János Kádár was arrested as part of the show trials against party leaders launched by Rákosi, also apprehended were Kádár's driver, typist, master of hounds (who was also a member of the Hungarian State Security as the head of the hunting department of the Ministry of Agriculture and had at one point been in charge of organizing Kádár's hunting trips),[49] and bodyguard. The bodyguard was arrested for having a concealed weapon, a detail that pithily captures the irrationality of the age.[50] When Kádár later rose to power, he almost immediately—at the end of 1956—put his fellow huntsman István Dénes back in his former position in the hunting department of the Ministry of Agriculture.

Villas in the 1950s were remodeled to meet the wants of the new leaders. In the trial of Gábor Péter, state prosecutor Andor Csapó described how a swimming pool had been built in his superior's garden:

> The pool had been dug out and the frame support was ready for the concrete. Then, the commander of the party guards complained that the pool was in a visible place, and that's when I learned that higher-ranking party leaders were also going to use it. We ordered

that the gradation of the ground be taken into consideration and the pool be relocated somewhere where it would not be visible. But then Gábor Péter ordered that the whole pool be turned around. So the entire iron framework and pit that had been dug had to be reversed, and in the end that's how the pool was built.[51]

According to Gábor Péter's testimony, Kádár was envious of the swimming pool and ordered one for himself, even though, as Péter said, "Financially, Kádár was better off, . . . of course, he enjoyed beauty and the good life too."[52]

János Kádár acquired the villa of a fellow representative in parliament—a delegate from the Independent Hungarian Democratic Party led by Father István Balogh. Kádár presumably acquired the villa in exchange for helping the politician, a man with a middle-class background, leave Hungary in late 1948 or early 1949, when Kádár was serving as minister of the interior.[53] Why did Kádár choose this particular house, since he could have picked any of the buildings on Rózsadomb? Though obviously the neighborhood has changed, walking around the area today, one notes that Cserje Street (the part of Rózsadomb called Józsefhegy) is the highest point. And something else made the villa special at the time, as revealed in a detail found in the design archive files on the surrounding lots. The 173-square-meter house was virtually the only edifice on Rózsadomb since the 1920s and 1930s that had no buildings on the neighboring plots. When Kádár moved in, he also procured the plots of land above and below his plot, parallel with Cserje Street. Apparently, he simply occupied, or rather annexed, them by putting up a fence. For about another decade and a half, no one asked any questions concerning the ownership of the parcels, nor was there any need to. Kádár was seen by the public as a man of modesty compared to his fellow party members and other East Central European party leaders; that is, he was a man who preferred to remain unseen.

But Kádár did not have much chance to enjoy the pool in his garden. By the time it was completed, he was in jail.[54] At the time of his arrest in 1951, his wife, Mária Tamáska, allegedly left the house with only one suitcase. The furniture was either seized by the new residents or transported to the central furniture repository. First, István Bata moved into the villa, followed later by István Dénes.[55] Hungarian writer and sociographer Árpád Pünkösti quotes Éva Katona, István Dénes's wife: "We were not aware that in the meantime a swimming pool was being built 'in full swing' on the property of the former Minister of the Interior, so by the time we had moved into the building, which as we later learned had been the Kádár villa, there was a pool there."[56]

After 1956, Kádár recovered the house. But following a deliberate image makeover in his new role, he had the pool covered up. Tamáska offers the following explanation of her husband's decision: "The water would have to be heated, which costs a lot, and my husband did not want people to be saying things like, 'oh, but the Kádárs even have a swimming pool.'"[57] The first secretary had hens purchased for the garden, and he fed them potato skins from the terrace. He always showed the most impressive sight to his guests: the Rózsadomb chicken coop. In the morning, government guards fed corn to the chickens, and they locked them in the coop in the evenings. With perhaps the exception of the fact that, as people noted in their memoirs, Kádár was fond of fresh eggs, this was obviously little more than a symbolic gesture.[58] In his 2003 book *Vállalom* (I take it upon myself), János Berecz, who was an influential politician under Kádár and indeed had written works under the regime in which he provided justifications for the suppression of the 1956 revolution, adds an intriguing detail to the legend: "On several occasions, he [Kádár] took delight in speaking of how his neighbor, Gyula Illyés, complained about the rooster waking him up early. He was surprised that Illyés was not accustomed to crowing."[59] Gyula Illyés was a poet and one of the so-called népi writers, or writers "of the people." Illyés did not actually live next to Kádár, but he did live nearby, one street up in the villa owned by his wife's family.

The first secretary had other notable habits, word of which spread among the people. For example, he always smoked the Hungarian brand of cigarettes, Symphonia, and he always used matches to light them. At the auction after his death, the small stool he had kept by his bedside was put up for sale.[60] The public saw János Kádár as a puritanical man.[61] Legend has it that he liked to eat his favorite dish, pasta with grits (or, according to other sources, pasta with cabbage or potatoes) on a kitchen stool in his Rózsadomb residence.[62] People were amazed by the "old man's" modesty and simplicity. Naturally, today we cannot see through the walls of the Cserje Street villa, and we cannot presume to have a more detailed grasp of the everyday life of the first secretary. However, since some photographs of the dwelling survived, we can take an imaginary walk in the apartment.[63]

János Kádár and his wife furnished their residence primarily with used neo-baroque furniture made in the interwar period. In 1989, Tamáska recalled, "As for the furnishings, we bought almost all of them by the piece after my husband had been released from jail. Some we purchased at the consignment store, and we paid for them in installments. The majority of the paintings are originals. Mostly works by [István] Szőnyi and [József] Egry. I bought them, one by one, for my husband's birthdays, at auctions, if I happened across something I liked, and we also received some as gifts."[64] Some of the furnishings the Kádárs quite certainly did not purchase. Rather, they picked them out from among the things in the storage rooms of the party, and many of the paintings were gifts. It is true, however, that they carefully designed the interior. In addition to the paintings by Szőnyi and Egry, the walls were adorned with compositions by József Rippl-Rónai, Gyula Derkovits, and Béla Czóbel—acclaimed Hungarian modernist painters. The floors in the entire apartment were covered with homespun and factory-made Persian rugs. The terrace offered a panoramic view of the city. The rooms for the staff (the housekeeper and the guards) were located in the basement.

The guards lived their own lives, but the comrade woman who served coffee and cognac or whisky for the guests was part of the everyday life of the Kádár family, and she was probably the only member of the staff to enjoy this distinction.

In the house, the living room was considered the space of great symbolic significance. One entered through a small hallway. The main feature was a historicist fireplace with a marble inset and a wooden frame. The living room was furnished as a parlor. In a distinctive manner, the interior combined turn-of-the-century historicism with the interwar neo-baroque. The most valuable piece of furniture was a turn-of-the-century historicist cabinet.[65] The antique interior furnishings were illuminated by an octagonal copper chandelier. Kádár's ornate baroque chess table stood in the living room. The board was fringed by an inlaid scroll. Few people were allowed to play chess here. According to memoirs, an "austere atmosphere" was characteristic of the leadership of the Kádár regime. In his free time, Kádár saw only the so-called club members[66]—the party leaders who were close to him: György Aczél, József Sándor, and Béla Biszku. Occasionally, they were joined by László Orbán, István Szirmai, and, in the early years, György Marosán. But most of the time, they did not meet at Kádár's residence.[67]

The first secretary placed the mini television set he had received as a gift in one corner of the living room, and, allegedly, he only turned it on for the May 1 broadcast. (This may have been one of the reasons why, in his old age, he withdrew and grew increasingly distant from the world outside the walls of the villa and the headquarters of the Central Committee.) On the rare occasions when official guests visited the house, Kádár sat down with them in the living room. For example, photos from a 1970 visit by the president of the Óbuda cooperative farm (which tended to the great park and ancient trees of the villa) indicate that he was offered scotch in a *pálinka* shot glass by Kádár (or, in all likelihood, by Kádár's housekeeper) in this room.

Two more rooms opened off the parlor that guests were able to see. The interior decor in the dining room was the simplest: a modern dinner table with six chairs and a sofa by the wall. A small wooden chest was placed in the corner, perhaps to highlight Kádár's (staged) modesty. The study or library also opened off the parlor. It was furnished with colonial-style and modern bookshelves that held Kádár's book collection. One of the party leader's pastimes (in addition to playing chess and cards) was reading.

Aczél recalls that Kádár "kept rereading Švejk by Hašek."[68] Kádár also liked detective stories and books on hunting. Among the latter, he enjoyed the writings of Zsigmond Széchenyi, with whom he went hunting on several occasions. He also liked the works of the aforementioned poet Gyula Illyés, and at the end of his life, Kádár read Dezső Keresztury's prose and poetry. Kádár was given books by a wide array of authors, so he always had plenty to read.[69]

In contrast with the two rooms described above, the most cozy, secluded place of the house, the bedroom, was elegantly furnished. It was illuminated by a crystal chandelier and lamps in brackets on the walls. Kádár and Tamáska kept the legendary stool beneath the bedside cabinet of the neo-baroque furniture set, which had been made in the interwar period. Photos clearly show that the primitive stool had been carefully stained to match the color of the elegant furnishings. The couple slept in a double bed. According to György Aczél, Kádár was a gentle and considerate husband.[70] The surviving correspondence between the husband and wife also suggests that Kádár had a strong emotional attachment to his wife. Tamáska once wrote a letter in which she beseeched her husband to come home: "My child, write to me, and do not fail to come, because I do not know what I will do to you if you don't listen to me. Perhaps, after all, I will beat you."[71] On another occasion, she wrote, "Goodbye, I promise I will finish for now and go to sleep. With love, Me."[72] It is also true that, when her rehabilitation in the party was at issue, Tamáska once addressed her husband as "comrade."[73]

By the end of the 1980s, the couple had been virtually abandoned, and they lived in the elegant home on their own, relying only on each other. After Kádár was removed from office, he left the party headquarters leaning on his wife. Aczél offered the following description of the scene: "After his fall from power, when he was walking down the stairs with his wife, there were no bodyguards around them, they were not even accompanied to the door out of courtesy, just two lonely old people going down the stairs, a woman in very poor health, taller than her husband, leading the old man by the hand."[74] At home, in an initial moment of agitation, allegedly Kádár turned to his wife and said, "Get dressed and ready, we are leaving this house."[75] In the end, however, they stayed.

"And what a primitive / animal he was: a dictator who loves paprika potatoes, / not tenderloin, didn't even have good taste," wrote poet György Petri, an emblematic figure in the democratic opposition that emerged in the 1980s and 1990s. The poem, titled "Marx," was about Kádár, the dictator, who in his close circles was called "the old man," and to whom the public referred as "Uncle John." But the poem seems unfair. Kádár's style did differ greatly from that of his comrades in Hungary and the other socialist states. Rather, the first secretary simply had a good instinct for public relations. When people thought of him, they did not think of a socialist incarnation of a feudal lord. He seemed different—both from his predecessors and from the other party leaders around him.

After the 1956 revolution, during what could be referred to (with some flair for the ironies of history) as the restoration period under Kádár, new people advanced from the second line to the first and became part of the ruling elite. As early as May 1957, a department of the party responsible also for their wellbeing proposed that the new cadres be settled in downtown villas, a "villa cluster," or a block of apartments similar to a villa.[76] In the Kádár era, the distribution of apartments, which had been under the purview of the Hungarian State Security (which, under Rákosi, evolved into an independent center of authority), was taken over by a party division—or rather, in practice, by Kádár himself. Beginning in the 1970s, the Department of Party Management and Administration of the Central Committee of the Hungarian Socialist Workers' Party controlled housing allocations. The head of the department was always one of Kádár's trusted confidants—first, László Karakas and, later, József Köböl. With the approval of the minister of finance, they could theoretically give a one-million-forint "loan" (which did not have to be repaid) to major cadres who were "in need."

In Kádár's totalitarian regime, the Hungarian State Security, which was made part of the Ministry of the Interior, became the "specialized" institution of oppression. Its sphere of activity was limited to the forceful preservation of domestic order and tasks related to intelligence. By this time, its leaders had no means of overseeing the lives of the members of the party apparatus. Although the system of allocations seemingly became more regulated in the 1970s, personal networks still determined housing allocations. The 1972 party budget earmarked a seven-million-forint housing management fund for the exchange of apartments of public interest. Between 1973 and 1978, 115 people were given state (party) subsidies (loans that did not have to be repaid) to purchase properties, and an additional 152 cadres were given interest-free loans. This was the more impressive side of the initiative. The less spectacular but more significant element of the system was that the (purely symbolic) prices of the apartments were set by the local councils. In Budapest, the Metropolitan Council picked the apartments, while outside Budapest the county councils used funds from their housing management budgets (2–3 percent of their total budgets) to provide dwellings. Local councils in cities and towns outside Budapest even had the residences of cadres remodeled at "moderate" prices. In 1983, a resolution was passed that stated, "If a public interest housing allocation is only feasible through the purchase of a National Savings Bank apartment or the construction of a detached house, it is still an eligible subsidy." The resolution constituted a formal acknowledgment that it had become customary for members of the elite to acquire private property. From this point on, various sums were allocated to subsidize the purchase of prominent apartments by cadres rising to the top ranks of the party leadership.[77] The era of seizing and occupying villas came to an end. The elegant villas of Buda were in the possession of the old members of the party elite.

The owners of the villas increasingly came to see the houses they had acquired after the Second World War as theirs. Like the former residents had done before them, they remodeled the buildings to meet their needs and desires. Beginning in the 1960s, villas were frequently inhabited by several generations of the same family. The reason was simple: It was no longer possible to acquire similarly prominent, elegant homes. In addition, residents did not have to fear that the houses would be expropriated. For them, the border between private and state property was essentially blurred beyond recognition. For example, in 1967, Sándor Gáspár, secretary general of the National Council of Trade Unions, had his villa remodeled as a private individual, but with funds provided through a loan from the National Savings Bank. A new wing was added to the house in Trombita Street, and two apartments were constructed within the villa. Plans were drawn up by the engineering department of the National Council of Trade Unions, and the building contractor was the maintenance division of the Iron and Metal Workers' Trade Union.[78] Communist politician Antal Apró (at the time, speaker of the Hungarian National Assembly) and his family had additions made to the villa in Szemlőhegy Street, transforming the two apartments to three apartments. In this case, the builder was the Central Committee of the Hungarian Socialist Workers' Party.[79] By the end of the socialist era, some of the valuable villas had become private property.[80] The rest were offered for purchase to their residents after the regime change.

The reclusive world of the 1950s proved a fleeting moment in the history of the Buda hills. From the 1960s on, relatively elegant homes were built in Buda, and members of the state and party bureaucracy had opportunities to move into new apartment complexes on the hillsides, close to the ruling elite.[81] The construction of conspicuously elegant villas gained new momentum in the 1980s, and the edifices often bore nostalgic and even atavistic stylistic features. The apartment complexes and villas springing up in the Buda hills were characterized by a complete break from modern architecture and, at the same time, by ostentation. As if in blunt rejection of the ideals embodied by the socialist housing complexes,[82] the contractors seemed to have been concerned first and foremost not with following any existing stylistic trends or creating any new ones but rather simply with "demonstrating status."[83] The buildings were expressive of the desire to establish a symbolic—and therefore in some way exclusive—space.[84] Members of affluent social groups, mimicking the lifestyles of the ruling elite, launched an unstoppable assault on the undeveloped areas of the Buda hills.

RESORTS AND VACATION HOMES

Traditionally, the most popular place to spend holidays in Hungary was Lake Balaton, a large freshwater lake in the western part of the country, where the villas of members of the elite and the middle class lined the shores. Before the Second World War, holidays on the shores of the lake were generally considered a privilege of the middle class or the elite. Initially, party leaders were given villas in Balatonaliga (also known and referred to simply as Aliga). Of somewhat lesser prestige than the villas allocated for private use and remodeled to the personal requests of cadres was a holiday in the Öszöd resort, in the complex located on the border of Balatonszemes and Balatonőszöd, which was available to members of the Council of Ministers. In 1944, the village of Aliga on the southeastern corner of the lake had a population of 130 residents, but by 1953 it was no longer listed among the settlements in Hungary. The village did not vanish. Rather, it was transformed into an invisible settlement, closed off from the public, because members of the ruling elite spent their holidays there.

Allegedly, it was Mrs. Zoltán Vas who discovered Aliga. She regularly vacationed in the village in the resort of the medical union, and she later rented a villa in the town. The visiting functionaries came to like the area, too. Aliga residents and owners of vacation homes were relocated to nearby villages. Houses that were in decent condition were kept, while others were demolished. The village hall located on a hill was converted into a restaurant for the new resort complex. The remaining vacation homes were gradually renovated and modernized.[85] Eventually, the functionaries came to Balaton and made the village of Aliga their own. The Balaton villas were attentively guarded. When Rákosi went for a swim in the lake, for instance, guards watched him from a flatboat.[86]

A modern building on the shore of Balatonarács, a village on the northern shore, was also converted into a resort for members of the party. In 1941, journalist Kornél Tábori described it in the *Balaton Kurír* (Balaton courier) as "the most magnificent piece of today's architecture by Lake Balaton."[87] The architect used a carefully crafted puritanism to indicate that the edifice "was built to serve as a residence for a twentieth-century middle-class man, true, one of the most prominent, well-to-do ones in the country."[88] Between 1938 and 1948, the resort was owned by the tycoon Zoltán Brázay. Later, János Kádár became very fond of the building. He often spent time in it, and when he was released from jail in 1954, he vacationed there with his wife.[89]

Later, when vacation homes for members of the party were popping up all over, Lake Balaton remained the most popular place. The Central Committee of the Hungarian Socialist Workers' Party owned resorts by Lake Balaton in Aliga, Arács, Földvár, and Tihany. If the functionaries and their families did not choose a vacation home near Balaton, they would often go instead to Dobogókő, a popular tourist area in the Visegrád hills north of Budapest, or Leányfalu, a village on the west bank of the Danube River, also north of Budapest. The former was mainly frequented by the cadres who held positions in the state administration, while the latter was used as a weekend resort for Politburo members.

There were two additional resorts in Budapest, one on the so-called Római-part (Roman shore, a reference to the nearby ruins of the Roman city of Aquincum), which was the most popular place for water sports on the Danube, and the other in District 6, in Munkácsy Mihály Street, part of the elegant neighborhood near Andrássy Avenue. Compared to the resorts in the countryside, the Római-part resort was less prestigious. It was used primarily by functionaries from outside Budapest who came to the banks of the Danube to relax, and occasionally party leaders would spend a weekend there. The park area included a twenty-five-meter swimming pool, table tennis tables, sports fields, and a snack bar for guests. In the summer, many Budapest residents used the resort's pool, because it was less crowded than other public pools in Budapest. The swimming pool of the Central Party School, part of the Ajtósi Dürer Street complex (later acquired by Eötvös Loránd University), was another recreational facility. It was mainly available to members of the apparatus. The hotel and restaurant of the resort in Munkácsy Mihály Street welcomed mostly foreign guests, but during the week, members of the Central Committee and the Politburo also dined there.

In the Kádár era, suites and rooms were designed on various levels of the resorts in which functionaries of varying ranks and positions were given lodging depending on their posts. In Aliga, for example, the grounds of the resort were divided into two parts.

The classy villas and elegant service units were located in Aliga II. (At the Club Aliga resort, villa number four, which was regularly used by the János Kádár and his wife, can be seen today.[90]) In Aliga I, in contrast, members of the administration were given rooms in stone buildings or wooden bungalows. The Arács villa, which was the smallest resort (and therefore was available to only a few people), seems to have been the most prestigious, followed by Aliga II, the Leányfalu resort, and villa four in Dobogókő. Most of the time, these resorts served as vacation places for members of the Politburo, secretaries and department heads of the Central Committee, county first secretaries, and leaders of the Budapest party committee.[91] By the time Kádár rose to power, the hierarchical order in the state party bureaucracy had taken form and become consolidated. In certain places (Aliga and Dobogókő), lower-ranking members of the administration were able to observe very closely how members of the top circles of leadership enjoyed positions of privilege.

In the Kádár era, the highest-ranking leaders of the party enjoyed significantly more (and better) opportunities than other cadres of the administration. The nomenclature law—or, as it was designated at the time, the "cadre sphere of authority law"—secured for people in power control over the most vital political posts. This meant the privilege of directly appointing candidates to the highest offices (which followed the Soviet practice described earlier). The number of key political positions in 1950 was between 2,700 and 3,000.[92] Studies of the sociology of power show that only people who served as the trusted confidants of a small handful of party leaders could make it into this exclusive circle. They were not part of the ruling elite. Rather, they formed a more comprehensive, so-called functionary elite. They were heads of organizations dependent in some way on the top political leadership and party leaders, representing a professional function (not only political power), or they held leading positions in the administration. They enjoyed only limited privileges, much as they were only entitled to limited power, but they had opportunities to move closer to both privilege and power in their later careers.

Party resorts offered a wide range of leisure activities. In Balatonaliga, for instance, the resort had a row of kiosks where vacationers could purchase fried dough and ice cream—in other words, they could engage in comparatively normal behavior, as if they were not in a restricted, fenced-off area. In the harbor, several sailing boats owned by the resort rocked on the waters of the lake, and a boat named *Győzelem* [Victory] was anchored in Földvár. *Győzelem* had a captain who had been contracted to pilot the boat. Balaton resorts purchased the first paddleboats in the mid-1970s, and also on-site were a movie theater, game room, and tennis and volleyball courts. Guests could sample Balaton wines in the Aliga and Arács cellars. In the winter, a horse-drawn sleigh tour was organized in Dobogókő, and cultural events were regularly held. Foreign guests were entertained by the Rajkó Orchestra of the Young Communist League Cultural Ensemble, the Symphonic Orchestra of the Ministry of the Interior Cultural Ensemble, and the Zánka Pioneer Orchestra. Occasionally, eminent artisans of Kalocsa folk art, such as the "embroidery women," were invited.[93]

The first member of the ruling elite who sought to ensure that his family would have a stable financial future by acquiring private property (perhaps because he knew the regime would not be in power forever) was József Darvas. Instead of having a house in Aliga furnished for him and his family, he had a private villa built in the hills, citing the healing effects of the mountain air. It was an unorthodox move for which he faced criticism.[94] Later, shrewd county first secretaries working on their own careers helped party leaders purchase vacations homes. Mrs. Ferenc Cservenka, Pest County first secretary, parceled out property to them in the elegant districts of Szentendre, as did János Pap, Veszprém County first secretary, in Almádi and Balatonfüred.[95] An increasing number of functionary families had vacation homes built by Lake Balaton, in Szentendre, or in Leányfalu.

"UNCLAIMED PROPERTY"

In his poem "Ballada egy balladáról" (Ballad on a ballad), László Kálnoky recounts the legendary heroics of poet Péter Kuczka (called Péter Koczka in the poem) and his visit to Mátyás Rákosi (Mátyási Rókus—an anagrammatic pun in the poem):

> one time he was a dinner guest
> of the great Mátyási Rókus, protocol
> in the company of other distinguished writers,
> and when the guests were saying farewell,
> Péter Koczka boldly,
> almost provocatively
> reached into the bowl of fruits on the middle of the table and said:
> With your permission, Comrade Mátyási,
> I'll nick one or two of these bananas
> and show them to my kids at home.

In stores and depots maintained exclusively for them, party leaders could obtain scarce food items, such as tropical fruits, Hungarian salami, and veal.[96] In addition, they did not have to cover the costs of utilities in the villas they were given. In fact, the party even subsidized the purchase of furniture and paintings.[97] Party leaders' apartments were equipped with modern refrigerators, which were a luxury at the time.[98] Furniture could be obtained in central depots maintained specifically for this purpose, and an interior designer helped the members of the elite pick just the right thing.[99]

In the 1950s, functionaries furnished their apartments with stylish pieces, such as settees and dressing tables obtained from the central depots. Varnished or painted antiques were particularly popular, as were marble-top furniture, golden ornaments, thick Persian rugs, and ornate crystal chandeliers.[100] Although strictly speaking they did not belong to the ruling elite of the age, many state security officers also enjoyed most of the privileges of the high-ranking members of the party. For instance, they, too, had acquired real estate and others kinds of movable property, and they had villas or upper-middle-class apartments allocated close to their workplaces in Andrássy Avenue. Thus, they indirectly and clearly un(self-)consciously reached back to the world and interior design of the turn of the century. As noted earlier, by the 1950s, top leaders had moved to the Buda hills. It was the second- and third-tier officials who filled the buildings in the neighborhood around Andrássy Avenue and the more elegant sections of Zugló, a popular district in Pest.

The record that was compiled when the furniture of state security department head Andor Csapó was confiscated[101] suggests a neo-baroque interior. The furniture indicates a traditional, historicist arrangement with no trace of modernism. For instance, the floors of the four rooms were covered with twenty-two Persian rugs.[102] His deputy, János Komendó, solved the problem of interior design with a single stroke: He moved into the Dohány Street apartment of a furniture retailer who had fled the country. The list of books seized in Komendó's apartment indicates that the volumes on the shelves did not match the carefully designed (in this case, appropriated) middle-class interior. In addition to works by Marx, Engels, Lenin, and Stalin, Komendó had a special decorative edition of the complete poems of Sándor Petőfi (the most widely known nineteenth-century Hungarian romantic poet), eighteen volumes of the *Pallas Lexicon*, and twenty-one other books in decorative bindings. Also on the shelves was Imre Madách's play *Az ember tragédiája* (*The Tragedy of Man*), the most famous Hungarian drama, first published in 1861 and the single most widely translated work of Hungarian literature today.[103]

Even in functionary circles, Rákosi was known as a devout collector. When the secretary general moved from Szabó József Street to the Lóránt Street dwelling in the Buda hills, some of the relics he had accumulated were left behind in the old villa. In late 1951, the ornamental pieces, which had become superfluous, were donated to the Institute of the Labor Movement. Thus, the institute acquired lace table runners, various statuettes (of bulls, eagles, and workers), crystal items, a shepherd's staff, and a sword.[104] The shelves in the china cabinets in Rákosi's new residence, however, still buckled under the weight of an overflow of baubles and other collectibles.[105]

It is perhaps worth noting that the contemporary inventories and registries do not paint a terribly impressive picture of the tastes of the middle class and the elites of the interwar period. After 1948, museologists compiled an inventory of the items that were going to be made part of the public collection of "unclaimed properties" and the objects that would be put in storage in the party depots. The list includes almost innumerable porcelain, crystal, and precious-metal devotional objects. People's dwellings, it seems, had been cluttered with kitsch of every shape and size, including statuettes of dogs, stags, swans, and little boys peeing.[106]

After the war, the state started "managing" the more valuable paintings among the "unclaimed properties." In principle, statues were entrusted to museums, but several ended up in private possession. The famous art collectors of the age laid the foundations of their art collections in this transitional period. István Balogh, for example, a Catholic priest who collaborated with the communist party, made significant additions to his collection. He served as the founder and director of ARTEX, the company that arranged the export to foreign countries of works of art that had been acquired by the state. He was also an undersecretary of state responsible as commissioner of unclaimed property.[107]

In the 1950s, there was a furniture depot in Mexikói Street and Mártonhegyi Street. Iron safes and furniture were stored in the building at the corner of Katona József Street and Újpest Wharf. Gábor Péter's "private" storage depot was located at 4 Liszt Ferenc Square; the building at 27 Személynök Street had a room reserved for Mrs. Pál Radnai (an accountant for the state security forces), which she used as storage space; and at 21 Személynök Street Ferenc Vándor (the other accountant) supervised a larger depot in which upholstery fabrics, carpets, draperies, blankets, and sheets were stockpiled. Another room in the same building was used for storing suits, winter coats, boots, shoes, shirts, undergarments, and raincoats. Clothing, pots, pans, and bed linens were also kept in an apartment at 58 Dembinszky Street. The "library" where confiscated books were kept was located at the corner of Damjanich and Dózsa György Streets. Shoe soles, leather items, and construction material were piled up at a place in Gyorskocsi Street. A depot for foodstuffs was at 81 Sztálin Street, and china vases and dinner sets for functionaries were kept at a storage site in Rózsa Street.[108]

Later, the party took over this task (as it took over many tasks) from the state security. Officials of the Hungarian Socialist Workers' Party made sure that the highest-ranking cadres had everything they needed. The party's central depot headquarters was located in downtown Budapest, at 9 Széchenyi Street, in District 5. Depot employees procured difficult-to-find food items for leaders in the highest positions, and they often provided the necessary supplies for receptions and for the resorts and institutions under the administration of the Central Committee. Archival documents suggest that it was not difficult to obtain the foods (such as veal and tropical fruits), but it was hard to purchase Western products—and by then, quality drinks, cigarettes, and cigars had become fashionable in functionary circles. As the author of one of the documents wrote, "Sometimes it is rather hard to meet the increased demand for imported goods, for instance German beer, hard liquor, and tobacco products. In the course of our work, we endeavor to meet the needs that arise at the events organized by the Central Committee and Politburo."[109]

For the historian, the records of the state security office during this period play a role somewhat similar to that of bequest registries in other eras. They are perhaps the most descriptive sources on the lifestyles and consumer habits of the elite of the time. However, one must be cautious when reading these documents, and one must always keep in mind that the aim of the procedures in question (the show trials) was to demonstrate that a given leader of the Hungarian State Security lived a life unbefitting of a true communist. One of the people against whom charges were brought made the following statement—obviously under duress—concerning his conduct: "I whored, I slept with men, and I drank, I drank a big glass of wine every day, I kept a lover, and I lived a lavish, wasteful life."[110] However, inventories and other documents indicate that there was some truth to the charges that were made in the show trials. For example, inspectors found forty-four kilograms of objects that "looked like gold" and eighty-one kilograms of objects that "looked like silver" in the apartment of Ernő Szűcs, Gábor Péter's deputy.[111]

Their luxuriant lifestyles notwithstanding, for a long time cadres lived under the threat of financial insecurity. Their privileges were dependent on their positions; thus, in order for them to maintain their standards of living, they had to be sure to stay "on course" in their jobs.[112] People who fell out of favor had to part not only with their positions but also with their apartments, their cars, and whatever belongings of value they might have managed to acquire. When the victims of the show trials were rehabilitated in 1956, there was at least a symbolic attempt to compensate them and help them reintegrate into "society." In fact, this meant helping them rejoin the circles of the elite, but many of them had indeed lost virtually everything. In addition to housing and cash, they were mostly given items that were in storage and were seen as unnecessary by the administration, such as books and opera glasses. Júlia Rajk, the widow of László Rajk, who had served under Rákosi as minister of the interior but had been put on trial and executed in 1949, was provided with an apartment "furnished with middle-class comforts." This was an attempt on the part of the functionaries to demonstrate that they considered the standard of living of the so-called middle class perfectly acceptable and even appealing, and they had not allowed it to disappear.[113]

It is worth mentioning a few other items that were symbolic of material prosperity under Kádár. Members of the hunting elite acquired valuable gun collections, including firearms such as Forgons, Holland-Hollands, and shotguns by the Belgian Halwa Company. Passionate stamp collectors sought valuable rare stamps, and communist party leader Ferenc Szűcs, lieutenant general of the Hungarian People's Army, served as vice president of the Federation of Hungarian Stamp Collectors.[114] Many people owned invaluable collections of paintings and furniture.

All the statistics that were compiled during the socialist era indicate a decrease in wage differences, but the regime only superficially aspired to lessen income inequalities. Higher positions continued to mean better incomes, and the many perks further contributed to the inequalities. In 1950, ministers earned 3,850 forints per month. Furthermore, they did not have to account for the additional 3,000-forint allowance they received for "entertainment expenses." Politburo members earned approximately the same amount. The average income at the time was 652 forints; thus, the income of a member of the ruling elite was six times the average. If one also considers the reimbursements they were given to cover expenses, it came to more than ten times the average, and more than seventeen times the 406 forints a month earned by the lowest-paid agricultural workers and employees.[115]

Throughout the Kádár era, the gap between the lowest and highest earnings essentially remained the same. From time to time, the incomes of party leaders were adjusted according to average earnings, so anytime incomes were raised for the middle class, the difference in incomes remained; the income gap, which might have appeared to have declined, was in fact maintained. In 1968, the salaries of party leaders and ministers were approximately six times the officially determined average income, and this figure did not include the allowances they were given as reimbursements of expenditures. The incomes of ministers and members of the Politburo remained roughly the same throughout the period, indicating the hierarchy between the party and the organs of the state, though after 1963 the latter began to earn a bit more. Incomes also reflected the hierarchy within the leadership. The secretary general and first secretary of the party consistently had the highest income. Next in line were the chairman of the Hungarian Presidential Council and the speaker of the Hungarian National Assembly, followed by members of the Politburo and ministers. The next level consisted of the undersecretaries, first secretaries of the counties, presidents of the county councils, and department heads of the Central Committee.[116] In addition to their incomes and expense accounts, most of the people who held high offices in the party or state also made money as representatives in the national assembly, which entitled them to additional emoluments. Wages showed a steady increase until the change of the regime, though in the 1980s they were far behind the top earnings in the private sector.[117] The status of party leaders, however, was strengthened by an array of privileges, of which a high salary had never been the most important.

Members of the ruling elite quickly realized that they could ensure the future financial security of their families only by obtaining private property. Efforts among the party leaders to acquire property increased significantly. Using their social capital and personal networks, the cadres profited from the process of reestablishing private property (within limits). The primary form of property accumulation, in addition to savings, was naturally the acquisition of real estate, the purchase of condominiums and vacation homes or apartments, and the purchase of valuable movable properties. Private land ownership was introduced in 1967. Restrictions on personal property were not applied to these estates. Consequently several "farms" were built with swimming pools.[118] The government put an end to the spread of this class of "new landowners" in 1971, after which a family (in fact, one individual) was allowed to own only a single apartment or housing plot and one vacation home or apartment. However, state and party leaders had little difficulty getting around both this law and a restriction on "possession of precious metals," which in principle was in effect until 1974. The law stated that a private individual could own no more than five hundred grams of gold.[119] It soon became clear that a position of authority not only meant temporary advantages but also helped ensure that an entire family would become prosperous and wealthy.[120]

CHEVIS AND THE KÁDÁR MERCI[121]

"The parliament is a captivating site on the bank of the Danube. It is a splendid building, and it radiates authority, dignity, and opulence. Its dimensions would be better suited to a great empire. A stream of Chevrolets (!), Buicks, Hudsons, and Chryslers rolled past the lions at the main entrance. I arrived in my father's car with Pál and my parents. Pál Justus got out of his DKW behind us, with his wife, Edit."[122] In her 1985 book *Fent és lent, 1945–1950* (Above and Below, 1945–1950), Klára Szakasits, the daughter of Árpád Szakasits, president of the Republic of Hungary for roughly a year between August 1948 and August 1949, mentions these details to characterize the mood at a reception organized for Romanian prime minister Petru Groza.

Along with elegant villas and sumptuous interiors, the automobile gradually emerged as another important symbol of influence, power, and wealth. In Hungary, the first people to begin using cars had been members of distinguished social circles and classes—either aristocrats or factory owners—and the car remained a mark of prestige. During the Horthy era, the automobile became part of the everyday lives and lifestyles of the ruling elites. The paradigm shift from the horse to the automobile was noticeable even in the habits of members of the regent's family. Miklós Horthy was not only an enthusiastic lover of horses, he was also captivated by the excitement of the motorcar. He obtained a driver's license and in 1936 began driving a Zeppelin DS8, a model that was referred to as the German Rolls Royce. His son István Horthy was something of a pioneer of motorcar driving in Hungary. At the turn of the century, owning a car was almost an obligation for a member of the elite, but gradually more and more people could afford an automobile. In the 1930s, many people working in professions that were typical of the upper middle class began to buy cars.[123] The Second World War, however, cut the number of available automobiles to one-tenth what it had been, and thus the car again became more of a rarity. Beginning in 1945, less expensive models (for instance, what in German was and is aptly called the Volkswagen, or "car of the people") entered the market, and minicars were promised to go into production, giving hope to people who sought to purchase an automobile. Politicians eager to give practical examples of the substance of the new political ideology emphasized that "quite visibly, the working middle class fell the farthest from the automobile.... In the past, car racing was the sport of the aristocracy and the industrial magnates."[124]

In 1947, Zoltán Tildy, who served as president from 1946 until he was forced to resign and was replaced by Szakasits in 1948, spoke about the democracy of the automobile in an interview printed in the periodical *Autó Magyar Sport* (Auto Hungarian sport). The interview was on the first page of the issue and included a photograph of Tildy, a member of the Independent Smallholders' Party, standing in front of a table on which rested an issue of *Autó Motor Sport*. According to Tildy, "First and foremost, we must make it widely understood that the automobile is not a luxury.... We must bring inexpensive automobiles into circulation that even workers with the most modest incomes can afford.... The automobile is not simply a tool, it also makes weekend days of leisure, hard earned following the gray weekdays, more enjoyable and more human. And this, I repeat, is not a luxury—as long as it is not enjoyed exclusively by a select layer of society." The periodical noted that the president had spoken in an "engagingly indirect fashion."[125]

After the war, the Royal Hungarian Automobile Club (Királyi Magyar Automobil Club) was renamed and became the Central Hungarian Automobile Club. In 1947, it was renamed again, this time becoming the Hungarian Automobile Club of the Republic (Köztársasági Magyar Automobil Club). Thus, the four-letter abbreviation by which it had been known, KMAC, remained unchanged.[126] In 1947, high-ranking members of the Ministry of Transportation and the Ministry of Internal Affairs were elected to leadership positions in the club, and Tildy and the minister of transportation Ernő Gerő were asked to serve as patrons. In 1948, the Budapest Grand Prix was held on a racetrack just outside Budaörs. Representatives of the new government were among those in attendance. Another race was organized that year for a grand prize that was offered by Lajos Dinnyés, who was the last noncommunist politician to serve as prime minister of Hungary before being replaced in December 1948 by István Dobi, a stooge of the communist party. Under the new system, the new club, which was determined to adhere to its own traditions, nonetheless had to give up its cherished and familiar abbreviation to accommodate another shift in the state. Its new name was the Automobile Club of the Hungarian People's Republic, or simply the Auto Club. It was some compensation, in the eyes of the members of the club, that on March 1, 1956, they were given the prominent Arizona building at 20 Nagymező Street. Until the end of the Second World War, the building had been home to the so-called Arizona Mulató, or Arizona tavern, where many of the great Hungarian musicians and actors of the twentieth century had performed. The elegant rooms of the building were restored, as were the frescoes and the wooden paneling, and a clubroom, reading room, and snack bar were created for the Auto Club.[127] Thus, representatives of the narrow circle of elite car owners were able to gather privately in a sumptuous space.

The promises made by politicians and ideologues notwithstanding, car ownership increasingly became the privilege of a narrow elite of state and party functionaries.[128] With the initial tightening and then elimination of the free market on which cars had been bought and sold, only high-ranking functionaries—and, in some cases, scientists, artists, and athletes—could even obtain a car for private use. It is hardly surprising that when a chauffeur was chosen for Mátyás Rákosi, the first consideration was trustworthiness. At first, an appropriate cadre was sought among the police force to serve alongside the deputy prime minister. A partisan who had been wounded in the chest was selected. He did not have a driver's license, and his war wound made him a less than ideal candidate, as it threw into question his health.[129] Another incident illustrates the way in which the automobile and car ownership were politicized. Hugó Koch, the technical director of the Gyula Meinl Ltd., was on his way to the wedding of one of his employees when he collided with Rákosi's car. The state security forces immediately took him to the building at 60 Andrássy Avenue, the building used by the state police for brutal interrogations, among other things. The man was accused of being "a recruited member of a group that conspired to commit acts of sabotage," and he was interned in a forced labor camp in the city of Recsk, one of the most infamous prisons in communist Hungary.[130] Pünkösti cites one of Rákosi's drivers, who presumably was speaking of precisely this case, recounting it from the perspective of the state security forces:

> We became the trailers [in the jargon of the state security forces, the vehicle that followed the car in which the prime minister or other important state figure was traveling], we accompanied Rákosi's car. They had not yet begun using a car to provide security in front, but they had developed a technique. They would pay close attention to what was coming, and if something ahead was threatening, they had to foil the malicious plan by deliberately crashing. Drapcsik [the driver] crashed into someone on the road to Gödöllő because he was coming in the opposite direction in an uncertain manner. It turned out he was an Arrow Cross man, and drunk, but they couldn't prove he had had any intention of wrongdoing. By that time, the cars were connected by radio, and Boda, Rákosi's bodyguard, gave the order to drive the other car off the road. Both cars were wrecked, but no one was injured.[131]

Later, a protocol was established. The party secretary traveled as part of a convoy. He rode in a limousine in the middle, which had a "forerunner" car ahead of it and a trailer car behind it.[132] The few other drivers who from time to time appeared on the streets were no longer in any direct danger. Gradually, the chauffeur and the bodyguard both learned the ins and outs of their jobs. State security was increasingly professionalized.

A Council of Ministers decree issued in 1950 specified who was allowed to use an automobile for private purposes. According to the decree, ministerial heads of departments, heads of national bureaus, chief municipal officers, the mayor and deputy mayors of Budapest, and leaders of companies that fell in the "A" wage category were entitled to use a car for private purposes, as were the "employees in leadership positions" for whom the authorized minister granted permission. In 1955, the already small number of people permitted to use an automobile for private purposes was made even smaller.[133] In the 1950s, in addition to members of the leading elite, artists and athletes were able to obtain cars. In 1952, one of the editors of the humorous periodical titled *Ludas Matyi*[134] wrote a letter to Rákosi in which he requested an automobile for Andor Gábor, the editor in chief. Gábor was becoming increasingly popular as the author of humoresques, and his request, made indirectly by one of his colleagues, was granted. He was allowed to choose from among the cars kept at the National Wreckage Depot.[135]

State offices primarily used cars that had been manufactured in socialist countries. These car manufacturers included Škodas, a Czech automobile manufacturer that was founded in the late nineteenth century as Laurin and Klement and remains in operation today, and Pobedas (later written as Pobjeda), a passenger car made in the Soviet Union from 1946 until 1958. But by 1956, the condition of these cars had drastically deteriorated. In contrast, high-ranking functionaries were able to purchase better cars (often ones that had been manufactured in the West) using the foreign currency accounts of the party or the state. The higher-ranking members of the Council of Ministers and the various ministries usually drove BMWs (primarily the 340 series) and sometimes Chevrolets. Party leaders primarily used Chevrolet Bel Airs and Chevrolet 57s, but the Soviet luxury cars, the ZIM and ZIS, were also used as a matter of protocol.[136] Rákosi's first car was a Horch.[137] The large black cars became symbols of power.

The institutions of the party-state had to find ways to get their hands on hard currency in order to obtain Western cars for the functionaries. In 1955, for instance, the president of the State Office for Church Affairs reached an agreement with the president of an international relief society according to which fifteen Chevrolets would be sent to Hungary instead of the $300,000 that had been intended for the Hungarian Jewry. The deal was advantageous for everyone. The money presumably got to the people for whom it was intended. According to the documents, the state provided the $300,000 for the Jewish community, plus an additional 30 percent, and new Chevrolets rolled across the borders of a country that was stuck behind the Iron Curtain.[138]

However, people also acquired Western cars through illegal channels. A man named Ferenc Kása oversaw a large network of agents and vendors in Hungary. He provided Western cars to prominent Hungarian artists and the coach and players on the Aranycsapat soccer team (called the "golden team" because of its many victories in major international matches and discussed in greater detail in chap. 4). In the 1950s and 1960s, one could only bring a car into Hungary from the West as a gift from a relative. Thus, anyone who received a car (or rather, purchased a car in the West) had to prove his or her family tie to the person who allegedly had made the gift. Kása issued numerous such letters from people living in the West who were purportedly giving a family member in Hungary a car, and he also helped people change forints into hard currency.[139] He had ties to auto mechanics in Budapest, who presumably did repairs and maintenance work on the Western models that had been brought into the country.[140] He was the only person who was able to obtain some components, so even functionaries in the Ministry of Foreign Affairs took their cars to Vienna to be serviced by him.[141] In the 1960s, Kása's wife traveled to Hungary as frequently as once every two or three weeks. She usually stayed with boxer László Papp, and when Papp was in Vienna, he would stay with Kása, his friend and business partner.[142]

While the use of an automobile for private affairs gradually became a natural part of the lifestyle of the ruling elite (and indeed was commonly regarded as such), a private individual was rarely able to acquire a car. A workers' council delegate, who in 1956 sought out Sándor Gáspár, the secretary general of the National Council of Trade Unions,[143] later said this of Gáspár: "It was common knowledge that he kept cars for his use, and I saw it myself, personally. In the courtyard of the [council] seat there were enormous cars, and he had dazzlingly pretty secretaries. It was also common knowledge that he was very fond of the gentler sex, and that he liked to drink. So in his own way, he was a spirited little man."[144]

As minister of foreign affairs, Endre Sík had the pleasure of owning one of the regal black cars. He later wrote about this experience: "Of course, it's nice if you have a car at your disposal. But one can have too much of a good thing. A person with a car has no free time at all. He becomes a slave to his car. He gets out of the habit of walking, and he realizes this with some dismay when, as he rumbles around the city tending to his affairs, he sees pedestrians and the hustle and bustle in the streets." Sík sometimes was able to resist the temptation to drive. He would use a car to get to the place where he would go for a walk, and his chauffeur would then drive the car back to his home: "From time to time, when I had managed to free myself up for an hour, I would drive to the Hármashatár-hegy[145] and then walk down the forest path. Those were the most pleasant hours of my time as minister."[146]

After the defeat of the revolution, the party leadership decided in 1957, as a gesture to the population of the country, to launch the commercial trade of automobiles. In January 1964, the Merkur state automobile commercial enterprise was created. Gradually, more cars appeared on the streets of cities, towns, and villages—Škodas, Wartburgs, Moskvitches, Zhigulis, and later Trabants (the P70 model). By the late 1960s, anyone with enough hard currency could buy Renaults, Fords, Peugeots, and even Mercedes from the Konsumex foreign trade company.[147]

In 1966, Kása came to Hungary in an official capacity with Alfred Ickovits, the Swiss representative of Opel, to enter into negotiations on behalf of Opel Works with the leaders of the Hungarian National Automobile Factory (Magyar Országos Gépkocsi Üzem Rt., or MOGÜRT), a socialist enterprise that handled trade in motor vehicle and automobile parts.[148] This was, in fact, an unfortunate development for Kása. Because the party leadership was willing to legalize the sale and purchase of automobiles, Kása's expertise was not needed, and the authorities no longer turned a blind eye on his dealings. He was arrested, and the highest court in the country sentenced him to sixteen months in prison and issued a 100,000-forint fine for crimes related to the illegal exchange of foreign currency. After serving his sentence, he was expelled from the country. Kása maintained ties to people in Hungary, however, and in the 1970s, he helped provide service and maintenance in Vienna for the cars used by Hungarian diplomats.[149] He managed to prevail on the authorities to close his internal affairs dossier in 1980, and thus was able to move freely in Hungary again.[150] Kása attracted the attention of the state security forces on one other occasion, when they sought to collect taxes that he allegedly owed in Hungary.[151]

In 1970, the Automobile Owners held an international ball in the Gellért Hotel, the most elegant hotel in Budapest. Automobile owners filled the banquet halls of the regal building. According to the invitation, the dress code for men was a dark suit. The organizers were tactful in their phrasing with regard to the dress code for women, but nevertheless insisted on the importance of appropriate garb: "Women decide for themselves what to wear anyway, and that has always turned out well." Two orchestras played, alternating, until dawn in the dance room, the vaulted hall. The Red Shirt Ensemble performed in the Marble Hall, and Roma musicians played dance music in the Danube Hall and the Tea Saloon. In the other rooms and the extravagantly ornate hallways, the elites strolled and chatted, with champagne glasses in hand.[152] The club still had an unusual, almost mystical (even prewar) mood, despite the fact that the number of car owners grew quickly (by 1970, it had reached almost seventy thousand). The automobile remained a sign of prestige for a long time, though by the 1970s only the rare Western models counted as something truly unusual.

Among the functionaries of the Kádár era, the Mercedes was all the rage. By the beginning of the 1970s, the Mercedes 280 had become the protocol car. Members of the elite would use a car for roughly two years and then trade it in for a new one.[153] In the early 1970s, 21 percent of the Mercedes in Hungary were owned by the state, though 58 percent of the 230s and the larger and newer models were owned by the leaders of the party-state.[154] It is also worth noting a phenomenon referred to as "Volvoism," as the Volvo emerged as the second-most-popular automobile among the members of this circle. The Chaika, or "Gull," the Soviet luxury car, was rare indeed.[155] When the luxury cars that were driven by the party leaders for "personal use" broke down, considerable problems were likely to result. Until the issue of acquiring parts was addressed, the government guard ordered parts duty-free from the Vienna office of the Mercedes factory with the permission of the Ministry of Foreign Trade. If the Vienna office could not supply the parts, they were brought in directly from the Federal Republic of Germany, though in principle this counted as smuggling. To be sure that the West Germans did not realize who Mercedes was providing the parts for, the order was placed by MOGÜRT. Thus, the Hungarian customs office not only put customs duties on the delivery but also sequestered it. In the end, the government guard had to ask the National Commandership of the Board of Customs and Excise to issue the parts and exempt them from customs duties. Otherwise, the cars used by the members of the Political Committee would simply remain stranded in the garage.[156]

The S-Class Mercedes, which was a symbol of prestige for the ruling elite, was given a fitting name by the next generation, a name that offered a pithy summary of the system: the Kádár merci.[157] Kádár and his wife had their own car (for private use) only once. It was a Volga that Mrs. Kádár was given by Nikita Khrushchev's wife, Nina Petrovna. In 1989, Mária Tamáska contended that they had sold the car to the state for thirty thousand forints: "They had appraised it at that much, and we did not want to haggle."[158] Nonetheless, they sold the protocol gift they had been given, because apparently they preferred cash to the car. Kádár also did not keep the Niva all-terrain vehicle that he was given by Leonid Brezhnev on the occasion of Brezhnev's visit to Hungary in 1979.[159] Kádár claimed not to be terribly fond of cars. He preferred to travel by the special train (the "silver arrow"), which was another symbol of prestige at the time.[160] When he was compelled to travel by car, Kádár used an S-Class Mercedes, equipped with bulletproof lead inserts. The first secretary of the party enjoyed the comforts that came with his position, and he adopted the customs of the elite and adhered to protocol.

The first train used by the government had been inherited from Miklós Horthy. Allegedly, Kádár himself made the decision to replace it. In 1964, when Khrushchev was pushed out of power, Kádár was in Warsaw.[161] The old radio on the elegant but somewhat antiquated train died, so Kádár was unable, on the way home, to keep informed of the events. As a result of this malfunction, a new train was ordered. The factory in Rába designed and made the carriages, and the Ganz factory provided the engines and machinery. After having ordered the construction of the train, Kádár summoned Ede Horváth, the director of the Rába factory, to Budapest. Horváth was accompanied by the person who designed the carriage. According to Horváth, András Benkei, Béla Biszku, Lajos Fehér, and Jenő Fock were present as representatives of the government for the meeting, where the plans were discussed in detail. The shrewd factory director, who was from the city of Győr, sought to corrupt the upper leadership. He offered to have the Rába factory make the train for free, but the functionaries did not accept his offer, and in the end the Ministry of Internal Affairs covered the costs. Kádár made a request that surprised all of them. He wanted the train to have a card room with two exits. Again according to Horváth, when he bid farewell to the delegation from Győr, Kádár asked whether there would be a red star on the front of the train. The director replied without hesitation that naturally they would make the train in accordance with the wishes of the office that placed the order. They left it at that. In the end, they did not put a red star on the front of the locomotive. In principle, the train had been made for the government, but in reality it was never the government's, nor even the party's.[162] The allegedly modest first secretary regarded the elegant train as his own.

Kádár took severe measures against the members of the apparatus (though admittedly with little result) in the 1980s, when new regulations were issued concerning the use of automobiles by party functionaries. In 1980, the Central Committee formed a fleet of cars that could be used by the cadres for functions where appearance and protocol mattered. The cars were kept at the Transportation and Technical Enterprise of the Department of Party Administration and Management of the Central Committee of the Hungarian Socialist Workers' Party.[163] At the same time, they reduced the number of cars in the possession of the various party organizations and the county party committees.[164] The laws stipulating the use of cars by functionaries were also changed.[165] In principle, the cars could only be used for official goals and according to a so-called taxi system, whereby the number of kilometers traveled was counted.[166] The Automobile Supervision Office of the Ministry of Transportation[167] was even empowered to fine an official who broke the rules and used a car for private purposes.[168] In practice, however, most of the cars in official use were essentially appropriated by the county secretaries and the first secretaries of the cities, in particular the county seats. If a functionary used a privately owned car for an official function, he was reimbursed for the costs. At the beginning of the 1980s, the monies that were given to cover travel costs were made part of the salaries of the party leaders, and these reimbursements often exceeded their monthly incomes.[169]

According to reports, in 1985 almost without exception the functionaries of the municipal party committees and the committees for settlements with the status of a municipality used their cars for "official purposes" as well. These cars were allegedly driven a total of almost ten million kilometers, meaning that every member of this cadre drove the distance of two and a half times around the country at its border. A total of almost forty-four million forints was paid in "compensation." Reports indicate that the larger village and municipal secretaries also traveled a great deal by car, despite the fact that their official responsibilities hardly extended beyond the borders of their relatively small settlements. The costs paid in compensation for this travel came to almost six million forints. With that amount of gas, they each could have traveled around Hungary one and a half times.[170] Until 1986, used cars that had been selected from among the fleet in the party garage for scrap or sale could be purchased on the basis of buyer designation—a process by which the authorities decided who could buy the cars and for how much. Later, these cars were sold by the used car branch of Merkur.[171]

The cars that were kept in the party garage, however, were not used much. The various organizations still had their own fancy cars for official purposes, so the number of cars kept in the garage continually declined. As was generally true in the government offices, the Mercedes in the party garage were gradually replaced with Ladas beginning in the mid-1980s. However, this attempt to maintain a strict sense of modesty was in vain. True, the black Mercedes were replaced with elegant but significantly less prestigious Ladas, painted a Turin blue, but in many of the garages on Cadre Ridge one found privately owned Mercedes.[172] By the 1980s, the Mercedes was a sign of conservative tastes, since many people had had elegant sports cars and vividly colored, sleek, streamlined limousines brought to Hungary from the West.

However, the functionaries who lived in the Buda villas stuck to their traditions.

BENEFITS: THE FOUR KS

"We all resemble the moon: no one shows anyone their dark side." This remark was made by András Hegedüs in one of his autobiographical writings.[173] A Stalinist prime minister in the roughly six months leading up to the outbreak of the 1956 revolution, Hegedüs was essentially the only prominent leader of the Hungarian communist party to confront (and speak about and write about) his past (sometimes from the perspective of a sociologist), though admittedly he only did so in the eventide of his life.

"As I attained higher positions, the size of our apartment increased," Hegedüs noted, offering a personal perspective on the history of the first half of the 1950s.[174] He and his family were given their first villa dwelling in Buda in 1951, in Bolgár Street. It was then that he became deputy minister of agriculture. His personal, or rather family, history, however, offers another explanation for the move: "Our third child was born that year. This gave some justification for us moving from an apartment with two and a half rooms, where we were living with our three children and a village girl [a euphemism for a servant] who looked after the children."[175] The building was a two-story villa, the basement of which was used by the secret police.[176] In the garden, "many fruits ripened from spring to autumn," and there was a heated swimming pool. The couple's third and fourth sons were born in the new dwelling, followed by their daughter. The Hegedüs family lived a very private life, closed off from the outside world, with the exception of one or two unpleasant incidents. "Back in our apartment in Pest, the bedbugs had been a source of discomfort and unrest. Here it was the mice (we had not yet realized that the best pesticide against them was a cat)."[177]

In the spring of 1956, the rapidly growing family got an even larger house, though they did not remain in it for long. When the revolution broke out, Hegedüs and his wife were expecting their sixth child. They felt that they had to flee. On October 28, 1956, they were taken in an armored car to the military airport in Tököl. From there, they flew to Moscow. The former prime minister's fate seemed uncertain for quite a while, as did the fate of his family. For some time, they fought to get back the possessions they had left at home.[178] Working together with the state security guards who had been on sentry duty outside the villa, the two housekeepers, who had also been assigned by the state security, plundered the house. Much of what was left had been pilfered by the people who had patrolled the abandoned cadre villas during the days of the revolution. After November 4, the remaining objects and items of furniture were taken to the repository of the Ministry of Internal Affairs. Working from Moscow, with the help of her sister, Zsuzsanna Hegedüs (András Hegedüs's wife) tried to launch an investigation into what had become of her family's belongings. She composed a long list of the items that had been left behind. It is worth noting that the list included not only the valuable set of Herend tableware but also some three hundred jars of jam and preserves. In one of her letters, Zsuzsanna both protested and lamented: "I still insist that we are not petty-bourgeois, but that does not mean that we should add to the blunders by remaining silent."[179]

After having returned to Hungary, the police and Zsuzsanna Hegedüs patrolled for a month the places where she thought her scattered possessions might be:

> Comrade [András] Tömpe [a major general in the Ministry of Internal Affairs] and the police are helping me make progress in the case. This keeps me very busy, because most of the time I have to go with them. I found the two lamps that had been in our bedroom in the possession of the captain who is living in our former home, as well as the brush machine, which they sold to them.

There will also be a few books there and, if he admits it, two armchairs. We also found a duvet, a great deal of needlework, the wall picture of Kim Il-sung, eight towels, your mackintosh, two pairs of your brown shoes, four of your button-down shirts, tableware, and two of your suits, which had been recut to make women's ensembles.[180]

One of the main subjects of the family correspondence was how to get back "the things that embody two people's twelve years of honest work."[181]

They tried to track down an array of household objects, including a tape deck, a movie camera, a projector, a television set, a blender, a record player, a vacuum cleaner, and a refrigerator. These items would never have been found in an average Hungarian home. Electronic household appliances only began to come into widespread use in Hungary at the end of the 1950s and the beginning of the 1960s. Statistics indicate that in 1960, out of every one thousand people, forty-five had a washing machine, eleven had a vacuum cleaner, and four had a refrigerator. In the 1950s, these items were clearly luxuries, in contrast with the "durable consumer goods" in more widespread use, such as a pedal-powered Singer sewing machine or a radio.[182] What Zsuzsanna and the police did not manage to find had to be replaced. Hegedüs helped the family put the household back together from Moscow. For instance, he sent a vacuum cleaner and a radio.[183] When he was finally able to return to Hungary, a comfortably furnished new home was waiting for him in Sarolta Street on Szemlő Hill.[184]

According to his recollections, in 1956 Hegedüs began a second life in Moscow. On March 15, 1963, he returned to Hungary, where he founded the Sociology Research Group of the Hungarian Academy of Sciences. He played an undeniably significant role in the emergence of sociology in Hungary.[185] In the eyes of the party leadership, he was a revisionist, and he was dismissed from his position at the academy and shut out of the communist party on the grounds of his alleged "unsuitability." Though he had once been a Stalinist politician, he had been troubled by doubts and concerns, and eventually he became an anti-Stalinist oppositional figure. He grappled with his past for the rest of his life. In his old age, he had a penchant for jotting down citations from Montaigne, and he wrote his own aphorisms in which he offered pithy summaries of wisdom gleaned through experience. One finds a characteristic example in his last book: "I was no exception. I always hated hunting, but as the minister of the State Farms and Forests, I had to hunt. On the last hunting trip I took, I shot a beautiful (!) stag. It hangs as a trophy on the wall of my pergola. It has the date on it: August 15 1956."[186] Why did this sociologist who had become critical of the system keep this relic of his own communist past in the pergola of his villa? Perhaps he was not entirely disinterested in hunting, or in the kill. However, he strove to distance himself from his Stalinist past and his old habits, though the trophy still hung in the hallway of his house in the 1980s.[187] Looking back on his life, he wrote about the privileges that separated the party leaders from everyday people and shaped their lifestyles.

Throughout the socialist era, the complicated system of perks and benefits assured the ruling elites a good living and a comfortable life, and these benefits were signs of their positions of power. Hegedüs wrote about this: "Naturally, symbols formed of the prestige of the newly emerged power, and with amazing cunning, these symbols designated quite precisely an individual's place in the hierarchy. A rise or decline in status was almost immediately followed by a change in the symbols of prestige."[188] The privileges enjoyed by the party leaders were referred to as the four Ks: the use of a car (in Hungarian, *kocsi*), the use of a so-called K line telephone, travel abroad (*külföldi út*), and access to the best medical care, which was provided at the Kútvölgyi Hospital (Kútvölgy is a neighborhood at the foot of the Buda hills).[189] Another version of the four Ks was in use among everyday people. The three Ks referred to the following: Kékestető (the highest peak in Hungary, in this case used as a synecdoche for the best vacation sites), the Kútvölgyi Hospital, and the Kerepesi Cemetery, where members of the elite were kept separate from the masses even in death.[190] Some variations included the words *kégli* and *kurva*, or "digs" and "whores."

The K Line

In the 1950s, having a direct city phone line in one's office was, in and of itself, a mark of status. The offices of the highest-ranking leaders were also equipped with K lines, which they could use to contact the party, council, company leaders, and the police in the rest of the country outside Budapest. The K line, which was called the "cadre line" by the general public, in fact referred to the separate administrative or public administration telephone network.[191] The ministerial line—or M line—was used by the highest leaders of the party-state. Leaders of the allied states spoke with one another on the direct international line.[192] In this circle, the maintenance of ties was as important as the creation of ties. The cadre line, which I have borrowed for the title of this chapter, can be understood as a metaphor for many things, including the privileges enjoyed by the cadres of the Kádár regime and the channels, both metaphorical and literal, that were accessible to the members of the elite.

The monopoly the party leaders held on information consisted of several elements. So-called closed-circulation books were marked "confidential" and were accessible only to the most influential leaders. These people were able to obtain books by Jean-Paul Sartre, Winston Churchill, and Milovan Djilas in order to have a sophisticated grasp of the opposition literature. In 1957, when ideological instruction and the re-education of functionaries who had wavered in their faith was considered particularly important, the party leadership decided to provide every member of the Central Committee with the books published by

Kossuth Publishing House, and they even allowed the members of the Temporary Executive Committee to choose from among the books printed by all the publishing houses. Even later, the privilege of reading certain restricted materials, summaries, and press reviews was reserved for the highest members of the ruling elite.[193] One clear sign of the strictness with which this monopoly on information was held is that members of the cadre who were working in the second line were not allowed access to all the materials. László Földes, a communist politician who at one time served as the deputy foreign minister, griped about this in his book *Második vonalban* (In the second line). According to Földes, when the Twentieth Congress of the Communist Party of the Soviet Union was held, news of the congress did not reach him directly:

> On one occasion, when I was hunting in the Vértes Hills, I spotted some small plastic bags. They contained the Hungarian translation of the speech that had been held by Khrushchev at the closed sitting of the Congress, printed on delicate paper. In all likelihood, the little bags and the papers with the text inside them had been launched from Austria with balloons. The speech offered many examples of the cruel acts that had been committed by Stalin against upstanding communists who had adopted a different stance on some question.... The radio stations in the West offered explanations of the speech that suited their tastes—and our party remained silent.[194]

Travel Abroad

Party and state leaders had paid vacations, and they were allowed to take trips abroad. True, in the beginning they could only visit vacation spots in other "people's democracies"—for instance, Zakopane in Poland or Karlovy Vary in Czechoslovakia. Later, however, they could travel to more distant countries, first on official trips and then as tourists. In the 1950s, most of the official trips were to other people's democracies, but beginning in the 1960s, the horizon began to broaden.

On October 1, 1954, András Hegedüs traveled to China as the first deputy chairman of the Council of Ministers (i.e., the deputy prime minister) for the fifth anniversary of the victory of the Chinese Red Army. He later wrote about one of his most memorable experiences in China:

> Of the colorful group of people who had been gathered together, for some reason of protocol (who knows what?), at every meal they put the Dalai Lama to my right and the Panchen Lama to my left. One of them was 18 years old, the other was 17. They were not even that much younger than me, but we could not manage to surmount the language barrier or the differences in our cultures. I was given only short answers to my questions, which made the young men seem like simple Chinese youths. But my view of the Dalai Lama changed entirely when I happened, quite accidentally, to see him entering a Buddhist temple, accompanied by a crowd of other priests. A divine sublimity radiated from his face. Standing a bit to the side, I watched his transubstantiation.[195]

In his memoir, which is permeated with ideology and therefore almost unreadable, communist politician György Marosán, who belonged to the inner circle of the party leadership after 1956, writes with almost palpable joy of the moment when he traveled to China in 1957: "I was overjoyed about the trip to China, not just because it was the first time that I was traveling to a country in the Far East, but also because our Chinese colleagues had asked Kádár to take me with him because they wanted to meet me."[196] Of course, Kádár himself had made the decisions concerning who would come as part of the delegation. On the plane on the way to China, Marosán played *ulti* (a popular Hungarian card game) with Kádár and Károly Erdélyi, Kádár's rapporteur, or personal secretary. Thus, he had a chance to get even closer to the most powerful man in the land. He wrote about this with great satisfaction: "I won. They realized that I was a good ulti player too."[197]

Kádár used his travels to get to know the people around him better, and the people he traveled with always tried to curry his favor. He did this himself when he traveled with his entourage as a guest of Khrushchev to New York in September 1960 on the *Baltika* for a general assembly of the United Nations.[198] He later proudly recounted to his wife how he stood his ground as a member of the team of the leaders of the European socialist countries. In 1989, Mária Tamáska offered her recollection of his account: "They crossed the ocean on a Soviet ship, and as a consequence of this, some of the group got seasick and was useless for days. The ship, a nine-ton coasting vessel, proved entirely unsuitable for the trip. The sea at the time was restless. My husband said that only he and Khrushchev showed up for the meals. According to him, he had to 'stand his ground for the nation,' but after the meals he too always got sick."[199]

János and Mária Tamáska Kádár's most significant travel experience came in 1977, when they visited Rome. Before the trip, while the preparatory diplomatic steps were still being taken, Kádár allegedly said the following: "If we are in Rome, it would be polite to look in on the pope." Rome captivated them. More than a decade later, Mária Tamáska still rhapsodized over the Italian capital: "We saw everything we could, but one could spend hours there. The Sistine Chapel is amazing, and since the Pieta was vandalized once, it is now kept behind glass, but they let us in there too, so we could marvel at the statue from up close. All of Rome is indeed an enormous and unrivaled museum, full of wondrous compositions."[200]

The state protocol was not much different from the protocol that was followed in the decade preceding the rise of the system or the decade after its fall. However, it is perhaps revealing to consider the countries to which the head of the state traveled as a representative of the country. In Hungary under socialism, it became a tradition to have a politician with a peasant family background fulfill the functions that were entirely a matter of protocol as a symbolic gesture to the peasant masses. Pál Losonczi, who had served as president of the farmers' agricultural cooperative of Barcs (a small town in southern Hungary), followed István Dobi, a smallholder politician turned communist, in this position.

We know a fair amount about Losonczi's travels, because after many mishaps his bequest eventually became part of a public collection. The museum in Barcs received the rich assortment of relics of Losonczi's career. He had served as chairman of the Hungarian Presidential Council—that is, the titular head of state—from 1967 until 1987. The socialist countries generally maintained ties with one another through the prominent members of the party. Diplomatic relations with the West understandably were not terribly lively. Thus, for the most part, the socialist head of state traveled to destinations in the third world. Pál Losonczi, a man of a peasant background, traveled to distant lands many times. He met with Idi Amin, the Ugandan dictator, and Jean-Bédel Bokassa, the emperor of Central Africa (who was accused of cannibalism by his political enemies). On several occasions, he observed the ritual dances of Africans garbed in national dress, and he had a chance to familiarize himself with the sumptuous ceremonies and luxuries of the Asian dictatorships. Indeed, in the course of one of his official trips, he rode on the back of a giant turtle.[201] He was given several distinctions, including the chain of the Iranian Order of Pahlavi, the Mongolian Order of Sukhbaatar, the chain of the Egyptian Order of the Nile, the chain of the Sudanese Legion of Honor, and the great cross of the Mexican Order of the Aztec Eagle with Collar.[202] He was a recipient of the Grand Cross of the White Rose of Finland with Collar. He received this distinction with Kádár in 1970, and it is worth noting, with regard to the international recognition of the system, that this distinction was also conferred on Hungarian heads of state Miklós Horthy (1931), Árpád Göncz (1995), Ferenc Mádl (2002), and László Sólyom (2005).[203]

Some trips were regarded by the functionaries simply as perks or rewards. The significance of these travel experiences is seldom conveyed in the memoirs, however, which are usually replete with clichés concerning the political importance of the trips. As the vice president of the world fairs, László Földes traveled extensively. When the United States organized an environmentally themed world fair in the city of Spokane, Washington, which lies not far from the Pacific Ocean, Földes boarded a luxury liner on his trip home: "However big the Queen's Elisabeth 2 [sic] may be, it still rocked, and my stomach revolted from the second day until we reached the harbor in Cherbourg. I watched my traveling companions with envy as they ate with hearty appetites. My plan to eat so much that it would end up costing the capitalist shipping company came to nothing. In spite of the discomforts, however, the sea, the meetings with ships coming in the opposite direction, and the spectacles were wondrous experiences."[204] In the end, Földes did not end up costing the capitalist shipping company money, and the discomforts notwithstanding, the socialist world fair expert still had the experience of a lifetime.

Among the party leaders outside Hungary, Kádár maintained close and even amiable ties with Tito and Khrushchev. At Tito's invitation, Kádár and his wife vacationed on the Brijuni Islands, and it was an experience they would always remember: "The sea was very pleasant. We spent part of the day by the seaside, swimming and walking," Kádár's wife Mária later wrote of the time they spent there. She described "a small paradise, colonized with tropical plants, or to be more modest with my phrasing, a botanical garden." Tito himself drove the motorboat when they set out on an excursion.[205]

Many functionaries also traveled to distant lands as tourists. Cultural politician György Aczél, for instance, at age forty had never left the country, but he ultimately traveled to more than fifty countries.[206] Zoltán Vas had a reputation for being quite the globetrotter, even among people in this circle. He traveled to the United States, Mexico, India, Nepal, and Israel. Back home in Hungary, he claimed of his travels that he only liked to go to places where he had at least one friend.[207]

The Kútvölgyi Hospital

As was the case in the interwar period under Horthy, under Kádár, the state provided particularly good medical care for members of the ruling elite. The best care was provided by the Kútvölgyi Hospital. The hospital was built in 1941–1942 (an outpatient clinic was added in the early 1970s), and until 1945 it was known as the Miklós Horthy Hospital. During the Second World War, the most distinguished figures in Hungary were given care here (and in private clinics). In 1945–1950, the hospital was used by officials of the party-state apparatus—that is, members of the National Official Health Service Foundation (Országos Társadalom Biztosítási Tisztviselő Alap, or OTBA). Not surprisingly, the hospital was given a new name after the war, and the change in the political system was accompanied by a change in the types of people who had access to the institution. From 1950 to 1956, the Kútvölgy State Hospital was under the direct control of the central leadership of the Hungarian Workers' Party, and a Soviet physician served as its director. Following the defeat in the revolution, it functioned temporarily as a general public hospital. In 1958, however, it was renamed the Central State Hospital and Outpatient Clinic, and it served as an institution that provided care exclusively for members of the privileged cadres.[208]

In 1955, the doctors at the Kútvölgyi Hospital set a strict everyday schedule for Mátyás Rákosi and Ernő Gerő, at least on paper. For instance, they established the following routine for the former first secretary of the party (who by then had been relieved of his position):

> Comrade Mátyás Rákosi's workday will last from 8:30 AM to 2:30 PM. He will then have lunch and then relax and if possible sleep in a darkened room until 5:00 PM. The telephone in this room should be disconnected. Between 5:00 PM and 7:30 or

8:00 PM he can work at home. After 8:00 in the evening he should only relax. He can spend his time reading (only belles lettres) or engaging in amusing diversions. Every evening, he should spend at least one hour strolling outside. He should go to bed between 10:00 and 11:00 PM. Comrade Rákosi should spend the weekends (Saturday afternoons and Sundays) doing nothing but relaxing somewhere outside the city.[209]

In addition to party and state leaders, the hospital provided care to another fifteen thousand or twenty thousand people in the 1960s. According to estimates made at the time, by the end of the 1970s, the hospital provided care for more than thirty thousand people. For gaining access to the hospital, there were various levels of privilege. The system was a reflection of a very hierarchical mentality whereby people of different orders and ranks in the party-state were given different levels of care. In principle, workers in the party apparatus also had access to care in the hospital, as did the leaders of state institutions, prominent figures in cultural and artistic life, and the people who worked for the Hungarian Young Communist League and the other mass organizations (and their family members).[210] From time to time, the responsible divisions of the Central Committee of the Hungarian Socialist Workers' Party, the Secretariat of the Council of Ministers, and the minister of health would issue detailed regulations concerning who could use the hospital and on what conditions. Someone who made it onto the list (and was referred to as "booked") was given permanent access to the hospital, along with his or her family members. The books noting who had access to the hospital were revised every two years. Anyone who, in the meantime, had fallen from favor lost the privilege of care in the Kútvölgyi Hospital.

Along with the people who had been booked were patients who had been granted permission. Permittees were given access to the hospital for one year. In the 1970s, there were approximately twenty-five thousand permittees (people who had been given the "For the Socialist Homeland" distinction, for instance). One could be granted permission to use the hospital a single time. This permission could be granted by the Party Center, members of the Council of Ministers, or the hospital superintendent on the basis of a preliminary request. This rule accommodated people who had access to the hospital and wanted to have an acquaintance or distant relative admitted, since it was widely known that patients in the hospital were given the best care available in Hungary at the time. Personal connections, however, were not the only way to get access. Signs suggest that one could also simply pay to gain admittance to the hospital. In the 1980s, the state security forces learned that people from the West (the United States, Austria, and Switzerland) had used "various connections" to obtain treatment at the Kútvölgyi Hospital.[211]

Even within the hospital, there was a hierarchy among the patients. The "protected leading comrades" received treatment in a separate part of the building. Rooms were kept at the ready in the C wing on the third floor of the hospital for the first secretary of the Hungarian Socialist Workers' Party, the president of the Council of Ministers, and the chairman of the Presidential Council. Their guards could be given accommodation in this wing. A clinic on the second floor also received and treated patients separately. The documents concerning the case histories of the prominent leaders were stored in a safe in a separate room. The Secretariat of the Central Committee issued a decision specifying who would be given care by the doctors at the Kútvölgyi Hospital (both family doctors and workplace doctors), and access was also specified in the Kútvölgyi authorization. Around-the-clock service was set up for the most influential cadres. The Ministry of Health installed an Altai radio telephone line in the secretary's office of the hospital superintendent, and the hospital was given service cars with distinctive markings that the doctors could use if they were asked to make a house call.[212] In the summer, the staff at the Kútvölgyi Hospital provided medical care at the party vacation resort in Balatonaliga and at the central resort of the Council of Ministers in Balatonszemes (in Őszöd). They worked in two-week shifts. The hospital also maintained a twenty-four-hour physicians' office in the Party Center, the parliament, the National Commandership of the Workers' Militia, and the Party College. Doctors were on duty for the sittings of the Central Committee of the Hungarian Socialist Workers' Party and the Hungarian National Assembly. There was also a division at 17 Mátyás király Street in District 12 with forty beds that provided rehabilitative treatment for national leaders who had exhausted themselves with work, as well as a "psychocal therapy" (*pszichikóterápia*) division at 10–12 Béla király Avenue with fifteen beds.[213] Psychocal therapy, of course, is not an actual concept. Thus, the name of this division can be regarded as an instance of linguistic inventiveness with *psychotherapy* and *physical therapy* or, simply, ignorance, which no one later dared to bother to correct. At this facility, the cadres could take a break from the stress and excitement of their professional lives and then return, well rested and revitalized, and begin to address new tasks.

Because of the high-ranking patients who sought care within its walls, the hospital came within the purview of the third branch of the Ministry of Internal Affairs. The independent III/III-A subdivision conducted "preventative operations" to avert sabotage or assassination attempts. According to an internal affairs report issued in 1963, there were eighteen people working in the hospital who earlier had been part of the ministry's network, and the ministry had eight agents officially stationed in the hospital. Several members of the board of directors submitted reports from time to time to the state security forces. These people included the hospital superintendent, the economic director, the head physician in the C wing, the "peak secretary" of the party, the heads of the technical and personnel departments, the head of the pharmacy, and the president of the union committee.[214] They did not uncover many sabotage attempts, however. On one occasion, a patient developed serious lesions because the hydrochloric acid had not been properly diluted, but the author of the report comforted his superiors with the reassurance that "the case did not involve a leading comrade."[215]

In 1980, an event took place in the Central State Hospital that was emblematic. An unfamiliar person presented himself. According to the descriptions given by internal affairs, he was a well-dressed man who wore a necklace with a large steel cross. He introduced himself as Dr. Csémi and then added that he was General Colonel Károly Csémi's son. According to the internal affairs report, he told the doctors that he had come from the "gynecology department of St. James Hospital, where he admitted a woman by the name of Mrs. Vadász" who had been bleeding badly and had contended that she had come from the central hospital and she was going to submit a complaint because of what had happened. Since the case involved one of his colleagues, he was willing to have the whole affair "smoothed over."[216] The man used the phrase "but you don't mind, do you" (using the informal form of address in Hungarian) remarkably frequently, presumably in an attempt to imitate the direct and fraternal style of the leading figures.[217] At the time, the authorities considered the act attempted blackmail, but today it perhaps might be better understood as an avant-garde criticism of the doctrinaire system. By using the name Vadász, which means "hunter," the protagonist of the story, like a figure from the oeuvre of François Villon, made clear that the case involved the wife of a high-ranking functionary who had had an abortion, because at the time, only party and state leaders were allowed to hunt. Adding gravity to his claim were his appearance in person and his claim that he was the son of a powerful general colonel. In the central hospital, however, which was kept under strict control, he did not attain his goal. He left without having managed to get his hands on any money. But when the case was investigated, the internal affairs officials discovered that earlier many calls had come in for a Dr. Csémi in the gynecology department of the hospital. Thus, in other places the shrewd trickster had introduced himself as a doctor who worked in the Kútvölgyi Hospital, and presumably he had been successful in his scheme.[218]

The Kerepesi Cemetery

In the 1960s, party members began to be buried in the Pantheon of the Workers' Movement in the Kerepesi Cemetery. The central memorial site of this pantheon, the sepulchral vault of the communist soldiers and functionaries, was inaugurated in 1959.[219] The party leadership first discussed the possibility of creating a memorial to the five great (at the time still unnamed) martyrs of the party and the victims of massacres that were committed in 1919 (following the fall of a short-lived communist regime in Hungary) in a "proletarian" neighborhood in 1949.[220] In the end, however, instead of erecting a monument in a working-class neighborhood, the party created a memorial as a burial site in the cemetery on Kerepesi Avenue. The question was discussed in March 1957, when the leadership was considering the question of the final resting place of the "victims of the counterrevolution." In the period of consolidation following the revolution, Kádár sought to legitimize the reprisals that had been taken and his own position of power by paying tribute to the memory of the alleged victims. Ultimately, however, the pantheon was created not just for these victims. Rather, it was made the resting place for communists and a mausoleum of the workers' movement. Beginning in the 1960s, members of the party leadership were buried here.

In earlier times, the cemetery (which today is also known as the Fiumei Avenue Cemetery) was already thought of as the resting place of prominent members of the elite. It had been declared a "resting place of honor" in 1885.[221] Many heads of state were buried here, including Gyula Gömbös in 1936, Pál Teleki and Károly Huszár in 1941, and Gyula Peidl in 1943. Each of these men had served at some point as prime minister in the tempestuous interwar period.²²² Today, the site is less a memorial to the tradition of the workers' movement than an embodiment of a kind of continuity in Hungarian history. To get to the pantheon from the main entrance, one first passes the graves of seven Hungarian Jacobins who were executed in 1795 by the Habsburgs and then the mausoleum of Lajos Batthyány, who served as prime minister under the revolutionary government in 1848 and was executed by Habsburg emperor Franz Joseph in 1849 for his role in the revolution. Once at the pantheon, visible behind the mausoleum is the sepulchral monument of Lajos Kossuth, who died in exile after having to flee the country following the failed revolution of 1849–1849, and Mihály Károlyi, who was the leader of a short-lived bourgeois democratic government in Hungary in 1918–1919 and who also died in exile.²²³ Continuing on, the visitor arrives at the graves of politicians who were prominent following the change of regimes in Hungary.

In the mausoleum, in the central building of the pantheon, one finds urn graves. Six pylons were erected next to the building. These pillars resemble towers and commemorate soldiers who were buried in other cemeteries. A plot was set aside in the shadow of the mausoleum where less prominent individuals were buried. Four additional plots and a so-called heroic plot were also considered part of the pantheon, and indeed some of the graves were even moved to these plots.

The mausoleum was designed by József Körner, the famous architect whose name was mentioned earlier in connection with the construction of villas. (Körner's second major commission was the design of the party building for District 2 in the 1950s; today, the building is home to the mayor's office of the same district.) The statues surrounding the building were made by Zoltán Olcsai-Kiss, who returned to Hungary in 1945 after having lived for twenty-three years as an émigré. He was successful in Western Europe as an artist, and the Sèvres porcelain manufacturer not far from Paris made replicas of his small statues.²²⁴ The people who commissioned the designs thought that the system would endure, for the building had space for 365 urns. I have found no sources indicating precisely why they chose this number, the number of days in a year. Perhaps this monument to the soldiers of communism was also intended to embody the inviolable unity of time. Presumably, the people who designed it were also thinking of the calendar of saints, which, as it is based on medieval tradition, has one saint for every day. In general, the symbolic language fashioned by the communists borrowed heavily from Christian tradition.

The system proved less durable than they had thought, however. By the time socialism fell, a total of seventy-five comrades had been buried in the mausoleum. The last such funeral was held in 1988. Thus, some of the urns in the building, which were made by the Zsolnay Manufacture (an internationally famous Hungarian porcelain factory), were left in storage, empty. In principle, the columbarium that was chosen for a specific urn was a sign of rank. The building had an upper and a lower urn room, and the names of the people buried in the upper room were written on the gate on the left, while the names of the people who were buried in the lower room were written on the gate on the right. According to the original plans, the ashes of the most prominent and high-ranking individuals were to be stored on the upper level, while the ashes of those who had had more modest careers were to be kept on the lower level. An esplanade of grave sites across from the mausoleum, which provided space for burials involving coffins, was to be used for the earthly remains of higher-ranking officials, while the plots on the sides were intended for the remains of those of lower rank. The pylons that were closer to the mausoleum were considered more distinguished sites for the names of the fallen.[225] In the end, however, the locations of the graves and the memorial sites did not reflect a clear hierarchy. Presumably, the family members of the dead exerted some influence on the selection of the sites.[226]

Many intellectuals who had communist sympathies were reburied in the mausoleum, including writer, poet, and aesthete Béla Balázs; painter István Dési Huber; and underground communist Endre Ságvári, who died in a gunfight with the gendarmerie in 1944. Later, the remains of leading functionaries were reburied in the mausoleum. These men include the following: József Révai,[227] the only leading figure of the Rákosi era on whom this honor was conferred; president of the republic Árpád Szakasits; Sándor Rónai, chairman of the Hungarian Presidential Council between 1950 and 1952; Ferenc Münnich, who, as chairman of the Council of Ministers of the People's Republic of Hungary from 1958 to 1961, was the second-most-important figure of the first decade of the Kádár system; the aforementioned István Dobi; Pál Ilku, who served as minister of culture; Endre Sík, who served as minister of foreign affairs; and Sándor Czottner, who served as minister of heavy industry. The remains of the great poet Attila József were reburied in the first of the left-hand-side plots surrounding the building. He was reburied in parcel thirty-five in 1994 because the democratic system that emerged after 1989 also sought to appropriate his legacy. The ashes of communist minister of internal affairs László Rajk, who was executed after a show trial in 1949, were also reburied here. Some of the high-ranking communists who died in the 1956 revolution were buried in the row of grave sites on the right. Later, politicians were buried here, including István Kossa, who served as minister of industry and later minister of finance, and Péter Vályi, minister of finance and deputy head of state. A few scholars and prominent figures of public life were buried here as well, including philosopher György Lukács and historian and philosopher Erik Molnár.[228]

There were also "communist plots and columbaria" in the Farkasrét Cemetery, which was considered perhaps the most beautiful cemetery in Budapest, for people who did not get spots in the Kerepesi Cemetery. In 1971, Mátyás Rákosi was laid to rest here. The Kádár system had endeavored to distance itself from Rákosi from the outset, so he clearly could not have been given a place in the sepulchral monument to the soldiers of communism.[229] The fact that the memorial site contained urns with the ashes of the party leaders made the Kerepesi Cemetery unpopular in the eyes of many: "In many cases, burial in the Farkasrét Cemetery came with an aura of deviance and even oppositionary sentiment," as Vilmos Tóth observes in an essay.[230] There were even members of the party leadership who did not like the pantheon. According to his wife, Zoltán Vas, who fell out of favor with and eventually was forced out of the party (but was fond of luxury and pomp), "said while he was still alive, some ten years ago, that he did not like that place, because it is dark and unfriendly, and he didn't want to be among the comrades who were buried there." Vas was buried in the artists' plot of the Farkasrét Cemetery.[231]

In 1989, János Kádár himself was laid to rest in side plot number twelve, not long after the reburial of Imre Nagy and his associates, in the presence of a crowd that was estimated to number several hundred thousand. Allegedly, the grave site was chosen by Károly Grósz, the last secretary general of the Hungarian communist party, and a raised sepulchral monument was erected in Kádár's memory that differed from the others in both its materials and dimensions. This is interesting because Kádár himself had once wanted the graves in the pantheon, which were adorned with five-pointed stars, all to be the same size.[232] After the regime change, representatives of the socialist system generally were no longer buried in the Kerepesi Cemetery for political reasons. Several of these men were buried in the Farkasrét Cemetery, including György Aczél, the most prominent politician of culture under Kádár; György Marosán, minister of state; Antal Apró, deputy head of state; Károly Grósz, first secretary and head of state; and Lajos Czinege, minister of foreign affairs. In 1996, Gyula Kállai, who had served as head of state, was buried in the Kerepesi Cemetery, but not in the Pantheon of the Workers' Movement.[233]

The change of regimes led to a decisive shift in attitudes toward the pantheon among the state, the wider public, and individual families. In 1992, the remains of László Rajk, who had been both a prominent communist and victim of communism, were moved to a new grave site. The same was done with the remains of poet and humorist Andor Gábor and poet Attila József in 1994, former head of state Sándor Rónai in 1998, and minister Pál Ilku in 2003. For József and Rajk, this was their second reburial. Slowly, the past became history, and it was given new interpretations by the next generation. Many families not only removed the remains of their family members from the pantheon, which had become something of a bad memory, but actually had them removed from the cemetery altogether. Árpád Szakasits was reburied in the Farkasrét Cemetery, and Károly Olt, who had served as minister of finance, was reburied in the Rákoskeresztúr Cemetery. The remains of a trade union leader were reburied, and he was given the last rites according to Catholic ceremony in the Saint László Church in Kőbánya.[234]

The burial of Antall József, who served as the first freely elected prime minister after 1989, was an event of tremendous symbolic importance in the history of the Kerepesi Cemetery. It helped lift the grim shadows of the recent past and restore some measure of continuity with the cemetery's past.[235] The system had changed, and the Pantheon of the Workers' Movement, with its crumbling walls, had itself become a monument to a bygone era and the unstoppable flow of time.

NOTES

1. Even today, "Buda hills" is understood to refer primarily to District 12, although earlier it referred to Districts 1 and 2 as well.
2. Éva Gál 2009, 45.

3. Running water was installed here in the 1980s. Since then, the buildings have been remodeled and bathrooms were constructed. Budapest Főváros Levéltára (Budapest City Archives, hereafter cited as BCA), fond XV, 17, box 329.
4. Éva Gál 2009, 49.
5. Gábor 1997, 38.
6. Ritoók 2000, 37.
7. G. D. S., "Szárnyaszegett fácános" [Broken-feathered pheasant garden], *Hegyvidék*, November 16, 2005, 18.
8. Éva Gál 2009, 57–60.
9. Ibid., 35.
10. Magyar Nemzeti Levéltár Országos Levéltára (Hungarian National Archives, hereafter cited as HNA), fond XIX-A-83, group a. 221/20. Az Elhagyott Javak Kormánybiztosságának felszámolása és az elhagyott javak leltározása [The liquidation of the State Commission for Unclaimed Property and the inventory of unclaimed property], gov. decree no. 1800/1948, *Magyar Közlöny* (Hungarian Official Gazette, hereafter cited as HOG), February 14, no. 37; 224/10. Az Elhagyott Javak Kormánybiztosságának megszűnése, Molnár Jenő kormánybiztos felmentése [The liquidation of the State Commission for Unclaimed Property, discharge of State Commissioner Jenő Molnár]. 236/3. Az Elhagyott Javak Kormánybiztossága felszámolási határidejének meghosszabbítása [Deadline extension for the liquidation of the State Commission for Unclaimed Property], gov. decree no. 5260/1948, HOG, May 16, no. 111; 245/5. Az elhagyott javak kérdésének rendezéséről szóló 1948. évi 28. Tc. végrehajtása. [Execution of Article 28 of 1948, Closing the issue of unclaimed property], gov. decree no. 8920/1948. HOG, August 27, no. 192.
11. Schiffer 1985, 64–70.
12. Nógrádi 1970, 277–278.
13. Állambiztonsági Szolgálatok Történeti Levéltára (Historical Archives of the Hungarian State Security, hereafter cited as HAHSS), fond 2.1, V-150238, VI/6, Tibor Érsek. Zoltán Vas, head of the Department of Finance in the party, had villas renovated and furnished for the "highest-ranking party and state officials" by the VII/4 and then the X/4 finance department of state security. The head of the department was Andor Csapó. His deputy was János Komendó. However, it was the so-called passport transactions that supplied the funds for the remodeling of the Korvin Ottó Hospital, children's resorts, and villas reserved for foreign guests. HAHSS, fond 2.1, V-150028/1, V/1-a.

14. Gábor Péter's girlfriend first lived in Normafa (a forested neighborhood high in the Buda hills), and later in Mártonhegyi Street. Péter arranged "special food service" and the use of a state vehicle for her. Sometimes he gave her small gifts, such as lingerie, paid for by Andor Csapó out of the expense fund. Péter also helped his girlfriend's mother acquire a new apartment. Péter's misuse of his position and funds was hardly exceptional. János Komendó furnished an apartment for his lover, who was a dancer on the Vasas culture team. HAHSS, fond 2.1, V-150244, VI/9, Komendó János. Andor Csapó used the funds for similar purposes. HAHSS, fond 2.1, V-150028/1, VI/1-a, Péter Gábor.

15. In Péter's trial, the Supreme Court declared: "Gábor Péter, who at the time of the accusation was a high-ranking state official, enjoyed all the special privileges that leaders at the time were generally granted, or could be granted. For instance, he had been given a spectacularly furnished Rózsadomb villa. The evidence that was produced in the course of the discussion concerning the new trial indicated that at the time leading party and state officials did not pay rent or utilities and were given free fuel and groceries. They could purchase clothes and textiles at a discount, too." HAHSS, fond 2.1, V-150028/3, VI/1-b. Supreme Court decision 19–20. In 1953, members of political committees earned the same amount as ministers (5,750 forints), and they received additional monthly perks valued between three thousand and ten thousand forints, depending on the size of their households. Rent and utilities (electricity, heating, and telephone) were covered, and fuel was provided, as were the costs of "garden maintenance" (the sum available was an annual two forints per square meter); the wages for the housekeeper, janitor, or caretaker, including rates and taxes (at most three household employees were allowed, depending on the size of the household); and extra costs related to household maintenance, such as interior repairs involving plumbing, heating, and electricity. When the cadres moved, the state covered the costs of the move, the onetime expense of furnishing the apartment, repair work, and remodeling up to fifty thousand forints (in the case of sums exceeding this amount, the committee determined the amount of money that would be made available). Exterior maintenance and renovation were the responsibility of the housing management company and the party. Food and drinks were reimbursed at a rate of up to seventy forints per day. HNA, fond M-KS 276, group 53, storage unit 131.

16. In the 1950s, free hunting licenses were available only for professional hunters or occasionally members of diplomatic bodies. For private, invitation-only hunting trips, special hunting permits were issued that

served in lieu of a license. Members of the elite often did not have either a license or a permit, so technically they were poaching. At first, the question of who was allowed to hunt was a matter of unspoken agreement. Later, members of the Egyetértés Vadásztársaság (Concord Hunting Society) were entitled to hunt on reserved areas. Sándor Tóth 2005, 130–132.

17. Kő and Nagy 2002, 176–178.
18. Pünkösti 1996, 126.
19. BCA, fond XV, 17, box 329, 32769, District 14, 25 Szabó József Street.
20. Ibid.
21. On the thirteen-hectare lot at 28 Béla király Avenue, social realist residences were built for Mátyás Rákosi (who never moved in), Ernő Gerő, József Révai, and Mihály Farkas. Hegedüs 1985, 138. Sándor Gáspár, interview by Márton Kozák, 1989–1990, 1956-os Intézet Oral History Archivum (1956 Institute, Oral History Archives, hereafter cited as OHA), no. 220, 60.
22. Of the homes designed by Körner, the two-apartment villa built in 1940 at 16 Palánta Street deserves particular mention. The design plans have not been preserved. On the design, see András Körner, "Körner József (1907–1971) építész emlékkiállítása a HAP galériaban (HAP sajtóközlemény)" [József Körner (1907–1971), memorial exhibition at HAP Gallery (HAP press release)], https://epiteszforum.hu/korner-jozsef-emlekkiallitas-a-hap-galeriaban.
23. Hegedüs 1985, 138.
24. Ibid.
25. At the 1953 convention of the Hungarian Workers' Party Secretariat, it was decided that three villas of the complex euphemistically referred to as the "Szabadság Hill housing estate" would be converted into resorts for the Central Directorate and the Politburo, and the fourth would be reserved for visiting foreign party leaders as guest houses. HNA, fond M-KS 276, group 54, storage unit 280.
26. Report no. 0235 of September 2002 by the State Audit Office of Hungary recounts the fate of the complex. The report is titled, "Audit of the Costs of Remodeling Attributed to Personal Protection Services at the Permanent Residence Allocated by the Government for the Prime Minister."
27. Archival sources indicate that the new leaders and their wives did indeed have special needs and wishes, and they were picky about the available buildings. Andor Csapó, for example, recalls one case: "Zoltán Vas commanded me to allocate a villa for Minister Czottner, but it took a long time, because the minister's wife insisted on a certain type. Consequently, I was given the following order by Gerő: 'C. [Comrade] Péter! Put

everything aside, and solve the Czottner villa question. What's taking so long? Gerő.'" Andor Csapó, letter to Károly Kiss, director of the Central Commission for Discipline Inspection, August 13, 1954, HAHSS, fond 2.1, V-150028/1, VI/1-a.

28. Villa design in Hungary maintained its relative independence of architectural styles dominating given periods, because the architects had to conform to the developers' stylistic preferences and values. Sármány-Parsons 1992. Architects who worked on commission, however, strove to assert their personal styles, occasionally even by misleading the affluent but naive developers. In 1940, for instance, György Rácz, who had been prohibited from setting up his own architecture business due to his illegal communist past, designed what was seemingly a "Swiss-style" villa—but actually he disguised his modern building under a "Swiss" rooftop. Parmer 2001, 109–111.

29. In the first decades of the nineteenth century, the villas in the Buda hills were typically built in the classicist style, with porticos featuring columns topped with Doric, Ionic, and Corinthian capitals. The first romanticist-style houses of the Buda hills began to appear in the 1840s, when "Swiss-style" villas became popular. They had wooden frames, wooden verandas, wooden pediments, and usually two stories. Éva Gál 2001, 26–27.

30. Aiming to create a national style, artists and architects reinterpreted and mixed earlier stylistic elements, resulting in buildings that bore an eclectic array of styles. Parmer 2001, 212.

31. Prior to the "modern turn" in his art, Lajos Kozma was an inspired representative of the neo-baroque style. Parmer 2001, 30–31. But the so-called Kozma baroque differs from the historicist neo-baroque buildings that were popular at the time.

32. Horányi 2006, 122.

33. Rainer 1996, 345.

34. See the inventory taken of Imre Nagy's villa at 43 Orsó Street on April 30, 1957. HNA, fond XX-5, group h, box 12, volume 1, 19–22. In most surviving photographs, Nagy is seated in his favorite historicist-style wing chair, which is on exhibit today at the Imre Nagy Memorial House located in the villa.

35. Schiffer 1985, 322.

36. Ritoók 2000, 37.

37. Nógrádi 1970, 430.

38. Ibid.

39. Eva Gál 2009, 49.

40. HNA, fond XX-5, group h, V 150 000, 4.
41. Ibid., 5.
42. His letter summarizes the events as follows:

> I have been living at 9 Lóránt Street in district XII since mid-October 1950. I moved here from Tatabánya, having been elected director of the reader's department of the Hungarian Writers' Association. Yesterday, my father, who had not yet come to see us in Budapest, paid us a visit. He is 77 years old, so it is difficult for him to find the energy to take such a trip. He wanted to see us before he dies. My father (István Koncser, tailor, mother's name: Rozália Zámoly, date of birth 1877) has been retired for the past four or five years. He is hard of hearing and his vision is poor, he is a sickly, crippled man. Today he was playing and chatting with his grandchildren in the garden. At around noon, he went out in the street to take a look around. He crossed the narrow street and looked around. It was here that he was shot by the state security guard. He was not in a restricted area. The guard may have tried to warn him first, but he did not hear him because, as I said, he is hard of hearing. He would not have tried to run away, since he is a slow-moving old man; he was surprised by the gunshot. My wife rushed out into the street, but they did not let her out, they did not even let her approach my father. They sat my father down on the cold ground and checked his wound. My wife wanted to go to his side and put a dressing on the wound, but they yelled at her harshly and did not let her go near him. (HNA, fond M-KS-276, group 65, storage unit 379)

43. HAHSS, fond 3.1, group 9, V 150305, VI/59, Mrs. József Szatmári.
44. After Gábor Péter's arrest, a state security officer recalled in a 1953 report that six months before,

> A lieutenant named Dalmi (who had an artificial leg) appeared at the Békés County department of the state security and declared that he had been given a confidential order by Comrade Péter to find a cook. The cook will be employed by Péter. He asked for my assistance in the search. Dalmi then presented the conditions and features, what figure Comrade Péter had in mind for the cook. Since it seemed unlikely that I would find a cook who would satisfy his preconception (I remember, her height, hair color, and figure were all specified, and her reliability), I took no steps to do so. (Kő and Nagy 2002, 153–154)

45. HNA, fond M-KS 276, group 53, storage unit 46.

46. Meeting of the central leadership, April 25, 1950. HNA, fond M-KS 276, group 54, storage unit 11, 4.

47. Losonczy 1948, 20; cited in Kövér 1998, 201.

48. Kövér 1998, 200.

49. Summary on individuals arrested, interned, and rehabilitated in the case of János Kádár and his accomplices. HAHSS, fond 2.1, Closed Archive, IX/9.

50. Pünkösti 2001, 373.

51. Trial of Gábor Péter, minutes of Andor Csapó's interrogation, April 3, 1957. HAHSS, fond 2.1, V-150028/1, VI/1-a.

52. "He told Csató 'to get me a pit like the one Péter has so that I can soak my feet in it.' He also said that 'it would be great also to have the adjoining garden so I could take strolls like Péter.'" HAHSS, fond 2.1, V-150028 I/1-e; published in Kis-Kapin 2007.

53. According to the design archives, the house at 21 Cserje Street, later to become the Kádár villa, was built by "Hon. Director István Vértes" and his wife, "Hon. Mrs. István Vértes." The couple carried out the construction under the wife's name. István Vértes's parents were Jewish. He converted to Christianity as an adult, joining the Calvinist Church. His father, József Vértes, a professor at the Székesfehérvár Trade Academy, was killed in Auschwitz. The son, apparently, was not threatened by immediate financial problems, since in 1943 he had purchased the lot, and construction must have begun during the war. In the summer of 1947, István Vértes joined the Independent Hungarian Democratic Party led by Father István Balogh. In the elections held on August 31, he won a seat in the legislature from the greater Budapest party list. At the January 19, 1949, session of the Hungarian National Assembly, Imre Nagy, speaker of the national assembly, presented a letter by representative Vértes in which he asked for a two-month leave on account of illness. In the May 15, 1949, parliamentary elections, Vértes was among the nominees on the greater Budapest list of the Hungarian Independence Popular Front, but by this time he may have emigrated to London.

54. After Kádár's release from jail, the couple lived in Fokos Street, Kőbánya in, according to Mrs. Kádár, a one-room and bathroom apartment. Later, they were given Rudolf Földvári's three-room apartment on Lékay Square. Meanwhile, István Bata moved into the villa. He was later replaced by a Zala County secretary. "Jóban-rosszban: Interjú Kádár Jánosnéval" [For better or for worse: Interview with Mrs. János Kádár], V, *Magyarország* [Hungary], no. 44 (November 3, 1989): 4–5. After

November 7, for a short while they lived in the parliament building. They later lived in the Foreign Affairs Hotel until May 1957, when they reacquired the Cserje Street house. "Jóban-rosszban: Interjú Kádár Jánosnéval," IX, *Magyarország*, no. 48 (December 1, 1989): 4–5. On October 29, István Bata fled to the Soviet Union. On November 2, he negotiated with János Kádár, who had arrived in Moscow, and Bata was present at the open convention of the Central Committee Secretariat of the Soviet Communist Party. On November 16, 1956, he was ousted from the party for being Stalinist. It was not until 1958 that he was allowed to return to Hungary.

55. Beginning in 1851, István Bata (1910–1982) served as a substitute member of the communist Hungarian Workers' Party (MDP) Central Directorate. He became a full member in 1963. He served as minister of defense from July 4, 1953, to October 24, 1956. In this capacity he was a member of the Hungarian delegation to sign the Warsaw Pact in 1955. On October 24, 1956, Bata divided Budapest into three military zones and gave the order to crush the revolution. Bata fled to the Soviet Union on October 29. On November 2, he negotiated with János Kádár, who had also traveled to the Soviet Union, and he may have been present for the open convention of the Central Committee Secretariat of the Soviet Communist Party. On November 16, 1956, he was ousted from the party for allegedly being Stalinist. It was not until 1958 that he was allowed to return to Hungary, and he was not allowed to return to the house on Cserje Street. István Dénes (1923–2005) was member of the communist Hungarian Workers' Party Central Directorate from May 31, 1950. He served as a member of the directorate's secretariat until May 30, 1954, and was a substitute member of the Organizing Committee of the MDP Central Directorate. In June 1950, he was appointed director of the Office of the Central Directorate. Dénes was secretary general of the Union of Working Youth between March 29, 1951, and February 11, 1954. Then he was elected first secretary of the Zala County MDP. After 1956, he was employed at the Ministry of Foreign Trade. He served as head of department, sales manager, trade advisor in Nigeria and the Belgrade Hungarian Embassy, and deputy director at Chemokomplex. In September 1985, he became the chief executive officer of ZENIT Ltd. He retired in 1987.

56. Pünkösti 1996, 322.

57. "Jóban-rosszban: Interjú Kádár Jánosnéval," VIII, *Magyarország*, no. 47 (November 24, 1989): 4.

58. Borenich 1995, 182–183.

59. On the other hand, János Berecz believes one of Kádár's childhood memories to be the inspiration for keeping poultry in the garden: "In one of our intimate conversations I asked him where his devotion for keeping chicken originates. To his heart, he would have only kept a rooster, but a poultry-run is incomplete... without hens. To my question about this infatuation with roosters he responded: when as a child he lived in the Dohány Street neighborhood, *he was so lonesome*, that he had only a rooster, whom he walked on a string-leash." János Berecz 2003, 348.

60. Borenich 1995, 178.

61. On Kádár's alleged, relative puritanism, see Huszár 2006, 248–253; Majtényi 2012.

62. Ibid., 251.

63. I describe the interior based on the catalog of the auction held after Mrs. Kádár's death. *Kádár Jánosné hagyatékának árverése* [Auction of Mrs. Kádár's bequest] 1993. The catalog section on furniture (with no pagination) begins with item 744 and ends with item 783.

64. Mrs. Kádár said of the interior: "There is no and has never been any luxury here. I did not crave it, and my husband would not have tolerated any of it." Yet even after her husband's death, she refused that any photographs be taken of the house. "Jóban-rosszban: Interjú Kádár Jánosnéval," V, *Magyarország*, no. 44 (November 3, 1989): 5. György Aczél describes the apartment in which the Kádárs lived (as we shall see, his description was not entirely fair): "Even in his house the most tawdry, kitschy fake fireplace was mingled with beautiful paintings by Szőnyi and Egry... it is typical of every self-educated man that no matter how much he improves, in a certain sense his tastes remain mixed." György Aczél 1999, 120.

65. I have art historian Péter Rostás to thank for this information. According to the auction catalog, the piece of furniture was an example of the transitional style of the Second French Empire, between the age of Louis Philippe and the rise of the Third Reich. *Kádár Jánosné hagyatékának árverése*, 1993 [Auction of Mrs. Kádár's bequest], 744.

66. Huszár 2002, letter 727, 30.

67. György Aczél 1999, 112. Only according to Mrs. Kádár had they frequently entertained guests: "As it is widely known, János Kádár loved parties, and he often had them in his apartment." "Jóban-rosszban: Interjú Kádár Jánosnéval," VI, *Magyarország*, no. 45 (November 10, 1989): 4.

68. György Aczél 1999, 120.

69. "Jóban-rosszban: Interjú Kádár Jánosnéval," V, *Magyarország*, no. 44 (November 3, 1989): 5.

70. György Aczél 1999, 122.

71. Huszár 2002, letter 691, 5.
72. Ibid., letter 706, 15.
73. Ibid., letter 714, 23.
74. György Aczél 1999, 124.
75. "Jóban-rosszban: Interjú Kádár Jánosnéval," X, *Magyarország*, no. 49 (December 8, 1989): 5.
76. HNA, fond M-KS 288, 1957, 1 storage unit.
77. The Central Committee of the Hungarian Socialist Workers' Party passed resolutions on November 8, 1971; February 26, 1979; and January 24, 1983, on the housing management fund of the party apparatus. "The housing management fund was to be used for housing transfers of public interest. According to the November 1971 resolution of the secretariat, "In justified cases, on the basis of individual preliminary approval by the Department of Party Management and Administration of the Central Committee, the Budapest Party Committee and county party committees may provide subsidies for the acquisition of housing under the control or disposition of the committee for comrades who have been transferred." HNA, fond M-KS, group 7, 1971, storage unit 389, 13.
78. BCA, fond XV, 17, box 329, 13045/4, Trombitás Street 39.
79. BCA, fond XV, 17, box 329, 15139/4. II, Szemlőhegy Street 42.
80. According to a 1989 sociological survey of party leaders, 71 percent of party members held clear title to the property they inhabited, and 22 percent were head lessees. Thirty-one percent lived in detached houses, and 41 percent lived in apartment blocks. Pál Tóth, "Az apparátus helyzetének komplex vizsgálata: Zárójelentés I, 1989" [A complex study of the apparatus's position: Final report 1, 1989], prepared on commission by the Institute of Social Science under the APB I. 2-01-04 subprogram, topic no. 2. 5. 7, supervisor Alfréd Lechóczky. Tibor Valuch called my attention to this source. For a detailed analysis of the document, see Balázs Varga 2009.
81. Szendrői et al. 1972, 40, 46. Includes descriptions and photographs of these apartment complexes.
82. György and Durkó 1993, 99.
83. Berta 1994.
84. Presich 1998a, 91.
85. Pünkösti 1996, 315–316.
86. Pünkösti 1992, 252.
87. Zoltán Brázay, "Nevezetes balatoniak," *Balatoni Kurír*, November 13, 1941, 1–2. Cited by Karkovány 2007, 3.
88. Karkovány 2007, 4.

89. "Jóban-rosszban: Interjú Kádár Jánosnéval," V, *Magyarország*, no. 44 (November 3, 1989): 4.

90. János Berecz 2003, 348.

91. HNA, fond M-KS 288, group 7, storage unit 537, November 21, 1977.

92. The cadre competence list is a collection of those offices that, in theory, were directly decided on by party leaders. The number of such offices was increased to 3,812 by the 1950 issuing of the list. In the mid-1950s, it included 2,414–2,261 positions. By 1966, this number had grown to 2,789; by 1987, it was 1,241, and in 1988, it had dropped to 435. György Varga and Szakadát 1992, 75; György Varga 1998.

93. HNA, fond M-KS 288, group 37, storage unit 385.

94. Hegedüs 1988, 169.

95. Huszár 2005, 81.

96. Hegedüs 1988, 167–168. On November 2, 1956, *Népakarat* (The People's Will) reported that two of its journalists had managed to enter Rákosi's villa. "But we were amazed not only by the furniture. We admired the thick Dutch cigars by Hoenson, the liquors, wines, champagnes, cognacs, and other drinks that we have never either seen or tasted, things from France, Spain, and who knows what other countries." Baranyai György and Nógrádi Gábor, "A Rákosi-villa rejtelmei" [Secrets of the Rákosi villa], *Népakarat*, November 2, 1956, 1. The Swiss Library of Eastern Europe at the University of Bern contains a few 1956 photos of the Rákosi chateau. These are described in Pünkösti 1996, 129.

97. In addition to being an invaluable source for art historians, interior design also offers insights for the social historian into the personality, values, and social networks of the person in question. Gyáni 1992, 51. In this case, it reveals the potentials of surviving traditions in the formation of individual and groups identities.

98. HAHSS, fond 2.1, V-150244 VI/9, János Komendó.

99. Hegedüs 1988, 168; Pünkösti 1996, 326.

100. HAHSS, fond 2.1, V-150262, VI/28, Mrs. Andor Csapó.

101. Andor Csapó was head of the X/4 Finance Department of the State Security.

102. HAHSS, fond 2.1, V-150262, VI/28, Mrs. Andor Csapó. Art historian Péter Rostás assisted in the analysis of state security inventories. I am grateful for his generous help in my research. A "pluralism of styles"—that is, an admixture of furniture bearing the traits of various styles and tendencies, had been the trend in interior design at the turn of the century. In fact, as Ilona Sármány-Parsons states, "The many draperies and jumble of ornaments, collectibles, and rugs from the East eventually covered every

surface." Sármány-Parsons 1992, 189. The proprietors of the villas, given the obligation to make a show of their status, took care to furnish the parlors and drawing rooms, and they used every means at their disposal to impress their guests.

103. HAHSS, fond 2.1, V-150244, VI/9, János Komendó.
104. HNA, fond M-KS 276, group 65, storage unit 79.
105. Schiffer 1985, 228.
106. HNA, fond XIX-L-20, group j, box 88-101.
107. Mravik 2003, 28.
108. HAHSS, fond 2.1, V-150244, interrogation record of János Komendó, February 4, 1953.
109. HNA, fond M-KS 288, group 37, box 385.
110. HAHSS, fond 2.1, V-150028/1, VI/1-a.
111. HAHSS, fond 2.1, V-150028/4; cited in Pünkösti 2001, 131–132.
112. Hegedüs 1988, 169, 188.
113. HNA, fond M-KS 276, group 53, storage unit 281. The Politburo discussed the method of rehabilitation at the meeting on April 19, 1956.
114. I would like to thank Dr. Sándor Tóth for sharing this information with me in the course of a conversation.
115. HNA, fond M-KS 276, group 53, storage unit 43; HNA, fond M-KS 276, group 53, storage unit 43 (January 12, 1950); HNA, fond M-KS 276, group 53, storage unit 180 (June 9, 1954); Honvári 2006.
116. HNA, fond M-KS 288, group 7, storage unit 439; Bányai 2005.
117. Centralized regulation of wages, the progressive taxation system, and the legal system itself hindered the emergence of high incomes. In 1983, however, the monthly average income of party leaders (9,100 forints) was far above the average, and 33 percent of the party leaders made more than 10,000 forints per month. Wages continued to increase until the change of regime, but functionaries' earnings were much less than the top incomes in the private sector. Their status was strengthened by the various privileges they enjoyed.
118. The notion of private land ownership was introduced with the 1967 IV land rights act. It stated that citizens' lands up to six thousand square meters within an inner-belt area, on farmsteads, or as garden plots were personal property, because they were used to meet "personal needs." This proprietary form was considered distinct from private property, although essentially it was little more than a socialist metamorphosis of the notion of private property. Thus, people were entitled to acquire property in outer-belt areas. The earlier 1897 act abolished the institution of personal land ownership. After this, the regulations that applied to plots beyond the

administrative boundaries of settlements applied to the plots within these boundaries as well.

119. Valuch 2001, 289.

120. János Brutyó, head of the Central Board of Inquiry, the "fist of the party," refers to these abuses in a speech titled "A közéleti morálról, moralizálás nélkül" [On public morality, without moralizing]: "Everyone has the right as a citizen to purchase a plot of land, for instance, and build a weekend home if he has the money. But if somebody exploits the opportunities, advantages, and privileges available to him due to his position (favorable allotment of land, access to transport, acquisition of building remains, etc.) this is not a matter of civil rights, but rather is an unethical acquisition of advantage and an abuse of authority." Brutyó 1983, 199.

121. I raised this issue in an earlier publication in Hungarian in a broader historical context. Majtényi 2000. For more on the social history of the "socialist car," see Siegelbaum 2011.

122. Schiffer 1985, 192.

123. On the social history of the automobile in the Horthy era, see Majtényi 2000, 101–109.

124. *Autó Motor Sport* 1/5 (November 1, 1946): 71.

125. Ibid.

126. Katona 2002, 47, 49.

127. Ibid., 58.

128. Historians who have written on the history of the Soviet Union have also tended to consider the use of an automobile (and, later, ownership of an automobile) one of the signs of membership in the elite. Gronow 2003, 34; Fitzpatrick 1999, 102; Hoffmann 2003, 143.

129. Politikatörténeti és Szakszervezeti Levéltár (Archives of political history and trade unions, hereafter cited as PHA), fond 274, group 26, storage unit 45.

130. HAHSS, fond 3.1, group 9, V-107373, Hugó Koch and Associate. György Faludy offers the same account in his memoirs, though in a different manner. Faludy 1989, 329–330.

131. Pünkösti 1992, 228.

132. Nógrádi 1970, 411–412.

133. Council of Ministers (CM) decree no. 65/1950 (III.2) on the regulation of questions concerning the maintenance of automobiles in public use; CM decree no. 66/1955 (XII.1) on the modification of the CM decree no. 65/1950 (III.2).

134. The title was a reference to the verse epic *Lúdas Matyi* by nineteenth-century Hungarian author Mihály Fazekas. The verse is

based on a folktale of unknown origin. In part because it tells of the triumph of a folk hero over a landlord, the poem was used in several different incarnations to provide a dramatic illustration of the superiority of workers over the traditional aristocracy.

135. Kő and Nagy 2002, 116–117.
136. HNA, fond XIX-H-12, box 1.
137. Pünkösti 1992, 9.
138. Dr. Ervin Haymann, president of the Societé de Secoure et d'EntrAide traveled to Hungary in March 1955 with the consent of the Politburo. The society had been formed in 1949 in Switzerland to provide social support for members of the Jewry. At the first discussion, Haymann suggested sending support to Hungary in two ways. First, in Switzerland, the organization would order so-called IKKA packages worth US$250,000. IKKA, which stood for IBUSZ Külföldi Kereskedelmi Akció, functioned as part of the government-controlled tourist industry and was essentially the only way people outside Hungary could send packages and aid to people in Hungary. They paid hard currency in exchange for aid packages, which were then delivered to people in the country. The second way involved the society simply providing merchandise or dollars. In the end, an agreement was reached whereby the organization would provide US$300,000 for aid for Hungarian Jews by allowing the Hungarian state to place orders of this amount in order to procure various items of merchandise. It also agreed that the merchandise to be provided during the first year would include fifteen Chevrolets, while the rest would be used for medicine and medical equipment. With the mediation of the Hungarian state, the Jewish community was given some six million forints (i.e., an exchange rate of twenty forints for one US dollar), while the Hungarian state managed to procure US$300,000 in merchandise. HNA, fond M-KS 276, group 65, storage unit 377; Pünkösti 2001, 277.
139. In 1966, a letter of denunciation was sent from Vienna to Hungary. The author of the letter first addressed it to *Szabad Nép* in the Corvin Palace, but he or she then corrected this mistake and addressed the letter to the "editorship" of *Magyar Nemzet* and *Népszabadság* on Lenin Boulevard (the author signed the letter first as Kati Horváth and then as Kati Kovács). The letter was also sent with some minor modifications to the Ministry of the Interior (the handwriting is different). HAHSS, fond 3.2, group 4, K-2795, 80–99.
140. Ibid., 81–82.
141. Report, Vienna, July 22, 1966, ibid., 101.
142. Report, Vienna, May 5, 1966, ibid., 69.

143. The National Council of Trade Unions was formed in 1948, after its predecessor, the Council of Trade Unions, had been dissolved. In principle, it represented the interests of the working class.

144. *Bácsi József-interjú* [Interview with Bácsi József], conducted by András B. Vágvölgyi in 1989, OHA no. 214, 158.

145. The Hármashatár-hegy is a large hill on the northwestern edge of Budapest. The name literally means "three-border hill." The hill used to lie on the border of the three cities of Buda, Óbuda, and Pesthidegkút. Buda and Óbuda are now parts of the city of Budapest.

146. Sík 1970, 250.

147. The type and year of the car that one drove indicated one's place in the financial and social hierarchy. In the 1970s, the Trabant became the inexpensive car used by the masses. Warsawa, Wartburg, Zaporozhets, Zastava, Moskvitch, Škoda, and Polski Fiat models were all more prestigious. Although the more successful were able to purchase cars from the West, automobiles imported from Eastern bloc countries were also marks of prestige. HNA, fond XIX-G-4, group ggg, box 58.

148. Report, Vienna, May 5, 1966, HAHSS, fond 3.2, group 4, K-2795, 68–69.

149. Instruction no. 164-2/80, ibid., 120–121.

150. HAHSS, fond 3.2, group 4, K-2795, 126.

151. Ibid., 129.

152. Katona 2002, 78.

153. Every year, the Ministry of Transportation and Postal Affairs prepared reports on the motor vehicle stock in Hungary, along with a separate report on the supply of cars that were used as perks by state and party officials and functionaries. HNA, fond XIX-H-11, box 1–40.

154. Péteri 2009, 315.

155. In 1976, for instance, there was only one Chaika in Hungary serving as a vehicle for official functions (or, as it was known in the public vernacular at the time, a personal car perk); it was the reserve car used by the Council of Ministers. If a council member's Mercedes broke down, he was compelled to use the "black gull." HNA, fond XIX-H-11, box 40.

156. HNA, fond XIX-L-3, group a, 004/1969.

157. Kiss 2006.

158. "Jóban-rosszban: Interjú Kádár Jánosnéval," V, *Magyarország*, no. 44 (November 3, 1989): 4–5.

159. János Berecz 2003, 360.

160. This special train, the luxury train of its era, can now be seen in the Hungarian Railway History Park in Budapest. Viewers can see the

fine upholstery in the compartments and the lavish interiors. On the police protection that was provided for the train, see A "K"-vonat (kormányvonat) biztosítási tapasztalatai [Experiences concerning protection for the K train (the government train)], 1963, Vera and Donald Blinken Open Society Archives (hereafter cited as OSA), fond 357, 2-1, box 7.

161. Baráth 2007 offers an account of the story along with the relevant sources.

162. Ede Horváth 1990, 38–39.

163. The Secretariat's Resolution of February 4, 1980, HNA, fond M-KS 288, group 37, box 374.

164. This took a considerable amount of time, as indicated by the fact that they used a statistic from more than a decade earlier in an attempt to demonstrate the effectiveness of the measure. "On 31 December 1985, 305 automobiles were rented from the Ministry of Transportation by the party committees of the 18 counties and Pest County, or 53.3 percent on the 572 automobiles that were rented in June 1972." HNA, fond M-KS 288, group 37, box 374.

165. CM decree no. 59/1982 (XI.16) of the Council of Ministers and Prime Minister decree no. 2/1982 (XI.1) of the Deputy President of the Council of Ministers modified some of the questions concerning the use of automobiles by public bodies. CM decree no. 33/1951 (I.31) addressed compensation for costs incurred when workers were sent out as part of domestic delegations or as part of the foreign service as well as the costs incurred when they were transferred. From then on, the earlier the regulations concerning "workplace automobiles" and "service automobiles" applied to the cars used by party leaders, which earlier had belonged to the category of "general purpose automobiles." The workplace automobiles could still only be used according to the taxi system. Memo, December 30, 1982, Department of Party Management and Administration of the Central Committee of the Hungarian Socialist Workers' Party. Transportation and Technical Enterprise. HNA, fond M-KS 288, group 37, box 374.

166. At the suggestion of the first secretaries of the Budapest and county party committees, the Central Committee secretary in charge of overseeing the Department of Party Management and Administration of the Central Committee could allow a worker of the party apparatus to use workplace automobiles to commute to and from work regularly if the worker had a particularly difficult time coming and going to work for health reasons. This had to be certified every six months. CM decree no. 59/1982 (XI.16).

167. Its official abbreviation was KPM.

168. The office could levy a fine of five forints per kilometer for the first one hundred kilometers, ten forints per kilometer for every kilometer traveled between one hundred and five hundred kilometers, and fifteen forints per kilometer for every kilometer traveled above five hundred kilometers. Department of Party Management and Administration of the Central Committee of the Hungarian Socialist Workers' Party, Transportation and Technical Enterprise, HNA, fond M-KS 288, group 37, box 374.

169. The secretariat's resolution of December 27, 1981, concerning the payment of travel costs as salary for workers in higher leading positions in the apparatus of the party and Hungarian Young Communist League. HNA, fond M-KS 288, group 37, box 374.

170. The precise sums were 43,845,400 and 5,712,000 forints. Department of Party Management and Administration of the Central Committee of the Hungarian Socialist Workers' Party, Transportation and Technical Enterprise, HNA, fond M-KS 288, group 37, box 374, 2, dossier. Memo on the development of automobile transportation in 1985, May 4, 1986.

171. Department of Party Management and Administration of the Central Committee of the Hungarian Socialist Workers' Party, Transportation and Technical Enterprise, guides, implementation plans, correspondence, 1980–1986, circular, May 16, 1986, HNA, fond M-KS 288, group 37, box 374.

172. Ibid.

173. Hegedüs 1988, 6–7.

174. Ibid., 168.

175. Hegedüs 1985, 132.

176. Ibid.

177. Hegedüs 1988, 186.

178. Révész 2008, 68–70.

179. Letter, February 23, 1957; cited in Révész 2008, 76.

180. Letter, June 14, 1957; published in *Moszkva–Budapest* 2009, 10.

181. Letter, February 23, 1957; cited in Révész 2008, 76.

182. The population's income and consumption, 1960–1978; Hoch, Kovács, and Ördög 1982, 156.

183. Letter, November 26, 1957; published in *Moszkva–Budapest* 2009, 10.

184. "In September, the four of us (István Bata, István Kovács, László Piros, and me), after having lived in one apartment in the 'tall' building built on Krasnye Vorota, were able to return home.... My family (my wife and six children) had already been in Hungary for almost a year, and they had set themselves up nicely in a state-owned villa on Rozsa Hill, where we still live today. (It is not far from the house in which I lived in the 1950s,

after the previous resident of the house, ÁVH Colonel Szűcs, was beaten to death in the torture chamber of his own office in the course of an investigation. . . . The apartment, with the kids and my wife, who had arranged everything as nicely as possible to welcome me, seemed like an island of peace." András Hegedüs, *Visszaemlékezések* [Recollections], 1958–1960. Árnyékban 1: Diliflepni és a Szívós söröző [In the shade 1: Diliflepni and the Szívós Bar], 1958–1960. 2. OSA, fond 361, 0-4, box 29. Following the change of regimes, the building at 5 Sarolta Street was then made into a block of apartments. The Hegedüs family also got possession of a vacation home in Fonyód. OSA, fond 361, 0-4, box 5.

185. Miklós Szántó wrote the following on András Hegedüs in a commemorative volume published in Hegedüs's honor: "In my opinion, Hegedüs was an independent, critical sociologist—he wanted and was able to become an ideal kind of creative intellectual like C. W. Mills." Szántó 2001, 270.

186. Hegedüs 1999, 24.
187. Hegedüs 1985, 85.
188. Hegedüs 1988, 167.
189. Huszár 2007, 101.
190. Kornai 2005, 62.
191. Hegedüs 1988, 167–168; Gyarmati 2009, 85.
192. Hegedüs 1988, 167–168.
193. Huszár 2005, 78–80.
194. Földes 1984, 226.
195. Hegedüs 1988, 219.
196. Marosán 1989, 240.
197. Ibid.
198. Sík 1970, 234.
199. "Jóban-rosszban: Interjú Kádár Jánosnéval," IX, *Magyarország*, no. 48 (December 1, 1989): 4.
200. Ibid., 4–5.
201. Komiszár 2007, 94; Magyari 2005.
202. Komiszár 2007, 95–99.
203. Ibid., 95.
204. Földes 1984, 299.
205. "Jóban-rosszban: Interjú Kádár Jánosnéval," VIII, *Magyarország*, no. 47 (November 24, 1989): 5.
206. Révész 1997, 73.
207. Mrs. Zoltán Vas 1990, 414.

208. Summary report, November 14, 1979, HAHSS, fond 3.1, 5, O-20009, 62–63.
209. HNA, fond M-KS 276, group 58, storage unit 4.
210. Report on the operational situation of the Kútvölgyi Avenue State Hospital and Outpatient Clinic, March 14, 1963, Budapest, HAHSS, fond 3.1, group 5, O-20009, Kútvölgyi Avenue State Hospital, 3.
211. Summary report, July 23, 1984, HAHSS, fond 3.1, group 5, O-20009, Kútvölgyi Avenue State Hospital, 94.
212. Summary report, November 14, 1979, HAHSS, fond 3.1, group 5, O-20009, Kútvölgyi Avenue State Hospital, 63–64.
213. Ibid., 65.
214. The fact that they were considered an "official connection" meant that they had not been recruited, but rather had to maintain ties with the state security forces as a consequence of their position. Report on the operational situation of the Kútvölgyi Avenue State Hospital and Outpatient Clinic, March 14, 1963, Budapest, HAHSS, fond 3.1, group 5, O-20009, 4–5.
215. Ibid., 3.
216. Report on the event that took place in the Central State Hospital, August 30, 1980, HAHSS, fond 3.1, group 5, O-20009, 72–73.
217. Memo, September 2, 1980, HAHSS, fond 3.1, group 5, O-20009, 75.
218. Ibid., 74–75.
219. Vilmos Tóth 1999a, 99.
220. Apor 2002, 179–184.
221. Plans had been drawn up in 1922 (i.e., under the Horthy regime) for arcaded sepulchral monuments on the paths surrounding the Kossuth mausoleum as an appropriate setting for ceremonial funerals. Vilmos Tóth 1999a, 64.
222. Ibid., 1–85.
223. Apor 2002, 191.
224. Vilmos Tóth 1999a, 99.
225. Ibid.
226. Vilmos Tóth 1999b, 237–256.
227. Révai was a member of the so-called group of four—that is, along with Rákosi, Gerő, and Mihály Farkas, he was one of the four Hungarian communists to return to Hungary after having lived in exile in the Soviet Union.
228. Vilmos Tóth 1999a, 99–100.
229. Ibid., 103.
230. Ibid., 120.

231. *Rendhagyó utószó* [An irregular afterword], excerpt from an interview with Mrs. Zoltán Vas by Gyula Kozák.
232. Vilmos Tóth 1999a, 101.
233. Ibid., 103.
234. Vilmos Tóth 2009, 29.
235. Vilmos Tóth 1999a, 121.

THREE

TRADITION AND INNOVATION
The Hunt for Concordance

THE RÁKOSI CADRE AND THE PAST

András Hegedüs made the following remarks in his recollections of the hunting trips he went on with Mátyás Rákosi, the general secretary of the party: "Rákosi hunted a great deal . . . and he loved to go skeet shooting too. This was a terrifying experience for me. Rákosi shot at everything that moved. He didn't bother to check to see if it was a rabbit or a person, he just shot. To be near him when he was hunting was perilous."[1]

During the period of Rákosi's rule, hunting was a distinct part of the lifestyle of the elites, though for a long time this was kept secret from the wider public, because in earlier eras, hunting had been a pastime of aristocrats and the nobility.[2] During the Second World War, the regent, who had a passion for hunting, had a bear-hunting ground created on what had once been the royal demesne estate of Szin (an area that today is in Borsod-Abaúj-Zemplén County, near Bódvaszilas and Szögliget, along the border with Slovakia). His intention had been to compensate for the loss of bear-hunting grounds in Transylvania, which, after the signing of the Treaty of Trianon, had become part of Romania. The actual work of establishing this hunting ground began in 1940,[3] when the Council of Ministers reached a resolution concerning the resettlement of the people of the town of Derenk (most of whom made their living by poaching), which lay within the territory that had been designated for the reserve.[4] During the war, measures were taken that did not attract much attention.[5] First, circus bears were brought to the reserve, but these "first generation" animals did not work out: "they attacked the locals" and "did a great deal of harm."[6] In 1946, the aldermen of the town of Szinpetri[7] and the local party organizations suggested to István Dobi, the minister of agriculture, that the borders of the Szin hunting grounds be changed because of the damage that had been caused by the bears. Dobi, who also liked to hunt, was not willing to do this. He explained his decision by referring to considerations involving wildlife management.[8] The story was of important symbolic value. It was a clear sign of the power of tradition and the passion for hunting, and also of the fundamental continuity in the customs and lifestyles of the elites, which survived changes in power and political and economic shifts and ruptures.

The political changes that had taken place notwithstanding, after the Second World War the hunting organization remained strongly bound to the traditions of the Horthy era.[9] Not surprisingly, the first people to form a hunting society were those who had hunted before, those who owned or had owned lands or even large estates, and those who were drawn to hunting as a kind of gentleman's pastime. The first hunting societies were formed under their names. As these societies emerged, the members of the new elite joined the ranks of the hunters.[10] After the war, the Gemenc Hunting Society was formed under smallholder politician Zoltán Tildy. Ferenc Nagy and Béla Varga were both members of the society and influential members of the Smallholders' Party, which was the most popular party in Hungary in the brief transitional period after the war.[11] As minister of internal affairs, communist party member Imre Nagy became the president of one of the new hunting societies.[12] Rank was clearly expressed in the hunting hierarchy, and hunting itself (i.e., the fact that someone hunted) was an expression of rank. It is thus hardly surprising that the leaders of the communist party, who were striving to acquire influence and power, all took hunting rifles in hand.

In the 1950s, the state maintained so-called ministerial hunting grounds and reserves. Members of the highest circles of the party and the government were able to hunt on these reserves, with or without hunting tickets (which were free of charge). This small group of elites consisted of roughly thirty people. Of the communist party leaders, Rákosi liked to hunt in Gyulaj, while Mihály Farkas preferred Gemenc, and Márton Horváth favored Galgamácsa.[13] Although the party leaders naturally created the hunting organizations in the name of the "power of the working class," they could not do without the skills and expertise of the older generation of hunters. Thus, many of these older hunters were able to remain in the world of hunting. In 1949, of the hunters who had been famous in the interwar period, many remained employed in the field, including Kálmán Kittenberger (who had hunted and pursued research in Africa), Count Zsigmond Széchenyi (who had gone on hunting expeditions in Africa), Count József Teleki, Count László Esterházy, Baron László Dudinszki, György Lelovich (a famous falconry master), and Emil Altai (who had once served as Miklós Horthy's master of hounds). They had all been members of the middle class or the elite under Horthy.[14]

In the 1950s, professional hunters represented a group that was retrograde according to the norms of the time, but also indispensable. The central personality of this group was Ákos Szederjei. Szederjei had worked for Miklós Horthy, and his grandfather had been a forestry engineer. In 1944, Szederjei was still working on the regent's bear-hunting grounds in Szin. By the time of the regime change in 1945, however, he was working for the State Forestry Works (Magyar Állami Erdőgazdasági Üzemek, or MÁLLERD), where he had been entrusted to serve as the head of the hunting department.[15] With great ambition, Szederjei dove into the work of reviving wildlife management, and he surrounded himself in his new workplace with old experts in the field. In November 1947, an article was published in an issue of the journal *Szabad Föld* (Free Land) on MÁLLERD titled "Where the Counts Are Still Swarming."[16] At the time, Counts László Esterházy, Zsigmond Széchenyi, and József Teleki were all working for MÁLLERD.[17] Communist politician Lajos Fehér was the editor in chief of *Szabad Föld*. According to Szederjei, after the article was published, Fehér sought him out to make amends: "When he returned home, his first trip was to see us, because he was afraid that he wouldn't be able to hunt anymore, because they wouldn't let him hunt since this article against us had been published. He came over to me and threw his lambskin hat—because he was wearing a lambskin hat—onto the floor and stomped on it in front of my desk. I told him you're stomping in vain, the article was published, and in response, he fired the journalist."[18] The old hunting experts could use their knowledge and know-how to blackmail the powerful figures of the era, and they had additional protections (beyond the goodwill of several national and local figures of prominence). Within the hunting organization, they employed the sons of leading politicians of the Smallholders' Party, including the son of István Dobi and Zoltán Tildy Jr.[19]

Personal relationships and trust had always played an important role in hunting. For instance, following the years of political transition, Endre Nagy, who at one time had served as a gendarmerie captain and was married to the daughter of Baron Hatvany, organized successful hunting expeditions for Rákosi and Márton Horváth, so he was welcomed into the circle of party leaders and gained their trust. He wrote about this experience in his diary: "It's quite inconceivable, but even though I am a one-time gendarmerie captain and the son-in-law of Ferenc Hatvany, Mátyás

Rákosi, János Kádár, Márton Horváth, the editor-in-chief of *Népszava*, Ferenc Donáth, Mihály Farkas, and László Rajk regard me as their pal."[20] As the state security officer who submitted reports on Nagy wrote with keen perspicacity, "He is undoubtedly on good terms with people in high positions, and he uses his relationships to do good business."[21]

THE HUNTING SOCIETY

Throughout Hungarian history, participation in the rituals of hunting often has been a precondition of membership in the ruling elite. Because hunting was tied to various positions of status and prominence, it influenced people's habits and gave rise to various cliques and circles. In these hunting societies, customs and habits became patterns of behavior, and, with the passing of time, they became traditions. They created a sense of identity and community, which was also a form of (possibly unconscious) identification with the social position and role one had managed to achieve.

In Hungary after the Second World War, four communist leaders were in positions of particular prominence and influence. Rákosi himself referred to this in a speech that he delivered to the central leadership in June 1953.[22] The inner circle consisted of Rákosi, Ernő Gerő, Mihály Farkas, and József Révai (in that order of importance), but many also would have included Zoltán Vas.[23] Although it was clear beyond any shadow of doubt that Rákosi had the most influence, these communists who had returned to Hungary from Moscow (Rákosi, Gerő, Farkas, and Révai, who were referred to, as noted in chapter 2, the "foursome") held positions of essentially equal power. Within their spheres of authority, they made decisions entirely on their own. They established their own clienteles, and they organized hunting trips as a way of consolidating and reinforcing these circles of sway. For the most part, they went on hunting trips in their favorite hunting grounds and in the company of their political circles. Gerő was the only one among them who did not hunt, which in all likelihood was due to the fact that this "bridge-building"[24] politician had bad eyesight.[25]

János Kádár had begun to hunt during the period of Rákosi's rule. Beginning in the late 1940s, Kádár regularly took part in the hunting trips organized by the party and the government. After he had consolidated his power following the 1956 revolution, he gradually distanced himself from the primitive manner of maintaining the dictatorship. Instead of using open aggression with the elite to maintain his hold on power, he adopted more traditional techniques of exerting authority. This shift cannot have been entirely deliberate. The personal reflections of Kádár as the first secretary of the party and the increased prominence of old patterns of exercising power set off a transformation of the ruling elite. Kádár arguably resembled Ede Minarik, the main character in director Pál Sándor's 1973 film *Régi idők focija* (Football of the good old days), which was based on Iván Mándy's novel *A pálya szélén* (On the side of the field). Minarik dreams of getting a football team (European football, that is, or American soccer) into the first-tier league, but he cannot manage to assemble a team. His repeated phrase, "We need a team," became a familiar phrase in Hungarian culture in roughly the last two decades of communism. Like Minarik, Kádár had to assemble a team; unlike Minarik, he was guided not by passionate conviction but by practical consideration. In 1963, when an amnesty was issued for people who had participated in the revolutionary events of 1956, Kádár decided to found the Concord Hunting Society. The political changes that took place in the wake of the Second World War had radically disrupted and transformed the traditional customs and institutions of the social elites. The National Casino had been shut down, as had the State Casino and the National Society of Hungarian Gentlewomen.[26] However, the social life and the customs and habits of the elite did not vanish entirely after the political turn.

By creating the hunting society, Kádár essentially revived a custom of social life among the elite in prewar Hungary, though he completely excluded the wider public. He personally instructed the responsible head of department in the Ministry of Agriculture to write the statutes for the society and to make a list of the people who could be members.[27] Sándor Tóth was the first forestry engineer at the forefront of the hunting organization. Earlier, officers in the state security forces had fulfilled this role. Tóth based his suggestions on the protocol lists:[28] "I was then asked to make suggestions, of course it was easy to make suggestions because I had been told which circles to choose from. The members and substitute members of the Political Committee who hunted, the secretaries of the Central Committee who hunted, the members of the Council of Ministers who hunted, and the heads of the institutions that had been singled out and the radio and television all were given permission to hunt, along with a few people in the army and in preventative operations."[29]

László Földes, first deputy to the minister of the interior, was also on the list, though he was something of an odd man out. He could not be excluded, however, since he was well known as a passionate hunter, and as a functionary who had undertaken the lion's share of the repressive measures implemented after 1956, he was one of the most influential members of the party (though he was later pushed to the margins). Sándor Tóth compiled a list of forty-one people. Not all of the most prominent figures of the party joined the society; some of them did not hunt, and others did not find the rigid frameworks of the society appealing. In the end, the Concord Hunting Society was formed with eighteen members.

The following people comprised the first members of the society: Antal Apró, member of the Political Committee and the deputy chairman of the Council of Ministers; Gyula Balassa, head of the National Forestry Directorate with the rank of deputy minister; András Benkei, member of the Central Committee and minister of the interior; Béla Biszku, member of the Political Committee and secretary of the Central Committee; Lajos Cseterki, secretary of the Central Committee and substitute member of the Political Committee; Lajos Czinege, substitute member of the Political Committee and minister of defense; Lajos Fehér, member of the Political Committee and deputy chairman of the Council of Ministers; Jenő Fock, member of the Political Committee and deputy chairman of the Council of Ministers; László Földes, member of the Central Committee and, as of January 1, 1965, head of the National Forestry Directorate with the rank of deputy minister; Sándor Gáspár, member of the Political Committee, vice president of the Patriotic People's Front, and deputy chairman of the Presidential Council; János Kádár, member of the Political Committee, first secretary of the party, and chairman of the Council of Ministers; Pál Losonczi, member of the Central Committee and minister of agriculture; Ferenc Nezvál, member of the Central Committee and minister of justice; Károly Németh, secretary of the Central Committee and first secretary of the Budapest Party Committee; János Pap, member of the Central Committee and deputy chairman of the Council of Ministers (in 1963, when the Concord Hunting Society was founded, he was still serving as minister of the interior); Zoltán Szabó, chief medical officer of the Kútvölgyi and later Róbert Károly Hospitals (he had treated Kádár after Kádár had been released in 1954); Major General Ferenc Szűcs; and István Tömpe, member of the Central Committee and president of Hungarian Radio and Television. Naturally, the leaders of the society were members of Kádár's inner circle. Károly Németh was the president, and Ferenc Szűcs was the master of the hunt. Since Németh was the president of the hunting society, initially the secretary of the Budapest Party Committee managed the administrative tasks.[30]

On weekends, Kádár's hunters would venture to forests all over the country. Kádár personally supervised the society. The hunting trips were organized by the hunting department of the Ministry of Agriculture, so Kádár was in direct contact with the head of the department, Sándor Tóth: "Initially, when the Concord Hunting Society was formed, we were in direct telephone contact with János Kádár. He would call us directly on the K line, and I would call him without hesitation anytime some organizational or other kind of problem came up. It was all on a kind of 'well stroll on over and we'll talk about what kind of hunting trip we're going to hold' basis."[31] For a long time, Kádár alone decided who could be a member of the society. Membership meant power for some and the antechamber to power for others, so people hungry for influence jockeyed for a position close to Kádár and the society. Of course, hunters also were always looking for good opportunities to hunt, and the society offered the best expeditions. Today, however, we see the organization and structure of the Concord Hunting Society from a different perspective than did the hunters of the time.

To describe the distinctive features of social groups, we must analyze the networks of relationships that formed in and across these groups, for we cannot simply assume that people in the past formed a group or a social class, layer, or elite simply because they occupied similar social positions, had similar lifestyles, or followed similar styles. Under Kádár, the nomenclature system also ensured that the party-state would be able to maintain control over the positions that were deemed important. The party resolutions concerning spheres of authority indicate clearly which offices and positions were considered the most important at various times. Membership in the ruling elite, however, depended not only on one's formal position but also on one's personal relationships and ties.

The order of rank among the people who were in positions of power was the following: Within the party, the first secretary, the members of the Political Committee, and the secretaries of the Central Committee were in the highest echelon of power.

In the government, the order was the chairman of the Council of Ministers, the members of the Council of Ministers, and the chairman of the Presidential Council. Not far behind them and always trying to catch up were the other influential figures of the time—the department heads of the Central Committee, the county first secretaries, and the heads of the offices with national jurisdiction. Not all of these people were automatically able to join the hunting society. In the race for membership in the Concord Hunting Society, personal relationships were often the decisive factor. More and more of the leading functionaries began to hunt, and a few Central Committee department heads and county party members who were shrewd in their maneuvers for position also managed to join. For them, the hunting expeditions with high-ranking party leaders brought the promise of promotion. Thus, the question of which of the prominent members of the leadership of the party-state would actually get into the group, which consisted of only some fifty or sixty people (with Kádár as its leading personality), was determined primarily by informal relationships, and the members of this group enjoyed the prerogative of reaching important decisions on issues that the country faced.

The so-called internal instructions issued by the Ministry of Agriculture and Food and the ministerial memorandums and records shed some light on the results of this race for membership in the hunting society.[32] As is generally the case in secret societies, the Concord Hunting Society had distinctive initiation ceremonies, and in the 1960s and 1970s, these rituals became established custom. Interestingly, a variation on spanking was part of these initiation rituals. After the game had been felled, the tenderfoot hunter was laid down on the quarry and flicked, gently, with the initiation switch, much as had always been done in forests in Hungary.[33]

Until the late 1970s, the number of hunters in the society continuously grew, until (presumably at Kádár's instructions) a halt was put on allowing any new members to join, and then the memberships of several of the hunters were examined. The rules for membership were revised, and the expulsions became permanent. Kádár presumably used this approach to supervise this privileged group of the ruling elite, and he made it clear that he had a central role in the society. According to memoirs, Kádár was annoyed by the family hunting trips, during which spirits were often high but discipline lacking, so separate hunting trips were organized for women and children. The Nimród Youth Hunting Society was formed, and a separate group was created of "Nimród women."[34] Later, a hunting society was formed for retirees who had been "left out," as it were. This new hunting society was euphemistically named the Friendship Hunting Society, but the Concord hunters referred to it as "the final resting place." The Friendship Hunting Society was founded with only fifteen members. At its largest, it had twenty-seven members.[35] If someone lost his position, he was expelled from Concord and sent to Friendship. Expulsion became a source of many grievances. Because many of the people in the highest positions hunted, and those who could, hunted with Concord, among the party and state leaders who hunted, membership in the Concord Hunting Society meant that one had joined the ruling elite. Similarly, the loss of membership was a token of exclusion.

JÁNOS KÁDÁR'S HUNTERS

Many functionaries became passionate hunters. In 1971, according to the ministry's report, party leader Jenő Fock had hunted the most, a total of ninety days. György Aczél, cultural politician and secretary of the Central Committee, came in second with sixty-four days. Major general and head of military intelligence Ferenc Szűcs was in third place with fifty-nine days, though trade union president Sándor Gáspár was close on his heels with fifty-four days. Many hunters brought their families with them for the weekend hunting expeditions. Children began to hunt, including the sons of Béla Biszku, Lajos Fehér, Jenő Fock, and Ferenc Szűcs. Even the communist first lady, Mrs. János Kádár, tried her hand at hunting, as did the wives of György Aczél and Lajos Fehér.[36] The professional hunters must have made the acquaintance of a wide array of different kinds of hunters among the party leaders.[37] Professional hunter Béla Rakeczky Jr. took a group hunting in Gyulaj: "I remember them well. Pozsgay [in the years immediately preceding the fall of communism in Hungary, party leader and author Imre Pozsgay was considered a reformer] was a gentleman, as he is today. Jenő Fock was a little bit aggressive."[38] Ottó Feiszt, after the regime change, served as the president of the National Hungarian Hunting Chamber. He was accompanying the head of state, who had become famous in hunting circles, in Zala and recalled: "They say that a stag is not a pheasant, so one cannot shoot let's say three stags. Jenő Fock did not keep to this rule. He was capable of shooting the tenth or eleventh or whateverth stag in a day. People who were hunting their own game only rarely shot three stags, let's say a Count Pálffy or a Zsigmond Széchenyi [a hunter famous for his expeditions in Africa]."[39]

Party leaders who were inexperienced hunters would do target practice to improve their aim. Before the hunting season began, they would go to the skeet and target shooting range in Gödöllő. In the 1960s and 1970s, the most prestigious weapon was a combination rifle with three barrels. Hungarian hunters usually used Merkel and Simson combination rifles, which were made in East Germany and were very expensive; of course, one needed to have good connections to get one. János Kádár received one of his guns from Yumjaagiin Tsedenbal, general secretary of the Mongolian People's Party. The ornate rifle, which is set in beautifully marbled walnut-root wood, is on display today in the Hungarian National Museum. The metal parts of the weapon are decorated with carvings depicting hunting scenes. A stag bells at the edge of a forest, a wild duck on the lake takes flight, a hunting dog peeks out from the reeds with a wild duck in its mouth. These are snapshots from the life of the forest and the hunter. A brass plate was nailed to the butt of the gun that reads: "Tsedenbal wishes his Hungarian hunting partner good luck."[40] Even in the West, János Kádár was known as a passionate hunter. He was given hunting rifles by Helmut Schmidt, chancellor of West Germany, and Franz Joseph Strauss, minister-president of the state of Bavaria.[41]

The hunters of the Concord Hunting Society brought home many trophies. In the Museum of Hungarian Agriculture, one sees the names of many famous Hungarian hunters. Covering the walls are trophies belonging to János Kádár, Antal Apró, Lajos Fehér, Béla Biszku, and László Földes (the one-time deputy minister of the interior, who also went on hunting expeditions in Africa). Kádár enriched the museum's collection with more than forty trophies, and he shot a world-record number of stags and deer with antlers.[42] Before his sixtieth birthday, the hunters of Gyulaj wanted to do something that would bring him a bit of joy by providing him a world-record fallow buck. For more than twenty years, Kádár held the record for the number of fallow bucks shot. In most countries, a fallow buck does not count as trophy-worthy game, so hunters outside Hungary were not aspiring to snatch the first secretary's laurels. In Hungary, however, for a long time, hunters did not dare allow others to shoot anything larger, and few guests sought to do so.[43] The most famous record, a world-record-setting roebuck, was shot by Lajos Cseterki. At the height of his career, Cseterki served as secretary of the Presidential Council, though he shot the roebuck when he was still a county first secretary.[44]

One finds several familiar names on the list of successful hunters in the trophy catalogs. The remarkable kills of the party leaders are among the gold and silver medal trophies.[45] In 1969, trophies from kills that Kádár had made were in first and third place in the gold medal stag antler competition held at the trophy exhibition of the Museum of Hungarian Agriculture.[46] During the long decades of socialism, Hungarian hunters held places of prominence in world rankings as well. The official statements and newspaper articles nonetheless were modest and restrained in their phrasing because they addressed wider audiences, and hunting continued to be perceived by the larger public as a pastime of the prevailing ruling elites.[47] At the first Hunting World Fair,[48] which was organized in 1971, in cases in which a party or state leader had set a world record, the name of the hunting association was given instead of the name of the hunter. One of the reasons for this may have been the simple fact that the event was open to and drew the attention of the wider public. An additional reason may well have been that the leaders of the new regime did not want their names to appear on a plaque alongside the names of prominent personalities of the Horthy era, such as Rudolf Hess, and this was more important to them than their vanity as hunters. Nonetheless, the publication that was issued as part of the exhibition paid tribute to the achievements of the "new hunters." According to the publication, which is diplomatically phrased but nevertheless tinged with pride, "Hungary has always been familiar to the hunters of Europe for its strong-antlered stags, does, roebucks, and wild boar. The carefully planned wildlife management of the past 26 years has produced particularly beautiful trophies."[49]

Hunting was always something of a ritual, and its ceremonial frameworks offered participants an opportunity to practice their marksmanship competitively.[50] Odescalchi Eugénie, a Hungarian duchess, wrote in her memoir of a hunting expedition that took place on the estate in Pusztaszer of Alfonz Pallavicini and of her husband's remarkable accomplishments: "Béla was in the lead: he shot six or seven hundred animals a day, rabbits, pheasants."[51] A few decades later, one of the members of the Concord Hunting Society offered the following remarks concerning the famed accomplishments of Sándor Gáspár, the trade union leader: "His personal pheasant record can be deservedly added to the familiar and openly-kept series of records for small game hunting.... On 21 December 1986, he shot 1,710 hatched pheasants, roosters, and hens in Lenes."[52] Hunters also competed with one another over who had shot which kinds of trophy-worthy game, which depended to a large extent on the circumstance. And for the most part, the professional hunters created the best circumstances for the most influential leaders.

From the perspective of the historian, hunting can be regarded first and foremost as a pastime that was characteristic of the habits and lifestyles of the elite of the era. It was a social practice that was shaped by the acts of individuals, but because of its significance as a leisure activity among the ruling elite, it offers a perspective for the study of the attitudes of a social group that sought to distinguish itself on the basis of its dominant position. The meanings of hunting, however, are clearly even more manifold than this would imply. It was expressive of personal attitudes and points of interconnection. Hunting has unquestionably been traditionally defined as a masculine pastime, and traditionally men have had a passion for it.[53] A superstition familiar among hunters is that if, "before the hunt, the hunter can fondle the breasts of an unfamiliar woman or, if god grants, a Gypsy girl, and he can bring a strand of her hair with him as a memento then it will bring him particularly good fortune during the hunt."[54] Even today, hunting is often considered a symbol of manliness, strength, and power. Hunters contend that you find out who someone really is in the course of a hunt. A professional hunter once recounted that when he had taken Valentina Tereshkova, the first woman astronaut, on an early morning hunting expedition and she suddenly saw a bellowing wild boar in the moonlight, the brave astronaut's legs had begun to shake.[55] This story and the popularity of hunting in elite circles also illustrate that hegemonic masculinity was a characteristic generally considered typical of members of the elite during state socialism (and throughout twentieth-century Hungarian history). Beyond the differences in the individual styles of aristocratic hunters and that of new leaders, the notion of hegemonic masculinity equally describes their behavior in certain situations, their interpretations of their roles, and perhaps also an ideology that served to reproduce masculine domination in different political systems.[56] Hunting among party leaders was a formative experience and the wellspring of the traditional macho culture of the prevailing Hungarian elites.

Although hunting is a socially determined pastime and therefore bears numerous social meanings, for the individual it is perhaps first and foremost a passion and a form of recreation. Hunters tend to be fairly unanimous in their contention that they are driven by an irrational, unfathomable urge, and they claim they have hunting "in their blood." These perceptions should not be ignored. The one-time director of wildlife management in Hungary made the following contention: "I have known many different kinds of hunters. . . . In many of them the ancient instincts still thrive, the superstitions, the profound humility before the forces of nature."[57] The following remarks were made about Lajos Czinege, who at one point served as minister of defense: "There were animals he had singled out and then sought for decades. The 'miracle stag' of Kaszó was one, for instance. Once, he saw a stag with antlers with an unusual flaw. He looked for it for decades, but he never managed to get his hands on it."[58]

Naturally, outsiders do not see hunting in the same way as hunters themselves do. Hobo, a Hungarian blues musician and the son of László Földes, shared the following recollection of the times when his father took him with him on his hunting trips: "It was ghastly to see the whole thing. I did not understand the pleasure in it. The whole hierarchy, the relationship between the hunters and the servants rests on a lie. The beater and the game warden looked after the animals in their own way, but then they led the gentlemen and the comrades to them so that they could shoot the shit out of them."[59] One of the moments in the process of driving the game out that is rich with symbolic meaning occurs when the beater kneels and the hunter rests the rifle on the beater's shoulder to take his shot. Whether this is a gesture of selfless assistance, as hunters tend to claim, or demeaning servility, as an outsider might contend, is perhaps a matter of perspective.

The members of the Concord Hunting Society brought guests to the reserves, including actors, foreign diplomats, Hungarian functionaries, and renowned hunters. Count Zsigmond Széchenyi, a hunter who was famous for having gone on hunting expeditions in Africa, was a much-loved guest of the society. He taught János Kádár's hunters how to hunt more effectively with two rifles. Master of hounds Pál Rosenberger recounted an occasion when, after a hunting trip, he had held a roll call. After reading the names of all the party comrades, Rosenberger reached Széchenyi's name. He ruminated for a moment and then read Széchenyi's name aloud as Comrade Count Zsigmond Széchenyi. This was met with considerable amusement and put everyone in good spirits for the dinner.[60] Antal Rácz, the head of the ministry's hunting department, discovered just how revered the count was when he heard the stories that the hunters of the Concord Hunting Society told about him. Széchenyi was the protagonist of most of the legendary tales of hunting adventures.

> They invited him to the hunting grounds used by Concord. I was not yet there. János Kádár recounted how Zsigmond had arrived with a three-legged stool. He was wearing a cape, and he sat down on the stool with the cape over his back, and he sat there, all the others were standing, they started to drive out the pheasants and the barrel pokes out of this heap and poof, one of the pheasants drops, again the barrel pokes out and poof, another pheasant drops. When the whole thing had come to an end, Kádár goes over to Zsigmond and says, "Well, Comrade Széchenyi, you're a very good shot!" To which Zsigmond replies, "Yes, but two got away." So two of the pheasants got away! Kádár had counted how many he had hit, while Széchenyi had counted how many he had failed to bag.[61]

SOCIAL LIFE AMONG MEMBERS OF THE CONCORD HUNTING SOCIETY

The Ministry of Agriculture and Food designated several stretches of the forests and wildlife management areas as primary wildlife protection areas for the Concord Hunting Society. Some of these areas were in old, traditional hunting grounds such as in Gemenc, Gyulaj, Telki, Gyarmatpuszta, Lovasberény, and Visegrád. A closed government reserve was established in 1968 as the State Forestry and Wildlife Reserve of Gemenc. This was followed in 1969 by the establishment of the State Forestry and Wildlife Reserves of Gyulaj, Mezőföld (Soponya), Gödöllő, and Telki. The last two were later merged to form the State Forestry and Wildlife Reserve of the Buda Region. They were all old, traditional, aristocratic or royal hunting grounds. The Concord Hunting Society later got the territory near Gyarmatpuszta, too, which was made part of the Buda Region reserve.[62] The enclosed wildlife management area of Gyarmatpuszta had once been the estate of Count Móric Sándor, a Hungarian nobleman and equestrian and hunter of European fame. In the 1960s, this territory was used for the most part by Deputy Prime Minister Jenő Fock, so it came to be known as Fock Land.[63]

Kádár, however, did not look kindly on it when a member of the Concord Hunting Society ended up in a position of privilege or particular prominence. The reserves were completely closed off to the wider public and were enclosed with fences as instructed by the ministry. In Gemenc, the archdiocese of Kalocsa had already had a fence constructed, so the new regime only had to complete it. This work continued in 1969 in Gyulaj. The enclosures that were created in Telki, Gyulaj, Gemenc, and Gödöllő cost more than seventy million forints at the time.[64] Hunting lodges were built that were lavish by the standards at the time, and thus they were expressive of the privileged status of the people who used them. The first of these lodges was built in 1964 in Telki, not far from Budapest.⁶⁵

Old traditions were associated with the hunting grounds, and most of the professional hunters had learned their vocations in the interwar period. The other members of the staff at the hunting grounds were reliable officers in the state security forces who had been recruited in the 1950s. A distinctive relationship based on mutual trust developed between the professional hunters and the visitors to the hunting grounds. A hunter acquired prestige in front of his colleagues if he accompanied an influential member of the state apparatus into the forest on a hunt. They proudly recounted their adventures to one another. The members of the Concord Hunting Society could observe the seasoned hunters and learn various tactics. The most famous of the professional hunters was János Berek. When he happened to chat with strangers in a tavern, he would introduce himself as permanent master of hounds for the Hungarian prime minister, since even under Horthy he had taken the prime ministers on hunting expeditions. Berek was famous for his ability to bring down even the largest stags. He was imprisoned several times, first in 1951 because of his alleged ties to Yugoslavia. In 1951, tensions between Yugoslavia and the Soviet Union were high, and Berek had been present when Tito, the leader of the party in Yugoslavia, had gone on a famous hunting trip in Kelebia, a village in Bács-Kiskun County. After the revolution, Berek was imprisoned again but later released, allegedly at the intervention of Kádár himself.⁶⁶ On several occasions, Kádár and his wife spent New Year's Eve with Berek and his wife on Veránka, an island in the Danube River that was part of the Gemenc hunting grounds. For his eightieth birthday, Berek, who was the master of hounds for the Gemenc State Wildlife Management Area, was given the golden rank of the Workers' Order by the Presidential Council. A short film was even made about him titled *Sose vagyok egyedül*, or "I am never alone."

The Concord Hunting Society was assessed, in a manner expressive of the ideology of the period of consolidation under Kádár, as an organization that provided a framework for hunting expeditions that were symbolic of rank and power, and thus it constituted a barrier to abuses of authority. In retrospect, the hunting society far more closely resembled a forum for the professionalization (in hunting) of the new elite. A system of individual and group hunting trips emerged, as did distinctive customs that were particularly characteristic of the members of the Concord Hunting Society. Initially, members wore garb that distinguished the "old" hunters from the "new" ones: "The people who had hunted earlier [before the rise of the communist regime] had proper hunting clothing: they wore green or camouflage loden pants and jackets, several of them had loden vests (the Hubertus brand), and their hunting caps were adorned with hunting badges. In general, the new hunters wore the practical items of camp clothing used by the army, the police, and less frequently the militia."[67] For shorter hunting trips, many hunters would simply wear everyday clothes. However, steps were taken, with respect to clothing, toward professionalization. The staff members on the hunting grounds were given uniforms, and, as revealed in pictures and caricatures of the time, more and more hunters themselves acquired traditional hunting garb.

The Concord Hunting Society always held a ceremonial dinner at the end of the year, usually in the Officers' House—a building that previously had been known as the Stefánia Palace. It had been built toward the end of the nineteenth century in a neobaroque style in an elegant district of Pest that was home to many sumptuous villas. Initially, it had served as a casino, or club, for the upper classes, and members of the higher nobility had gathered inside its walls. Even members of the Habsburg family and foreign rulers had walked its hallways. After 1947, the building ended up in the hands of the Hungarian army and was used to host members of the party elite.

At the annual hunting society dinner, members were given copies of *Fácán Matyi*, or "Mattie the Pheasant Boy." The title is an allusion to the humor magazine *Ludas Matyi*, mentioned in chapter 2, and *Fácán Matyi* was drawn by the same caricaturists as *Ludas Matyi*. *Fácán Matyi* was a secret, exclusive publication made solely for members of the Concord Hunting Society, and it depicted events in the life of the society. The magazine, which in general was published once a year, was edited by the executive committee of the hunting society. The caricaturists had to follow instructions closely. Clearly, they knew who their readers were, just as they knew who had ordered the magazine, and this had a crippling effect on their art. One of the expedient iconographical tools of their self-restraint was the practice of using photographs—not caricatures—of the state and party leaders in their drawings.[68] *Fácán Matyi* often alluded to Hungarian hunting traditions. The party leaders were referred to as the sons of Nimród, partly in jest and partly seriously, and in their own way the party leaders adhered to tradition, if perhaps according to reassessments and reinterpretations. On some occasions, well-known parodists and actors were invited to the hunting society's events to create a more relaxed and casual atmosphere. They presented "mildly indecent numbers," patriotic poems, sketches, and parodies.[69]

In 1980, when he became minister of agriculture and food, Jenő Váncsa joined the Concord Hunting Society and took part in the festivities at the end of the year:

> There were always one or two artists who also hunted, and they performed as part of the program. We always found [Géza] Hofi's performances the most interesting. [Hofi was a famous parodist and humorist who, in his popular cabaret performances and radio programs, caricatured party leaders, if perhaps cautiously.] Hofi was good because he was able to tell jokes with a political and ethical critical edge, which a lot of us liked. Some people shook their heads, but even the Old Man [Kádár] nodded and smiled. As the alcohol on hand dwindled, spirits rose, but I am hardly saying anything new in that. János Kádár and his wife

were always the first to leave, after which the gathering soon came to a close.⁷⁰

In the years of team building under Kádár, membership in the hunting society became almost an expectation among ministers and members of the Political Committee, as did participation in the weekend training sessions and the group hunting trips, which were intended to forge a tight sense of unity. The expeditions, which lasted for several days, also included group dinners, card games, and wine spritzers.⁷¹ After the hunt, the functionaries would line up in smaller groups. Kádár himself remained unapproachable to members of the Political Committee. He regularly played cards with Jenő Szűcs (a major general who was also the head of the hunting society), and they were joined by the head of the hunting department and the local head of hunting. Sándor Gáspár, a trade union official, sat at another table, and Central Committee secretaries Károly Németh and Béla Biszku and the doctor for the society, János Zoltán, shuffled the cards. They played *ulti* (a popular Hungarian card game) and chatted. It was forbidden, however, to bring up affairs of state in Kádár's presence. Most of the men drank wine spritzers. The first secretary preferred dry white wine, and he drank in moderation. When it came to the card game, however, he was less modest. His opponents regularly let him win (presumably prudently).⁷²

During the dinners after a group hunt, the staff at the Gundel restaurant (one of the most elegant restaurants in Budapest even today) served food and drink. Károly Marton, who worked at Gundel and later became the deputy general manager of the upscale Hungarian hotel chain Hunguest Hotels, was one of the waiters on these occasions and recalls: "They referred to us as gastronomical commandos. We could do anything. Once, when they were holding a celebration following the vineyard harvest, they opened up half a hillside to us so we would be able to serve the guests properly."⁷³ Sándor Tóth was among the guests when Kádár and the members of his closest circle were passing the time with their merrymaking: "The food was usually modest, a pheasant soup, a stew, Kádár's favorite was savoy cabbage and pasta with fried cabbage, so they always served them as a side with the most delicious dishes, and everyone loved savoy cabbage and pasta with fried cabbage, because it was not good manners not to love them."[74]

According to the servers who were on call for these events, Kádár never failed, after the evening had come to a close, to shake hands with the members of the staff and to bid farewell to them. He behaved in a similar manner with the professional hunters. In Telki, however, where he usually went to relax, accompanied only by his wife, he made a very different impression. The caretaker of the lodge, Mrs. Kálmán Berényi, tended to the needs of the first secretary and his wife:

> He looked right through me, as if looking through a pane of glass.... On one occasion, we were waiting for him, they always arrived on Saturday afternoon, once a year when the stags began to bell, around the time of Mary's name day. The four of us, the professor of internal medicine, the commander of the government militia, the medical officer of the government militia, and me, were sitting in the little dining room waiting for him and trading stories. I asked what would happen if comrade Kádár were to come in and I were to jump into his arms and say how overjoyed I was that he had arrived. The professor said, "Edit, where do I sit at dinner? Where do I sit during the meals?" "Well," I said, "next to the Old Man." "And how do you feel my situation?" "Well," I say, "the professor is a full member of the circle at the table." "I am? Then let me tell you, once, I interfered, I interrupted one of the conversations, and János Kádár says to me, 'doctor, you are here to be sure I don't light up, and me, I do as I please.' That's what he said, Edit! We are servants here, all of us, just one of us sits in one place, another in another place." So we had to know very well our place, and we had to be disciplined and orderly.[75]

As first secretary, Kádár always avoided shows of luxury or sumptuousness, and he presented himself to the public as a man of an almost puritanical lifestyle. He behaved in this manner not only when on the public stage but also among the members of the Concord Hunting Society, and his shows of restraint set the boundaries. This conduct best suited the role he had chosen for himself. If Kádár was present, the mood of the hunts was more orderly and disciplined. György Tollner, the director of the State Forestry and Wildlife Reserve of the Buda Region, organized several hunting trips for party leaders. According to Tollner, "János Kádár, comrade Kádár was our best, most patient guest. We always kept our fingers crossed, or at least I did, that he would be present for the group hunts. Because if he was there, everyone was disciplined, everyone was serious, they didn't make demands or complaints, how come you didn't drive out the game for me, how come you drove game out for him. If Kádár wasn't there, then, alas, people behaved differently."[76]

The party leaders had to address several issues of discipline. Antal Rácz, the head of department of the ministry in charge of protocol affairs, was responsible for ensuring that order was maintained during the hunts. For group hunts, this task was performed not by Rácz but by the leadership of the Concord Hunting Society, with Ferenc Szűcs, the stern master of hounds (who also bore Kádár's arms), at the head. For individual hunts, Rácz had to intervene personally. Naturally, he sometimes needed the assistance of the highest-ranking leaders and, on some occasions, even of Kádár himself. Rácz recalled a few particularly dramatic episodes: "There was one guest who shot the roof of the UAZ [an off-road vehicle manufactured in the Soviet Union], and there was another who propped his rifle on the back of the car and took aim, but without realizing that the barrel was in front of the mirror, and he totally blew the rearview mirror to smithereens. Once, while they were disemboweling the game, the driver ran into the hunting lodge and called me on the phone to ask for help, saying that the guest was so drunk that he was shooting indiscriminately, and it was terrifying."[77]

Kádár organized the hunting society around himself, and he maintained permanent control of it. The rules that he set and the patterns of conduct he exemplified were only effective as standards if he could keep his central place in the group. When he took part in group hunts, he had to conduct himself with the appropriate gravity to ensure that both his presence and, later, when he did not take part in a hunt, his absence would be felt. When Kádár did not come on a hunt, the group did indeed fall apart, and the hunters showed a remarkable lack of discipline. Kádár created balance among the hunters, who had different personalities and often nurtured feelings of enmity toward one another. Jenő Váncsa, minister of agriculture and in charge of supervising the members of the hunting society, had to rely on Kádár in any confrontations with the other hunters:

> He didn't let us behave rowdily during the hunts. The question always came up in the course of the hunts of whether or not we could shoot pheasant hens or just the pheasant roosters. Once, one of the high-ranking members of the Political Committee asked me before the hunt had begun, "We're going to shoot everything today, right?" János Kádár had not yet arrived, because if the gathering were to begin at, say, 9:00 or 9:30, and we were there a half-hour ahead of time, János Kádár arrived one minute before the hunt was scheduled to start. If he arrived early, then he had the car stop at the edge of the forest and he smoked a cigarette, saying that he didn't want to bother the Society, and he meant it. He was precise in other things too. Suffice to say, my colleague came over to me and said we'd shoot everything, and I said, "Well, let's wait a bit on that," and the Old Man arrived and asked me, "According to the rules, we are only going to shoot the roosters, right?" I glanced at my friend [who had asked about shooting hens] and replied yes, we'd only shoot roosters.[78]

TOWARD THE CHANGE OF REGIMES

In the 1980s, Kádár went into the forests less frequently, and he rarely participated in the group hunts. Until 1979, the Hunting and Wildlife Management Department of the Ministry of Agriculture and Food had overseen the organization of hunting in

Hungary. Sándor Tóth, the head of the department at the time, often discussed with Kádár in person the issues that arose in connection with the Concord Hunting Society. Several members of the society, however, complained that the two puritans, as they referred to Kádár and Tóth behind their backs, made decisions without their input. They created a Wildlife Management Supervisory Main Department, which in 1982 took over control of forest and wildlife management.[79] This step left Kádár even more distant from the affairs of the Concord Hunting Society.

The new main department remained outside the formal structure of the Ministry of Agriculture and Food. Even the agriculture minister had no power over the new wildlife management department. Essentially, the department's only task was to organize and supervise the operations of the Concord Hunting Society and provide the funds necessary for the hunts.[80] In the 1980s, with the support of some members of the Political Committee, this main supervisory department, which was responsible for overseeing the more important hunts, launched some rather grand developments. Sándor Csányi, the ambitious manager of financial affairs for the department, appeared in the political arena. After the change of regimes, Csányi became the head of the National Savings Bank, the largest bank in Hungary, and today he can regularly be seen next to Prime Minister Viktor Orbán at soccer games. Csányi is also president of the Hungarian Football Federation. Under his fiscal leadership of the Wildlife Management Supervisory Main Department, new forestry centers and hunting lodges were built.

Hunting lodges in traditional prewar hunting reserves, such as Valkó, Gemenc, and Lenes, were completed for the 1971 Hunting World Fair, and additions were made to the lodges in Soponya and Gyulaj. In 1975, the executive committee of the Concord Hunting Society compiled an inventory of the lodges that were only available for use by members.[81] New cars were acquired to appease the party leaders, who had a passion for automobiles.

Mercedes-Benz cars were becoming popular in the circles of the party leadership at the time, and since the ministry's hard currency allotment could not be used to purchase all-terrain vehicles,[82] Mercedes-Benz executives were invited to go on paid hunting trips. Enough game was set aside for them from Concord's quota, with skins and antlers that could be taken home as trophies to cover the purchase price of the cars. In 1984, ten new Mercedes-Benz cars arrived in Hungary.[83]

Boar gardens were also created in the enclosed areas, the first one in Isaszeg. This made hunting considerably easier for the guests. The swine could not escape, so grand hunting trips could be organized with a large number of kills. In 1975, after a hunting trip in Gödöllő, the carcasses of one hundred wild boars were spread out in the clearing beside the hunting lodge. The animals were decorated with branches and leaves, and the hunters lit the tremendous pyre in celebration of the successful hunt.[84] Animals were brought from abroad to replenish the stocks. In Gyarmatpuszta, for instance, the stocks included bison that had been brought to Hungary from Poland.[85] One of the bison, which had been given the name Pupi, allegedly chased one of the members of the Political Committee. In the end, the animals, who clearly showed no respect for protocol, were turned over to the zoo in Veszprém.

A so-called light program was launched for use with partridges, pheasants, and ducks. In the 1960s, they had used brooding hens to hatch the eggs, and after an appropriate amount of time had passed, the birds were taken to the hunting grounds. Later, the hunters got their hands on incubators, and they used so-called Lohmann houses (technology for large-scale production made by German company Lohmann Tierzucht) to hatch and nurture the chicks in the right light and under the right thermal conditions. On the hunting grounds, feeding paths and artificial feeders were built for the birds that were turned loose.[86]

Hunters with similar temperaments and frames of mind soon made one another's acquaintance. Thus, smaller circles were formed within the Concord Hunting Society. One group consisted of the most passionate hunters. They enjoyed one another's company, and they loved to pursue game together and set new records, one after the other. Sándor Tóth, who was part of the society when it was founded, watched with amazement as Kádár and the Concord hunters grew ever more distant from each other. Tóth observed:

> In this circle, Kádár played the role of moderator. He compelled the members of the Society to be modest, i.e. the quest to bag game and get big trophies should not be the primary consideration, but when it came to small game, the quest to mimic some prewar or aristocratic mold had started. János Kádár, however, did not give up his rhythm, the animal could come to him in the mist and he would shoot, reload, shoot, reload, and all nice and calmly, and in the end he put down his gun and didn't hunt. Clearly, he had declined so much physically, and he had slowed down, psychologically it was such a burden to stand in his position that he did not want to hold the hunting trips, but the core of Concord still got along excellently.[87]

As Kádár began to lose power within the society, membership came to depend more and more on formal positions. Clearly, it was hardly in Kádár's interests to have others use the hunting society to develop their own clientele. In 1983, György Lázár, chairman of the Council of Ministers, issued a special directive specifying who could hunt on the territory of the forestry and wildlife management areas—in other words, the territory under the control of the Concord Hunting Society. In doing so, he officially excluded all the retirees among the members and all the people who had lost their earlier positions. Of the people in government, state secretaries could become members of the society, and of the people in the party, Central Committee heads of department and county first secretaries could join. Earlier, membership had depended in part on informal relationships such as ties to Kádár or the people in his immediate circle.

From 1983 on, however, position counted. On January 1, 1984, nineteen people were stripped of their membership. According to people's recollections, the leadership of the Concord Hunting Society spoke with each of them in person, and in the end, they found some opportunity for everyone to hunt. József Veres, one of the retirees, had close ties to Kádár. They had been in prison together back in the early days, and they used the informal form of address in Hungarian, which was exceptional even in the circle of hunters. At Veres's request, Kádár intervened on his behalf, and in the end, Veres was allowed to remain in the society.[88] In the 1980s, as the wider public began to become increasingly well informed of the workings of the regime, the Concord group became increasingly secretive. There are very few bits of evidence (scattered memos, lists of kills, memorial certificates for the group hunts) on the basis of which one could determine who went hunting as a member of the society. While many of the older members of the Concord Hunting Society were driven out and forced to join the Friendship Hunting Society, many of the young Turks in the party were able to set foot on the reserves, and members of the Hungarian Young Communist League began to bag ever larger game.

In December 1986, the Concord hunters crowned their achievements by setting a new record for pheasant hunting. The spoils of the hunt were a global sensation. In the course of the expedition, which was held in Lenes on December 21, 1986, the Concord team brought down 8,974 pheasants with 20,800 bullets.[89]

When the ethical norms for hunting were again laid down following the regime change, hunting experts spoke critically of these shooting competitions and rivalries. One of them wrote the following:

> The pile of animals that were shot is "repulsive," and the person who shot them would be better described as a "carrion-record setter." It is a shocking spectacle, for instance, that there are shooters (I am deliberately avoiding using the word hunters) who are

capable of firing off a volley of rounds at a pheasant, a bird which can't even fly properly (and without taking into consideration whether the bird is a hen or a rooster), or a meek, recently hatched wild duck, which is forced to take short flights. The heap of boars shot in the boar gardens is equally repulsive. It is reprehensible to shoot more than one animal with antlers during the roebuck or stag hunts. Alas, the uninhibited leaders of the dictatorship were at the vanguard in this.[90]

At the beginning of the 1980s, the press began to pay attention to the hunting expeditions taken by members of the government, and they were mentioned with increasing frequency in public forums. In 1984, Imre Szász's sociographical book *Ez elment vadászni* (which, since it echoes a children's counting rhyme, could be translated as "And This Little Piggy Went Hunting") was published as part of a series titled "Magyarország felfedezése," or "Discovering Hungary." Before it was published, the book was examined by the party committee to be sure that it was censored to the regime's tastes. It concludes with a conversation with Károly Grósz, who at the time was the first secretary of Borsod County. In the interview, Grósz, who later became secretary general of the party, did not completely deny or refute the contentions made concerning the transgressions committed by influential leaders of the regime. He only denied them when they concerned him or the hunting trips in which he took part: "Once, a friend of mine invited me to come to Szabolcs [Szabolcs-Szatmár-Bereg County], there was something there they badly wanted me to shoot, the hunter who accompanied us showed me a buck with six-pronged antlers and told me to shoot him. I asked him which set of antlers this was for the buck, and he said the third. I could tell that he would grow into a better buck, so I left him alone. The hunter urged me on, telling me to go ahead and shoot, but he was relieved that I didn't."[91] Grósz offered the following characterization of his relationship to hunting and to nature: "Even today, sometimes after it has rained I go out at dawn, lean my rifle against a tree, and instead of hunting, I pick mushrooms."[92] The attempts to craft a portrait of the ambitious Grósz that would evoke sympathy indicates the growing role of public forums and the public sphere, as does the fact that Grósz strove to distance himself from other party leaders. The professional hunters likened his customs, conduct, and attitude to the habits and conduct of his predecessor (even if he was not able to forge a unified group out of the Concord society, as Kádár had done before him). Hunter Ottó Feiszt accompanied Grósz on many hunts, and party general secretary Grósz walked a well-worn path in the footsteps of János Kádár. "The first time I met him, he was the First Secretary of Borsod County, and he was a very pleasant hunter. On the next occasion, he came to Zala to hunt, by then as General Secretary of the party. He remembered me, and he greeted me by saying, 'Howdy Ottó' [using the informal form of address].... The last time Károly Grósz came to Zala to hunt was in 1990. He arrived in a 1200 Lada, and he introduced his companion hunter as someone who was unemployed."[93]

In 1984, the Political Committee discussed the question of hunting and fishing. According to the report, "No noticeable social tension has been experienced in fishing."[94] This statement clearly had an important implication as the document discussed at length the inequalities that were palpable in "the area of hunting."[95] The hierarchy in the world of hunting and the exclusive nature of the hunting societies could not be brought to an end in a single stroke, and presumably the regime did not even wish to do this. In a letter written in 1985, Kádár described the question of membership in the hunting societies as a "proverbially difficult issue for us."[96] It is perhaps characteristic of what could be called the style of the era that the people applying for admission into the Concord Hunting Society emphasized in their applications their knowledge of hunting. In other words, despite the fact that a position of importance was a precondition of membership, applicants still thought it significant to acknowledge the "professionalization" of hunting and their professional skills. This was even the case, for instance, when a deputy minister sought admittance to the exclusive hunting society of the Ministry of Finance.[97] The leadership of the Hunting Federation (the National Executive Committee, the Committee, the county executive committees) had many county secretaries, council chairmen, leaders on the National Council of Agricultural Cooperatives, and leaders in the ministries and the bodies of the highest authorities.[98]

In the regime's period of transition, the question of the hunting practices of the party leaders again was raised.[99] In 1988, a retiree from Balatonakarattya turned, with the assistance of Zoltán Király (a parliamentary representative who had been expelled from the party because of his oppositional conduct), to the Council for Constitutional Law of the Hungarian National Assembly to request that the decrees concerning hunting free of charge be repealed.[100] In the end, the chairman of the Council of Ministers declared null and void the directive concerning hunting on the territory of the government reserves. The waves of change eventually reached the Concord Hunting Society, and indeed they submerged the society in their eddies. During the sitting on February 7, 1989, the Political Committee essentially ordered that the Concord Hunting Society be dissolved. Those present resolved to acknowledge a decision taken by the society itself if the society were to announce its dissolution at the next assembly. In the debate concerning the resolution, György Fejti suggested continuing to ensure opportunities for the members of the society to hunt. Karoly Grósz, general secretary of the party, felt that it would be important to be evenhanded: "We cannot suggest that János Kádár join, I don't know, the Veres-Szamos hunting society [a small, local hunting society]." Grósz also noted that it would be important to inform the soldiers in the army, because "they have something like this too." Someone then interrupted and said, "Speak up in time, Comrade Grósz, because we want to go on over there."[101]

On February 16, 1989, after the Political Committee had issued its resolution, minister of agriculture and food Jenő Váncsa convened a discussion in the ministry in which Miklós Villányi, the minister of finance, and the responsible staff members at the two ministries took part. Beginning on May 1, they brought an end to free hunting on state territories. Váncsa moderated the discussion: "We said that this should come to an end before the change of regimes. There was some debate on this. I cited a few examples of how people were talking at the time about our hunting trips in the taverns, and how could you explain it, if people were saying that after a hunt, when they would slice open and disembowel a sow in farrow, the little piglets came tumbling out shrieking, well, I can't explain that, I said. If you can, then please do! This was more persuasive than any other reasoning."[102]

The Concord Hunting Society was refashioned and redubbed Silvanus. The Friendship Hunting Society kept its old name. On the recommendation of the Ministry of Agriculture and Food, Silvanus was entitled to rent the hunting grounds at Galgamácsa, and Friendship could rent the hunting grounds at Vértestolna. Whereas the hunters had previously referred to themselves as the sons of Nimród, now they marched under a different mythical figure. Silvanus is a Roman deity of forests and fields who lives in the dense underbrush and watches over the trees, the woodlands, and the woodcutters. As the forest dwellers slowly begin to form social groups, Silvanus also begins to keep watch over fields, farmers, flocks, and even vegetable and fruit gardens. Alas, Silvanus's Hungarian adherents never actually had time to organize group hunting expeditions on the old (now new) hunting grounds.[103]

The government set aside ten million forints to meet any demand that arose for hunting expeditions. The forestry office was given responsibility for organizing official hunting trips, and the Gyarmatpuszta reserve was designated a hunting ground for the government.[104] Hunting, however, essentially was dropped from government protocol. In 1990, a plan was proposed for the designation of new government reserves, but József Antall, the first prime minister of the new regime, indignantly dismissed it.[105]

In the pivotal years of transition, there was good reason to fear that the changes that were taking place would eventually reach the famous hunting grounds. Several hunters approached politicians with their anxieties concerning the fate of Hungarian wildlife, but their fears proved unfounded. Hikers and nature lovers got back the forests around Buda, but the fences remained around the hunting grounds in Gemenc, Gyulaj, Soponya, and some smaller enclosed areas. Finally, in 1995, a hunting society was formed for parliamentary representatives, and it has featured many times since on the front pages of newspapers and the covers of magazines, as have the hunting trips of some prominent politicians.[106]

Today, the circle of hunters has grown considerably wider, but this has not led to any fundamental change in attitudes toward hunting as a sport and pastime, and it most certainly has not brought an end to the inequalities in the world of hunting. The most affluent hunters go on expeditions abroad, and there is now a Hungarian branch of the Safari Club International.[107] The branch holds annual meetings at the Hilton Hotel in Las Vegas. One of the secretaries of this society began his career in the Nimród Youth Hunting Society, as did the head of Vadcoop, the first of the "renting" hunting societies—those that do not own or lease their own hunting grounds, but rather pay other hunting societies on a trip-by-trip basis for the use of their grounds. Thus, one finds continuity not simply in the customs and habits involved in the hunting world in Hungary but also in the personalities.

NOTES

1. Hegedüs 1985, 85.
2. When the press asked the politicians what they did during their free time before the 1945 elections, Ferenc Nagy was the only one who mentioned that he liked to hunt. Rákosi, in contrast, contended that in his free time he also focused on politics. Hajdú 1983, 5.
3. József Pitlik, a real estate agent from Miskolc, was entrusted with the task of finding "appropriate properties" for the population of Derenk

and resettling "all real estate owners of Derenk" to these properties. Magyar Nemzeti Levéltár Országos Levéltára (Hungarian National Archives, hereafter cited as HNA), fond K 27, May 24, 1940 (46).

4. HNA, fond XIX-K-I, group y, box 342-343. For an almost novelistic account of the resettlement, see Szűts 1965.

5. The community of Derenk had earlier won the title "the most faithful settlement," when, after Trianon, the Polish population of the village decided in a referendum to remain part of Hungary instead of becoming part of the new state of Czechoslovakia.

6. Later, under Ákos Szederjei's oversight, they managed to settle the next generation of animals. With regard to the importance of expertise over time, it is perhaps worth noting that on December 15, 1944, Szederjei was brought from the forestry office of Szin to the Ministry of Agriculture. After he had been approved by the authorities in 1945, he worked in the hunting department of the ministry. In 1948, he became the department head of the State Forestry Works. Pápai 2003, 263; Sándor Tóth 2005, 40.

7. The settlement was on the border of the hunting reserve, like Bódvaszilas and Szögliget, also on the Hungarian side.

8. HNA, fond XIX-K-1, group ii, box 4, 161.280/1946. The primary territory of the reserve consisted of lands that had been reacquired by Hungary from Czechoslovakia following the First Vienna Award and the estate of Szin. The new border that was drawn in accordance with the Paris Peace Treaties at the end of the Second World War, however, severed part of this territory from Hungary. In 1947, the reserve experts recommended to the Council of Ministers that they contact the Czechoslovak government in the interests of the three bears that lived on the territory of the reserve. However, at the time, population exchanges were underway (which involved the forced resettlement of large Hungarian-speaking populations to Hungary), and so the authorities did not consider it the "opportune" moment to take such steps. Thus, the animals were not given any protections from Czechoslovakia hunters. HNA, fond XIX-K-1, group ii, box 8, 125.725/1947; Sándor Tóth 2007, 182, 191–192.

9. I have raised this issue in several essays: Majtényi 2006, 2008, 2016.

10. The transformations and alterations that were underway allegedly took place in the name of democracy and social justice. For instance, in his request for admission, Árpád Sas, secretary of the Trade Union Council, who in 1946 had joined the hunting department of the Ministry of Agriculture, offered the following argument: "For the working class, the fact that there is an individual from the Trade Union Council who has the

confidence of organized labor in the Hunting Department of the Ministry of Agriculture is particularly reassuring." Sándor Tóth 2005, 41.

11. Sándor Tóth 2009a.

12. The Society of the Sport Section of the Free Trade Union of Hungarian Public Employees (Közalkalmazottak Sport Egyesülete, or KASE, the Public Employees' Sport Society) elected Imre Nagy as its president. Sándor Tóth 2007, 138. Presumably, Nagy hunted later as well. The records concerning a house search that was conducted in his residence on April 30, 1957, contain the following items: "One two-barrel, break-action hunting rifle," "36 hunting rifle shells," "2 hunting rifle licenses with photograph," and "2 authorizations to purchase ammunition." HNA, fond XX-5, group h, box 12, volume 1.

13. Sándor Tóth 2005.

14. HNA XIX-K-1-ii 11. c.; Sándor Tóth 2005, 65, 343.

15. On the basis of Finance Ministry Decree No. 15.120/1945, the first central guidance organ of state forestry was created. It was called Magyar Állami Erdőgazdasági Üzemek, or MÁLLERD, the State Forestry Works.

16. *Szabad Föld*, November 20, 1947.

17. Pápai 2003, 271.

18. Ibid., 272.

19. Ibid., 275–276.

20. Katalin Beretz 2001, 27. Katalin Beretz, Endre Nagy's widow, compiled and edited the surviving reports, diary fragments, and sections of interviews into a unified first-person narrative.

21. Állambiztonsági Szolgálatok Történeti Levéltára (Historical Archives of the Hungarian State Security, hereafter cited as HAHSS), fond 3.2, group 4, K-2248 "Szarvas."

22. "It was thanks to my leadership that no unified, broad collective emerged in the leadership of our party. Instead of collective leadership, together with two or three comrades, first and foremost Gerő, Farkas, and Révai, I handled the leadership." HNA, fond M-KS 276, group 52, storage unit 24.

23. Nógrádi 1970, 433; Nánási 1983, 229, 252.

24. Gerő was made minister of transportation in 1945, and the Communist Party's propaganda organs dubbed him the "bridge builder."

25. Hegedüs 1985, 85.

26. Huszár 2005, 35.

27. Interview with Sándor Tóth, Budapest, September 10, 2005.

28. Sándor Tóth 2005, 126.
29. Interview with Sándor Tóth, Budapest, September 10, 2005.
30. *Fácán Matyi*, 1964.
31. Interview with Sándor Tóth, Budapest, September 25, 2008.
32. HNA, fond XIX-K-9, group b, box 345.
33. Interview with Károly Marton, Budapest, November 6, 2008.
34. Sándor Tóth 2005, 91–92.
35. Ibid., 132–133.
36. HNA XXVIII-K-10 1. c.
37. Ibid.
38. Interview with Béla Rakeczky Jr., Gyulaj, October 10, 2008.
39. Interview with Ottó Feiszt, Budapest, November 10, 2008.
40. "Kedves Gyula: Ajándék Keletről; A nyugati ipar remeke" [Dear Gyula: A gift from the East; A first-rate work of Western industry], *Kaliber: Önvédelmi, vadász-, katonai és sportfegyverek szaklapja* [Caliber: A specialized journal on weapons for self-defense, hunting, military, and sports], April 14, 1999, 16–18.
41. "Kedves Gyula: Kádár-vadászfegyverek; Ajándék a túlsó partról" [Dear Gyula: Kádár's hunting rifles; A gift from the far bank], *Kaliber: Önvédelmi, vadász-, katonai és sportfegyverek szaklapja* [Caliber: A specialized journal on weapons for self-defense, hunting, military, and sports], August 1999, 34–36.
42. Magyar Mezőgazdasági Múzeum [Museum of Hungarian Agriculture], Vadászati Kiállítás.
43. Interview with József Bányai, Budapest, November 10, 2008.
44. Interview with László Sándorfalvi, Soponya, October 10, 2008.
45. Hunting exhibitions and trophy presentations, Budapest, Hunting and Wildlife Management Department of the Ministry of Agriculture and Food, 1970, HNA, fond XIX-K-9, group aj, box 44.
46. Trophy exhibition. The gold medal and silver medal trophies of Hungarian hunters from 1969–1970, 1970. VI. 20–30. Ministry of Agriculture. Stag antlers 1969, gold medals: 1. János Kádár, 2. Ferenc Kárpáti, 3. János Kádár, 4. Dr. Béla Horváth, 5. István Kovács, 6. Andor László, 7. Károly Csémi, 8. Sándor Gáspár, 9. László Földes, 10. László Mátyás, 11. Mátyás Timár, 12. János Borbándi, 13. Jenő Fock, 14. Lajos Czinege, 15. Lajos Cseterki. Hunting exhibitions and trophy presentations, 62, HNA, fond XIX-K-9, group aj, box 44. At the hunting exhibition organized the same year in Győr, the antlers of stags that had been shot by Horst Gerlach, Witzl Jürgens, Rudolf Hess, and Helga Hess led the list. Ibid., 132.

47. A 1967 issue of *Szabad Föld* carried a short item praising the merits of Hungarian hunters:

In Novi Sad, Yugoslavia, at the international exhibition held between 12 Sept and 5 October, some ninety Hungarian trophies were on view among the others. 76 of them won gold medals, 10 won silver, and 4 won bronze. Two of the stag antlers from game felled by Hungarian hunters almost competed with the world record. The clearly superior antlers of a roe from Martonvásár put the Polish antlers which had held the world record for 70 years in second place. The stag antler from a deer that had been brought down in Gyulaj also set a new world record. All things considered, in the competition for European big game, Hungary won first place. Most of the Hungarian trophies that were on display in the exhibition, which closed with a presentation of the great success of Hungarian wildlife management, were placed side by side in the Museum of Hungarian Agriculture. The trophy exhibition will be open to the public as of 7 November. *Szabad Föld*, October 29, 1967, 2.

48. The importance of the event within Hungary and the popularity of hunting at the time are both made vividly palpable by the host of influential luminaries who participated. Among those present at the opening were Lajos Fehér, deputy president of the Council of Ministers; Sándor Gáspár, secretary general of the National Trade Union Council (Szakszervezetek Országos Tanácsa, or SZOT); Károly Németh, first secretary of the Budapest Party Committee; members of the Political Committee; Miklós Óvári, secretary of the Central Committee of the Hungarian Socialist Workers' Party; and Mátyás Timár and Péter Vályi, deputy chairmen of the Council of Ministers. HNA, fond XIX-K-9, group aj, box 40.

49. Guide to the Hunting World Fair, Budapest, 1971, Ministry of Agriculture and Food Exhibition Office, 11, HNA, fond XIX-K-9, group aj, box 40.

50. Kövér and Gyáni 1998, 200.

51. Odescalchi 1987, 170; cited by Gyáni Gábor. Kövér and Gyáni 1998, 201.

52. Zoltán 1996, 46.

53. Hadas offers this interpretation of the history of hunting. Hadas 2003.

54. Kopa 1999, 26.

55. Interview with György Tollner, Budakeszi, September 2005.
56. Raewyn Connell (R. W. Connell) defines four main types of masculinities: hegemonic, complicit, subordinated, and marginalized. Connell 1987; Connell and Messerschmidt 2005.
57. Sándor Tóth 2005, 182.
58. Zoltán 1996, 81.
59. Interview with László Földes (Hobo), Budapest, October 2005.
60. Interview with Pál Rosenberger, Solymár, October 26, 2008.
61. Interview with Antal Rácz, Budakeszi, November 6, 2008.
62. HNA, fond XIX-K-9, group ah, box 1-2.
63. Interview with Pál Rosenberger, Solymár, October 26, 2008.
64. Zoltán 1996, 23.
65. In Gemenc, in addition to the hunting lodge on the bank of the Danube River and the house named Keselyűs (The Vulture's Dwelling), one more wooden building was erected on Pandúr Island (the island is named after the Pandours or Pandurs, originally soldiers in an infantry unit in the Habsburg army, but later used to refer more generally to guards and patrol soldiers). In Gyulaj, a building was erected on the hill next to the fishing ponds in 1982 that was even bigger than the adjacent Rákosi villa. In Telki, the two-story hunting lodge in the middle of the State Forestry and Wildlife Reserve of the Buda Region (which had all the amenities of a modern dwelling) was built specifically as a place to welcome guests of the government. In Gyarmatpuszta, there was a small hunting lodge on the hillside. In 1984, a three-story guest house with numerous rooms was built on the elevated area above the lake. There were only two, relatively modest hunting lodges in Gödöllő, so a three-story lodge was built in Valkó. After 1975, modern buildings were erected in Gyarmatpuszta, Soponya, and Karapancsa with room for twenty to thirty people. These edifices made it possible to increase the export traffic of the wildlife management areas.
66. Antal Rácz, who was later the head of hunting in Gemenc, knew the legendary hunter and the stories about him:

> They took János Berek off in 1956, and when things had gotten back to normal after 1956, Kádár and his bunch went to Gemenc to hunt. They were accompanied by István Dénes, head of the hunting department, and Kádár was looking for János Berek. Everyone mumbled, no one dared say where he was. But come on, where's Berek? So they told him, Comrade Kádár, the police took him off. Where? Don't know where, but they took him off. So Kádár tells Dénes to get Berek out immediately. Then they left, they went hunting, they

played cards, at midnight, when they had been playing cards for a long time, Kádár asks Dénes, comrade Dénes, did you take care of things? Dénes says no, later, tomorrow morning. What? Tomorrow morning? You don't understand that in prison even five minutes is hard, what are you talking about, tomorrow morning? Take care of it now! So he took care of it. I heard the other side of the story from János Berek. Berek said, when they apprehended him, that he wanted to write a letter to János Kádár, at which the prison guard hit him in the mouth with a rubber cane and told him not to dare even let that name cross his lips. And when notice came that János Kádár had ordered them to release Berek, the prison guard had cleaned János Berek's boots. So Berek says, I told you that if I write a letter, you might even get a promotion. I would have allowed it, but now I won't let you get ahead at all. Interview with Dr. Antal Rácz, Budakeszi, November 6, 2008.

67. Zoltán 1996, 33.
68. The magazine can be found in the public collection. In his book, János Zoltán published some of the caricatures. Zoltán 1996. Sándor Tóth put issues of *Fácán Matyi* at my disposal.
69. Zoltán 1996, 40.
70. Interview with Jenő Váncsa, Budapest, September 20, 2008.
71. Zoltán 1996, 34–36.
72. Ibid., 34–35.
73. Interview with Károly Marton, Budapest, November 6, 2008.
74. Interview with Sándor Tóth, Budapest, September 25, 2008.
75. Interview with Mrs. Kálmán Berényi, Budapest, October 10, 2008.
76. Interview with György Tollner, Budakeszi, September 25, 2008.
77. Interview with Antal Rácz, Budakeszi, November 6, 2008.
78. Interview with Jenő Váncsa, Budapest, September 20, 2008.
79. Almost nothing has survived in the archives of the ministry's written documents concerning the protocol hunting expeditions. This is typical of the archival practices of the time, and more specifically of the practices for disposing of archival materials. See HNA, fond XIX-K-9, group ah.
80. Antal Rácz ended up at the head of the main department.
81. Zoltán 1996, 15–18.
82. In 1979, a resolution issued by the Political Committee limited the use of automobiles for official or ceremonial purposes. HNA, fond M-KS 288, group 5, 1979, storage unit 786.

83. Zoltán 1996, 14.

84. Ibid., 23.

85. Gesing, the Polish minister of forestry, gave the Gyarmatpuszta bison to Gyula Balassa in 1957 and 1961. In 1965, the hunting department of the ministry gave the animals to the Budapest zoo because it could not manage the difficulties that arose in connection with their maintenance. At the time, there were seven bison in Gyarmatpuszta, including calves. Some of them were given to the zoos in Debrecen, Pécs, and Veszprém, and some were taken abroad as animals for trade. Interview with Sándor Tóth, Budapest, September 25, 2005.

86. Interview with Antal Rácz, Budakeszi, November 6, 2008.

87. Interview with Sándor Tóth, Budapest, September 25, 2008.

88. Zoltán 1996, 63.

89. The hunters on the expedition were Sándor Gáspár, Lénárd Pál, Péter Várkonyi, József Szakali, Lajos Papp, Ferenc Szűcs, László Papp, Sándor Rácz, János Pap, Lajos Lénárt, József Farkas, János Zoltán, Antal Rácz, and János Berek. The trip was organized by Kornél Böröczky, and Károly Árva was the guide. It was held in the State Forestry and Wildlife Reserve area in Gemenc. The list of kills is in the hunting lodge in Lenes.

90. Bán 1996, 31.

91. Imre Szász 1984, 268. When replying to a question, he also recalled the following: "I bagged one stag that is beyond the limit of the gold medal by one point and one that is one point below it. I have the invitation of comrade Czinege to thank for the latter. I shot it in Kaszópuszta." Ibid., 270.

92. Ibid., 270.

93. Interview with Ottó Feiszt, April 30, 2008.

94. Notice for the Political Committee concerning society's demands arising with regard to hunting and fishing. At its meeting on September 25, 1984, in the course of a debate concerning the suggestion of the economic policy department of the committee, the Political Committee entrusted the Ministry of Agriculture and Food with the task of "addressing the questions that arise with regards to hunting and fishing, while the Council of Ministers will put the suggestion concerning the solution to these questions on the agenda at an appropriate time." HNA, fond M-KS 288, group 5, 1984, storage unit 921.

95. In 1984, 17 percent of the hunting grounds in Hungary were used by people who were entitled to participate in the hunts organized by the state. There were fewer than one hundred such people. The National Hungarian Hunting Federation and its associated societies (767 hunting societies in

total with some 31,200 members) used the other 83 percent. In accordance with party directives, beginning in 1985, opportunities to hunt were made available to more "sportsman hunters." For the most part, this involved hunting grounds that were distant from Budapest. A directive was issued to focus more on efforts to breed game, "in particular the small game and big game in enclosures sought by the new sportsman hunters." The county councils were instructed to determine whether the amount of hunting territory per hunter could be decreased. "Renting" hunting societies were founded to create opportunities for people living in big cities to hunt. In 1985, a change was made to the laws concerning hunting to extend the privilege to hunt to members of the agricultural cooperatives. On a case-by-case basis, state farms that were determined to have engaged in "intensive wildlife breeding and wildlife management" were given this privilege. HNA, fond M-KS 288, group 5, 1984, storage unit 921; Sándor Tóth 2005, 162–166.

96. HNA, fond M-KS 288, group 47, storage unit 774 (69). The general secretary of the party had approached Pál Vallus, the president of MAVOSZ (Magyar Vadászok Országos Szövetsége, National Association of Hungarian Hunters), in the meantime to ensure that the president of the Óbuda agricultural cooperative would be able to keep his membership in the society.

97. HNA, fond XIX-L-1, group vvv, box 1. I did not find any submission for admission by a higher-ranking individual, in all likelihood because by the time someone had become a minister, he was already hunting.

98. In the mid-1970s, Sándor Tóth suggested, unsuccessfully, that these institutions be pronounced incompatible, since people in the state offices used their sway to influence the affairs of the federation.

99. In 1989, a periodical titled *Reform*, for instance, became embroiled in a prolonged debate with *Nimród* (a hunting newspaper) and regularly dealt with hunting and the individuals who hunted.

100. Decree 13/1983. VI.9, issued by the Ministry of Agriculture and Food, repealed them. Sándor Tóth 2005, 137.

101. HNA, fond M-KS 288, group 5, 1989, storage unit 1051.

102. Interview with Jenő Váncsa, Budapest, September 20, 2008.

103. HNA, fond XXVIII-K-10, box 1.

104. Sándor Tóth 2005, 129–130.

105. Interview with Sándor Tóth, Budapest, September 25, 2005.

106. Sághy Erna, "Vadászgató magyar politikusok" [Hungarian politicians on the hunt], *Figyelő*, December 18, 2005.

107. *Nimród*, October 22, 2005. Their "ideology of legitimacy," it seems, is charity. As members of the Hungarian branch of the Safari Club International write on their web page, "Our plans include the organization of auctions. By devoting the monies we bring in to wildlife protection and charitable causes, we hope to exert a positive influence on public opinion in the interests of the sport of hunting." The Hungarian text is available at www.vadaszat.net/sci.

Mátyás Rákosi, secretary general of the Hungarian Workers' Party, next to one of the statues of him, 1952

Mrs. János Kádár, the widow of party first secretary, in the Kádár villa, 1989

Villa, party resort at Lake Balaton, in Aliga, 1970s

Ferenc Nezvál, member of the Central Committee and minister of justice, with a rifle, circa 1970

Chevrolet Bel Air, protocol car of the 1950s

Mercedes 280, protocol car of the 1970s

János Kádár, first secretary of the Hungarian Socialist Workers' Party, skipping stones, Soviet Union, Crimea, August 1972

János Kádár relaxing, Crimea, August 1972

The Honor Guard at the bier of Ferenc Münnich, ex-chairman of the Council of Ministers, 1967

János Kádár, the "weary hunter," Telki, in the territory of Concord Hunting Society, the hunting club of Hungarian party leaders, in the late 1970s

Mátyás Rákosi in the hunting dugout, early 1950s

Fidel Castro, first secretary of the Cuban Communist Party, after his hunt in Telki, 1974

"The Nimród women" come together, *Fácán Matyi*, humor magazine of the Concord Hunting Society. "Gentleladies, I have saved women's honor! The leadership should know that they can count on us," circa 1971

János Kádár's views concerning the acquisition of new hunting clothes, *Fácán Matyi*. "New clothes? I have to think about this ... (1967, 1968, 1969 ...)"

Géza Hofi, famous Hungarian humorist of the time, at a dinner held by the Concord Hunting Society, late 1970s

The antler exhibitions of the Concord Hunting Society, Telki, 1970s

The "Lenes record" of Hungarian party leaders: 8,974 pheasants, Lenes, 1986

The Hungarian soccer team in the Bern world championship, June 1954

Comrade Kónyi, the Stakhanovite of Ganz Electric Works, a painting by Béla Bán, 1950

The Gellért Hotel, the most elegant Hungarian hotel of the time, in the late 1960s

Diplomatic relations are established between Hungary and Cuba, minister of foreign affairs Dr. Endre Sík and Dr. Ernesto Che Guevara sign the minutes, December 18, 1960

Mátyás Rákosi at a party meeting in Zala County, 1952

Mátyás Rákosi in his study, 1952

János Kádár playing chess. Detail of the wall painting in the hall of the party seat, by Aurél Bernáth, titled *Munkásállam* (Workers' state), 1972

Children's drawings made for Mátyás Rákosi's sixtieth birthday, 1952

FOUR

MEETINGS BETWEEN THE SYSTEM AND ITS PEOPLE

PARTY LEADERS AND SOCCER

The Golden Team

The manner in which the party leaders related to the pastimes and passions of the ruling elite depended, to some extent, on how such pastimes were viewed by the public. Horse racing, for instance, was less popular than hunting among the elite (perhaps because the competitions were more exposed to the public eye). Like hunting, horse racing had begun as a pastime of the (aristocratic) elite, but by the turn of the twentieth century, it had become all the rage among wider swaths of the population. Beginning in the 1950s, the roughly ten thousand members of the displaced upper classes and members of the lower middle and lower classes hoping to win money attended horse races in throngs.[1]

The passion among the party leaders for soccer, however, can be considered an expression of their attachment (at least on the level of symbol and ritual) to the ethos of the workingman. The coryphaei of the regime certainly served as midwives, as it were, at the birth of the famous Golden Team, a Hungarian national soccer team that won several surprising victories in the 1950s over highly competitive international teams (including a match against the Soviet Union in September 1956, one month before the outbreak of the 1956 revolution). Minister of defense Mihály Farkas and Ferenc Puskás (one of the luminaries of the team, after whom the major soccer stadium in Budapest was renamed in 2002) were famously close. The symbiosis between party leaders and the soccer players was emblematic of the relationship of the elite to the masses (or, to be more precise, their relationship to the public sphere and their own social roles).

The term *masses* in this context is not intended in the usual categorical sense in which it is used in the social sciences; rather, it conveys the notion often employed by historians of the prevailing social elites—that is, as a counterpole to the elite. This dichotomy is used to characterize a society that has been neatly bifurcated by power relations. In a manner typical of the commitment on the level of image and ritual to the ethos of the workingman, members of the elite during the socialist era tried to cross and even efface the borders that separated them from other social groups as a manner of justifying their own social positions and roles. The working class and the industrial workers—which were allegedly the foundation of the regime but certainly never actually existed in the form envisioned by the ideologues of the system—were the "masses" with and to which the representatives of the system continuously had to maintain a relationship.

One of the basic needs of any regime is to win acceptance—that is, to create the impression that its survival is in the fundamental interests of its "subjects." Even dictatorial systems strive to establish some kind of social legitimacy. Innumerable theories have been proposed concerning the power relations of the socialist systems.[2] According to the most widespread understanding, the legitimacy of a dictatorship rests on the belief that it cannot be toppled.[3] Everyday people, living in a system governed by power relations that seemed permanent and immutable, could only hope for change to come from above. The people in power counted on and exploited this when they strove to establish a paternalistic relationship with their "subjects."[4] In most cases, this striving was coupled with the personal cults of the party leaders. The propaganda offered portrayals of these men that suggested that they were willing to undertake issues that were of importance to society as a whole as a kind of favor or an act of kindness. In other words, they were indispensable to a functioning society.

In Hungary, soccer had been one such issue—that is, an issue of national importance—since the beginning of the twentieth century. The symbiosis between power and soccer, however, dates to the 1950s. Communist politicians who rose to power recognized the political uses of soccer. Florin Poenaru, in an analysis of soccer in Romania in the 1980s, argues persuasively that the soccer stadium became a symbolic site in the socialist era, where the representatives of power strove to craft the image of the regime and its omnipotence or, as Poenaru writes, "the imaginary unity, grandeur, and omnipotence of the regime."[5]

In Hungary, the new regime tried to transform and rearticulate the meanings and social identities attached to sport associations. The clubs were reorganized and renamed. On the soccer fields, teams representing various trades and professions, trade unions (for instance, the mining and railway workers' trade unions), and bodies of law and power enforcement (the army, the police, and the state security forces) competed.[6] The latter regularly won the championships. Appearances suggested that the working class was the most prominent player in Hungarian society and the "leading force," and the state that "represented" it was sturdy and consolidated. The symbolic meanings that were attached to soccer and to individual teams and local and group identities, however, naturally could not be changed from one day to the next; indeed, to some extent, the heads of the regime had to take these identities into consideration and even adapt to them.[7]

The question of which team someone rooted for was also part of the party leaders' social identities, which were formed amid the pull of ideologies new and old. Ferenc Münnich was the head of the Ferencváros Sports Club (or Ferencvárosi Torna Club, known by the abbreviation FTC, or simply as "Fradi") from March 1948 until January 1950. Fradi traditionally had a right-wing fan base. In his inaugural address, Münnich made the following contention: "FTC is in fact a national institution in Hungary. We must watch it closely. We must lead it properly and develop it properly so that it can be a firm pillar of the sports world of the Hungarian people's democracy."[8] Beginning in 1948, representatives of the nomenclature held positions in the presidiums of the sports societies. These positions, however, obliged them to engage in continuous lobbying activities, and they often were unable to perform their supervisory roles. As a result, beginning in 1950, the Political Committee had them withdraw from this sphere of public life.[9] Members of the highest circles of the party leadership also felt that the prestige of the party leaders might be negatively affected if, in the wake of a game, the fans were to regard the defeat of their team as a personal failure of the party figure associated with the team.[10]

The functionaries loved to make public appearances in the company of the deservedly revered players. In 1949, for instance, as a kind of reward for their remarkable performances (specifically, victories against the Austrian, Bulgarian, and Swedish teams), the eleven players on the Hungarian national soccer team were given the privilege of being the first people behind minister Ernő Gerő to cross the chain bridge that had been rebuilt after having been destroyed in the war.[11] Soccer offered a remarkable opportunity for upward social mobility. The simple sons of the people became celebrated world stars, and the players became representatives of the democratic nature of the system. The members of the ruling elite treated the players like the king in a Hungarian folktale treats the simple peasant boy who, if he demonstrates his mettle, wins the king's daughter's hand in marriage and half his kingdom.

And the story often seemed true. When Ferenc Puskás (perhaps the greatest star on the Golden Team, referred to by players and fans as "Puskás Öcsi," or "Little Brother Puskás") was celebrating his fiftieth match as a player on the national team, Mihály Farkas asked him the following question before the game: "So, Puskás, what kind of present do you want?" Puskás modestly replied, "I am perfectly happy to ask for something for others, but I do not place orders for something for myself! Fine, he replied, trust it to me." In the end, the legendary player received a silverware set for twelve people and a Persian rug from Farkas at a celebration on Svábhegy, or "Swabian Hill," one of the wooded hills of Buda. The other soccer clubs also brought presents to the event.[12] Later, during his life in emigration, Puskás made the following remarks concerning Farkas: "Minister Mihály Farkas did a lot for the team. Why would I speak ill of him now if he helped me then?"[13]

The dictatorship offered the best players numerous opportunities to get rich. Some players were made military officers (like Puskás), while others were made parliamentary representatives (for instance, József Bozsik), and they were given additional emoluments for their roles in these positions. The most important and most widespread advantage enjoyed by the players, however, was simply that the state turned a blind eye to their black-market dealings. In the files of the state security forces, the name of Viennese automobile dealer Ferenc Kása is frequently found side by side with mention of the Golden Team. Kása was the thirteenth player, as it were (right after György Szepesi, the radio announcer whose reports on the games were legendary), and, later, when the regime began to dangle the sword above the players' heads, he brought misfortune on many of them. (Today, we know that Szepesi, as an agent of the state security forces, was also working in the services of the state.) In addition to his involvement in transactions involving automobiles, Kása helped convert forints into hard currency. Hungarian soccer players played their biggest games for hard currency in Vienna, which was not far from Budapest but was on the other side of the Iron Curtain. The talented and well-to-do smuggler was a recurring figure in the files on the soccer players, and the notable players of the 1960s inherited Kása from the Golden Team.

Professional sports offered everyday individuals opportunities to escape their ordinary lives, and victories in sports helped the masses forget their everyday problems—or at least, such was the hope. Thus, it was hardly surprising that the state provided broad support for sports and athletes—and in particular, the Golden Team, which in 1954 won second place in the FIFA World Cup. In his poem "After Defeat," Hungarian poet Lőrinc Szabó offers the following portrayal of the symbolic victories of the Hungarian soccer players from a distance of cathartic disappointment: "The war-beaten people (and with them, perhaps the world) / not long ago believed victory / mere symbol." In the years following the political turn, the first larger manifestations of discontent broke out on the streets on July 4, 1954, the evening of the Golden Team's loss to West Germany in the World Cup match in Bern, Switzerland. Outrage in Hungary gave rise to protest. One could interpret this as a clear sign of the importance of soccer as an instrument of the regime in its attempts to assert its legitimacy. In other words, the defeat helped undermine the perception that the regime was immune to any challenge. Humorists in Budapest later characterized the event as the "*focialista forradalom*," a pun in Hungarian that could be translated as "soccer-ialist revolution."[14]

It was incomprehensible that the Golden Team, which consisted of some of the most creative talents of the art of soccer, could have lost to the West German team, thought to be composed of unimaginative, if industrious, players who brought little imagination to the game. As evident from the archival films that were made on the occasion of the fiftieth World Cup match, for most of the game, the Golden Team played almost entirely on one side—the offensive side—of the field. In most cases, the shots hit the goal post or were blocked by the superb German goalie, or the Germans simply were saved by a bit of luck. Head coach Gusztáv Sebes later wrote a book in which he blamed the loss primarily on the English referee.[15] The defeat was so shocking that the fans assumed the players, the leaders of the sports world in Hungary, or the party leadership had accepted a bribe from the Germans to throw the match.

Reports on the prevailing mood at the time convey a sense of the gossip that spread in the wake of the defeat.[16] People said that Sebes had not returned to Hungary, and that he had committed suicide. Some people claimed that Puskás had gone to Australia after the loss; "according to others, Puskás had announced that he had a gun license, and he would shoot anyone who behaved insolently with him."[17] People also claimed that Sebes had been bribed, and that he had let Mihály Tóth play on the team because Tóth was his daughter's fiancé (Tóth had played in the decisive match, and this had come as a surprise to most): "Mihály Tóth, however, said that he would never have married Sebes' daughter, even if in exchange he would have been allowed to play on the team. According to others, Tóth was related to Mándi, the second-tier coach, and this was how he had gotten on the team. And Puskás had insisted on being made part of the team because he had wanted to accept the trophy himself."[18] Fans sought those responsible for the defeat not only among the players. On the streets of Budapest, a rumor spread that the party leaders received fifty Mercedes in exchange for letting the German team win (the first Mercedes-Benz cars were just beginning to appear on the streets of Budapest at the time). People outside Budapest claimed that Germany had given Hungary combine harvesters.[19]

In West Germany, the unexpected victory was celebrated euphorically as a kind of rebirth of the nation, while in Budapest the sense of disappointment led to protests in the streets. The defeat of the Golden Team was a disappointment for Hungarian society as a whole, and it stirred a kind of impotent rage among the populace. As people began to gather on the streets and form groups and even a sizable crowd or mob, they also began to engage in different kinds of collective action. As Elias Canetti writes in *Crowds and Power*, "Most of them do not know what has happened, and, if questioned, have no answer; but they hurry to be there where most other people are."[20] The crowd temporarily forgot about the rules of the game that it collectively had established.

While outraged fans protested on the streets, the members of the soccer team were having a protocol lunch with members of government. According to his memoir, Gusztáv Sebes first learned of the protests during this lunch, when minister of the interior László Piros turned to him and asked, "Are you nervous? Don't worry. We have protected and we are protecting your apartment."[21] The way members of the elite behaved under the circumstances was characteristic of their approach to power, conflict, and risk. While they assured the team members of their enduring goodwill, not one of the leaders of the regime openly took a stance in support of the players. The party leadership had done everything to ensure that the masses would attribute the successes of the team to the system, and now the protesters were looking for the people who could be held responsible for what they regarded as a humiliating fiasco.

In his book *Tollforgató forgószélben* (Writer in a whirlwind), journalist István Hajduska offers the following description of the protests: "I had not seen anything like it since the liberation. A protest, which had broken out in an improvised manner, with neither the knowledge nor the approval of the authorities or the party, or any mass organization."[22] Although it may seem like something of a cliché, sports really did represent the "valve of hope" under socialism. This explains, to some extent at least, the tremendous disappointment with which the Golden Team's defeat in the finals was met; though gradually the disturbances in the streets began to die down and life returned to normal. People seemed to acknowledge this defeat along with the others of the recent past. And yet, as Tamás Aczél and Tibor Méray claim in their book *Tisztító vihar* (Cleansing storm), which analyzes the 1956 revolution and the reasons behind it, "There was something that they did not forget. The protest."[23]

Plays Off the Field

After 1954, even party leaders became critical of the Golden Team. One report that made it to the table of the central leadership condemned the lifestyles of the soccer players and took exception to the smuggling operations: "The many games abroad, which are necessary and proper, gave our players an opportunity to establish connections with the criminal underworld abroad. Some of the players have debts of several thousand forints or schillings, and this is characteristic of the gravity of these relationships."[24] The report mentioned midfielder József Bozsik, who, as a soccer player for the army, was allowed to travel with the team. In December 1955, when the Vörös Lobogó, or "Red Flag" (the Magyar Testgyakorlók Köre Budapest Futball Klub, or Budapest Football Club of the Hungarian Athletes' Circle, or MTK, the first Hungarian team to play in the European Cup) was traveling back to Hungary, a well-known "nepman" (i.e., someone with connections to the smuggling world) named Schwarz was waiting for the team: "He yelled in a shrill voice in front of the whole team that if Bozsik did not pay his 300,000 forint debt he would have him arrested if he ever went abroad again."[25] An inquiry was launched into the matter, and some representatives of the regime wanted to compel Bozsik to resign from his position as a parliamentary representative so that they could hold him responsible. The supreme public prosecutor and Gyula Egri, the secretary of the central leadership of the Hungarian Workers' Party, both made this request to the secretaryship of the party's central leadership.[26]

However, Ernő Gerő, a highly influential member of the Rákosi party leadership, stood up in Bozsik's defense in a handwritten memorandum: "He deserves it, but politically, this is not the opportune moment."[27] Presumably, given that the Olympic Games were approaching, the party leaders did not wish to weaken the team and risk an embarrassing defeat. The leaders of the army also supported the team, since most of the eleven members of the national team played for the army. Colonel and minister of foreign affairs István Bata and major general Jenő Hazai, commander of the Political Main Group Directorate of the Ministry of Defense, wrote a joint letter to the central leadership in which they defended both the players and the coach.[28]

Although the international team suffered a few affronts to its pride after the loss in Bern, the leaders of the sports world in communist Hungary were still preparing for the 1956 Melbourne Olympics in the spirit of national pride. For instance, a memorandum drawn up for the prominent figures of the National Committee for Physical Education and Sports ranked the teams Hungary would face according to how they compared with other Hungarian league teams. According to this ranking, the English team was comparable to the teams that played in the second tier of the Hungarian national league, the United States and Australia were comparable to the Budapest first-tier teams, Vietnam was comparable to the county championship teams, and the world championship German team could play in the second half of the first tier of the national league. The Bulgarian and Turkish teams were comparable, according to the memorandum, to the teams in the national championship. The Yugoslav and Soviet Union teams were not given a ranking, presumably for political reasons.[29]

In the end, the Soviet Union won the Olympic soccer tournament, with Yugoslavia, Bulgaria, and India coming in second, third, and fourth, respectively. Germany faced and lost to the Soviet Union in the first round. The Hungarian team, which was seen as a likely winner, withdrew from the tournament. Thus, the long-awaited moment of revenge, which, from the perspective of the party leadership, would have been useful as a means of soothing public unrest, never came. In 1956, the unbeatable Golden Team, which the new regime had reared and which the system had sought to use as a symbol of its potential, broke up, and many of its members never returned to Hungary, choosing instead to pursue their careers abroad. Never again did the team win laurels, neither for Hungary nor for the regime.

Zoltán Czibor was the only member of the team who took part in the fighting in Hungary in 1956. To be more precise, he patrolled the city for days, armed, and he was in contact with the group of rebels who fought on and around Széna Square in Buda. Allegedly, Czibor was the favorite player of the enemies of the regime.[30] He was one of the legendary players of the Golden Team, and he was also legendary for making trouble. Once, for instance, he quarreled with some customers in a coffeehouse, and the clash was sufficiently serious to attract the attention of the police, who prepared a report on the event. Ferenc Puskás intervened on Czibor's behalf by seeking the assistance of Mihály Farkas, and in the end the whole affair was hushed up.[31] According to reports received by the minister of the interior, during the revolution, Czibor had chased the commander of the Ministry of Defense garage in Ezredes Street from the building with a machine gun, and he had turned the ministry's cars over to the revolutionaries.[32]

Czibor later recalled that he had gotten his hands on a gun when he had gone to his workplace, the garage of the Ministry of Defense (at the time, he was a player on the army team), to get gas. There, he had asked one of his colleagues for a gun and two boxes of ammunition.[33] On October 30, he left the country with the army team for what was to become the famous "tour" in South America (the Ministry of Foreign Affairs document refers to the trip as a "tour"), from which only a few of the players returned to Hungary. Czibor was one of the team members who chose to remain abroad. He trained with Associazione Sportiva Roma, where he was given a preliminary contract. However, because of the strict rules concerning transfers, he soon had to find another team with which to play.[34] The intelligence agencies in Hungary, it seems, did not have very good contacts abroad at the time. While half the world knew that Czibor was playing with the Barcelona team, according to the May 1958 resolution concerning him (i.e., concerning the surveillance on him), he was living in Italy, where he had joined one of the club teams.[35]

In 1958, the intelligence services began to take more interest in Czibor, as his presence abroad was considered dangerous "from the perspective of the people's republic": "Presumably, the imperialist intelligence services use him against our homeland, and they may send him home with a task to perform."[36] By 1959, the intelligence services had gathered all the information on Czibor held by the Ministry of Internal Affairs. His name, it turned out, was mentioned in the registry of the state security agents, but the dossier on him had been destroyed. Czibor's last tie to the state security forces was Lieutenant Jenő Erdélyi, an officer of the Budapest Army Sport Association (Budapesti Honvéd Sportegyesület) in charge of preventative tactics.[37] In 1958, at the order of the intelligence services, Erdélyi provided a characterization of Czibor and a summary of the alleged contents of the reports he submitted.[38]

Although one can hardly put much stock in Erdélyi's claims, his characterization of Czibor may nonetheless be revealing, since he knew Czibor well. His description rests on aspects of Czibor's character, but he could not have painted a portrait of Czibor that would have evoked sympathy. Nonetheless, the characterization offers glimpses into the Bohemian world in which actors and athletes moved against the seemingly grim backdrop of the 1950s. According to Erdélyi's reports, Czibor spent most of his free time with members of the Operetta Theater, and he usually sold his smuggled goods to artists. He also had an expansive network of ties to people in the smuggling world in Hungary, and they sold the other contraband wares that he brought to the country.[39] Czibor was on friendly terms with several prominent singers of the time, including Zoltán Szentessy, Pál Homm, and János Sárdy, and some high-profile actors, such as Kálmán Latabár and Iván Darvas. In general, they met in the coffee bar in the Operetta Theater or the Fészek Művészklub, an artists' club founded in 1901 and nationalized by the regime in 1950. The name, which means "nest artists' club," is an acronym consisting of the first letters of the words "painters," "architects," "sculptors," "musicians," "singers," and "comedians" in Hungarian). Czibor was a regular at both places. He drove a Tatra 600, a large family car manufactured in Czechoslovakia. Lieutenant Colonel Lajos Sumet, president of the army soccer division, had helped him purchase the car.

According to Erdélyi's reports, Czibor adopted his actor friends' habits, parodying and caricaturizing them, and he was well known for his fondness for jokes.[40] According to one report, "His favorite phrase was 'nix komplett,' with which he expressed his opinion that the person with whom he was speaking was stupid. His other favorite phrase was more drastic, no matter who they were talking about in his presence, or directly with him, he would always reply, 'he can suck it.'" Allegedly, he would regularly tell women, "You are pale, angel, take some Citoricilin drops." His friends simply called him "Meanie." Erdélyi also noted that Czibor liked "to show his money and play the big spender, often he would toss several thousand forint on the floor and have one of his friends pick the money up, for which the friend would get one-hundred forint."[41]

Although the description provided by Erdélyi had perhaps a bit too much flair (it was made at the order and according to the tastes of the intelligence officers), in the closed world of the 1950s, Czibor was able to play the part of the Bohemian and the socialist dandy. In the 1950s, a few figures of Hungarian social life lived and behaved quite deliberately as if they were completely oblivious to the fact that they were living under a dictatorship. Most of them had been members of the urban bourgeoisie. Czibor, who became a legendary soccer player, had been the son of a railroad employee from the city of Komárom. The system gave him the opportunity to become part of this milieu. However, the reports of the state security forces at the time reveal that this world was nowhere near as free and independent as it seemed at first glance.

In October 1956, most of the legendary soccer players traveled to Bilbao, Spain, for the European Cup. From there, they traveled to South America with the Budapest army team, after which they did not return to Hungary. Ferenc Kása and Schwarz, the two contacts in Vienna with ties to the smuggling world in the West, again began to become involved with the team. (Schwarz is mentioned in the files only by his family name. To the players and the authorities, he became a symbolic figure of the black market, without personality or defining characteristics, much as today we tend to relate to companies that provide services—without personal interest or sentimental attachment.) While the army team was playing in Spain, Schwarz contacted the players and offered to get their wives out from behind the Iron Curtain. Ágoston Garamvölgyi, one of the players, allegedly paid Schwarz $2,000 to get his wife out of Hungary.[42] In Vienna, Kása again facilitated the purchase of cars by the players.[43]

Puskás, perhaps the most domestically and internationally famous Hungarian soccer player, was among those who did not return to Hungary. He played with Real Madrid from 1958 until 1967. The state security forces launched proceedings against him for treason, and they opened a dossier on him under the name "Vándor" (which means "wanderer"). The file on Puskás was started on May 20, 1958, and closed on June 26, 1972.[44] According to Ministry of Internal Affairs documents, Erdélyi also corresponded with him.[45] Erdélyi addressed Puskás in his correspondence as "My Dear Little Brother," and Puskás addressed

Erdélyi as "My Dear Jenő." A passage from one of Puskás's letters offers a sense of the distance between Hungary and the West at the time:

> And now it is my turn, I noted before what I will write, that I am well, true, sometimes I miss old friend, but in vain, we can do little to solve this, and I have not yet felt homesick. Perhaps this is because I have tobacco and I live a calm life, I do what I want to do in the moment, no one speaks up about it. True, I have to work for the tobacco, they play a completely different soccer game here than back home, and no misunderstanding, not better, but rather much weaker, but you have to run that much more, of course that was just a question of habit for me, true, for the first few weeks it was hard, but it's always hard at the beginning, but you get used to it, like a dog gets used to being beaten.[46]

With the hard work and all the "running," however, came a new clarity and openness: "Everything is calm here, you don't have to deal with any fishy stuff. You can earn your money and you don't have to fear that if they ring the bell, then ok, now who's gotten caught, and what for."[47]

The fates of the players who remained in or returned to Hungary can also be interpreted as characteristic of the system and the Cold War era. József Bozsik was one of the emblematic figures of the Golden Team. After the revolution and Puskás's decision not to return for the foreseeable future to his homeland, Bozsik became the leader both on and off the field. The Kádár era began badly for Bozsik. In 1957, he was kicked out of parliament. One can only guess why, though he may well have been regarded by the new regime as someone who had been too close to Rákosi. On the field, however, he reasserted his place. A midfielder who, next to Puskás, seemed restrained, Bozsik gradually began to emerge from the shadow of the world-famous Puskás. In 1958, he played again in a world championship as a right halfback, and he was even made a forward. In 1962, at age thirty-seven, Bozsik retired from the team. First, he became the president of the army soccer division, and later he was entrusted with oversight of the entire club. He was famous, and his shop, the Bozsik Boutique in Kígyó Street (which was run by Bozsik and his family), was considered an exclusive place. As a reward for their performances on the field, retired popular soccer players were allowed to work and earn money in the private sphere of the Kádár system (which in many cases was flourishing), because shopkeepers were permitted to rent business spaces, and in particular inns, from the government.[48]

In 1964, internal affairs agents arrested Mátyás Benkő, a Viennese merchant, for a criminal offense involving currency exchange. Benkő was one of Kása's business partners, so he had good ties to the Hungarian soccer players of the 1960s. The threads of the case led back to József Bozsik. Benkő had met regularly with Bozsik and Lajos Tichy, another star soccer player of the 1960s. On several occasions, Benkő had smuggled luxury items into the country with their assistance and exchanged forints for schillings. Bozsik's wealth had attracted the attention of the agents working for internal affairs. The agents were interested in the villa that he had had built that year in Ménesi Avenue, his summer vacation home at Lake Balaton, and his Peugeot car. They searched Bozsik's boutique in Kígyó Street, looking for items that had been acquired under suspicious circumstances, and they noticed that Bozsik was in contact not only with business partners in Vienna but also with Ferenc Puskás. Bozsik confessed that, from time to time, Puskás had given him hard currency as payment for an earlier debt. Probably, however, Puskás was still working as part of the commercial network between Hungary and the West. In the end, Benkő was convicted, and Bozsik was given a suspended sentence of three years in prison.[49]

The question of the reform of soccer in Hungary and the redemption of the country's reputation as an international contender was a recurring topic during meetings of the various bodies of the party throughout the Kádár era.[50] At times, the party leadership proclaimed that it would set things straight and create a clean slate in the world of Hungarian soccer. Kádár himself, who was not only fond of chess but also was an enthusiastic soccer fan, paid attention to the team. After the world championship in 1958, György Szepesi allegedly approached Kádár in person and asked him to put Gusztáv Sebes at the head of the team again. Kádár, however, feared that protests might break out again were the team to suffer a defeat under Sebes.[51] In any event, Kádár regularly attended the soccer games, and he never made a secret of the fact that he remained true to his roots and was a fan of a "workers' team"—the Vasas, or "iron" team, which was founded in 1911 by the Hungarian Union of Iron Workers as the Vas-és Fémmunkások Sport Clubja, or the "Sports Club of Iron and Metal Workers." The Kádár regime made a symbolic gesture in 1957 by allowing two of the clubs that looked back on a proud tradition in soccer—the Ferencváros Club and the MTK Club—to use their old names. When "Fradi" finally won a championship in 1963 for the first time in fourteen years (which must have seemed like an eternity), according to soccer legend, in their overjoyed giddiness, the fans chanted a rhyme using Kádár's name: "Bajnok lett a Ferencváros / fasza gyerek Kádár János," or "Ferencváros is the champion / That János Kádár's a slick prick kid."[52]

The story of Puskás's return to Hungary is also an illustrative episode in the history of soccer in the Kádár era. The Kádár regime postponed Puskás's rehabilitation for a long time. The legitimacy of the system rested on people's assessments of 1956, after all, and Puskás's decision to remain abroad was hard to reconcile with the notion that the regime had quashed a counterrevolution (this was the official interpretation). However, as time passed and Hungarian soccer boasted fewer and fewer successes (and eventually none), the aura and the memory of the Golden Team grew stronger. Finally, in 1981, Puskás, the prodigal son, returned to his homeland for a visit. He played in a gala game organized before a match between Hungary and England as part of the world championship series. He scored two goals, reminding the spectators of the good old days of Hungarian soccer. At the end of the match, when the team went up to the grandstand, Puskás bowed to Kádár, as photographs of the event show, and Kádár responded to this gesture with a polite nod of his head. In the sports stadiums, which, as memorial sites of great victories, were and are symbolic social spaces, the party leaders strove repeatedly to legitimize their hold on power.

Miklós Németh, the prime minister from November 1988 until May 1990, tried to represent a new style in the bleachers. He made the following contention to *Sport Plusz*, a periodical whose first issue was published in January 1989: "It is an entirely different matter that many of the earlier party leaders and members of the political committees rooted for Vasas and watched or continue today to watch their games. That does not make Vasas the party team. For instance, since my childhood, I have rooted for the Ferencváros team."[53] Thus, a new head of state bid farewell to an era by expressing his support not for Vasas, the team that had been the ideological favorite of the communist regime, but rather for Ferencváros, the team that had always been seen as a kind of counterpoint to Vasas and, with its hooligan fans, represented the presocialist world when it came to soccer.

WORKERS AND THE WORKERS' STATE

In the Limelight

The power of the working class was the foundation on which the system rested, at least according to the propaganda of the regime. Many of the party and state leaders of the Kádár era who ended up at a considerable distance from the workbench (or, indeed, had never sat on one) were nonetheless regularly depicted in the press and on election placards as members of the working class, and they presented themselves as workers at the party congresses. This was a symptomatic phenomenon of the era, and in general it was considered proper to introduce oneself accordingly. For instance, the following exchange took place between János Kádár and his interrogators in 1954: "Occupation?" "Mechanic, former Minister of the Interior."[54]

Clearly, these assertions of working-class identity were hardly enough to ensure the legitimacy of the system, and even as reference points they provided only a fragile foundation. It was hard for someone to claim convincingly while in office that he was a mechanic *and* a minister, and not the other way around. The intention was to demonstrate to the citizenry that socialism had created new opportunities for members of the working class. The workers' competitions, however, offered an opportunity to do this.[55] Beginning in 1948, "outstanding workers" were recognized in festive ceremonies, and, as of 1950, so-called Stakhanovites were decorated for their contributions to the construction of socialism.[56] These competitions were based on the Soviet model. The Stakhanovite was a sedulous and unflagging worker who followed the example of Aleksei Grigorievich Stakhanov, a Russian miner who in August 1935 allegedly mined more than 102 tons of coal in less than six hours.[57] The Stakhanovites had an important symbolic role in Soviet society. The headlines concerning their alleged achievements were affirmations of the well-being, strength, and power of the working class.

The Hungarian press regularly provided reports on the accomplishments of the outstanding workers and the Stakhanovites and about the rewards they were given in exchange for their diligent work. Workers who were given this recognition seemed to live very good lives. They were given money and consumer goods such as bicycles, motorcycles, radios, clothing, and books.[58] Sometimes they were even given free tickets to the Budapest theaters, the opera, or the circus,[59] and some of them were given summer vacations in Galyatető, a popular spot in the Mátra Mountains that lies on the southern side of Galyatető, the third tallest mountain in Hungary. Many of them received significant sums of money, sometimes even more than a minister's salary. According to the February 1950 cadre characterization of Imre Muszka, the most prominent Stakhanovite in Hungary in the 1950s,[60] "He makes an average of 1,500–1,600 forints a week, but sometimes he made 3,000 forints a week."[61] Three thousand forints was several times the monthly salary of the average worker.

More than 100,000 workers were given distinctions as outstanding workers or Stakhanovites.[62] In newspapers and the radio reports, however, only some thirty or forty Stakhanovites, the names of whom were familiar to the wider public, were mentioned with any regularity. Indeed, they were mentioned in the national news reports more than some of the ministers. The coryphaei of the party and the trade union chose these workers very carefully, because in their private lives and their careers they had to exemplify the changes that had taken place in the circumstances of the working class since 1948. At the congresses of outstanding workers and Stakhanovites, the workers, who relatively suddenly found themselves in the limelight, regularly praised the achievements of the socialist transformation and reconstruction of the country, referring to their own good fortunes as evidence of the success of the new system.[63] Their comments and the stylized presentations of their life histories clearly conveyed the message that the workers' state had accomplished a great deal for the working class.

The outstanding workers and Stakhanovites played important roles in public forums, and their performances (as it were) were carefully planned well in advance. Although the organization of the workers' competitions was the responsibility of the trade union, the party regularly gave its approval for the scheduling of the outstanding worker and Stakhanovite congresses.[64] Before holding a speech at a Stakhanovite congress, Antal Apró requested information of the cadre class, since at the congress he would have "to mention the accomplishments of the 10–15 best workers in the country, who can be presented to Rákosi and the others as paragons."[65] In 1951, a trade union functionary nonetheless pointed out to the trade union leader that, of the workers who had been recognized as outstanding in 1948 and had been immortalized (if temporarily) in the postcard series titled "Új idők új hősei" (New heroes of new times), one was in prison, two now led a dissolute lifestyle, and nothing was known about the others.[66] As this observation plainly illustrates, the fates of the workers who were recognized for their efforts ceased to interest the party leaders as soon as they were no longer needed for publicity and propaganda campaigns.

It is symptomatic of the regime and its propaganda practices that the outstanding workers and the Stakhanovites were presented to the public as if they were in direct personal relationships with members of the elite and party leaders, and as if they enjoyed similar lifestyles. In other words, according to the images that were presented to the rest of the citizenry, the outstanding workers and the Stakhanovites were able to obtain the kinds of luxury items that very few people at the time could get their hands on.[67] The press, for instance, reported on how Imre Muszka had sat next to János Kádár and Antal Apró at the conference of the Greater Budapest Party Committee,[68] and he had been given the chance to travel as one of the members of the Hungarian delegation to Moscow to present the "gifts of the Hungarian workers" to Stalin on Stalin's seventieth birthday.[69] On many occasions, the Stakhanovites found that they were decidedly unpopular because of their public roles. For instance, neither the wider public nor Muszka's coworkers in Csepel forgot that, as part of the ceremony organized on Heroes' Square as a tribute to the memory of Stalin, Muszka had bid farewell in the name of the Hungarian workers to the Soviet dictator (allegedly while shedding tears), to whom he had referred to as "our loving father."[70]

The lifestyles of the Stakhanovite workers, including the furnishings in their apartments and their possessions, were based on the customs and tastes of the elite. This was one of the ways the workers displayed their privileged positions to other members of their social circles. At the time, there was no officially accepted model of a middle-class lifestyle that could have served a function similar to the image of the working-class elite in the interwar period by providing an ideal to which to aspire. The outstanding workers, however, found themselves side by side with the party leaders only in public forums. Although at times they were given excellent salaries and were allowed to make appearances at official events and ceremonies, they were never actually able to achieve a high standard of living for long, the reports in the press notwithstanding.

Muszka, for instance, who worked as a wood turner, was given a dwelling in Csepel, which was presented to him by Ernő Gerő. On the basis of press reports of the time, however, one might get the impression that Muszka had been given one of the villa residences. In fact, the home was an apartment in a series of one-story town houses in a workers' housing development in one of the greener parts of Csepel. Writer Ferenc Karinthy, the son of famous Hungarian writer Frigyes Karinthy, wrote an article on Muszka for *Szabad Nép* in which he offered the following description of the furnishings in the apartment: "He designed and made all of the kitchen furniture. There is a small chest of drawers. On the left side, there is a children's washbasin that can be pulled out, on the right, there is one for adults, in the front a drawer for finery, underneath an ice chest with two big watermelons chilling inside it. If you close it, you can't see any of this. It's a very cute little commode." The Muszka family did not have an entirely peaceful life in Csepel—a traditionally working-class neighborhood. One of their neighbors continuously played the radio at high volumes, and it seems that the noise was a constant disturbance: "The plaster has come off the bedroom wall in a spot about the size of your palm: they must have hit it with the heel of a shoe."[71] This unpleasantness notwithstanding, Muszka had a fairly good life in comparison with his coworkers. There was a serious dearth of apartments in the 1950s, and it was very difficult to get an apartment in any of the larger cities in the country, and particularly in Budapest.

While the party leaders in the more exclusive neighborhoods of the city (Rózsadomb, Zugliget, and Pasarét) preserved the lifestyles and interior design traditions of the interwar middle and upper classes, after 1945, modernist architects dreamed up new, up-to-date urban housing developments for the Hungarian capital. Sketches of comfortable housing projects and sunny point blocks and town houses cluttered the design tables. With much of the city under reconstruction, however, there was not enough money to transform these visions into reality. Indeed, there was not enough money to renovate the buildings that had been left in ruins. The shortage of apartments in Budapest became a permanent condition, and this shortage had particularly dire consequences for the workers in the industrial establishments. The construction projects that were eventually completed were regarded as prestige investments by the party-state. Every system strove to reward its social base with new, impressive homes. For instance, several housing developments had been built for civil service employees before the war,[72] one of the best-known of which is the Wekerle Estate.[73]

The question of who the leaders of the new system chose as the recipients of newly constructed apartments was a matter of no trifling importance. After the Second World War, the largest construction project in Budapest took place between 1948 and 1950 at Lehel Square (named after Lehel, a Magyar leader and member of the Árpád House).[74] According to reports in the press, the new buildings were being constructed for so-called outstanding workers. To ensure that this message was driven home with sufficient clarity, the name of the square was changed to Outstanding

Workers' Square. The very site of the construction project suggested that the new system sought to reward and pay tribute to the foot soldiers of the people's republic, since the area of the city (Váci Avenue and Angyalföld, or "Angel Land") was part of a traditionally working-class neighborhood with workshops and factories.[75] The new buildings, like the point block on Mónus Illés wharf[76] and the residential housing blocks on Béke Square (Peace Square) in Csepel, were comparatively high-quality edifices with comfortable, well-equipped apartments (meaning they had electricity and hot and cold running water). The buildings had central heating and elevators, which at the time constituted genuine luxuries.[77]

The press also offered accounts of the families of outstanding workers moving into the new, high-quality buildings. And yet most of the residents in these buildings were not actually outstanding workers and their family members. The outstanding workers wrote requests and, later, outraged letters, but in vain. Less than a tenth of them were given apartments. Kádár, who was serving as minister of the interior at the time, oversaw the distribution of the apartments. He tended to favor the military, the state security forces, and the police.[78] It seemed that the new system, like the old ones, favored officials and bureaucrats, even while striving to convince the population that finally a regime had come to power that rewarded workers. In the building at 2 D, Ernő Berda, Gyula Pap, Márk Vedres, and later Dezső Bokros Birman—four visual artists who were loyal to the regime—were given studio apartments,[79] revealing the prestige in which the apartments were held and the workings of the system according to which they were apportioned. The ninety-six new apartments on Béke Square in Csepel, ostensibly for outstanding workers, were distributed according to a similar logic.[80]

An unusual event offers a glimpse into what went on behind the scenes in this would-be workers' state. Several of the working-class families could not afford to pay the high cost of utilities in the centrally heated apartments. They complained about these costs, and eventually their protests became a rent strike, against which the authorities were compelled to take action.[81] Another case offered clear proof of the superior strength of the functionary class. In late 1954 and early 1955, the army was given only sixty-two of the apartments in a housing block on Hungária Boulevard consisting of 174 apartments. The soldiers also complained that they had not been given apartments that all opened off the same stairway. They staged an unmistakable demonstration of force in the new building.[82] The author of a report on the prevailing mood at the time offered the following description of the events:

> After the apartments had been apportioned, they presented their demand that the members of the army be given the apartments in the corner high rise building. On the morning of 30 December, soldiers came out and put sentries armed with machine guns on guard at the entrances to the stairhalls and announced that the civilians living in the building had to leave the apartments immediately so that the soldiers could move in. They refused to let anyone in the building. Later, however, after negotiations with the leaders of the council, they acknowledged the facts of the situation and withdrew their forces. It is in any event quite clear that it was wrong for the army to turn against the resolutions issued by the council in this way.[83]

In response to public protest and increasingly dire social problems, the party-state later tried to limit the power of officials and civil servants by strengthening the roles of the local councils vis-à-vis the ministries and the other organs of the state in the distribution of apartments.[84] It was quite clear, however, that in the system whereby the state allotted properties, the workers usually were at a disadvantage.

All signs suggest that, for the regime, it was more important to win the sympathies of the functionary class than it was to reward the members of the working class. Nevertheless, the functionaries were envious of the benefits the workers received. When the first outstanding worker decorations were awarded, according to the reports in places where the party secretary or the chairman of the factory committee had been nominated for the distinction, the overall mood was not good; the workers, "forming smaller groups," were indignant.[85] As early as June 1949, the National Council of Trade Unions, which officially organized the competitions, suggested that "the best administrative colleagues working in the National Party Center, the Greater Budapest Party Organization, and on the county committee should receive distinctions as outstanding workers and excellent workers."[86] Most of the Stakhanovites who were celebrated day in and day out in the press were removed from their jobs performing physical labor and were given other positions with better incomes. (One reason for this may have been the desire to create a functionary class that was loyal to the regime.) Muszka fell out of favor precisely because he turned down the chance for such a promotion. According to Karinthy's report, when declining the offer, Muszka told the local party representatives, "Thank you, you are not going to promote me. You are not going to make a ticket collector in the wood yard out of me."[87] After this, Muszka was not allowed to work the lathe and produce assembly-line pieces in the factory for a high wage. Indeed, he was criticized several times in public forums. He had not subscribed for peace loans, he had not shared his working practices, he did not compete with other Stakhanovites. At a meeting of the central leadership on February 10, 1950, Rákosi himself criticized Muszka in his speech.[88]

The party functionaries, however, created, at least virtually, a group that symbolized the prosperity and power of the working class. They published propaganda pamphlets on the lives of the outstanding workers and the Stakhanovites, and the indefatigable worker became the recurring character in the new type of literature. *Újítók Lapja* (Reformers' journal) announced a literary contest for compositions touching on the workers' competitions, and flurries of poems were written celebrating the accomplishments that had been made in the construction of socialism.[89] The subject, however, soon proved too important to be entrusted to hacks and rhymesters. Forging the figure of the heroic worker in belle lettres became the task of renowned writers. The archetype was already a familiar face in international literature.[90] As early as 1936, poet István Vas lamented the trend: "As a poet, I am outraged by the disgrace of seeing Demyan Bedny, the poet who studied the Stakhanov movement for one or two weeks and praises the higher speeds of a locomotive and the work of the leader."[91] After roughly a decade, no one could have voiced a similar complaint; indeed, the poets and writers in Hungary had been made a part of the regime's propaganda machine. Eszter Tóth, for instance, the daughter of famous poet and translator Árpád Tóth, wrote a poem about passing on work practices; Péter Kuczka, who would later emerge as a major science fiction author in Hungary, wrote a poem about output percentages;[92] and Karinthy published writings about the Stakhanovites in *Szabad Nép*.[93] It was relatively easy to write the accounts, given that Karinthy vacationed in Galyatető with several Stakhanovites. In 1953, when the party decided to forgive Muszka, he was rehabilitated with the publication of an article by Karinthy.[94]

It was quite clear, however, that the drama being performed onstage bore little resemblance to what was taking place behind the curtains. Perhaps the defining stylistic element of the era that best captured the reality of the socialist world was that of the Grotesque. Hungarian writer István Örkény, one of the most prominent authors of the Hungarian Grotesque, wrote an unfinished novella entitled *Babik*.[95] The protagonist of the novella, Babik, is an outstanding worker in a skeleton key factory. But Babik is merely the invention of the factory's trained craftsman and the quality control inspector, who use Babik to get their hands on more money. No one has ever actually seen Babik, but the equipment with which he works is decorated in recognition of his achievements, and the director's enthusiastic secretary even marries him. The word *babig* was invented by the Vienna Circle, a group of philosophers and scientists who met regularly at the University of Vienna between 1924 and 1936. *Babig* was offered as an example of the human ability to invent words that have no empirical referent and are therefore (according to the Vienna Circle) meaningless and make any sentence in which they are used meaningless.[96] Örkény's protagonist Babik is arguably a similar example of a signifier with no signified. He designates precisely the thing that does not exist—much like the diligent Stakhanovite, who allegedly produces ten times his allotted quota.

The Fates of Workers?

The fate of Imre Muszka, the best-known Stakhanovite of the 1950s, was characteristic of the age. He was still working in Csepel in October 1956, when András Bordás, one of his close coworkers, was murdered.[97] Bordás was killed by the insurgents on October 26. Allegedly, the Stakhanovite turner had intended to show the Soviet soldiers where the police building was, but others assert that he was mistaken for a member of the state security forces. According to the records for the case, the people who lynched Bordás had no idea that he had been recognized as a Stakhanovite. Later, a technical school in Ferencváros was named after him, as was a street in Csepel.[98] The school was renamed in 1993, but the street still bears his name. Muszka left Hungary in January 1957. Some of his coworkers believed that he had fled the country for Belgium,[99] while others heard he had left for Denmark. One person even claimed to have seen him serving as a *pufajkás*—a member of a militia organized by the security forces:[100] "In the autumn of 1956, I was about to cross the Erzsébet-Csepel Railway Bridge [the bridge connecting Pesterzsébet and Csepel, two districts of Budapest]. All the brigands were still standing on the bridge, the security forces and others, to make sure no enemies could go across. And there stood Muszka. I asked, 'What the hell are you doing here?' To which he replied, 'I joined the government.' He was wearing a pufajka. I took the news to the guys in the factory, telling them that he was standing on guard on the bridge with a machine gun in hand."[101] I have found no documents in the records indicating that Muszka actually became a *pufajkás*.

In January 1957, Muszka fled to Yugoslavia. Later, the state security forces interrogated anyone who had returned to Hungary from one of the neighboring countries, for whatever reason. Muszka's name is mentioned in the reports and records: "Imre Muszka, roughly 45 years old, 172 cm tall, former Kossuth Prize winner, recognized on several occasions as a Stakhanovite."[102] The legend of Muszka continued to evolve in the recollections of those who had fled the country, and also in the rumors they heard. The story can be summarized roughly as follows: In early 1957, Muszka was in the refugee camp in Novi Kneževac, a town in northwestern Serbia whose Hungarian name is Törökkanizsa. He was planning to go to the United States and sign a contract that would allow him to bring his family.[103] According to another refugee who knew him, the state of Yugoslavia had offered to let Muszka work as a turner in Belgrade, but he had declined.[104] Around April, he left the camp in Novi Kneževac for the camp in Bajnabástya. There was a rumor among the people at the camp that he had become an informant. Muszka was last seen leaving the camp in a jeep with four of his colleagues. He never returned to the camp.[105] In the second half of 1957 and early 1958, he was in a refugee camp that had been set up in a resort in Szelce.[106] The other inmates said Muszka was afraid because he had left his family in Hungary. He was also afraid that the Yugoslavs would send him home. Allegedly, he said he would sooner kill himself than return to Hungary.[107]

In September 1957, the leaders of the Budapest Csepel Machine Tools Factory submitted a proposal to the appropriate party and state officials that they revoke Muszka's distinctions. The proposal, which is signed by the leaders of the factory, offers the following official explanation for why Muszka left the country: "During the period of counterrevolution in October, he and several other decorated workers were harassed and hunted down with the intention of killing them."[108] However, the implication that Muszka feared for his life during the turmoil of late October and early November hardly explains why he fled the country months later, only crossing the border on January 18, 1957. Since the Csepel functionaries had no other information concerning Muszka, in all likelihood he did nothing during the revolution that would have compelled him to leave the country.[109] He may well have sought to flee his coworkers' wrath, given the prominent role he had played earlier and the role he allegedly played in 1956. He could hardly have been sure that the system would provide adequate protection for him and his family. The support it had from Soviet tanks notwithstanding, the new regime did not seem to wield much power on the local level at the end of 1956 and the beginning of 1957. It is also not difficult to imagine that Muszka simply had grown weary of a system whose representatives sometimes hoisted him on high as the archetypal worker and sometimes simply let him fall.

In the camps, representatives of Western powers conducted interviews with the refugees, on which they based their decisions about whether they would admit them into their countries. For a long time, it seemed that Muszka would not be given refugee status by any of the Western countries. In the end, however, he was allowed to travel to England. According to one agent's report, in 1958, Muszka paid a call on Ignác Pióker, a Kossuth Prize–winning planer, at the World's Fair in Brussels. Muszka complained to Pióker that he could not succeed in the West because the "'great publicity campaign' [of which he had been part] in Hungary stymied him."[110] There were all kinds of stories and rumors about how he later fared. According to some people, he lived abroad, and prostitutes had taken him in,[111] while others claimed he had returned to Hungary.[112]

Ideally, a storyteller, and particularly a historian, leaves no loose strings. However, for now we know nothing certain about Muszka's ultimate fate. In the 1960s, he vanished from the stage of Hungarian history. The memory trace he left later proved anachronistic. In 1967, the Hungarian daily *Szabad Föld* published an article with the following remark concerning Muszka and the ideal he had once represented: "We still remember the time when they assiduously strove to secure nationwide popularity for people like Imre Muszka, the Csepel turner. (Rumor says he went abroad to flee the deviously 'organized' 1,000 percent performances and his oppressive fame.)"[113] In the Kádár era, the functionaries no longer used individual workers in their publicity campaigns; rather, they used worker collectives, the brigades,[114] perhaps because they thought it would be less difficult and less risky to popularize a more abstract collective.

Most of the Stakhanovites remained on the workbench, but a few of them were mentioned in later news reports because of their careers. Ignác Pióker, for instance, became a recurring character in the drama of the socialist system. He was active as a parliamentary representative from 1953 until 1985, and in 1975 he was made a member of the Presidential Council (the body that represented the president of the state). Photographs of Pióker figured on the placards used for the May 1 ceremonies and in the elections. Newsreels offered narrative portraits of him in his workplace and in his home, surrounded by his family, telling his sons about the Kossuth Prize. A photograph taken by photographer Imre Benkő of Pióker with his medals and decorations laid out in front of him became an iconic image of the age.[115]

Of the famous Stakhanovites, however, Ede Horváth had perhaps the most impressive career. He served not only as a figure in the store display of the Kádár regime; he was also an active player in the power games. Horváth's career began at the Hungarian Train Car and Machine Tool Factory, where he started as a turner and was later made director.[116] As far as Horváth was concerned, the secret to his success lay in the fact that "they saw the love of work, the aggressive will to achieve in me. I always had that."[117] As the director of an enterprise, Horváth developed a distinctive style. Allegedly, when asked by the minister of metal and engineering industries János Csergő what he would need to realize his vision for the enterprise, Horváth replied, "two train cars of petrol so that I can wash the factory out of the dirt."[118] Later, when serving as the director of the factory, he fired the second-highest-ranking person at the factory because he found him asleep under a palm tree in his office, a newspaper in his hand and a bottle of cognac by his feet. (More precisely, Horváth pensioned the man off, making a concession to the man's age, which was not the standard practice at the time.)[119] There was a kitchen next to the office of one of the leaders of the factory. Horváth once opened the door on a man while the man was cooking, and Horváth immediately called for a car, into which he had everything packed up that was in the kitchen. He also took the dramatically unusual measure of selling the factory hunting lodge.[120]

Horváth became a well-known enterprise leader under socialism, and, in the course of his career, he even made it to the second line of the party leadership. After the Political Committee, the Central Committee was the second line; it was not easy to move any higher than this in the party hierarchy. As noted earlier, he also became a parliamentary representative. Horváth was a new figure among the old faces in the party leadership, and as an outsider he brought a new style. After the Second World War, the leadership of the Hungarian Communist Party consisted almost entirely of people from bourgeois social backgrounds.[121] Under Rákosi, they had symbolized the assumption of power by the working class, and so during public ceremonies they liked to appear alongside workers. After the revolution, Kádár again selected people to serve in the leadership of the new regime from the second and third tiers of the old nomenclature. Without exception, the newcomers to the elite were politicians who had climbed up all the various ladders in the life of the functionary.[122] The proportion of politicians who had working-class backgrounds only appeared to grow in the years of the Kádár system, since the new people became part of the regime as officials, and, as György Gyarmati observes, "They further strengthened the profile of the Hungarian Socialist Workers' Party as a workers' party and bureaucrats party."[123] Later, the party leadership very methodically reared a subsequent generation of leaders. Many of them, after having had careers as functionaries in the Hungarian Young Communist League, were then able to assume positions in the highest bodies of the party, and many people also moved from careers on the county level to positions of national leadership.

Although it does not appear to have been an important part of Horváth's identity, with the exception of Horváth, few people among the representatives of the workers' state had actually begun their careers as workers, and he was the single person among them who in the 1950s was still performing physical labor. (A man named István Szabó had a similar or even more spectacular career. He went from being a peasant farmer to serving as a member of an agricultural cooperative, then as the president of the cooperative, and finally as a member of the Political Committee.) Horváth represented a new style from several perspectives, but he does not seem to have had any difficulty learning the ropes in the Kádár system. He used the same tools that the other powerful figures of the era used to further their careers. For instance, in 1961 and 1962, the Political Committee and the Central Committee began to examine abuses and misuses that had taken place at the train car factory in Győr. It came to light that the factory had given engines for motorboats to local and national-level "potentates." In the course of the inquiry, it was established (and this was characteristic of the era) that the functionaries had not kept a "test log" on the "trial factory." More problematic than this was the fact that after the engines had been tested, presumably on Lake Balaton, the aforementioned potentates had been able to purchase them at prices that meant a loss for the factory. Horváth was one of the people who was condemned for his participation in the affair.[124]

Although Horváth adapted to his environment, as someone who had arrived in a position of influence from the outside, he found himself embroiled in several conflicts—at the company, at the county level, and on the Political Committee. In the mid-1960s, for instance, he had a clash with Ferenc Lombos, the county first secretary and, as such, the most powerful person at the county level. Lombos and Horváth may have come into conflict because of their common past; Lombos had been an engine mechanic at the train car factory in Győr. It was common knowledge in the city that Lombos's wife had gotten herself into some trouble. In May 1961, the Central Board of Inquiry of the Hungarian Socialist Workers' Party convicted her of smuggling.[125] In 1965, Horváth openly accused the woman of stealing (at the time, she worked as a member of his staff in the factory). When the case came before the Political Committee, Ferenc Lombos did not deny the charges so much as raise objections to the steps Horváth had taken. "It would have been better," Lombos complained, "had he submitted a report to the Political Committee or had he called me in and said, 'you fool, look at what you are stealing.'"[126] In the course of the inquiry, the case of the motorboat engines again came up. Lombos had purchased an engine for two thousand forints with ministerial authorization. In August 1963, he sold it, used, at a pawnshop for ten times as much to the sports division of the factory. In 1965, Lombos's wife was also accused of having had girders taken to the couple's plot on Tihany, a peninsula on the northern shore of Lake Balaton, and of having issued invoices with exaggerated sums for the enterprise's guest house on the peninsula (she was responsible for the factory's vacation affairs). The couple was also accused of having had Lombos's privately owned car repaired at the factory. To clear himself of the charges, Lombos requested a police investigation, and the police determined, on the basis of witness testimony, that there had never been any kind of girder on the couple's plot in Tihany. Lombos was found guilty of the other two accusations, but the authorities also reproached Horváth for having caused the affair to blow up in the first place: "For reasons unknown to us, comrade Horváth has seriously compromised comrade Lombos and taken the affair into the streets in a manner befitting neither the party nor the conduct of a comrade."[127]

As the leader of one of the most important enterprises in the country, Horváth yearned to play a role of national prominence. In 1989, the year of the regime change, at a sitting of the Central Committee, Horváth, a one-time member of the working class who had become a performance-oriented enterprise leader, harshly criticized Károly Grósz, the last secretary general of the party, and called on him to resign. Horváth claimed that he was not satisfied with Grósz's performance, and he called on "the new Political Committee to create circumstances in which the government will be capable of functioning and keeping its word."[128] The stance he adopted in this pivotal year can be regarded as broadly symbolic of the seismic shifts that were underway. It is similarly symptomatic of the mechanisms according to which the party functioned (or failed to function) that Károly suspected that a lobby associated with cultural politician György Aczél—that is, a lobby that was seen as led by the intelligentsia and shaped by influential Jewish figures—was behind the attack on him, at least according to Horváth's recollections.[129] The functionaries identified themselves with the workers' state and, from time to time (when it concerned their positions), with the working class as well.

The practice of identifying with the working class, however, was not limited to the level of principle or rhetoric. The ideological foundation of the ruling elite in the Kádár era was a system of relationships. As soon as the functionaries became a part of the stratum of officials, which represented the power of the working class (as it were), they found themselves in a complex relationship with the working class. Regardless of their professions or the trajectories of their professional lives, as individuals they became representatives of the working class. This was little more than metaphorical talk, however—a way to buttress the position of the individual in an abstract system of interrelationships. With the consolidation of the ruling elite, the real issue for the individual became not the reinforcement of the alleged legitimacy of the system, but rather the search for ideological justification for individual interests in an ongoing battle for position. In other words, one had to contrive ideological explanations for efforts either to revise the existing (power) relations or to maintain the status quo in the face of such attempts. The battle, which was fought under the flag of asserting and confirming the legitimacy of the system, was actually being waged by the functionaries on an entirely different front.

NOTES

1. Even under the Kádár regime, which fostered an image of itself as the representative of the working class and the embodiment of the power of the worker, the equestrian world in Hungary still gave horses names like Imperial and Kabbalah, both of which were successful in international competitions. László Gál 2005, 194. Zeidler offers a summary of the history of horse racing under the subtitle "Horse Racing—The Sport of the Magnates." Zeidler 2006, 76–83.

2. The basic reference point for theories of legitimization is Max Weber's theory of power. Weber 1978, 53; Lüdtke 1991, 9–15. The main function of legitimization is the stabilization of political power, but at the same time, the legitimized power (or domination) that is created as a result constitutes a power that is, from the perspective of its leaders, at least somewhat limited. Beetham 1991, 39.

3. Hollander 1988, 135.
4. Kornai 1999, 93.
5. Poenaru 2013, 241.
6. According to a suggestion made by the National Sports Office, "a new system of sports associations" needed to be created "modeled on the

example of the Soviet Union." Magyar Nemzeti Levéltár Országos Levéltára (Hungarian National Archives, hereafter cited as HNA), fond M-KS 276, group 54, storage unit 116.
   7. Hadas and Karády 1995.
   8. Béla Nagy 1987, 54.
   9. As noted in the memorandum concerning the case, "They are hiding questionable things beneath the names of our leading comrades. The peculiar grouping of the members of the Political Committee in the various fanatical camps of fans of the different associations is harmful, in the end, to the reputation of our party." Gyula Hegyi added the following: "Often, the sports associations use the personality of the given comrades for bad purposes." HNA, fond M-KS 276, group 54, storage unit 85.
   10. Földes 1984, 269.
   11. Sebes 1981, 132.
   12. Hámori 1982, 149.
   13. Ibid., 148.
   14. Mária Ember offers a summary of the events in a writing entitled "A kis magyar 'focialista forradalom'" (The little Hungarian "socc(ialist)er revolution"). Ember 2001.
   15. Sebes 1981, 260–263. In the book, Sebes uses italics to draw emphasis to the following passage: "It was a big mistake on my part during the halftime, at the instructions of the president, to put Czibor on the left wing and Mihály Tóth on the right wing." Ibid., 266. Presumably, Sebes was acting under the instructions of Gyula Hegyi, the president of the National Committee for Physical Education and Sports.
   16. From time to time, the party would have functionaries submit reports on the prevailing mood. Naturally, these reports can hardly be regarded as accurate estimates of the mood of the population at a given time. Rather, they offer an impression of what the members of the local party apparatus dared to suggest, on the basis of some inquiries and information gathered from various sources, in the name of the citizenry.
   17. Budapest Főváros Levéltára (Budapest City Archives, hereafter cited as BCA) fond XXXV 95, group c, storage unit 308 (1954, 14 July).
   18. Ibid.
   19. Ember 2001, 42.
   20. Canetti 1984, 16.
   21. Sebes 1981, 267–269.
   22. Hajduska 1988, 91.
   23. Tamás Aczél and Méray 1982, 216.

24. Report of the Administrative Division of the Hungarian Workers' Party on the implementation of the December 1954 resolution of the central leadership concerning sports, June 13, 1956, HNA, fond M-KS 276, group 69, storage unit 50.

25. Ibid.

26. Proposal submitted by Gyula Egri to the secretaryship, July 23, 1956, ibid.

27. Gerő added the following remark: "He should be very seriously cautioned." According to all signs, this was little more than an oral reprimand. Ernő Gerő's memorandum, July 25, 1956, ibid.

28. In their letter to Gyula Egri, the secretary of the Central Leadership of the Hungarian Workers' Party (dated June 18, 1956), Bata and Hazai initiated a kind of counterattack. They asked the committee to examine the work of the National Committee for Physical Education and Sports; ibid.

29. Report of the chairman of the National Committee for Physical Education and Sports on the playing strength of the teams that had made it to the finals in the Olympic soccer tournament, August 16, 1956, ibid.

30. Kasza 2004, 53.

31. Szöllősi 1997, 128–130.

32. Állambiztonsági Szolgálatok Történeti Levéltára (Historical Archives of the Hungarian State Security, hereafter cited as HAHSS), 3.1.5. O-11911 "Vasutas," 16.

33. Czibor 1998, 37–39.

34. Confession of Ágoston Garamvölgyi, Budapest, March 20, 1958, HAHSS 1.5. O-11912 "Vándor," 8–18; 13.

35. Resolution, Budapest, May 13, 1958, HAHSS 3.1.5. O-11911 "Vasutas," 6.

36. Ibid.

37. HAHSS 3.1.1. B-91315 "Eperjesi."

38. Report. Budapest, April 11, 1958, HAHSS 3.1.5. O-11911 "Vasutas," 7–8, 9. Czibor was given the code name Péter Sztojanovits by the state security forces. Ibid., 7.

39. Ibid., 13.

40. Ibid.

41. Ibid., 14.

42. HAHSS 3.1.5. O 11912 "Vándor," 18.

43. Ibid., 17.

44. Ibid.

45. Puskás first replied to Erdélyi in a letter dated June 17, 1959, and then again in a letter dated September 24, 1959. Ibid., 54–58, 59–61.

46. Ibid., 55.

47. Ibid., 54.

48. People who worked in these positions were known as *gebines*. The word presumably comes from the German word *Gewinn*, meaning profits or winnings. Beginning in 1957, there were stores in Hungary that essentially were not under any direct supervision by the larger enterprise, which only monitored gross turnover. The *gebines* were also allowed to choose their staff, like a real entrepreneur might, and they could bring family members into the business. Tamás 1997, 50.

49. HAHSS, fond 3.1, group 9, V-149869 12–118.

50. For instance, in 1974, the National Office for Physical Education and Sports drew up a plan for the secretaryship of the party that allegedly sought the causes of the problems and offered solutions. The resolution of the secretaryship was taken to Hungarian radio and Hungarian television, and later an open discussion was organized concerning it. "The public pays close attention to the achievements" of the team and the clubs, so it may have seemed to the party leaders that by taking a resolute stance they might be able to strengthen "trust" in the party. HNA, fond M-KS 288, group 7, storage unit 445.

51. Kő 1997, 319–321.

52. Hadas and Karády 1995, 104.

53. Miklós Németh added the following remark: "I also do not agree with the idea that Ferencváros is the team of the Ministry of Agriculture and Food, the Budapest Army Team is the team of the Ministry of Defense, or the Újpesti Dózsa team is the team of the Ministry of Internal Affairs." As his statements indicate, the state was already attempting to distance itself from and indeed free itself of the soccer clubs, which brought the country nothing in the way of renown or prestige in the international sphere, but nonetheless constituted a significant cost. Németh 1989: 5.

54. Minutes of the negotiations concerning the readmission of János Kádár, Ferenc Donáth, Gyula Kállai, and Sándor Haraszti, July 22, 1954, HAHSS, fond 3.1, group 9, V 150 322/2, 1–90, 463–464. Kádár was in fact a typewriter mechanic, which at the beginning of the 1930s was unquestionably an "elite" profession within his social class.

55. The first national workers' competition was held in March 1948, following the nationalization of private enterprises. On April 30, 1948, several hundred workers were presented with the badges that distinguished them as outstanding workers. There was not enough room in the hall where the event was held for all the winners of the competition, so ceremonies were also held in factories and workshops). At the end of

1945, the Stakhanovite movement began. In honor of Stalin's seventieth birthday, the Organizing Committee of the Hungarian Workers' Party issued a resolution launching a work-pledge movement from October 28 to December 21, 1949. This was the overture to the Stakhanovite movement in Hungary. The first Stakhanovite emblems were awarded in February 1950. See Sándor Horváth, Majtényi, and Tóth 1997, 1998.

56. Politikatörténeti és Szakszervezeti Levéltár (Archives of Political History and Trade Unions, hereafter cited as PHA), Szaktanács (Council of Trade Unions) 1–2/49; PHA Council of Trade Unions 1948, 18/126; PHA Szakszervezetek Országos Tanács (National Council of Trade Unions), Bér és termelés (Wages and production, hereafter cited as WP) 1949, 16/96; PHA Council of Trade Unions 1948, 19/132.

57. Siegelbaum 1988, 66–76.

58. PHA Council of Trade Unions, 1948, 19/132; PHA National Council of Trade Unions, WP 1949, 11/66; PHA, National Council of Trade Unions, WP 1949, 13/77.

59. PHA, Council of Trade Unions, 1948, 19/132.

60. A propaganda publication offered an account of Muszka's circumstances in the 1950s: Tokár 1951. For a discussion of his life's story, see Sándor Horváth 2002.

61. PHA, National Council of Trade Unions, WP 1950, 11/71.

62. Between 1948 and 1950, more than 16,000 outstanding worker emblems were awarded, and between 1950 and 1955, 115,000 workers were presented with Stakhanovite certificates. In 1956, the practice of awarding these distinctions was brought to an end. Initially, the Council of Trade Unions made a centralized decision concerning the number of distinctions that would be awarded. In August 1948, the Organizing Committee of the party decided that the individual factories and workshops would nominate workers for the distinction, and the Workers' Competition Committee would examine their proposals. HNA, fond M-KS 276, group 55, storage unit 15, August 6, 1948.

63. PHA, National Council of Trade Unions, WP, 1950, 10/65.

64. The first Outstanding Workers' Conference was held on August 1, 1948. László Piros, Ernő Gerő, and Árpád Szakasits were among the party leaders who gave speeches. HNA, fond M-KS 276, group 55, storage unit 15, August 6, 1948. In February 1950, a Stakhanovite conference was organized. HNA, fond M-KS 276, group 53, storage unit 45, February 9, 1950.

65. PHA, National Council of Trade Unions, WP, 1950, 10/65.

66. PHA, National Council of Trade Unions, WP, 1951, 23/157.

67. According to Jukka Gronow, the privileges that were bestowed on the outstanding Soviet workers and Stakhanovites were a symbolic expression of the idea that they, too, belonged to the elite. Gronow 2003, 148–149. Sheila Fitzpatrick contends that the outstanding worker and Stakhanovite movements created a new consumer culture among members of the working class that evoked the culture of the earlier elite. Fitzpatrick 1999, 102–103.

68. *Szabad Nép* [Free people], December 6, 1949, 9.

69. *Szabad Nép*, December 31, 1949, 3.

70. According to the report printed in *Szabad Nép*, Muszka said the following words of farewell to the Soviet dictator: "Our dear Stalin has died. Our truest friend has died. Our dear father has died." He continued: "We never had a more loving father. The Hungarian and the Hungarian working-class people never had a better friend." *Szabad Nép*, March 10, 1953, 3. Many people remembered Muszka's performance. Allegedly, he sobbed "more impassionedly" than anyone else on the dais. Péter Kovács 2008, 1477.

71. Karinthy 1953, 2.

72. For instance, one of the housing developments for civil servants is in Józsefváros. Pap and Pruzsinszky 2000–2003.

73. Found in District 19 of Budapest, the Wekerle Estate was built between 1908 and 1925. It was named after Sandor Wekerle, who served as Hungarian prime minister from 1906 to 1910. The estate was primarily intended to provide housing for government employees, though from the outset it was also home to many of the employees who worked in the nearby factories. It remains a popular neighborhood in Budapest today.

74. *Szabad Nép*, February 8, 1950, 7. On the histories of the buildings in which the outstanding workers lived, see Sándor Horváth 2007, 32–41.

75. Prakfalvi 2009, 126, 138.

76. In 1945, the wharf, which had been called Margit Wharf, was renamed after Illés Mónus, a social democratic politician and journalist who had lived in the neighborhood. In 1926, Mónus, who had been born to Jewish parents in a settlement in what today is the Ukraine, converted and became a Lutheran. However, according to the Second Anti-Jewish law, which was passed in 1939, he was legally defined as Jewish. In the autumn of 1944, he was captured and killed by the Arrow Cross. A few years later, the name of the wharf was changed a to Bem József Wharf, after József Zachariasz Bem, a Polish engineer and general who served under

Lajos Kossuth in the Hungarian Revolution and War of Independence of 1848–1849.

77. Prakfalvi 2009, 123–128.

78. Employees of the Hungarian State Railroads' Machine Factory were given dwellings in the B building (one of the four). Ibid., 132. The electoral register contains the year of birth and the occupation of every resident of the four buildings. The occupations included kindergarten teacher, boiler mechanic, dependent, engineer, doctor, factory worker, party functionary, state security official, and officer. Ibid., 137.

79. Ibid., 137.

80. Ibid., 134.

81. The wife of one of the outstanding workers told people at the market that the system had duped the outstanding workers by giving them the high-rent apartments. In the building housing employees of the Hungarian State Railroads' Machine Factory, many people were renting out one of the rooms in their apartment. Sándor Horváth 2007, 36–37.

82. Prakfalvi 2009, 134–135.

83. Report, Budapest, January 8, 1955. The document can be found in Gáspár and Szabó 1985, 352.

84. Proposal to increase the pace of residential building construction and bring prices down, and also rethink the system according to which apartments are distributed. HNA, fond M-KS 276, group 53, storage unit 263, December 29, 1955.

85. PHA, Council of Trade Unions, 1948, 19/132.

86. National Council of Trade Unions proposal concerning nominations for the distinction of outstanding worker. HNA, fond M-KS 276, group 55, storage unit 77. Organizing Committee of the Central Leadership of the Hungarian Workers' Party, July 4, 1949.

87. Karinthy 1953, 2.

88. In his autobiography, Rákosi offers the following recollection: "I cited Muszka, an iron turner who in his remarks sincerely and repentantly confessed that for an entire year he had kept his working practices a secret, lest one of his apprentices outdo him." Rákosi 1997, 820.

89. *Szabad Nép*, October 10, 1952, 2.

90. David Ovadia offers the following depiction of the busy everyday lives and struggles of the Bulgarian outstanding workers: "6:00: first change of shift in the factory, but I was already preparing to leave at 5:00. And who else left early? Only the party secretary came before me." At an assembly of party members, the outstanding worker gives the following response to news of sabotage: "As of tomorrow, comrades, / I will work at

two machines." His stern features grow soft when he gazes on his children: "And the state stands with me here too, / I raise my son to be happy." Literary works that focus on the lives and achievements of the outstanding workers include David Ovadia's "The Outstanding Worker" and Vladimir Mayakovsky's "Outstanding Workers" and "Marching Song of the Outstanding Workers' Brigade."

91. István Vas 1935, 336–337. Demyan Bedny was the pen name used by Yefim Alekseevich Pridvorov, a devoted supporter of the Bolsheviks who emerged as a prolific writer of so-called agitprop (propaganda writings with explicit political messages) during the Russian Revolution. He was a party favorite in the Soviet Union until the early and mid-1930s, when he began to fall from Stalin's graces. He was expelled from the Communist Party in the Soviet Union in 1938, but he gradually managed to regain Stalin's sympathies over the course of the war, and he did not suffer the fate of many of the poets who fell out of favor with Stalin—for instance, his more famous contemporary Osip Mandelstam, who was arrested and died in a transit camp in 1938.

92. Eszter Zsófia Tóth, "A munkamódszer-átadásról" [On passing on work practices]. Péter Kuczka, "Háromszázötven százalék" [350 percent], *Szabad Nép*, December 25, 1949, 13.

93. Ferenc Karinthy, "Hazai tudósítások" [Domestic news], *Szabad Nép*, December 25, 1949, 15; "Knechtl Nándor élete" [The life of Nándor Knechtl], *Szabad Nép*, December 11, 1949, 4; "Kőművesek" [Stone masons], *Szabad Nép*, April 30, 1950, 14; "A képviselőjelölt egy napja" [One day in the life of a candidate for parliament] (on iron turner Sándor Bátriás, who was given as award as a Stakhanovite twice), *Szabad Nép*, May 3, 1953, 3; "Az első magyar munkás, aki befejezte ötéves tervét" [The first Hungarian worker to complete his five-year plan], *Szabad Nép*, December 1, 1951, 4; "Hol van Muszka Imre?" [Where is Imre Muszka?], *Szabad Nép*, September 11, 1953, 2; Karinthy 1950, 1954.

94. Karinthy offered the following description of Muszka: "His hands were photographed for film, his pronouncement were published in the press and reported on the radio. Two years ago, we vacationed together in Galyatető. There was not a single person in the huge restaurant that did not know who this narrow-faced young man next to the window with smoothly brushed hair was: Muszka, the Kossuth Prize–winning turner. After breakfast, he strolled out into the space in front of the hotel, put a ten fillér coin on the stone wall, and shot it from 25 paces away." Ferenc Karinthy, "Hol van Muszka Imre?" [Where is Imre Muszka?], *Szabad Nép*, September 11, 1953, 2. In another writing, Karinthy recalls having met Ignác

Pióker in Galyatető: "Ignác Pióker, the Kossuth Prize–winning Stakhanovite, the best planer in the country, recipient of the Order of Labor, one of the best-known people of our homeland. Anytime he turns up, people start to whisper. They know his face from the newspapers and the films. There is even a book about him. I met with him in Galyatető last autumn, in the Grand Hotel, where as it so happens a portrait of him hangs from the walls. But I had already heard a great deal about Pióker." Ferenc Karinthy, "Az első magyar munkás, aki befejezte ötéves tervét" [The first Hungarian worker to complete his five-year plan], *Szabad Nép*, December 2, 1951, 4.

95. *Babik* was first written as a short story for film in 1954. Working with directors Péter Bacsó and Károly Makk, Örkény transformed the story into a screenplay, but it was rejected by the film authorities. Örkény then rewrote it as a novel, but it remained unfinished. In 1982 and 1983, it was published in three different formats, first as a stand-alone novella, then in a collection of Örkény's unfinished compositions, and then as a screenplay in the third volume of Örkény's dramas.

96. Carnap 1972, 66–67. Péter Dóka pointed out this parallel to me.

97. Eszter Zsófia Tóth 2005, 89–90.

98. József Bácsi, deputy chairman of the Central Workers' Committee of the Csepel Iron and Steel Works, interview conducted by Eszter Zsófia Tóth and György Majtényi, 1997. Elek Nagy, president of the Central Workers' Committee of the Csepel Iron and Steel Works, interview in Kozák and Molnár 1993, 21–22. *Nagy József és társa: 1956 utáni perek gyűjteménye* [József Nagy and associate: Collection of trials after 1956], National Széchényi Library Manuscript Collection, 3. b. 1991/57.

99. Interview with Ferenc R. conducted by Eszter Zsófia Tóth, unpublished manuscript, 1998.

100. The Hungarian word *pufajka* comes from the Russian word *fufajka*, a quilted jacket that was worn by the militia. *Pufajkás* means a person wearing such a jacket.

101. Interview with Ferenc M. conducted by Eszter Zsófia Tóth, unpublished manuscript, 1998.

102. HAHSS, fond 3.1, group 5, O-16391. They were granted an amnesty and returned to Hungary. Minutes of the interrogation of dissident András Leéb, Budapest, April 28, 1960, 240. The Kossuth Prize was one of the most prestigious state prizes of the era, because it was given not only to artists and scientists but also to workers.

103. HAHSS, fond 3.1, group 5, O-9611. On April 2, 1957, they returned to Hungary from Yugoslavia, having been granted an amnesty. Minutes, Szeged, March 8, 1957, 46.

104. Ibid., 54.
105. HAHSS, fond 3.1, group 5, O-16391. They returned to Hungary, having been granted an amnesty. Minutes, Budapest, April 28, 1960, 240, 242.
106. HAHSS, fond 3.1, group 5. O-16665. They returned to Hungary from Yugoslavia, having been granted an amnesty. Minutes, Budapest, July 22, 1959, 102–106.
107. Ibid., 106.
108. BCA, fond XXXV 1, group a 4, storage unit 8, October 7, 1957, 124–125.
109. For a summary of the history of the Csepel workers' council, see Eszter Zsófia Tóth 1999.
110. HAHSS, fond 3.1, group 5, O-16665. They returned to Hungary from Yugoslavia, having been granted an amnesty. Minutes, Budapest, July 22, 1959, 106.
111. Pünkösti 1979, 20.
112. In April 1962, a man named Imre Muszka was nominated for the position of president of the Vas County Alliance of Industrial Cooperatives and Enterprises (Vas Megyei Ipari Szövetkezetek és Vállalkozások Szövetsége) for the city of Szombathely, though in the end he was not elected. HAHSS, fond 3.1, group 5, O-12857. Mixed materials on 1956, Agent "Lajos Kiss," Ministry of Internal Affairs Vas County Police Headquarters, Report, Szombathely, April 17, 1962, 167. I found no other information concerning him, but it may well simply have been a case of two different people with the same name, and Muszka may have died abroad.
113. Bajor Nagy Ernő, "Korszerű eszmék—korszerűtlen példaképek" [Up-to-date ideas—Out-of-date examples], *Szabad Föld* [Free earth], October 22, 1967, 9.
114. In 1948, the Organizing Committee of the Hungarian Workers' Party had entrusted the Workers' Competition Party Committee with the task of drafting suggestions concerning the organization of group (brigade) competitions. HNA, fond M-KS 276, group 55, storage unit 15, August 6, 1948. Later, in the Kádár era, endeavors to make the brigades popular became common practice. According to government resolution 1.068/1957. (VIII. 4.), which bore the title "On production deliberations and the rewards to be provided for workers and enterprises who are at the head of the socialist workers' competitions," established the regulations for the workers' brigades competitions. Point B of the first paragraph of the resolution states, "The form of the competition that best corresponds to the goals and the local circumstances should be determined at the production deliberations, in consultation with the workers (i.e. individual

competitions, brigade competitions, competitions between workshops, etc.)." Point 1 of chapter 5 states, "The assessment of the production achievements of the individuals and the brigades will begin on 1 July 1957." For a microhistorical examination of the socialist brigade, see Eszter Zsófia Tóth 2007.

115. For contemporary portrayals of Ignác Pióker's life history, see Zolnay 1951; Déri 1952. For an analysis of the Stakhanovite movement from the perspective of his life, see Sándor Horváth, Majtényi, and Tóth 1998.

116. For a study on Ede Horváth's life in the 1950s, see Kántor 1950. For more recent summaries, see Ede Horváth 1990; Dusza 2003.

117. Ede Horváth 1990, 66.

118. Ibid., 17.

119. Ibid., 25–26.

120. Ibid., 28.

121. András Hegedüs offers the following description of the social backgrounds of the four main leaders:

> Four young men set out, it's interesting to note that they have very similar family backgrounds. They are all Jewish, yes, but they are from the middle layer of the Jewry, which had not yet integrated itself into the ruling classes in Hungary, but which had abandoned the strict norms of the Jewish ethnic group. They embarked down the path of assimilation, but their attempt to assimilate were not successful. In 1892, Rákosi was born in Abda. The era of the millennial celebrations is a good time, his parents are shopkeepers. They are doing reasonably well. The turn of the century also is so promising that this shopkeeper takes the bold step of founding a large family. They have six children. Gerő was born in 1898 in a small village, Tergemenc [sic; Terbegec, Trebušovce in Slovakia], today I think it is part of Czechoslovakia. Révai was also born in 1898, in Budapest, to a family of middle class Jewish merchants. Mihály Farkas was born six years later in Abaújszántó. No one knows who his father is. His mother owns a wash house. If I want to, I call her a washer woman. If I want to, I call her a business woman. "A nagy Mezei András-interjú" [The big Mezei-András interview], I. 3. OSA 361-0-13 2. d.

122. Gyarmati 2009, 79–82.

123. Ibid., 82.

124. HNA, fond M–KS 288, group 5, storage unit 247. Minutes of the sitting of the Political Committee of the Hungarian Socialist Workers' Party, October 17, 1962; HNA M–KS 288. f. 4/45. s. u. Minutes of the sitting

of the Political Committee of the Hungarian Socialist Workers' Party, February 9, 1962.

125. HNA, fond M–KS 932, Központi Ellenőrző Bizottság (Central Supervisory Committee), Mrs. Ferenc Lombos, 1961.

126. HNA, fond M–KS 288, group 5, storage unit 373, August 31, 1965.

127. Ibid. For an analysis of the case, see Csaba Szabó 2006. The English translation of this citation is considerably more eloquent than the original Hungarian text. The Hungarian text contains two words, *pártszerűtlen* and *elvtársiatlan*, that could have easily been translated as "un-party-esque" and "un-camraderiely." These kinds of ungainly neologisms were not uncommon and were symptomatic of the need to craft a new terminology in the service of an ultimately failed attempt to establish the ethical code of a new ideology.

128. The event took place during the sitting of the Central Committee on April 11, 1989. Ede Horváth 1990, 60. According to the minutes of the meeting, Horváth made the following request: "After having given it considerable thought and having felt considerable anxiety, I respectfully ask comrade Grósz again to think over whether he should accept the position as general secretary of the Political Committee that remains to be selected." 1989 Records Books of the Central Committee of the Hungarian Socialist Workers' Party, vol. 1, 727. According to the collection of interviews with Ede Horváth, the text of this request was the following: "I respectfully ask comrade Grósz not to accept the position as general secretary of the Political Committee, which remains to be selected." Ibid., 60. Horváth allegedly showed a copy of the proposal to the editor of the collection. Ibid., 111.

129. "Well, you know what Grósz said about me? That I was in cahoots with the Jewish elite, that the big industry lobby was behind me, and that he was sure that Aczél was urging me on." Ibid., 60.

FIVE

LUXURY
Public and Semipublic Spaces

CONSUMER HABITS IN THE HOSPITALITY INDUSTRY

Budapest is famous for having been a city of cafés. What is perhaps less often mentioned is that at the turn of the twentieth century, alongside the wide array of cafés, innumerable similar establishments opened, including bars, taverns, music halls, and cabarets. These places were not simply sanctuaries for writers, artists, and musicians; they were, more generally, "the symbolic spaces of dissolution and sexual libertinism."[1] They were distinctive institutions of public life, and as meeting places and sites for trysts, they constituted a semipublic space between the public and the private spheres.[2] It was very much in the interests of the new elite to bring under its control not only symbolic public spaces and the press but also these spaces, which existed in the overlap of the hospitality industry and culture.[3]

The representatives of the new social order strove not simply to restructure and transform individual habits or practices; they openly sought to put an end to certain ways of life. According to the ideology of the new system, the spaces of the hospitality industry were symbolic of the "sinful" bourgeois values of the interwar period, and they were seen as allegorical embodiments of the mentality and milieu of the society of the Horthy era.[4] The state adopted firm measures to bring these spaces under its control. In the process of nationalization, the cafés, bars, and nightclubs were closed or turned into simple countertop coffee shops. In 1946, for instance, an inquiry was launched against the owner of the Bagdad Café. Allegedly the authorities were simply examining the establishment's permits, but in fact someone envious of the owner had denounced him. Making little effort to conceal their repugnance, in their reports the inspectors characterized the art nouveau style of the café, which at times straddled the border between decorative and kitschy, as unethical. According to the report, "The entrance to the restaurant opens onto a cloak room with mirrors where guests are greeted by an erotic painting that has been painted on the wall; the exposed thighs of a fully-clothed, brazen woman in an inviting pose. . . . There are even two black men on the staff." As a consequence of the inquiry, the café was closed, despite protests of the establishment's "organized labor."[5]

As the majority of studies on the era of state socialism have noted, with the reduction of disparities in income and the creation of standardized prices and services, the differences in the lifestyles of individual social groups became far less striking than they had been. These changes and shifts, however, by no means put an end to social inequalities. The business managers of the restaurants, taverns, and other similar establishments that had been nationalized often were confronted with the fact that not all guests are created equal, and different groups of customers frequented different establishments, much as (and partly as a consequence of this) the cafés, bars, and taverns served different functions.

In 1953, the Representative Hospitality Industry Company was given the building of the New York Café (which until then had been used as a sports gear center). This was an event of important symbolic significance. The company set up the Hungária Café in the building. True, the café no longer functioned as a gathering spot for wine-ruddied merchants or for the authors and editors of *Nyugat* (West), a prominent literary and cultural journal of the prewar period (many well-known authors whose writings had regularly been published in *Nyugat* had frequented the New York Café). But it was quite clear to everyone that the regime had failed in its efforts to rid the streets of Budapest of its cafés.[6] According to rumor, the head of the Newspaper Publishing Company wanted an elegant building with a café that he could use as a headquarters for the press, but he had difficulty convincing Zoltán Vas, the party leader, to agree to his request. However, when the publisher mentioned that he would have the café set up again, Vas immediately gave his consent and then noted, "but only because of the café."[7]

During an interview with me, Károly Hetényi, who had worked as a busboy and then headwaiter at the New York Café in the interwar period, offered the following description of some of the most famous regulars at the café (whom he was clearly proud to have known):

> [Dezső] Kosztolányi [a prominent Hungarian writer and poet] was a dull guy who was quite full of himself, and he had stupid habits, 'cause he would eat the soft inside part of the bread, and he drank Romanian coffee with it, he called it Romanian coffee, half a deciliter of Puerto Rican rum, the glass filled with hot coffee, Kosztolányi drank that with sugar, and he ate the soft part of the bread. They all had some crazy habit. Endre Ady [another prominent Hungarian poet] always ordered the same thing: lentils with gravy.... [Frigyes] Karinthy didn't have any favorite food, he ate whatever they shoved in front of him, so he was nutty too.

Later, Hetényi had watched as the Hungária Café tried to conjure something of this past, and though the circle of guests had changed, the café again became an important gathering place for writers, poets, and the like. Though Hetényi concedes, "True, it was not the same as it had once been."[8] According to a widespread rumor in Budapest, György Aczél grew bored of the mood of prewar liberty in the so-called crimson salon of the Hungária, and in the early 1970s he had the New York/Hungária closed. The truth of this rumor is unknown, but it is true that the restaurant-café was redesigned in the early 1970s, and the crimson salon was made into a cloakroom.[9]

The various social profiles of the people who frequented different restaurants, cafés, and buffets clearly show that the members of the various social groups maintained their traditional leisure habits and customs in public spaces. Such habits and customs were expressions and affirmations of identities, both individual and group. In continuing these practices, they re-created the old world of the hospitality industry and nightlife in the city. People seem to have craved the sultry air of the nightclubs and bars. By the end of the 1950s, the Bagdad Café, for instance, had already opened its doors again to customers seeking to indulge in evenings of revelry.[10] Gradually, an approach to the hospitality industry based on recognition of customers' differing tastes and interests was revived.[11] In Budapest, the Museum Café, the Astoria Café, and the Gundel restaurant, which reopened in the mid-1950s, established reputations as places that offered a high standard of service. In other words, they became the "elite" establishments of the hospitality industry. Their design and interiors represented the traditions of the interwar period. Even the most prestigious establishments were obliged to offer canteen-style meals with at least two menu choices. The complaints that were made at the time, however, suggest that the restaurants did everything they could to discourage people from taking advantage of this service.[12]

The coryphaei of economic policy assigned an important role to the hospitality industry in the revival and cultivation of tourism, which brought significant amounts of hard currency into the country. An episode involving Miguel Ángel Asturias (a Nobel Prize–winning Guatemalan poet, novelist, playwright, and journalist) and Pablo Neruda (the pen name and later legal name of Chilean poet and politician Ricardo Eliécer Neftalí Reyes Basoalto, who was also a Nobel Prize winner) is emblematic of one of the main functions of the hospitality industry in socialist Hungary. The two writers had come to Hungary for a peace congress. Their wives had wanted to purchase clothing at the world-famous Clara Salon. Asturias and Neruda first checked to see how much money they were owed in Hungary as royalties, but the sum they were owed, they learned, was not even close to enough. In the end, they decided to make an offer to the government to popularize the country and, more precisely, its hospitality industry abroad.[13] Thus, the propaganda publication titled a *Megkóstoltuk Magyarországot* (We sampled Hungary) was born.[14] Asturias and Neruda enjoyed their time in Hungary, drinking, eating, and writing prose and poetry, all while singing the praises of the country and its cuisine.[15] The two gourmands wrote enthusiastically of traditions that had been preserved: "The inns, taverns, restaurants, and cafés function according to ancient and excellent norms."[16] At the end of the book, they thanked their "friends," "from whom [we received] delectable advice," with a heart-shaped gingerbread cookie on which the words of the farewell were written with frosting. Their "friends" included communist politician György Aczél and poet and literary translator György Somlyó.[17]

Initially, the world of the restaurants, cafés, taverns, and clubs—which were open to the public—and the leisure pastimes and customs of the ruling elite—which drew on the traditions and lifestyles of the interwar period but were kept hidden from the public eye—remained entirely separate. In the 1950s, "team-building" Sunday lunches were held in the guest house on Béla király Avenue in the Buda hills for members of the highest echelons of the party leadership.[18] In 1945, the central leadership reserved a count's villa in the area as a weekend resort.[19] The building was surrounded by a huge park, where the children of the cadres could play. When lunches were held, all the prominent figures of the party and the state sat at white tables with their families. Participation in these events was virtually obligatory, since Mátyás Rákosi himself regularly came to the venue,[20] though he and his wife were seated separately, in a small, freestanding building in the garden. All other prominent figures of the party, from Mihály Farkas to János Kádár, sat at the grand table in the main building.[21] One Sunday, Gyula Kállai, who served for a time as chairman of the Council of Ministers and for two years as speaker of the national assembly (he is also credited with initiating the proceedings that led to the execution of Imre Nagy), saw the infamous "foursome" playing cards: "They were playing 21. Rákosi was playing too. Every time he hit the bank he never failed to say, 'As Marx said, you never joke about money.'"[22]

The party leaders had not forgotten the traditions of the prewar world or the customs and habits they once enjoyed. When merrymaking, they sometimes also sang. Party leader Géza Losonczy, the son of a Calvinist preacher, was a gifted singer not only of psalms but also of Hungarian folk music. One of his favorite folk songs was "My Rose Bathes in Milk When She Gets Up."[23] When they drank together, the functionaries usually had Roma musicians play their favorite folk music and then lively dance music. They referred to this relaxed form of revelry as *cigányozás*, a racist word that might best be translated into English as "Gypsy-ing."[24]

In the Kádár era, these regular weekend gatherings came to an end. The members of the Central Committee and the Political Committee were able to eat in the stately party resort building in Munkácsy Mihály Street, which opens off of Andrássy Avenue.[25] There was a room in the building for ceremonial events, and elegant receptions were held here. On weekdays, Kádár regularly ate in this building. On weekends, he ate there with his wife.[26] The organized common meals were moved to weekdays and thus kept separate from the functionaries' private lives. This was arguably symptomatic of the fundamental difference between the approach to power under Rákosi and the approach to power under Kádár. Whereas Rákosi had sought to push the state into every nook and cranny of life, the Kádár regime thought it preferable to allow for at least the appearance of private life. However, this was also a consequence of one of Kádár's personality quirks. Kádár preferred to keep his distance from the other functionaries. The so-called PC lunches were always held after a meeting of the Political Committee. According to trade union leader Sándor Gáspár, the lunches were a "release for the tension that had gathered during the Committee sitting." In 1958, some sociable functionaries organized gatherings in Leányfalu. According to Gáspár, "At one time we tried to introduce the practice of sitting down without an agenda and talking." Kádár, however, considered these meetings "fruitless," and the fact that they were not continued was due fundamentally to his aversion to the idea.[27] The exercise of power became increasingly professionalized, and the amicable groups of elites were replaced by a bureaucratic official order.

The restaurant in Munkácsy Street had the feel of a cafeteria, though clearly not because the functionaries had lost their preference for luxury or culinary delights. They formed smaller groups and indulged their tastes for fine dining elsewhere. In the Kádár era, because of favors he granted the functionaries, Lajos Onódy, the head of the Restaurant and Buffet Company (a state company that enjoyed a monopoly in the food services industry), became a trusted confidant of the state and party leadership. On festive occasions, Onódy would surprise leading comrades (for instance, Béla Biszku and Sándor Gáspár) with valuable beverages, and he would send them silver platters with assorted cold cuts (they did not have to return the platters). He founded small hunting societies for them named Mackó (Bear Cub) and Diána. The functionaries regularly met in Mézes Mackó, or "Honey Bear," a restaurant in a basement in Kígyó Street. Rumors, often unfounded, spread about activities that took place at some of these gatherings that remained hidden from the public eye, including orgies that allegedly were held in the establishments and hunting lodges under Onódy's supervision.[28]

In the Kádár era, the Gundel restaurant—next to the Városliget, or city park, at the end of Andrássy Avenue—was used for ceremonial events held by the party and the government. It is worth taking a deeper look into everyday life in this peculiar world of a luxury restaurant under socialism. Gundel was able to take orders from the Hungarian Socialist Workers' Party, the Council of Ministers, the Presidential Council, the Office of the Parliament, and the protocol departments of the Ministry of Foreign Affairs. The events were usually held in the elegant private banquet halls of the restaurant, though also sometimes in the parliament building or at the guest house of the Ministry of Foreign Affairs. The staff at Gundel also cooked for and provided service at receptions hosted by embassies and trade delegations, the celebrations held for April 4 and May 1, the gala performances held in the theaters of the city, and banquet meals held on special trains and boats and in forests and hunting lodges. When important delegations arrived, Gundel was entrusted with planning and preparing the meals for the events in the countryside or in settlements outside Budapest. Sometimes, the Gundel staff even accompanied party and state leaders when they traveled abroad.[29] During the revolution, some staff were brought to the parliament to provide food for the comrades who found themselves stuck in the building.[30] At the receptions, the newcomer politicians were able to sample unusual specialties. As Kállai writes,

> We began to taste black and red caviar, which counted as an aristocratic delicacy, and I must confess, initially we did not think much of it. Or of the various kinds of smoked fish. The lobster, which had been cooked until it was deep crimson, gave us the shivers. Zoltán Vas's wife taught us how to pull off the lobster's tail, clean its legs and claws, remove the red shell, and eat the white meat inside.

We were also impressed by the roasted pheasant-cock, which was always resting almost ostentatiously in the middle of the meat platters, with its feathers still attached, almost ready to take flight.[31]

László Somogyi, who worked in Gundel in the 1950s, offers the following account of the people who attended the receptions: "In general, they were normal people. The one you had to be very afraid of was Mihály Farkas, at the drop of a hat he would have someone sent off to the army, so we were cautious. They didn't take any of our people off, but there must have been some reason for that."[32]

Gundel was overseen by the National Tourist Hotel and Restaurant Company (which later became the Hungária Hotel and Restaurant Company, or more generally known simply as HungarHotels). In addition to Gundel, the company managed several elegant establishments in Buda, including the Rózsadomb Restaurant, the Hármashatárhegy Restaurant,[33] and later the Restaurant Alabárdos.[34] In the second half of the 1960s, government receptions were held in the Grand Hotel Restaurant on Margaret Island.[35] These establishments were the most exclusive places in the city.

Gundel functioned as a "semi-independent unit," which in practice meant that it had an interest in increasing its revenues. The primary source of revenue was not the protocol events but rather the many tourists from the West who came to the deservedly famous restaurant. The management of the restaurant therefore developed a "business policy." In the summer months, when the tourist traffic was considerably higher, many people were added to the staff. At the end of the tourist season, many of the employees were dismissed, because few customers came to the restaurant in the winter. The Ministry of Internal Affairs had considerable difficulty keeping track of the people who were added almost indiscriminately to the staff at the beginning of the tourist season, having learned of the opportunity through employment agencies and newspaper advertisements.

In 1961, state security officers examined the "cadre situation" of the restaurant,³⁶ and in general they found the staff suitable for the food industry tasks involved with important state occasions and ceremonies. According to the Ministry of Internal Affairs report, "With the exception of the storage and delivery staff, the striking power for terror-diversion prevention is satisfactory." As was typical of the strategies adopted by the regime to maintain an expansive network of contacts, the state security forces had some kind of "relationship" with twenty-two people "among the employees of the company and the chefs and servers who are brought in from other companies for the events." Two of them were informants, and the other twenty were considered to be in a "social relationship" with the security forces. The Ministry of Internal Affairs also had three "official relationships" with people in the restaurant at the time.³⁷ To add the necessary shade of nuance, it should be noted that these "relationships" in Gundel essentially remained dormant throughout the Cold War.

The part of the Ministry of Internal Affairs responsible for "the prevention of sabotage and attacks" in the exclusive restaurants never had much to report to its superiors. The reports that were submitted at the time mention, for instance, that when Czechoslovak president Antonín Josef Novotný came to Hungary for an official visit, "an entire roll of ham [was found] in a spoiled state injurious to health."³⁸ No attempts at sabotage cast any shadow over the restaurant, however. Gundel was not the only "hospitality industry object [*objektum*] kept under watch for the prevention of sabotage and attacks." The Ministry of Internal Affairs kept a close eye on all the establishments that served food, drinks, and baked goods at the protocol events. Thus, by the 1960s, the Vörösmarty patisserie, the Pannónia Restaurant and Buffet Company, the Pushkin Cold Kitchen, and the Margaret Island Filling

Unit of the Budapest Mineral Water and Ice Company were all under observation by the state security forces, because they all provided food and drink for official events.[39]

A distinctive coterie frequented Gundel. One of the reports submitted by the state security forces offers the following description of this peculiar world: "Traffic around the company is lively and dense. The zoo, which is not far from the restaurant, and the other, more distant amusement sites draw crowds. The crowds which come to the area are very mixed, ranging from tourists of various nationalities to representatives of all of the different social strata in Hungary." When official events were held, "forming a broad line, the passers-by" would stare at the black cars in which the potentates were brought to Gundel. Not far from the restaurant, a gang of some twenty-five or thirty people had formed "with the Amusement Park and Circus bar as its center" (the amusement park and circus were on the far side of the zoo, not distant from the restaurant, along with one or two bars). This was a source of considerable consternation for the state security officials, since the appearance and conduct of a gang clearly stretched the official interpretive framework of socialist ethics.[40]

The Ministry of Internal Affairs had to make sure that the area around the restaurant was safe. One report offers the following summary of the steps that were taken to protect the "object" (*objektum*): "In order to increase operational security at the events within the company, we contacted the head of the district 14 police. On the basis of our conversation, they have entrusted their network in the area of the company (the ice-cream vendor, the street sweeper, etc.) with the task of averting attack by studying the composition of the groups of people who frequent Gundel and their behavior, and throwing light on their potentially hostile intentions. We will inform each other of our observations."[41] Today, it is difficult to imagine the ice cream vendor and the street sweeper working to avert attacks by watching people come and go from the banks of the lake in the city park. Comic as the idea may seem, however, it actually fits well into the surreal world of the time, where a luxury restaurant welcomed tourists, guests from the West, diplomats from other countries, and the most powerful leaders of the communist party.

In the everyday life of the Gundel restaurant, "the prevention of sabotage and attacks" was the furthest thing from anyone's mind. Behind the veneer of strict adherence to the system's Cold War doctrine, a culture of catering and hospitality services that drew on prewar traditions flowered. In a manner that was generally inconspicuous, it brought gourmets from abroad who took delight in the delicacies offered by Gundel under the same roof as Hungarian devotees of the restaurant. The company manager, the cooks, and the waiters involved in ceremonious dining craved the money brought into the country by guests from the West. In the background, the allegedly socialist state also yearned for the hard currency brought into the country by Gundel's reputation. This type of fine dining exerted an influence on the tastes and desires of the party and state leaders that was based on old traditions and fundamentally Western habits. The tastes and desires of the party leaders in turn influenced the rest of Hungarian society. Members of the elite did not merely turn a blind eye to the fact that the old theaters of luxury consumption were gradually taking on a new life; they actually supported this shift with their policies, and with their behavior they helped the consumption of quality items and luxuries gain ground.

In December 1973, Gundel was closed for general renovations and redesign. The members of the staff were given positions in other restaurants and hotels. Indeed, most of them were given positions in the Gellért Hotel, another distinguished establishment that belonged to HungarHotels and was the most elegant hotel in Buda. From then on, the Gellért Hotel restaurant was chosen as the site for "high-level state and protocol events."[42] The state security forces took the necessary (or at least allegedly necessary) operational measures in the Gellért Hotel to ensure safety from sabotage. In the summer of 1980, Gundel was reopened with only part of the restaurant in operation, and the renovation work still underway.[43] It was not until January 1, 1981, that protocol events could be held in Gundel again. The other rooms and chambers in the building were reopened, including six rooms next to the convention hall, the garden, the ice cream bar, the cocktail lounge, and the buffet.[44]

In 1980, the Ministry of Domestic Trade decided to restructure the entire hospitality industry. In January 1981, the Gellért Hotel was put under the oversight of the Danubius Hospitality and Medicinal Bath Company. Gundel was put under the management of the Fórum Hotel Regional Directorate, along with the Restaurant Alabárdos.[45] (Before the Second World War, there had been a famous row of hotels on the bank of the Danube River in Pest. The buildings were reduced to rubble in the war. In the 1970s, an agreement was reached between the Hungarian government and the Austrian government concerning investments in the tourist industry. The Fórum Hotel, the first modern hotel on the Danube in Budapest, was built using Austrian loans—that is, loans from a Western country—and with the participation of Austrian construction companies.) These measures, which obviously did not harmonize with the ideology of the socialist state, were driven by the fact that the flagships of the hospitality and tourist industries at the time were the luxury hotels that lured tourists from the West to Hungary. All the available money and expertise was concentrated here.

LUXURY IN EXCHANGE FOR HARD CURRENCY

After the war, some of the remaining hotels in Budapest were confiscated for administrative or other purposes. In March 1948, with the exception of the Gellért Hotel, which was municipal (capital) property, only a few, privately owned hostels were in business. The remodeling of the Gellért had begun after the war, and the government planned to use the luxury hotel to receive foreign visitors and host official events. Although there had been some debate over whether to renovate the building in the tradition of its original art nouveau style or with a simpler facade, eventually the decision was made to use the original style.[46]

Generally, the development of the socialist system did not offer much of a promising future for hotels and their proprietors. In March 1948, when large-scale businesses were being nationalized, Hotel Nemzeti (National Hotel), which had previously been an investment of the Dreher Haggenmacher Brewery, came under state control, as did, in May 1948, Astoria, Britannia (later known as Béke), Continental, and Bristol (later Duna). The Gellért was nationalized in July. The remodeled Grand Hotel on Margaret Island reopened in August as a state-owned enterprise. In December, during the new wave of nationalization, the state—or, to be more precise, the National Hotel Enterprise, which had been founded in May—took over control of Szabadság (then Imperial), Opera, Erzsébet, and the Szabó hotels. (This was also when the state confiscated most of the hotels outside Budapest.) In the 1950s, several renowned downtown Budapest hotels reopened, which indicates that the party-state saw significant potential in the hotel and catering industry. In December 1951, the palace was reopened as a hotel. In 1953, Vörös Csillag (Red Star, which had gone by the name Golf until 1950 and today is Panoráma) was reopened, followed by Royal in 1954, Park in 1957, and Metropol in 1958.[47] The state exercised close control over these establishments and introduced a strict system of ranking.

Sources suggest that the leaders of the hospitality industry and commerce world recognized the traditional structures that had survived and the existence—and even diversity and complexity—of social inequality much more quickly than did prominent sociologists. In the 1960s, sociology was gradually taking on a new life and confronting the ideology of the regime and the Stalinist model of the unified working class, peasantry, and intelligentsia. Hotels and restaurants were ranked according to the quality of the services they offered, and stores were categorized in a similar fashion. The national theoretician of the hospitality industry, Sámuel Schnitta, described the hierarchy of catering enterprises in his 1962 work: Premium businesses were the highest rank, followed by first, second, third, and fourth-class businesses.[48] In addition to premium hotels, Schnitta introduced an extra category that ranked even higher: luxury hotels.[49] These could be classified further as A, B, and C hotels. Their interiors reflected more the historicist, obsolete taste of the ruling elite and the lifestyle it embodied than the official ideology of the socialist era. In his handbook, Schnitta offered the following example of a hotel meeting the requirements of the luxury category: "The Budapest Gellért Hotel is the absolute manifestation of the luxury hotel as the term is universally understood. The façade, with its columns and palace-like features, grandiose ells, rooms with balconies, impressive main entrance with a glass roof stretching all the way to the curbside, driveway, and parking spaces in the front." Schnitta noted minor decorative features of comfort: "There is recess carpeting in front of the main entrance, a carpet of fitting color covers the entrance staircase to the hotel, often there are evergreen trees on both sides of the main entrance: this all gives the hotel its sense of luxury."[50]

It worth noting that Persian-style carpets were also made in Hungary, and in the 1950s luxury hotels were the most likely to purchase them. These rugs were considered of high quality; like real Persian rugs, they were elegant and vivid in their colors. A hotel expert heaped praise on them: "The properly made Hungarian Persian has 60,000 knots, it weighs 3 kilograms per square meter, and it is durable."[51] In the more exclusive hotels, suites were characteristically furnished with antique furniture, while rooms had more modern interiors.

The history of the Hotel Royal, which in the 1960s was considered the veritable acropolis of the Hungarian hospitality industry, merits a closer look. Following the Second World War, the Royal was reopened with 170 rooms on two floors. The rest of the building hosted various offices. For example, it served as the headquarters for the socialist rail company, Hungarian State Railways. During the revolution, the hotel, in which revolutionaries had taken refuge, was attacked and damaged by Soviet tanks. The building was burned, and the roof collapsed. Already in 1957, leaders of the hotel industry announced that the Hotel Royal would be renovated. The reopening of the chic hotel was intended to tempt visitors to the 1958 Brussels World Exhibition to come to Hungary (and bring their hard currency with them). The renovation work, however, was delayed, and the reconstruction of the Royal was not completed until 1961. The total cost of renovation and remodeling came to 140 million forints. As György Kalmár-Maron, the former chief doorman of the Royal, recounts, guests had been arriving prior to the opening. "The opening was scheduled for 21 August, and on the evening of the 20, a couple arrived from the Pécs division of the Hungarian Young Communist League, claiming that they had reserved a room for that night. Of course, no one had ever confirmed their reservation, but they showed up anyway! With an arrogance that was simply astonishing they managed to get accommodation in the Royal, which only opened the following day."[52]

In the 1960s, after Gellért, the Royal was considered the most exclusive hotel in both Budapest and Hungary. Malév, the Hungarian airline, opened its office on the first floor of the building.[53] The Royal had a first- and a second-class restaurant, where both deviled eggs and caviar were served on silver trays, but half portions of tripe and pork lung stew could also be ordered, and guests could reserve seats in the palm garden for tea. There was a bar with booths, and the hotel had its own confectionery as well as a movie theater. In the evenings, there was even a nightclub.[54]

The idyllic atmosphere of the Royal was disrupted by an unexpected event in 1963. Two employees held their wedding reception at the hotel, and the following day the newlywed wife had a strange rash all over her body. The physician feared it might be smallpox. The apparatus of the totalitarian regime immediately leaped into action. The authorities instantly closed the hotel; guests and employees were to remain inside the building. Employees who were not on the hotel premises were assembled and transported to the quarantine hospital.[55] State security officers secured the neighborhood. The rash soon disappeared from the woman's body, and the doctor turned out to have misdiagnosed her malady.[56] Many people thought that the hotel had been closed as part of a planned state security operation. At the time, politics permeated all aspects of life, and the average citizen was unlikely to believe that in a closed world in the middle of Budapest, tourists from the West were living a life of luxury. From the sidewalks, prying passersby tried to figure out what was going on inside.

One of the employees at the Royal at the time was a man named Tibor Vadnai. He received a phone call at home about the quarantine, and he was instructed to report to the hotel immediately: "I packed some essentials, my guitar and a bottle of whiskey, and I joined the others. . . . Initially, nobody knew whether it was serious or not. Everybody responded according to their individual temperaments; some thought they had only three weeks to live, and they went from room to room behaving like people who believed the end was near. I did not sense any panic, we thought it was a great party, the only unpleasant thing was that we were vaccinated against variola."[57] György Kalmár-Maron, who, as the Royal's doorkeeper, knew everything about what was going on, had similar recollections: "At night, the women shagged in the rooms, since the staff and the guests were all locked up together."[58]

It took three weeks for the quarantine to be lifted, during which eight hundred guests, including many tourists, were stranded in the hotel. Meanwhile, life went on in the marble-covered halls, as it once had on the sinking *Titanic*. Two bands were continuously playing music. Staff members were able to immerse themselves in the world of seemingly unattainable sumptuousness that the regime had created for Western tourists. Nine months after the quarantine, several Hotel Royal staff members gave birth.[59] The movie *Meztelen diplomata* (The naked diplomat) was shot that year (1963). It was based on *Vesztegzár a Grand Hotelben* (*Quarantine in the Grand Hotel*, available in English translation by István Farkas), a novel by Jenő Rejtő. Rejtő was a journalist, playwright, and pulp-fiction author who was put in a forced labor unit in the Second World War because of his Jewish origins and died of typhus on the Eastern Front. (One of Rejtő's comic novels is about a surprisingly similar incident. Guests at the Java Grand Hotel are placed under quarantine after one resident is determined to have contracted the plague.) Allegedly, some of the film's scenes were shot in the Hotel Royal; regardless of whether that is true, the setting did indeed evoke the interior design of the Hungarian Grand Hotel.

Béke (Peace) Hotel was a similarly elegant establishment not far from Hotel Royal. In Béke's sweetshop, coffee was brewed in a Zsolnay porcelain brewer (Zsolnay porcelain was and is world-famous for its elegance and quality), and the guests were seated at tables covered with lace tablecloths. The hotel also had a night bar, a first-class restaurant, a bar, a wine cellar, and a hunters' hall. The domed hall was famous for its roof, which opened at the press of a button, and guests could enjoy clear summer evenings under the moon and stars. As Tibor Meskál, an expert in the hospitality industry, recalls, as was the case in other places, "uniforms were not uncommon in Béke, since wearing them was compulsory and even fashionable at the time."[60]

Developments and investments in luxury increasingly began to address the demands of Western tourists who paid in foreign currency. Gradually, the traditions and lifestyles of party leaders and Western tourists became indistinguishable. Members of the ruling elite also desired the best of everything, and the two very different groups of people frequented the same places. A member of the Executive Committee of the Budapest City Council, who on weekends took his family for lunch to the Citadella (an elegant restaurant on Gellért Hill in Buda), complained at a meeting of the council that he had been required to pay the two-forint entrance fee, although he took no interest in the view.[61] The account given by minister of the interior János Pap suggests that members of the elite were becoming less cautious about appearing in public, and they saw little incongruity in the fact that, as representatives of the working-class state, they were enamored of luxury. In 1987, Pap commented on his "everyday" habits:

> I believed then and still believe today that a state leader, in fact, especially a state leader ([!] lives a life in which it is not a sin if he drinks a beer in a bar or a coffee in a confectionary in the afternoon. Or if, on Sunday, he invites his wife to have lunch in Fortuna, saying we always loved that place, it was a classy spot, or let's go to Margaret Island, to the Grand Hotel. So you made a phone call, reserved a table, got in the car, had the driver drop you off there, had a great meal you could easily afford, and had fun. We took advantage of these opportunities, and some were displeased. And somehow it became a trend. I do not know how many of today's state leaders would go once a week to Hotel Duna, Fórum, or Hilton and have dinner there with their wives, but for my part I can't think of a single one.[62]

The first new hotel was Hotel Budapest, located on Szilágyi Erzsébet Avenue. It was built in 1967 specifically to serve Western tourists. From 1967 to 1969, the Duna Intercontinental was constructed on the Pest bank of the Danube River. The hotel was based on designs by József Finta, who appeared like a blazing star on the Budapest architectural scene and left a permanent mark on the cityscape. With the Duna, Intercontinental became the first international chain to enter the Hungarian market.

Characteristic of the gradual abandonment of even the illusion of social equality by the regime, the authorities approved the plans of the building despite the fact that it was utterly monumental in scale in comparison with the buildings that surrounded it, and thus it created a stark contrast. A building that dominated the entire cityscape was erected for the Western world in the middle of Budapest, on the Duna promenade, even though in the Hungarian capital—unlike the capitals of other Eastern and Central European countries—no new edifices had been constructed to stand symbolically for the socialist regime.[63] The second of the new line of hotels, the Fórum, today known as the Intercontinental, was completed in 1981, financed with loans from Austria. The new hotels were symbolic spaces. The elite created a transition between the prewar and postwar worlds, but perhaps more importantly, by supporting the growth of the hospitality industry in the pursuit of their own interests, they also opened up toward the West.

On August 19, 1968, after three years of negotiations, HungarHotels signed a contract for the construction of the Budapest Hilton.[64] According to urban legend, János Kádár himself decided that the Hilton would be built in the Buda Castle district when he was watching fireworks from the balcony of the newly completed Duna Intercontinental. He supposedly was taken by the panoramic scene and the view of the floodlit Buda Castle. At the time, the ruins of the tower of the Saint Nicholas Church of the Dominican Order and the Louis XVI–style building of the old Ministry of Finance stood on the property that had been selected for the construction of the hotel.[65] Since the archeological excavations of the site took five years, experts in architecture had plenty of time for a public discussion of the proposed design of the building.[66] Opinions differed as to whether the modern structure would harmonize with the historical monuments in the area, and the debate continued long after the hotel was completed.[67]

In addition to the stylistic features of the building, the question of interior design posed further problems for architects and developers. Although work was supervised by a special interior designer and applied and fine arts teams, furniture manufacturing in Hungary could not meet the requirements set by the American hotel chain, and Hungarian companies lacked well-established export networks. Therefore, each piece was designed individually, and the furniture was imported from Czechoslovakia and Austria. These measures were met with serious criticism. Modern furniture of various designs stood in astounding contrast to the historicist interior.[68] Debates surrounding the Hilton's design and interior had political overtones, too, since all the design features that were adopted (a combination of the traditional and the modern, the historicist on the one hand and seemingly Westernized kitsch on the other) were in stark contrast with everything socialist architecture was supposed to represent.

The fact that representatives of the workers' state, which was eager to bring in hard currency, were making concerted efforts to attract elegant Western hotel chains was not without political overtones. The fact that these representatives themselves had no aversion to luxury also drew attention to the contradictions between ideology and practice. For example, in an article published in *Új Tükör* (New mirror), journalist Árpád Pünkösti examined whether a blue-collar worker would be allowed to enter the Hilton. The report was prompted by news that carpenters Géza Hungler and György Hermann had been denied entry. According to the official explanation, the two workmen, who had made a few of the pieces of furniture, wanted to take a look around before the official opening. But the manager of the hotel ensured Pünkösti, "Regardless of occupation, anyone is allowed to order goose liver, frog legs, or, if they wish, they may even book the presidential suite."[69] The article reveals that Hungler and Hermann were not simple carpenters; rather, they worked for a company that manufactured exclusive furniture. For example, they had replaced the wooden wall panels in the parliament office of Pál Losonczi, chairman of the Hungarian Presidential Council. They would gaze on the hotel from the balcony of Losonczi's office and enjoy the panoramic view of Buda. But even seasoned visitors were appalled by the prices in the Trubadur bar and the Tower restaurant.[70]

The Buda Hilton opened on December 31, 1976, with a New Year's Eve dance. Notwithstanding the debates concerning the design of the hotel and its ideological and architectural incongruity with its setting, the Hilton soon became a popular tourist attraction and theme for photographers. Contemporary postcards showed images of the building with the recognizable auburn glass panels reflecting the lines of the neo-gothic Fisherman's Bastion in the citadel. The bastion, built in 1895, resembled an old sepia-colored photograph in the windows of the Hilton. The hotel came to symbolize the wealth and prosperity of the socialist era. In the 1970s, it was considered the most exclusive establishment in Hungary. The renowned Hotel Royal responded to the challenge by opening a new restaurant, Ízek utcája (Street of flavors), in 1976. The restaurant had a show kitchen intended to lure guests, which included hamburger, the symbol of popular culture.[71] Hotels gradually became the sphere of everything allegedly forbidden by the ideology on which the regime was founded.

In Hungary, exclusive hotels also served as sites for prostitution. In the 1950s, prostitutes were deemed a public danger as people who avoided taking normal jobs.[72] Beginning in 1955, "lechery" was punished as a crime, and sometimes it was considered a breach of the peace. Women who had obtained licenses to work as "women of pleasure" were put in various institutions, where they were "reeducated." They were usually reassigned (as it were) to certain occupations. Reflecting on the 1970s,[73] a Hungarian writer remarks with a slightly malicious tone, "If the woman driving the Pobjeda taxi was elderly, you could take it for granted that she had been assigned to a driving course when the brothels had been broken up."[74] In 1961, these offenses were entered into the criminal code. Socialism, however, hardly managed to put an end to prostitution over the long decades of its reign. Indeed, it grew more tolerant of the practice. The black book of complaints at the Hotel Royal, for example, contains a 1962 entry by a New York tourist who complains that the authorities did not allow him to have a guest to his room. The guest happened to be (to quote the complaint) "a lady friend."[75] László Somogyi was the manager of the Royal's nightclub in the 1960s. He kept careful watch to ensure that the prostitutes observed the unwritten codes of night life:

> I had a talk with these women. The essential condition was that if there were no guests, they would order at least a coffee or a soda, and if they came with a customer, both of them would order something. They were not allowed to be loud, to shout at other tables, or to pick fights, and if anyone broke these rules, they were banned from the bar for a week. There were, maybe, two women who were permanently banned from the premises. The doorkeeper was given instructions as to who to let in and who to keep out. We didn't let anyone in from off the streets whom we didn't know. There was another rule: if a woman left with a guest on business, she was not allowed to come back the same day.[76]

In 1977, in response to an interview question, the service manager of the Hilton revealed a small secret about the hotel's business policy: "We keep a close eye on the high standard set by the hotel, and we ask the young women looking for foreigners to leave, but we turn a blind eye to the presence of two or three escort women who know how to behave."[77]

Beginning in the 1960s, the state security had planned to monitor foreign visitors, and through them the Western world in general, with the assistance of socialist Mata Hari. As early as 1967, intelligence proposed the establishment of a hotel equipped with bugs and hidden surveillance cameras. Eventually, they decided on a "simple, smaller, friendly, Italian-style bar," and thus an establishment named Sole Mio was opened in an elegant neighborhood of Buda.[78] Prostitutes were also employed at Sole Mio. The agent who went by the alias "Balikó Mária" and officially worked as a bartender had earlier been given an operational mission in 1967 in Esztergom, where she had been assigned the task of seducing members of the clergy—a task in which, to the extent that the sources can be trusted, she was unsuccessful.[79] In 1989, the intelligence agent under the cover name "Koh-i-noor" planned to open a massage parlor in Solymár using foreign capital investment and assistance. Business partners from West Germany were going to "import" fifteen Thai women as well. According to the Ministry of Internal Affairs report, a member of the Hungarian government, a council leader, and an executive also joined the enterprise, which promised significant profits, but ultimately the business plans fell through.[80]

Of course, information on prostitution under socialism is fragmentary at best. The bulk of it is found in the internal affairs reports. Few accounts can be considered authentic or descriptions based on actual experience. The memoir literature, however, contains a number of courtesan stories, and one story is arguably emblematic of the era. In her autobiography *Vörös alkony* (Red dusk), Éva D. Kardos, Mátyás Rákosi's niece, gives an account of her life beginning with her time as a member of Sándor Nógrádi's partisan unit and going all the way to the 1970s and 1980s, when she joined the world of hotel prostitutes. Kardos met István Dékán, her future husband, during the Second World War in a partisan group. First, she served in Ukraine as a partisan radio operator and then as a nurse. Later, she came into Hungary through Slovakia as a member of Nógrádi's group.[81] After the war, because of her family connection to the party, Kardos was given classified and confidential tasks. She worked as a secretarial assistant to Gábor Péter, the head of the state security forces and the leader of radio wiretapping. Her husband became a state security officer and was appointed to serve as the head of counterintelligence in 1950.

Dékán's fate is characteristic of the era: He was dismissed, then called on to return, and immediately promoted to major general and the position of assistant minister of the interior. He was discharged again on October 22, 1956, the eve of the revolution. He later became a school principal and, equally importantly, a devoted hunter and the author of several books on hunting. He died on his fifty-sixth birthday in Moscow in 1975. He had traveled to the Soviet capital to commemorate the thirtieth anniversary of the end of the Second World War, and he was found dead in his hotel room. The memoir, most of the biographic details of which can be checked (with the exception of the details concerning prostitution), contains one numerological oddity. The number fifty-six, the year that shattered the world of the cadres, pops up repeatedly in the story.

The widowed Kardos turned to the world of bars. In her memoir, she recounts her first move: "Loneliness and solitude pushed me out into the streets. I was fifty-six years old, and I was again at a point at which I had been so many times before, where I did not know what to do."[82] She walked into the bar of the hotel across from her apartment and was about to leave when "a tall, intelligent-looking man, with glasses and only one arm came down the stairs. He looked at me and said in utter candor, 'Come with me. You'll get 150 marks. Will that do?'"[83] One hundred fifty West German marks was the equivalent of eight thousand forints—one month's salary. The one-armed man took Kardos to another hotel, where he paid two thousand forints at the reception desk in exchange for the staff turning a blind eye to the fact that he was violating the law and taking a prostitute up to his room. When Kardos left, she had to pay two hundred forints to the bellhop for his discretion.[84] Little by little, Kardos learned the rules of nightlife. Her new friends advised her to learn both German and English, since "it wasn't too helpful in this profession that I only spoke Russian."⁸⁵ The bar in the Hotel Royal was her primary haunt, but she occasionally did business in the Átrium, the Gellért, and Hotel Béke.⁸⁶ Allegedly, the police were aware of her history with the Ministry of Internal Affairs, and they left her alone, because they suspected she was dealing with important connections and pursuing high-level missions, though by that time she was working only for herself.

CLOTHING AND BUDAPEST FASHIONS

"How was an imperialist spy spotted at first sight, arrested, and thwarted? He was not wearing a loden coat and did not start the paper with the sports section." This joke circulated in the streets of Budapest in the 1950s. The Pest humor also created a "female" version of this bon mot, highly critical of public morals: "How was a female imperialist spy spotted at first sight, arrested, and thwarted in Budapest?" one pedestrian wearing a loden coat asked another passerby in the street. If there was no reply, he immediately replied: "She was not wearing a loden coat, and she was not pregnant."

Public imagination came to associate the decade with the gray (or green) loden coat. This bygone era is also generally depicted in history books as gray and blandly dull in its homogeneity, despite the fact that former traditions inevitably persisted in post–Second World War Hungarian society, and every social layer, including the elite, had to adapt to the habits and tastes of earlier generations. Although nothing seemed to threaten the hegemony (or monotony) of the loden coat, differences of shade, tone, and colors nonetheless survived under the surface.⁸⁷

In this social milieu, the role of the elite in the establishment of trends to be followed and the ways in which the elite blazed new trails in the survival and revival of old traditions were of particular importance. Initially, the material culture of the nomenclature explicitly had drawn on the traditions of the prewar middle class and elite; indeed, it had practically relied on this heritage and these values.[88] As is well known, when a member of the ruling elite fell out of favor, the state security forces immediately bore down on him. His villa and all his personal belongings were confiscated, and the state security compiled a detailed inventory of the items confiscated. Unfortunately, despite the mandatory meticulousness, these inventories testify to the ignorance of the agents who drew them up with regard to furniture and clothing. Usually, the lists merely indicate the quantity and, occasionally, the colors of the coats, suits, shirts, pants, underwear, and socks that were confiscated. Only when an item, such as lace, silk, or women's undergarments, attracted attention would a more detailed description be given. Along with items of clothing, expensive and out-of-stock fabrics were sometimes confiscated, which indicates that several people had their clothes tailor-made using fabrics they had obtained or sequestered for themselves (since ready-to-wear clothes apparently did not meet their expectations, and tailors and saloons did not have valuable fabrics readily available). In the apartment of a state security department head, for example, the wife's wardrobe contained several slips: three knitted, twelve silk, two satin, and one lace. In addition, she had forty-eight new and two used nylon stockings, four silk stockings, and one pair of lace stockings, altogether forty-seven slips (twenty-three of which were made of silk). The husband's wardrobe contained six pairs of shorts and eight Swiss and three artificial silk, eleven short, and six long pairs of underpants with embroidered initials. They were all confiscated. The goods saved for tailoring included white silk, white raw silk, printed silk, pink silk, and striped silk.[89]

As this example aptly illustrates, lace lingerie and silk stockings, sometimes covered by sober factory-tailored clothes, were very popular in the Kádár era. The fact that Gábor Péter used money from the budget for the secret police to buy lace suitable for lingerie for his girlfriend offers a further example of the popularity of the clothing and the delicate materials out of which it was made, not to mention the casual corruption of the time.[90] Socialism by no means managed to do away with traditional preferences or Western fashions. It merely confined them, temporarily, to a narrower space. There were, after all, only limited opportunities under the socialist regime to follow Western fashions by donning clothing that differed from the garb worn by the rest of one's social group yet was not overly conspicuous or striking—for instance, delicate undergarments or well-tailored dresses and garments that were made of more expensive fabrics.

Clothing has always conveyed messages about one's social place and attitudes.[91] The elite of the socialist era in Hungary were able to use dress to express their places of privilege.[92] The available sources reveal relatively little about the clothing worn by the people in the highest echelons of the party leadership. There are only a few sources, which came into being in the wake of some "unusual event," that offer detailed descriptions of their garments and their customs with regard to dress. These sources suggest that members of the elite, too, strove to meet the obligations that arose in the course of official events and the expectations that were placed on them because of their positions. One such source is the long list that was drawn up by Zsuzsanna Hegedüs, András Hegedüs's wife, of all the belongings they left behind in their villa when the family had to flee in 1956.

What kinds of items did the couple have in their wardrobe, and what did they take with them when they fled? According to the list, in addition to two suits that were essentially out of use, Hegedüs owned seven other suits: one light-colored Burberry suit, one light-colored wool suit, one coffee-colored suit, one black wool suit, one dark-blue striped suit, one medium-blue striped suit, and one brown suit with two pairs of pants. He also had an entire army captain's outfit, with all the necessary accoutrements for winter and summer and for ceremonies. And he had two hunting suits. Zsuzsanna Hegedüs only listed items from her wardrobe that she did not want to part with or to have to replace, including a few unusual items, such as a beige tropical worsted coat and skirt, a matelassé gown, and a long, medium-blue beadwork evening dress. Like her husband, she also had a green loden coat.[93] In her book, Éva D. Kardos shares her recollections of the ways the wives of cadre members were expected to dress: "They sewed my evening dresses in Váci Street, because there was always one reception after the other. I hated the receptions, but it was still gratifying to have them gaze in awe on my dresses, and I just hovered next to Stevie [István Dékán, the head of Hungarian intelligence], who sometimes wore his uniform, which was adorned with medals."[94]

Given its social prominence (not its actual role), the elite always constitutes something of an example to be followed in terms of customs, habits, and fashions. However, in the 1950s, the nationalized clothing industry was not able to meet the demands of the elite or, for that matter, other social groups. The clothing industry struggled with all the problems and difficulties that other industries faced. Poor labor organization and the decoupling of supply and demand left their mark on the products. After the state nationalized private industry, the factories where quality products, such as suits and women's coat-and-skirt ensembles, had been made were filled with tradesmen who brought their workers with them too. Initially, they continued, in their work at the socialist companies, to use small-scale industry approaches and methods, and they were only gradually compelled to shift over to large-scale factory production. The system nonetheless failed, however, to maintain the standard of quality that had prevailed earlier. When the state tried to gain a foothold in Western markets with the clothing produced by the ready-to-wear industry in Hungary, the foray was an ignominious failure.[95]

It is not difficult to understand why Western products remained popular in Hungary in the 1950s and indeed grew increasingly popular precisely because they were difficult or impossible to obtain for the vast majority of people. In 1948—that is, in the earliest stages of the new system—*Szabad Nép* ran the following advertisement for a skin cream made in the United States:

> Back to the stirring spoon, the leaders in their brown and black shirts [referring to the uniforms worn by the Schutzstaffel, or SS] proclaimed the slogan. They tried to push women into the background in every sphere of life. In contrast with this retrograde effort, democratic society gives women the equal right to success, in every domain of society and private life. Women, however, are women, and whatever first-rate intellectual qualities she may have, a good appearance is always to her advantage. For success, a flawless appearance is a big advantage, and the most important prerequisite of a flawless appearance is a clean complexion. PARCOL-American Skinfood's superb nutritive cream has an unparalleled effect on a woman's complexion, and it can be purchased in any specialist's shop for 10.90.[96]

Quality declined, as did the selection of items available in stores, and yet many people nonetheless found ways to get their hands on the clothing and materials they yearned for. One of the ways of doing this was to bring clothes and fabrics from the West, or to have them brought by someone else. According to Sándor Sebes, the head of the Economic Division of the Hungarian Communist Party and then the Hungarian Workers' Party, initially he loaned party money to a businessman who promised to bring enough high-quality fabrics from Italy to Hungary to provide every member of the apparatus with enough to make one full suit and every member of the Political Committee with enough for two.[97] In 1968, György Péter, the chairman of the Central Statistical Office and one of the theoreticians of the economic reforms, was accused of having sold silversmith works and coins in Vienna and of having brought smuggled nylon stockings and stolas back to Hungary. He was later arrested and driven to commit suicide or perhaps murdered.[98] According to the accusations that were brought against him, he had taken advantage of his frequent trips abroad, and he had used his diplomatic passport and his service car with its A license plate.⁹⁹ He was also accused of having purchased a "fashionable nylon underskirt and 1 kilogram of purple woolen yarn" in the West as a gift. Today, it is difficult to determine whether there was any truth to the accusations that were brought against Péter as part of a state security conspiracy to bring him down, but his case offers an illustration of the buying habits of the nomenclature and the opportunities they had to obtain items that were otherwise almost entirely out of reach.¹⁰⁰

The members of the ruling elite were not the only people to engage in these kinds of dealings. The clients of the party leadership did so as well. Soccer players brought cars to Hungary and traded in car parts. Japanese kerchiefs and shawls, nylon stockings, cotton yarn and thread, and silks were in high demand in Hungary, so in the course of their trips abroad, the players purchased these items in large quantities. These dealings were actually socially legitimized acts, since the system could only mitigate and manage the crises that arose in Hungary because of the economy of dearth by adopting or at least turning a blind eye to illegal activities.¹⁰¹

In the 1950s, fashion in Hungary and Budapest was set by two salons in Váci Street, as indeed had been the case a century earlier: Clara Salon (Specialty Women's Clothing Salon) and Budapest Fashion Salon (the Fashion Salon of the Capital Council of Made-to-Measure Tailors). The wives of party and state leaders purchased their clothing at these two establishments. Klára Rotschild, the manager of the Clara Salon, paid close attention to fashion trends in Paris and brought them to Budapest. Her rival, Mrs. Ferenc Arató, preferred a more conservative, English style. She made a soberer elegance fashionable among the elite circles.¹⁰² Rotschild had learned her trade at her father's side during the Horthy era. In 1934, she opened an independent shop, and after the shop was nationalized, she continued to manage it as the artistic director. The system, however, was not willing to overlook entirely her bourgeois past. Her name was on the registry of "politically compromised individuals" kept by the Budapest police. She was considered a "class enemy" who "had ties to suspicious people as an informant."[103] The intelligence agency kept a close eye on Rotschild. The officers wanted to know with whom, among the salon staff, the foreign journalists, the press photographers, and the diplomats, she maintained secret relationships.[104] The clothing she designed, however, had to satisfy the demands of the members of the highest circles—that is, the ruling elite—so Rotschild paid close attention to fashion trends in the West, and she was able to travel abroad whenever she wanted.[105] She also organized fashion shows that were held in Gundel and in the Officers' Club of the People's Army.[106]

In Paris, Rotschild did not simply hit the streets, examine the shop display windows, and memorize the trends in French fashion, as the rumors or legends about her all suggest. She also had a network of relationships. Margit Halász (Mme Achmed Tulgay) was married to a Turkish diplomat, and Erzsébet Wessely ran an elegant milliner's shop in Paris (Wessely was a minority shareholder). Rotschild regularly met with them when she was in Paris, and they gave her the newest fashion designs.[107] In the August 1957 issue of *Ez a Divat* (This is fashion), the fashion magazine of the time, Rotschild offers the following enthusiastic account of her two-week trip to Paris: "Lace and fur, the two classic fashion items, have again been given the place they deserve. The muslin is in fashion, and in the evening, the brocade."[108] Rotschild was not only attentive to trends in fashion in Paris, she also thought it important to maintain customs and fashions from the prewar period. Her employees were compelled to meet strict requirements to ensure that the salon and the esteemed Rotschild name lost none of their prestige. For instance, even in the 1970s, her models were required to wear corsets.[109]

Initially, socialist haute couture meant that the elite and the social strata that imitated and followed the styles of the elite adopted fashions from the West. Designs were based on Western models, or least on models that were seen from behind the Iron Curtain as Western. Since it kept its attentive eye on trends in Paris, the elite constituted a model for the rest of society in terms of dress. However, the retrograde leaders of the new system, who had conservative tastes in every field of life, were not able to dictate fashion entirely. Even from this perspective, the elite was unable to rule over Hungarian society. Indeed, when it came to the creation of various fashions and styles, other, often marginal social groups and subcultures played considerably larger roles.[110] It was, of course, in the interests of the regime to leave the individual a degree of freedom for expression in everyday life, and in the symbolic spaces of consumption, everyone could find their bearings according to their means and tastes. In 1967, Kádár himself expressed his opinion on the new fashions at the Hungarian Young Communist League Congress. If perhaps with some disapprobation, he nonetheless spoke with a tone of concession: "I do not wish to concern myself with the pants and beards and hairstyles from the wild west.... What is important here is that the party and the youth alliance is not a fashion company or a hairdressing trade cooperative, and they need not deal with this sort of thing."[111]

As the examples given above show, the fashions of the 1950s and 1960s in Hungary were by no means gray or lacking in variation, all appearances to the contrary. The increasingly diverse selections in stores, furthermore, only made these differences more varied and vivid. Beginning in the 1960s, the leaders of the regime established a hierarchy among the stores that regulated and monitored supplies according to consumer habits.[112] They strove ever more doggedly to ensure that the revived network of businesses would be able to satisfy the demand for luxury items.[113] Fashion took on a new life as a profession. "Comrade Zamushkin," the director of the Tretyakov Gallery in Moscow, who in the 1950s visited the College of Applied Arts in

Budapest, complained that "the vast majority of the clothes in the [college] sketches were made for young, slender, urban women." He noted, almost as an admonition, that in the Soviet Union the peasants on the kolkhozes wore exactly the same clothing as the workers in the city. The college's curriculum and disciplinary regulations emphasized that "the decadent and formalist art of the West serves the interests of the imperialists and the warmongers." But they did so in vain, for the fashion magazines from Paris and London made it across the sealed border anyway.

In the 1950s and 1960s, op art and maxi dresses became increasingly popular and trendy, and cocktail dresses and pantsuits were all the rage. The fashion designers who completed their studies at the college were later employed by the Hungarian Fashion Studio, which was created in 1958. The studio was founded by the minister of cultural affairs with the explicit goal of shaping public tastes. The slogan was "fashion for the working woman," but most of the clothing that was made as part of the series consisted of ten to fifteen items that were purchased by actors and women working in radio and television.[114]

Beginning in 1954, alongside the state department stores that sold ready-to-wear clothing, the clothing stores of Budapest, and the Röltex network, a series of businesses opened that sold delicate ready-to-wear clothes and items of clothing that were made only in small quantities. In the summer of 1955, the so-called Model House opened in the heart of Pest, on Liberation Square (which earlier had been Ferenciek tere, or Franciscans' Square, and now again goes by its old name). In the 1960s, two of the most important moments in the rising importance of fashion were the introduction of the "Queen of Spades" collection, which entered the marketplace via the Clothing Store Company, and the opening of a store targeting people in their twenties, which demonstrated that members of the younger generation were following new Western trends and styles.[115] Beginning in the 1960s, department stores that specialized in select items began to pop up in

Budapest. For instance, in November 1963 the Luxus (Luxury) department store opened its doors on Vörösmarty Square, in the heart of Pest. For the people who came to the capital from other parts of Hungary, the department stores such as Verseny and Corvin on Rákóczi Avenue, a large artery in the center of Pest, were the fanciest places to shop. Initially, in the county seats the Centrum department stores represented high quality. In 1976, the Skála Budapest Grand department store opened its doors in Budapest, and a few years later the Skála Metro department store opened on Marx Square (today Nyugati Square, in front of the Western Train Station). At the time, they constituted modern, consumer-oriented shopping centers.[116]

In the 1970s, boutiques began to spring up. The National Association of Small Tradesmen (Országos Kisiparosok Szövetsége, or OKISZ; today Magyar Iparszövetség, or Hungarian Industrial Association) opened a boutique in the Budapest Hotel named Belle Boutique and then Beauty Boutique (using the English word *beauty* and not its Hungarian equivalent) in the Duna Intercontinental. The Módi boutique chain also offered prospective customers an array of elegant items of clothing.[117] In October 1982, Pierre Cardin reached an agreement with the Hungarian state concerning the production and sale of its products in Hungary. In 1983, the first boutique that sold brand-name products from abroad opened at 8 Tanács Boulevard (today Károly Boulevard). In 1986, a Benetton store opened in the Skála Metro department store. Stores that sold only select luxury items of clothing, such as the S-Modell chain, also planted their feet in the capital. The S-Modell Studio of the Applied Arts Company was the high-end state-owned fashion design enterprise in Hungary at the time.[118] Consumer habits under socialism were also reflective of social relations and social stratification, and they made social differences increasingly visible. Abandoning dissemblance, many people left their loden coats at home in the closet.

The practices and customs that were developed and adopted by the various social groups naturally exerted an influence on the habits of the elite as well. As soon as a new fashion trend became widespread, people in positions of power began to look for new styles to give expression to their exceptional places of privilege. In the 1950s and 1960s in Hungary, the elite and the groups that were close to the elite opened the gates to the West. With the spread of Western fashions, however, the dress habits of the elite actually become more staid and conservative, and they turned back toward more traditional models. They were thus able to give expression to their privileged status, and the fashion experts who surrounded them, such as Klára Rotschild, used old styles and patterns to form their tastes. The wives of state and government leaders were almost the only people who shopped in the Clara Salon.

Rumor had it in Pest (and in the 1980s, newspaper articles also made the claim) that Jovanka Tito, the wife of Josip Broz Tito, the leader of communist Yugoslavia, sent a bust of herself carved out of marble by famous Croatian sculptor and architect Ivan Meštrović to Rotschild. When Jovanka did not have time to try on clothes, the bust could be used to tailor the pleats and folds.[119] This was merely one of the many rumors that circulated about the habits of the socialist leaders, but Jovanka Tito was in fact a regular patron of the Clara Salon, where indeed there was a mannequin that had been made to correspond to her measurements. Sometimes Rotschild would travel to Belgrade for the final fitting. Mária Tamáska Kádár offers the following recollection: "I was not a good customer for them, because when I did occasionally drop in, I brought not only the material but even the lining with me. Jovanka, she was a good buyer, because she would order several dresses at once."[120]

Another episode that is perhaps characteristic of the role of clothing as a symbol of social status took place on November 14, 1970, when Nada Budisavljević went to Klára Rotschild's salon with Jovanka Tito, with whom she was friends, to have clothes made for Jovanka. They parked their Citroën in front of the Astoria Hotel, reserved a room, and had dinner in the hotel restaurant. In the meantime, their car was broken into and their suitcases were stolen. Along with the suitcases, the valuable items of clothing and fabrics that they had intended to take to Rotschild's salon (including a black Persian turban and a mink stole) were also stolen (in all likelihood, they had belonged to Jovanka). The wife of the man who was imprisoned for the crime later submitted a plea for clemency on behalf of her husband.[121] She offered an account of how she and her husband had tried to dig their way out of poverty. As the woman explained in her plea, one evening, her husband, who had completed his studies at the Marxist university, had said in despair, "You don't have to feel sorry for the stinking bourgeois, it's not a crime to take a bit from them." At the time, she did not realize who the aggrieved party was.[122]

RESPECT FOR TRADITION, PROTOCOL, AND ETIQUETTE

Klára Rotschild was unflappable in her devotion to tradition, and she represented and strove to popularize Parisian fashions as both a profession and a calling. Yet her efforts, to some extent, were in vain, because it took time for the new elite to familiarize itself with and adopt the old customs and learn the unwritten rules of diplomatic conduct. There were innumerable anecdotes about gauche functionaries who stood out at social events because of their awkwardness, their poorly tailored clothes, and their out-of-place neckties. Archival sources mention suits worn by functionaries that were too big and diplomats who were less than elegant in both their dress and conduct. For instance, in a letter written in 1949 to the Ministry of Foreign Affairs, Károly Ráth, the Hungarian ambassador to Greece, observed,

> In the eyes of our center, evening wear, a tuxedo, and a dinner jacket, which in capitalist countries are indispensable items of

clothing and are often necessary, are accoutrements which can simply be borrowed. This is one of the reasons why the representatives of our people's democracy often make appearances wearing these items of clothing, but absurdly tailored and sized, at official ceremonies, since they borrow them from one another or from places that rent out fancy dress. When I presented my credentials, the three of us were wearing formal attire of the most varied cuts and eras, and this can hardly have helped boost the esteem in which our country is held. The top hat worn by one of the other two was so small that he could not put it on his head, and his formal wear must have been made no less than 40 years ago, and you could have fit two of him in it.[123]

The representatives of the new state proved able to learn, however, and they strove to master the subtle rules and ruses of diplomacy. In his memoir, Endre Sík, who served for a time as minister of foreign affairs,[124] writes about how, when he arrived in Washington, DC, in 1948 as a diplomat, one of the first things he did was to furnish the Hungarian embassy appropriately. He reacquired items that the United States had confiscated from the embassy of the Habsburg monarchy when it had entered the First World War, including antique furniture, Persian rugs, and expensive curtains. Sík made the following remark concerning his first step as a diplomat: "A few weeks later, the English diplomats who had come to the embassy expressed their amazement at seeing what wonderful antique furniture we have."[125] He expressed similar satisfaction at having seen that the British ambassador had been very impressed by his evening wear, which he had had made by a tailor in Budapest. This also won him the ambassador's sympathies, which, at least according to his recollections, he managed to keep even over the course of the diplomatic wrangling that was taking place because of the Mindszenty affair (József Mindszenty, the archbishop of Esztergom and head of the Hungarian Catholic Church, had been arrested and defamed).[126]

When the Soviet occupying (or liberating) forces pushed the last German soldiers from the territory of Hungary in 1945, the temporary national assembly moved from Debrecen in the east to Budapest. The mood at the protocol receptions that were held in the parliament after the move was characterized by an unusual familiarity and even intimacy. The representatives and the guests, after listening to the obligatory welcoming speeches, "dispersed in the corridors of the building, the Hunting Room, the Gobelin Room, the salons of the chambers, the vaulted hall under the cupola, and everywhere they began to eat and drink."[127] According to Gyula Kállai, a communist politician, as spirits began to rise, some of the people began to sing. In general, the communists sang marching songs associated with the workers' movement, while the representatives of the self-styled peasant parties sang folk songs. In other words, songs such as "Harcban nem lehet megállni" (We cannot stop in the fight), whose lyrics are typical of the international communist movement (with references to "comrades" and the "new order"), were sung alongside songs such as "Megismerni a kanászt fürge járásárul" (You can recognize the swineherd by his nimble gait), a Hungarian folk song with a distinctive pentatonic melody characteristic of some of the oldest layers of Hungarian folk music.[128] In the short-lived era of multiparty coalition between 1945 and 1948 (when the communists completely consolidated their exclusive hold on power), "the leaders of the parties joined one group or another, at least for the duration of a song or two." Kállai also notes, with a slightly malicious tone, "The statues of our great kings, Stephen, Ladislaus, Louis I, Matthias looked down on us in amazement from the gallery of the vaulted hall."[129]

The new politicians soon adopted the style and manners of the old guard. For instance, in 1951, minister of agriculture Ferenc Erdei—who had a background in the social sciences and, perhaps not incidentally, a working-class mentality—offered a Lipizzaner stallion as a gift to Soviet general Semyon Mikhailovich Budyonny. Quite satisfied with his gesture, Erdei then informed Rákosi that Budyonny had thanked him for the present and sent his greetings to the government of the Hungarian People's Republic.[130] Several prominent politicians set an example with their behavior that, it was hoped, would be followed among the elite circles. In 1961, Sík, who had once been a Piarist novitiate, allegedly said the following when he passed the baton on to János Péter, himself a former Calvinist bishop, at the head of the Ministry of Foreign Affairs: "What I have begun, not ingloriously, continue, my friend, in glory."[131] After the change of regimes, former communist politician and diplomat Mátyás Szűrös shared his recollections of Péter: "His mere appearance radiated prestige. He was a tall man, like a full-grown tree, and he always wore a black suit. He had preserved his look, his good posture, and his elegant dark clothes from his time as a bishop."[132] Szűrös offered the following anecdote to give a shade of nuance to his portrait of the stern personality of the former bishop, who had converted and become a supporter of the people's republic: "János Péter knew that [Lothar] Bolz [the East German minister of foreign affairs] was an art collector, and for some anniversary he gave him a wild cattle head that had to be put in an enormous box. What I am trying to suggest is that he had a sense of humor too.... He also showed his sense of humor in company from time to time."[133]

The new system placed considerable emphasis on training for diplomats. A two-year and then three-year diplomatic academy was founded, where students who had completed grammar school could study diplomacy. Because this approach did not prove to be a convincing success, some changes were made. Instead of allowing students who had completed grammar school to enroll, the academy accepted people who had completed college or university studies in history, law, or economics or in one of the national language and literature departments. The students spent one year studying diplomatic history, international law, and foreign trade. In 1955, the academy was closed. Eight years later, a special international faculty was founded at the University of Economics.[134]

The contemporary literature concerning etiquette and protocol, which constitutes a distinctive but heretofore largely ignored corpus, offers insights into the ways in which traditions survived and were reinterpreted. The rules of protocol continued to dictate how leaders and diplomats dressed. The so-called half-ceremonial garb consisted of a jacket during the day and a tuxedo in the evening. Ceremonial garb meant full formal evening wear.[135] Guides to Hungarian etiquette censured mustaches and signet rings, both of which were in fashion among the leading circles. According to a 1961 publication, "Most men live their everyday lives here with shaved faces, with neither moustaches nor beards. It is more hygienic and more customary."[136] Furthermore, "The only jewelry for a man is the wedding ring on his hand, which is the mark of his family life."[137] A book of advice and guidelines entitled *A dolgozó nő otthon* (The working woman at home) contains a chapter on beauty care and cosmetics as well as passages on "unnecessary hair" and "cosmetics for evening merry-making."[138] The literature on etiquette cautiously strove to limit the use of the word *comrade*. According to one of the books containing advice on comportment and manners, "If the insulting aftertaste which inevitably is tied to the form of address 'uram' [this term in Hungarian literally means "my lord," but in everyday conversation today, it is still used to mean "my husband"] should disappear, then indeed there will be no reason not to use this beautiful and original, Hungarian and respectful form of address, since the 'lords' in Hungary today are not the same 'lords' as 200 or even 20 years ago."[139]

The guidelines for interior design emphasized the many alleged advantages of modern furniture, but they had praise for antique furniture as well, and they offered advice on how to arrange furniture tastefully. For instance, according to Blanka Simon, the author of *Házi mindentudó* (Know-it-all homemaker), when "modern furniture can be arranged alongside 'period' furniture, the effect is not disturbing. Biedermeier and neo-Baroque furniture go together best with the 'modern' pieces of furniture; but an Empire-style wardrobe or a Baroque table with two armchairs also go well alongside them."[140] Simon also noted that "a good painting in the apartment is the touchstone of our tastes. It offers proof of our keen sense of beauty. We go to exhibitions and shows, we examine the paintings and statues. We study and educate ourselves in this field too. And we must not think that we can only decorate our dwellings with the works of renowned, recognized masters."[141] Simon also provided readers with practical information concerning how to clean an oil-on-canvas painting, a precious stone, or marble.[142]

According to those who gave advice concerning interior design, it was almost essential to have antique pieces of furniture complementing and adding a bit of flourish to the interiors in modern apartments.[143] They made these recommendations in part simply because the production of furniture in Hungary at the time could not meet the demand, but also because traditional tastes had survived and indeed were flowering.[144] At the end of the 1950s, the Budapest Furniture Industry Company resumed making neo-baroque furniture for domestic consumption and even for export to the Soviet Union.[145] Poet József Romhányi (Rímhányó) wrote a humorous poem titled "Egy szú végrendelete" (Last will and testament of a woodworm): "To my mother-in-law, last but not least, / I leave my new metal furniture, quite a feast" (the English translation makes some attempt to approximate the playful rhymes of the original).

Comedians flourished under socialism in Hungary. Cabaret performer Béla Salamon, a legendary figure of the so-called Mirthful Stage (Vidám Színpad), did a memorable skit titled "Dad Finds a Job."[146] In the short parody, a family has invited the father's boss to dinner, but they have to find a way to get Dad out of the house, because he has a tendency to deliver tirades beginning with "Well, back in my day" and heaping praise on the gentlemanly world of the prewar era. The other members of the family fear that, with his rants, he may offend his boss. Dad, however, is not interested in going out to the movies, and over the course an ensuing chat, he speaks his mind. Gradually, it turns out that the prewar world he recalls fondly is not all that different from the world in which his boss moves. At the end of the story, Dad decides to get out the hidden silverware. The story would not have been effective had it not touched on an essential aspect of so-called socialist society—that almost everyone looked back on the prewar period with some degree of nostalgia.

Traditional tastes and codes of ethics were not the only aspects of social life to survive and even flourish in the socialist era. Everyday customs and roles also endured. While at social occasions the men spoke about issues of state or more generally fraternized, women did charity work and endeavored to exert some form of indirect influence. Árpád Szakasits's daughter offers the following recollections of one of the receptions held by her father:

> The shadows of the guests who had gathered behind the lit windows of the Presidential Palace on Museum Square could be seen on the curtain. The doors to the rooms in which the reception was held were all left open. In the banquet hall, the old furniture and the new furniture seemed to have gathered at various places under the high ceiling with its white plaster. The silverware and porcelain at the table-settings shimmered on the heavy damask. Everything was elegant, as protocol demands.... My mother, however—and I was very much aware of this—was thinking of the "Snow Flower" children's home, which was soon going to close. The former palace of Archduke Joseph in Tapolcsányi Street had been redesigned on the basis of designs by Anna Szabó to create a home for kindergarten-age children.... I watched her squeeze a promise out of Károly Olt, the Minister of People's Welfare, and then she badgered

Minister of Public Education Gyula Ortutay with questions. Finally, she turned to József Darvas, Minister of Construction. She used the occasion to squeeze donations out of them for the children's home.[147]

After the system had been consolidated, the rites and ceremonies of state holidays gradually acquired concrete form. The events that were held in celebration of the new ideology drew heavily on the old, prewar customs, and they took place in spaces where ceremonies had traditionally been held. On April 4, 1950, for instance, the new leaders who were finding their way in their new positions held a major celebration. The event was planned by the Greater Budapest Party Committee and the Ministry of Foreign Affairs as well as a party committee that had been formed specifically for this purpose, working together with the army, the state security forces, and the police.[148] Delegations from the other communist countries were invited to the celebration, along with representatives of the communist parties in the West. The Ministry of Foreign Affairs handled the government delegations, and the Foreign Affairs Division of the party handled the party delegations. The leaders of the people's republics were given two-bedroom and three-bedroom apartments, as were the members of the political committees and the ministers. The government delegations were met at the train station by a guard of honor.[149] Parades, changes of the guard, and fireworks shows were held to give the city of Budapest a particularly festive mood. In the larger cities of the country, ceremonies were held at which prominent members of the government and party delivered speeches.[150] On April 5, the leaders of the Hungarian Workers' Party held a banquet lunch in honor of the guests from abroad in what earlier had been the presidential palace (the elegant building was still used for official receptions at the time).[151] As had been tradition, a gala performance was held in the Opera House to emphasize the importance of the occasion. The organizers welcomed the guests in the two banquet halls, the Crimson Salon and the Székely

Bertalan Room. The former was named after the upholstery on the walls, and the latter was named after the Romantic painter Bertalan Székely, who had painted the frescoes on the room's walls. When the enormous chandelier lit up the theater during the breaks, the audience could see the prominent members of the party and the guests from abroad in the royal box, a stately space gilded with twenty-four-carat gold in the center of the three-story neo-baroque gallery. At the suggestion of minister of public education József Darvas, representatives of the Catholic episcopacy had even been invited.[152] Their presence added to the prestige and importance of the occasion.

Under socialism, the county balls also had a prewar mood. For instance, the festive occasions that were held in the Savaria Grand Hotel[153] in the city of Szombathely had patrons, and the organizers invited high-ranking guests from public life and treated them to elegant food and drink. According to the invitation for the county ball that was held in 1959, the patrons were minister of labor and parliamentary representative Ödön Kisházi, deputy minister and parliamentary representative Pál Ilku, deputy minister Károly Dapsi, Kossuth Prize–winning writer and parliamentary representative Ernő Urbán, first secretary of the county party committee and parliamentary representative János Gosztonyi, county president of the Patriotic People's Front and parliamentary representative Dr. László Zsigmond, and, finally, chairman of the County Council election committee György Gonda. As was typical of the style of the era, on the invitations to the county balls, after or next to the national dignitaries, one finds the names of works council chairmen, police lieutenants, and "outstanding" tractor drivers, textile workers, and foremen as patrons. In other words, efforts were taken to ensure that the events harmonized, at least on the surface, with the ideology of the regime, which supposedly championed the working class.

The balls attempted to conjure the mood of the bygone era. The caterer provided "first-rate food and drink." Music was provided by the Savaria orchestra and by a folk ensemble led by Géza Horváth and Károly Sallai. The dance program began with an old Hungarian ballroom dance (the *körmagyar*, or Hungarian round), which was followed by a Csárdás (another traditional Hungarian dance), a waltz, a tango, a fox-trot, a hesitation waltz, and a slow-fox.[154] The national potentates and the local council members and party functionaries opened the revelries with appropriate solemnity, as their predecessors once had under the system of landlords and overseers, and they danced the very Hungarian round, which had been created in the nineteenth century by Hungarian choreographers with the specific purpose of pushing French and German ball dances out of the dance halls of the Hungarian nobility.

THE FIGHT FOR SITES

After the devastation of the war, in the spirit of traditional tastes and customs, the new state leaders tried to create new spaces and symbolic sites for ceremonial shows of power. The traditions of the earlier elite tied their hands in many ways, for they had to adapt to their new positions, and most of them came from social groups that had always followed the lifestyles of the old elite (if admittedly according to their significantly more modest means). Thus, one discerns a kind of petty bourgeois banality in their values and tastes. As far as they were concerned, period furniture, historicism, and the neo-baroque were synonymous with style and elegance. In 1946, for instance, the palace of the president of the republic was furnished to resemble the Renaissance-style palace of the Esterházy family.[155] Furniture and tile stoves were taken from several places, including the Kiscell manor house (from the bequest of interior designer and art collector Miksa Schmidt).[156] Paintings and sculptures from the royal palace in Buda were also used to adorn the interior spaces of the presidential palace. Other works of fine art from the castle were given to the prime minister's office, and the rest—for the most part works that were unacceptable to the ideology of the system because of their historical connotations (for instance paintings of the Habsburg rulers and busts of Miklós Horthy)—was given to the Hungarian National Museum.[157]

Artist and decor and interior designer Elek Falus, who had traveled in Western Europe before the war and was a man of considerable experience in his profession, did the interior designs of the palace. On the basis of these designs, he seems to have had the prewar aristocratic traditions very much in mind. The interior spaces were transformed in the neo-baroque style, with the exception of the butler's pantry, where modern cabinets were installed. New historicist lamps, lamp brackets, and bodyguards' racks, clothing racks, and gunacks were also designed for the building. The communist politicians took their first steps on the path leading to power amid these decorative additions. On August 5, 1948, János Kádár, László Rajk, and István Kossa (the new members of the government under Lajos Dinnyés) took their oaths of office in front of president of the republic Árpád Szakasits. When the office of the president of the republic was abolished, the building was given a new function. It was turned over to Hungarian Radio.[158]

Later, the Hungarian Young Communist League Club opened an office in the building. The furnishings and decorations conjured the building's past even in events organized for youth. The members of the younger generation danced underneath the coffered ceiling, which was as old as the edifice itself, and an ornate fireplace and a carved mirror affixed to the wall had been made by the Esterházy family. The coat of arms of the Esterházy family above the mirror was another unambiguous reminder of the history of the building. The image on the coat of arms is a griffin in profile perched on a crown and facing to the left. It holds three flowers in its left front claw and a saber in its right.[159] History may have taken a turn to the left, but the past could hardly have been said to have disappeared without a trace. The fact that the "people" were able to take possession of a building used for symbolic and ceremonial functions by one of the most prominent families of the earlier elite was a mark of the democratic nature of the new system. Innumerable manor houses were made into schools, colleges, hospitals, and other institutions serving public interests. The party coryphaei, however, did not always strive to wipe away all traces of the prewar world. Rather, they sought to put the imposing buildings of the earlier systems, which were rich in their styles and scales with symbolic meanings and functions, into the service of the new regime.

Initially, the leaders of the communist party wanted to use the royal palace in Buda as a party and state administrative center. The wing of the building that looked out over Krisztinaváros (a neighborhood west of the castle) would have housed the offices of the center—for instance, the secretaryship of the Hungarian Workers' Party and Mátyás Rákosi's office.[160] In 1951, the plans were completed under the supervision of István Janáky and Iván Kotsis Senior, two famous architects working at the Public Building Planning Institute.[161] The neo-baroque designs for Rákosi's study were evocative of the throne room of the castle itself, which was "two-stories in height." The throne room was going to be used as a reception room.[162] At a meeting called to discuss the reconstruction and redesign of the castle, Rákosi harshly criticized the designs, and he argued in favor of more modest, modern spaces, referring to the Kremlin as an example.[163] In the end, however, Rákosi came to like, or at least accept, the designs. In the resolutions concerning the plans, the following recommendation was included at his suggestion: "Cannons could be put on the round bastion and a small garden could be made."[164] In general, the functionaries were fairly resolute and sometimes, as I have pointed out, innovative in questions concerning the fine arts.[165] In his memoir, Kotsis, who worked on the designs for almost three years, notes with palpable bitterness, "The Bolshevik government began to disfavor the modern approach in architecture, and it made the 'bygone architectural forms' the official style, furthermore, in an Asian variation."[166]

The neo-baroque survived the years of the political turn, too. Traditional tastes and preferences, which initially had been resolutely rejected, gradually began to permeate the customs and lifestyles of the elite, breaking through the cordons set up by the ideologues of the regime. Although the neo-baroque style was officially rejected throughout the socialist era, as certain aspects of prewar neo-baroque society were adopted, the style gained some degree of acceptance. In principle, the representatives of Hungarian socialist realism completely rejected the styles and tastes that had dominated between the two world wars, and they also rejected modern functionalism. Traditional elements of style, however, repeatedly popped up in the new designs of the old masters, in particular when the plans concerned adornments, furnishings, and interior design for prominent public buildings. When working on these kinds of designs, they gladly drew on the traditional formal languages and on their own earlier designs.

The party leaders prepared for a long time to move into the royal palace, as indeed Horthy himself had done before them. As work on the restoration of the building after the damages of the war dragged on, they nonetheless took the necessary preparatory steps for the move. In 1951, they purchased antique furniture for the castle so that they would be able to furnish their offices in a style that harmonized with the surroundings.[167] Between 1953 and 1955, the furniture designs for the palace interiors were completed. The designers wanted to use the Mátyás Hunyadi Room as an official elite chamber. This room almost certainly would have been Rákosi's study had he not fallen out of favor by then.[168] In an essay on János Flach's furniture designs and Flach's borrowings from the historicist style, art historian Péter Rostás observes that "the neo-Classical furniture, the lines of which are stern, combines elements of the Louis Seize and Empire styles, in general the proportions and structures that emphasize gravity and stability."[169] Flach, who earlier had worked at the Lingel factory, would have added five-pointed stars to several of the individual pieces of furniture to bring the old world style a bit closer to the symbols and ideology of the age.[170] With their tendency toward historicist style, the plans for the redesign of the palace's interior spaces harmonized with the surroundings. But the designs of some of the rooms suggested that the interiors be faithfully restored.[171] In the end, the party leaders abandoned—admittedly reluctantly—their plan to use the royal palace as a government center, in part because the restoration would have taken a very long time.

In 1945, the offices of the Hungarian Communist Party were temporarily housed in the building at 17 Akadémia Street. Rákosi's secretaryship was set up on the second floor of the building.[172] Care was taken to ensure that the furnishings were expressive of the importance of the office. In the 1950s, for example, elegant colonial-style furniture was ordered for Rákosi's office, which later was moved to the room of the director of the Institute for Party History.[173] As the party became a state-party and the state became a party-state, the apparatus began to swallow up everything around it, a bit like an enchanted creature in a folktale. First, it swallowed up the neighboring corner house. Then it occupied the buildings on either side of Árpád Street, which opens off of Akadémia Street. Then a party office was created in the parts of the buildings that looked onto Nádor Street, which is parallel to Akadémia Street. The party office continued to devour the buildings around it. As journalist Béla Szász observed, the party "is in the fever of permanent relocation, not permanent revolution."[174]

Before 1945, the ministries and important state institutions were located in the Buda Castle, the castle district, and the immediate surroundings. The two most important such offices were the seat of the regent, which was in the royal palace, and the office of the prime minister, which was in the Sándor Palace. When Budapest was under siege, these buildings were badly damaged. Thus, after the Second World War, state officials were obliged to move to Pest. When the upper house of parliament was abolished, spaces were left empty in the building of the national assembly. The office of the president (the Presidential Council of the People's Republic), for example, was moved from the Andrássy Palace to its new home in the parliament building, and the Office of the Council of Ministers also set up house in the building.[175]

Since the most important organs of the party and the state had pitched camp, as it were, in District 5—that is, the inner city in Pest, not far from the parliament—a new officials' quarter took form. Whereas the kingdom without a king, as Hungary was sometimes wistfully called in the interwar period (since technically it was a kingdom but the regent himself had thwarted the efforts of the Charles I of Austria to reclaim the throne twice in the immediate aftermath of the war), had set up its offices in the royal palace and the surrounding area, the people's republic, which in practice functioned at the time without a parliament, took control of the building of parliament and the surrounding parts of Pest. By taking possession of the sites of institutions that had embodied the former Hungarian state in some way—institutions that meanwhile might have been marginalized or become defunct yet still bore symbolic meaning—the party established at least symbolic ties to the traditions of the earlier regime to strengthen its own legitimacy. In the 1950s, new buildings for government offices were built near the parliament. In 1950, a new office building for the Ministry of Internal Affairs was constructed on the east bank of the Danube River, not far from parliament. It was the first prominent government building to be built after the war. Party and government buildings that still stand today grew like mushrooms in District 5, creating a kind of party and government quarter.[176]

The royal palace was never actually restored in the Rákosi era, and the ruling elite set up shop (to vary the earlier metaphor) for the long run in the inner city of Pest. Under Kádár, the party leadership very deliberately and strategically sought to distinguish and distance itself from the prewar elites. As a powerful symbolic expression of this intention, the Buda Castle was given an entirely new function under Kádár. In November 1957, journalist and politician Ernő Mihályfi suggested in an article in the daily *Magyar Nemzet* (Hungarian nation) that the royal palace, "which they had wanted to turn into a closed government quarter during the time of the personal cult, should be made a palace of culture."[177] Clearly, Mihályfi had been prompted to make the suggestion by someone in the upper echelons of power, for soon after the article was published, official measures were taken.

The castle district began to be rearranged and redesigned, and several historicist buildings fell victim to the changes. Institutes of the Hungarian Academy of Sciences and other cultural institutions moved into the ministerial buildings of the Horthy era that had survived the siege. The interior spaces of the royal palace were redesigned. Exhibition halls and workrooms were created, and elements of the interiors that conjured the old architecture were removed as unsuitable for the new functions of the spaces. Red and white marble, which was one of the characteristic decorative materials of the age, dominated, and it gave the spaces the necessary prestige. The Budapest History Museum was placed in the southern wing of the rebuilt palace, and the eastern wing and center building housed the Hungarian National Gallery. Until 1989, the northern wing was home to the Museum of the Workers' Movement.[178]

This peculiar mixture of destruction and construction was an emblematic act that symbolized a reckoning with the Horthy era, a break with the Rákosi era, and the consolidation of the Kádár era. This interpretation of the transformation of the human geography of the city is supported by the fact that the Kádár system did not always give up easily on claims to prominent and symbolically meaningful buildings, even when these buildings were found in the castle, although the regime considered the fate of the castle symbolic. For instance, in 1967, the system was considering using the Sándor Palace, which had been left in ruins by the fighting in January 1945, for the Museum of the Workers' Movement, but by 1969, the plans had changed and it was to serve as a guest house for the government. By 1971, the plans for the renovation had been completed.[179]

Under Kádár, the Central Committee of the Hungarian Socialist Workers' Party, an organ of government even more powerful than the Ministry of Internal Affairs, moved into the modern office building on the Pest bank of the Danube River. Kádár himself, who had once walked the steps of the building as the minister of the interior, may well have played a decisive role in the move.[180] Thus, the first secretary of the party had his office set up in a familiar place. The building, which is just south of Jászai Mari Square (on the Pest side of Margaret Bridge, named after actor Mari Jászai) was also used for meetings of the supreme body of the party, the Political Committee. The members of the committee discussed affairs at a large, oval table, where everyone had a specific and permanent spot that mirrored his or her place in the hierarchy. At one end of the table, Kádár presided over the sittings until the last two years of the regime's rule, when he was replaced by Grósz Károly.[181]

The hall of the party seat contains an enormous wall painting by Aurél Bernáth and his colleagues titled *Munkásállam* (Workers' state). Bernáth was a famous Hungarian painter whose art bears the influence of an array of styles, but perhaps most prominently expressionism. The secco painting was unveiled in 1972. According to the security guards who worked in the building, Bernáth and the other artists used linseed oil and eggs to cement the painting to the wall.[182] Among the people depicted in the painting, one recognizes several of Bernáth's writer and artist friends, not to mention János Kádár himself. Kádár is playing chess with an anonymous figure (suggesting that Kádár is a man of the people), while György Aczél looks on. Somewhat like the artists of the Renaissance, Bernáth includes the people who commissioned the work in the painting. Kádár is playing white, and he has just taken his opponent's queen. His head casts a shadow on the wall that resembles a halo. The painting has been interpreted as an allegorical expression of submission to the dictator, but also as an ironic comment on the regime. The figures in the secco are not working. At most, they mimic working. One person is pushing a wheelbarrow, but he is wearing flip-flops. Others merely look on. One could argue the painting presents the workers' state as little more than adornment, with the shrewd chess player in the background. Bernáth even included Imre Nagy, the former prime minister put to death at Kádár's order, in the painting. Bernáth depicted Nagy wearing his distinctive pince-nez, but the artist later removed this feature lest it get him in hot water.[183]

After the change of regimes, the building was turned into offices for parliamentary representatives. The wall painting was covered with a gray curtain, though in 2004 the curtain was taken down. The secco then became the subject of controversy again, since the politicians in the opposition (who very decidedly crafted an image of their party as one that stood in stark opposition to the socialist legacy) recognized the figure of Kádár.[184] Thanks to the linseed oil and eggs, *Munkásállam* has indeed withstood the upheavals of time (better than the ideology it purportedly represented), and it remains as a reminder of the country's recent past.

NOTES

1. Szigeti 2002.
2. Szigeti 2002.

3. Jürgen Habermas writes about the role of the public sphere in connection with Greek democracy: "Only in the light of the public sphere did that which existed become revealed, did everything become visible to all." Habermas 2011, 200. This is one of the reasons that it is important for all ruling regimes to restrict, or least keep watch over, the public sphere. Richard Sennett analyzes the transformation of the public sphere from the perspective of the phenomena of public life. In other words, he focuses on various manners of expression and the ways in which individuals and groups use their behavior, speech, and dress to transform the substance of the public sphere—that is, everything that has become visible. Sennett 2002. Despite the fact that, from time to time, the people who were in positions of rule made clear shows of their power in front of crowds that were summoned for ceremonial occasions (which could be characterized as sites and manifestations of the symbolic public sphere) and kept close watch over the media (which became the manipulated public sphere), the tools that were at the disposal of the public (behavior, speech, dress) gradually acquired increasingly significant roles, and the representatives of the system quickly recognized their importance.

4. Havadi 2006, 320.

5. Magyar Nemzeti Levéltár Országos Levéltára (Hungarian National Archives, hereafter cited as HNA), fond XIX-G-5, box 2, 480/1946. 2.

6. Ruffy 1965, 226–227. On the history of the New York Café, see Csapó 1996; Ferenc Vadas 1996.

7. Saly 2005, 47.

8. Interview with Károly Hetényi, Budapest, March 23, 2009.

9. Zelei 2003.

10. People seeking vibrant nightlife found it in the Bagdad, the Shanghai, and the Zöldfa restaurant. Gundel and Harmath 1979, 48. In the late 1940s and the 1950s, Savoy and Abbázia, both on Andrássy Avenue, were popular. Erki 1996, 59.

11. Havadi 2006, 347.

12. Ibid., 338–339.

13. Szentgyörgyi 2005. Szentgyörgyi, who was with Asturias and Neruda as an interpreter, makes the following remark: "The two greats got down to work with bombastic 'Latin' elegance and practical 'petty-bourgeois' thoroughness." Ibid., 79.

14. Asturias and Neruda 1968.

15. Hungary, "where they make the world's paprika and pepper." Ibid., 20.

16. Ibid., 22.

17. Ibid., 109.

18. Hegedüs 1985, 137–138.
19. Kállai 1984, 208.
20. Kövér 1998, 119–120.
21. Pünkösti 1996, 324.
22. Kállai 1984, 208.
23. Kövér 1998, 199.
24. Zoltán 1996, 88.
25. HNA M-KS 288. f. 37/385. s. u.
26. János Berecz 2003, 305.
27. Interview with Sándor Gáspár, National Széchényi Library, Collection of Historical Interviews, 149.
28. Tischler 2004, 251.
29. Report on the operational situation at the Gundel restaurant, Budapest, November 14, 1969, Állambiztonsági Szolgálatok Történeti Levéltára, Historical Archives of the Hungarian State Security (hereafter cited as HAHSS), fond 3.1, group 5, O-20004/3, 9.
30. According to the report, two people took part in the revolution. Report on the operational situation at the Gundel restaurant, Budapest, June 8, 1961, HAHSS, fond 3.1, group 5, O-20004/3, 9.
31. Kállai 1984, 271.
32. Interview with László Somogyi, Budapest, March 18, 2009.
33. Report on the operational situation at the Gundel restaurant, Budapest, June 8, 1961, HAHSS, fond 3.1, group 5, O-20004/3, 8; Report on the operational situation at the Gundel restaurant, Budapest, November 14, 1969, HAHSS, fond 3.1, group 5, O-20004/3, 21.
34. Report on the operational situation at the Gundel restaurant, Budapest, November 14, 1969, HAHSS, fond 3.1, group 5, O-20004/3, 9.
35. Resolution, Budapest, September 9, 1968, HAHSS, fond 3.1, group 5, O-2004/1, 4.
36. Report, Budapest, June 8, 1961, HAHSS, fond 3.1, group 5, O-20004/3, 9.
37. Ibid.
38. Ibid., 11.
39. Resolution, Budapest, September 9, 1968, HAHSS, fond 3.1, group 5, O-2004/1, 4.
40. Report on the operational situation of the area around the Gundel Company, Budapest, August 1, 1962, HAHSS, fond 3.1, group 5, O-20004/3, 14.
41. Report, Budapest, June 8, 1961, HAHSS, fond 3.1, group 5, O-20004/3, 12.

42. Report on the operational situation at the Gundel restaurant, Budapest, October 28, 1980, HAHSS, fond 3.1, group 5, O-20004/3, 25.
43. Summary report, Budapest, June 8, 1981, HAHSS, fond 3.1, group 5, O-20004/3, 29.
44. Report on the operational situation at the Gundel restaurant, Budapest, October 28, 1980, HAHSS, fond 3.1, group 5, O-20004/3, 25.
45. Summary report, Budapest, June 8, 1981, HAHSS, fond 3.1, group 5, O-20004/3, 30.
46. Preisich 1998b, 148.
47. Rózsahegyi 1962, 20.
48. Schnitta 1965, 16.
49. Ibid., 285–286.
50. Ibid., 285.
51. Rózsahegyi 1962, 143.
52. Interview with György Kalmár-Maron, Budapest, March 11, 2009.
53. Augustin 2002, 113–120.
54. Interview with Tibor Meskál, Budapest, November 27, 2009.
55. Interview with Tibor Meskál, Budapest, November 22, 2008.
56. With regard to the Hotel Royal, the Historical Archives of the Hungarian State Security contain only the dossiers of the staff members who were active as informants during the 1956 revolution. If the quarantine had indeed been ordered by the state security, presumably there would be some written trace of this among the documents. HAHSS 3.1.5. O-16591.
57. Interview with Tibor Vadnai, Budapest, March 13, 2009.
58. Interview with György Kalmár-Maron, Budapest, March 11, 2009.
59. Interview with Tibor Meskál, Budapest, November 20, 2008.
60. Interview with Tibor Meskál, Budapest, November 20, 2008.
61. Havadi 2008, 176.
62. Interview with János Pap conducted by Márton Kozák in 1987, OHA no. 106, 139–140.
63. Preisich 1998b, 148–149.
64. The firm in charge of operations later changed because Hungar-Hotels did not have sufficient credit. In 1972, Danubius Hotels was formed to take its place in the health sector of the tourist industry.
65. The building complex burned to the ground in the Second World War.
66. In 1969, Béla Pintér and his colleagues won the internal invitation announced by the Public Building Planning Institute for tenders for the construction of the Hilton Hotel.

67. Bojár 1998.
68. After the opening, in an article in *Élet és Irodalom* [Life and literature], art historian József Vadas poked fun at the striking dissonance of modern articles for personal use in Biedermeier interiors. Vadas 1977.
69. Pünkösti 1977, 6.
70. Ibid., 8.
71. Augustin n.d., 136.
72. According to Decree No. 160.100/1926 issued by the Ministry of Internal Affairs in 1926, records had to be kept of the females who worked as "women of pleasure," and in principle the state authorities were allowed to take action against a woman who was suspected of prostitution only if the woman in question was not listed in the public records as someone who had been given a license. This decree was valid and in force until the passage of a new decree (no. 17) in 1955, although after the war, the official records were no longer kept and the state prosecuted people for prostitution.
73. On the issue see, Sándor Horváth 2017, 247–258.
74. Zelei 2003, 61.
75. "I was going to take an old friend of mine who happened to be a lady up to my room to discuss private matters. In the elevator, I was rudely stopped by the porter and humiliated in front of several people." Complaint book of the Hotel Royal.
76. Interview with László Somogyi, Budapest, March 18, 2009.
77. Pünkösti 1977, 8.
78. According to the resolution reached by the Ministry of Internal Affairs concerning the foundation of the Ámor háza, or "House of amour," "in the interests of increasing the effectiveness of the intelligence activities concerning the Vatican and, more generally, Italy and making this intelligence more productive, it has become necessary to create and use on a domestic basis an Italian-style bar and, in the same building, IBUSZ (Idegenforgalmi Beszerzési Utazási és Szállítási Részvénytársaság, Tourism Procurement Travel and Transport PLC) guest rooms to serve our operational goals. If the appropriate technical prerequisites are met and informants are supplied, this will enable us to monitor, study, and compromise the target people who interest us, and also to learn of meetings and other hostile activities." "Ámor háza" resolution, Budapest, May 16, 1968, 7, HAHSS, fond 3.2, group 5, O-8-143/1.
79. Tabajdi and Ungváry 2008, 346–360.
80. Ibid., 428–435.

81. In their book *Utak és ösvények* (Roads and paths), István Dékán and Éva D. Kardos offer an account of the history of the partisan group and how they met each other. Dékán and Kardos 1975. On the history of István Dékán's partisan group, see Ferenc Tóth 2002.
82. Kardos 2004, 260.
83. Ibid., 261.
84. Ibid., 262–263.
85. Ibid., 279.
86. Ibid., 281, 298, 290, 293.
87. On fashion in socialist countries, see Bartlett 2010, Simonovics 2019.
88. At the end of the war, the state security took possession of fabrics and items of clothing as "abandoned property." The items were then distributed among the functionaries. A similar fate awaited the personal belongings of people who had fled the country or been deported, and indeed later the same thing was done with the possessions of functionaries who had fallen from grace, as it were.
89. HAHSS, fond 3.1, group 9, V-150262.
90. Ibid.
91. Like language itself, fashion and clothing can be interpreted from the analytical perspective of semiotics. Clothing always acquires meaning through its context. Barthes 1990.
92. Barbara Papp makes the following observation on the basis of the recollections of Imre Nagy's secretary:

> She could recall nothing of the files that went through her hands or the politicians who came into her office. I found it even more surprising that, when listing Horthy's wonderful qualities, she digressed and gave a detailed description of Horthy's wife's clothes (one recognizes on the basis of the description the clothing Mrs. Horthy wore for the Eucharistic Congress, which presumably she [Nagy's secretary] too could only have known from pictures). About Imre Nagy or [Kliment] Voroshilov she also offered only the vague "he was a dear, good man," about the latter, "he was a polite man," but with her descriptions she could make the clothes worn by the women who were in her company seem almost palpable. "Oh, what was his name, Mr. Voroshilov, he was a polite gentleman; when they came to bid farewell, there was a young Russian soldier woman with him, perhaps his daughter." She continues, outraged, like someone who was protesting before the fact against the ill-willed contention: "But not in pants, noooo! She was wearing an attractive little coat and skirt." Papp 2006, 216–217.

In 2004, Papp interviewed a ninety-eight-year-old woman who had once served as Imre Nagy's secretary.

93. Vera and Donald Blinken Open Society Archives (hereafter cited as OSA), fond 361, o-6. Miklós Tamási called my attention to this source.

94. Kardos 2004, 199.

95. As a simple example of the lack of organization and planning that crippled the attempts of the socialist state to compete in the Western marketplace one could mention that the National Hungarian Foreign Trade Enterprise imported balloon cloth from Switzerland while the National Men's Clothing Industry Enterprise was exporting ready-to-wear coats made using balloon cloth to Holland. The Dutch clients did not accept the exports, and they made the following objections: "1. The sleeves of the coats are abnormally short given the size of the coats. 2. They found pencil marks on the collars. 3. The pockets were too small and were so high on the coats that part of them was covered by the belt. 4. The pockets were lined with two different materials. 5. The quilting was ugly and poorly done. 6. The buttonholes had not been cut out. 7. Only half of the hood was lined." The state security launched in inquiry into the affair, which arrived at the following conclusion: "The leaders of the National Enterprise are all petty-bourgeois individuals, who were owners of fancy tailored clothes and even now look down on the workers." HAHSS, fond 3.1, group 5, O-9478.

96. *Szabad Nép* [Free people], March 11, 1948, 3.

97. Pünkösti 1992, 285.

98. András Hegedüs wrote the following remarks about the tragedy of György Péter in a manuscript that survived as part of his estate:

> I can imagine what it must have been like when this Grand senior, who was so proud of the empire he had created, was taken into custody by a few political officers whom he regularly denied entrance into his office. How humiliating it must have been for him to be interrogated about his unfortunate medal-collecting partners. He had not confessed anything to the Horthy police, under much harder circumstances. I sense the horror of this humiliation, I don't understand how it got to the point that in the sick room of the internal affairs hospital, which was kept under strict watch, he managed to stab himself in the heart with an apple-peeling knife. "There was blood everywhere," a witness told me years later. I suspected and I still suspect that they helped him perform hara-kiri, which is unbecoming of a Hungarian. György

Péter, *Visszaemlékezések: Portrék* [Recollections: Portraits], OSA, fond 361, 0-4, box 30.

99. Cars used by offices of the state had license plates beginning with the letter A.
100. HAHSS, fond 3.1, group 9, V-155912/1–4.
101. HAHSS, fond 3.2, group 4, K-2795; HAHSS, fond 3.1, group 5, O-11911; HAHSS, fond 3.1, group 9, V-149869.
102. Dózsa 2003, 110. The Clara Salon was at 12 Váci Street, and the Budapest Fashion Salon was on the corner of Váci Street and Haris Lane.
103. HAHSS, fond 3.1, group 5, O-15671.
104. Report, Budapest, September 15, 1967, HAHSS, fond 3.2, group 4, K-839 "Szöszi," 17.
105. Dózsa and Déri Hegyi 2003, 155.
106. HAHSS, fond 3.2, group 4, K-458.
107. HAHSS, fond 3.2, group 4, K-1058.
108. Klára Rotschild, 1957, "Ez Párizs" [This is Paris], *Ez a Divat* [This is fashion], 8, no. 4–5. Cited in Valuch 2004, 62–63.
109. Simonovics 2008, 212.
110. Barthes 1990, 244–245, 264–265.
111. Comments by János Kádár at the Seventh Congress of the Young Communist League, 1967; in Kádár 1968; cited in Valuch 2009, 99.
112. Internal trade organizational documentation, January 1, 1964, HNA, fond XIX-G-4, group xx, box 130.
113. Work plan for implementation of directive no. 10-32/49/1965 of the Ministry of Domestic Trade; Report on the inquiry into the implementation of the work plan prepared on the basis of directive no. 10-32/49/1965 of the Ministry of Domestic Trade, HNA, fond XIX-G-4, group xx, box 130.
114. Between January 12 and June 4, 2006, an exhibition was organized in the Museum of Applied Arts titled "Fashion for the Working Woman! Fashion Sketches from the 1950s and 1960s and Selections from the Materials in the Documentation Department. Re-Vision Series I." Judit Fekete offers a summary and analysis of the fashion designs presented at the exhibition and their histories, along with citations from the remarks made by Igor Zamushkin, the director of the Tretyakov Gallery in Moscow and the curriculum and examination regulations of the college, which were issued in 1953. Fekete 2006, 8–10.
115. Simonovics 2008, 209.
116. Valuch 2006, 85.

117. At the time, the more elegant salons were called boutiques. Later, this word came to be used for the smaller stores run by one self-employed person. Simonovics 2008, 209.

118. Valuch 2006, 85.

119. Ungvári Tamás, "A herceg, Zsazsa és a szépségkirálynő" [The prince, Zsazsa, and the beauty queen], *Új Tükör* [New mirror], December 7, 1987, accessed July 10, 2009, www.molnarcsilla.hu/sajto_halal/uj_tukor87dec7.htm.

120. "Jóban-rosszban: Interview with Kádár Jánosnéval" [For better or for worse] (VIII.), *Magyarország* [Hungary], no. 47 (November 24, 1989): 5.

121. The woman's husband was sentenced to six years in prison. As an accomplice, she was sentenced to serve eighteen months in "severe" imprisonment. Budapest Főváros Levéltára (Budapest City Archives), fond XXV-41, box 394, 964/1971. Sándor Horváth called my attention to this source.

122. BCA, fond XXV-41, box 394, 964/1971.

123. HNA, fond XIX-J-1, group j, Greece-II-13 t.-004821-1957; published by Kurecskó 2001.

124. As a young man, Endre Sík was a Piarist novitiate, as mentioned above. He later completed university studies in law. Naturally, he was not from a working-class background. In 1947–1948, he began his career as a diplomat nonetheless.

125. Sík 1966, 239.

126. Ibid., 247.

127. Kállai 1984, 270–271.

128. Ibid., 271–272.

129. Ibid., 272.

130. HNA, fond XIX-K-1, group ah, box 2.

131. *Református püspökből külügyminiszter: Péter János külügyminiszterről beszél Szűrös Mátyás diplomata politikus* [From Calvinist bishop to minister of foreign affairs: Mátyás Szűrös speaks about minister of foreign affairs János Péter]; in Bakó, Hajdú, and Marik 2005, 276.

132. Ibid.

133. Ibid., 278.

134. Sík 1970, 15–22.

135. Réczey, Pekáry, and Gondi 1961, 226.

136. Ibid., 232.

137. Ibid., 234.

138. Almár et al. 1961, 152–163.

139. "Thus, the terms 'comrade' and 'female comrade' can remain as honorary forms of address for political relationships in which politics and party work weld together even more strongly the sentiments of the individual." The books also cautioned against using the terms *kartárs* (fellow worker or colleague), *szaktárs* (another variant on fellow worker or colleague), and *öregem* (something like "old man," implying familiarity and fraternity) "with people we do not yet know." Réczey, Pekáry, and Gondi 1961, 60–61.

140. Simon 1957, 19.

141. Ibid., 22.

142. Ibid., 157, 168, 173.

143. Koós 1959, 77, image 38; Koós 1960, 72; Zsuzsa Kovács 1968, 99, 103, 142, images 85, 87, 239, 240, 249, 361.

144. Because some items of furniture were in short supply and others that were in production were of poor quality, one comes across statements such as the following in the interior design magazines and books: "A Biedermeier writing-cabinet is a practical convenience for writing and work. The upper drawer, pulled out a bit, and the folded-down front form the writing surface. The inner drawers serve as places to keep documents and objects of value. This item of furniture holds its ground in a modern interior." Zsuzsa Kovács 1968, 103, image 249. In 1961, three modern pieces of furniture were in circulation: Varia wall units, Hangulat (mood) furniture suites, and one kind of kitchen furniture. József Vadas n.d., 179.

145. Fóris et al. 1964.

146. Béla Salamon entertained audiences with a character he created named Pomócsi, the embodiment of the perennial average Joe. Pomócsi may have been the first to have uttered the sentence that later became something of a byword of the era (he was certainly the person who said it the most frequently), "And if I ever open my mouth!" With this cautionary admonition, he manages to ensure that his bosses will not reassign him and compel him to leave Budapest for a position in some other city or town. Pomócsi does not come up with the idea himself. Rather, his boss's secretary arms the everyday hero with the mysterious warning. She assures him, "Everyone has a skeleton in his closest." (The Hungarian saying is colorful enough to merit a note of explanation. More literally translated, it is "Everyone has a bit of butter behind his ear." The saying stems from a time when butter was something of a treat, and the implication is that everyone has snitched a bit of butter once or twice when no one was watching.)

147. Schiffer 1985, 284.

148. On eight occasions, the secretaryship of the central leadership of the party discussed the question of the organization of celebrations and public holidays. HNA, fond M-KS 276, group 54, storage unit 83., 84., 86., 87., 89., 90., 91., 92. On the morning of April 2, István Kovács (as a representative of the party) and Mihály Zsofinyecz (as a representative of the government) placed a wreath on the monument in Vecsés, a statue by Sándor Mikus of Miklós Steinmetz, as part of the so-called liberation holiday. The history of the monument itself is characteristic of the era. The propaganda machine crafted a legend about two Soviet officers who actually existed, Captains Steinmetz and Ostapenko, both of whom died at the end of the Second World War in mortar fire after attempting to launch negotiations with the Germans. According to the legend, before the Soviet forces laid siege to the city of Budapest, Steinmetz and Ostapenko approached the German enemy forces bearing a white flag. Their aim, the story goes, was to spare the city from a long siege, but they were murdered by the Germans. In 1948 and 1951, at the entrance and exit to the city, statues were erected in their memory. In 1956, the statue of Steinmetz, which stood at the border of Budapest and Vecsés, was taken down. In 1958, a new statue by Sándor Mikus was erected in its place. The Hálaszobor, or "Statue of gratitude," a tall obelisk that still stands on the north side of Liberty Square in Pest and remains a subject of controversy, was also unveiled on April 2. Two members of the government and two members of the Presidential Council took part in the ceremony. On April 3, prominent members of the government and the party placed wreaths on the monuments in the most important sites of the city—Gellért Hill and Liberty Square. People belonging to the first rank of the ruling elite took part in the events on Gellért Hill, while people who belonged to the second rank of the hierarchy took part in the ceremonies on Liberty Square. At the ceremonies on Gellért Hill, Ernő Gerő represented the party and Árpád Szakasits represented the Presidential Council. Prime Minister István Dobi represented the government, Minister Mihály Farkas represented the army, Gábor Péter represented the state security forces, and Gyula Balassa represented the police. On Liberty Square, Kádár and one of the deputy chairmen of the Presidential Council represented the government. György Marosán represented the government, Sándor Nógrádi represented the army, Gábor Péter again represented the state security forces, and Gyula Balassa again represented the police. HNA, fond M-KS 276, group 54, storage unit 92.

149. Separate measures were taken in preparation for Soviet marshall Kliment Voroshilov's visit. According to the plans, if his train were to arrive during the day, a "mass reception" would be organized in

Nyíregyháza, Debrecen, Szolnok, and Budapest. HNA, fond M-KS 276, group 54, storage unit 92.

150. Árpád Házi traveled to Tatabánya, Mihály Zsofinyecz to Salgótarján, János Beér to Pécs, István Ries to Miskolc, József Prieszol to Ózd, Károly Olt to Győr, László Sándor to Debrecen, and József Köböl to Szeged. Backup plans were made in case one or more of the ministers were to prove not up to the task. Imre Molnár, Mihály Földes, Aranka Károly Döbrentei, and István Szirmai were prepared to fill in if necessary. HNA, fond M-KS 276, group 54, storage unit 92.

151. The organs of the party checked the preparatory steps that were taken for the reception of István Dobi, lest the chairman and staff of the Presidential Council, who had a relatively narrow sphere of authority, commit some political blunder. Ibid.

152. Ibid.

153. The name of the hotel is the Roman name of the city of Szombathely.

154. Magyar Nemzeti Levéltár Vas Megyei Levéltára (Hungarian National Archives – Vas County Archives) fond XIV-64, box 47.

155. The palace on Mihály Pollack Square, on the plot between Szentkirályi Street and Múzeum Street, was built in a neo-Renaissance style on the basis of designs by Antal Baumgarten. József Rozsnyai offers an overview of the history of the building. Rozsnyai 2009.

156. In 1947, the Office of the President had sixty cotillion chairs that were on consignment in the national museum brought to the palace, where they were needed for receptions. Rostás 2001b, 36, 74–75. In late 1949, after the Office of the President was abolished, the chairs were not returned to their original location. Some of them went missing.

157. A registry of the works of art that were turned over is found in the appendix to the article: Szvoboda Dománszky 2001, 447–453.

158. Rozsnyai 2009, 29–31.

159. Ibid., 23. Rozsnyai refers to a winged lion. In fact, the image depicts a griffin.

160. Prakfalvi 2001, 348. HNA, fond M-KS-276, group 65, storage unit 276, published by Kókay 2001, 327; HNA, fond M-KS-276, group 54, storage unit 191, published by Prakfalvi 2001, 352.

161. Prakfalvi 2001, 345–348.

162. HNA, fond M-KS-276, group 65, storage unit 276, published by Kókay 2001, 327.

163. Ibid., 328–329.

164. Ibid., 330, 331.

165. See, for instance, Ernő Gerő's resolute stance on the reconstruction of the palace: "In my opinion, the castle palace should be exactly the same after it has been restored as the old palace was. This of course does not mean that the decorative elements cannot be simplified and the superfluous adornments omitted. We essentially restored Margaret Bridge to look exactly as it once looked, but we left out all the Baroque embellishments and made the whole thing simpler and, thus, more beautiful." Ernő Gerő's memorandum on the reconstruction of the castle palace, ibid., 325.

166. Iván Kotsis, "Életrajzom" [My biography], unpublished manuscript; cited in Prakfalvi 2001, 345.

167. Documents of Deputy Minister János Szabó, 2. b. item 18, HNA, fond XIX-D-3, group j; Report of the Investment Bank, August 15, 1961, 28.

168. See HNA, fond M-KS-276, group 65, storage unit 276, published by Kókay 2001, 327.

169. Rostás 2001a, 511.

170. If the plans had been followed, the marble veneer, gold, and brass in the room would have glimmered in the glow of the ornate, twenty-four-armed chandelier that hung from the rose-tree ceiling. Flach also drew up plans for sculptures of the trunks of palm trees made of gilded wood and brass for the tables in the study as well as lamps with parchment shades. Rostás 2001a, 511–513.

171. Ibid., 513–514.

172. Pünkösti 1992, 275.

173. Ibid., 274.

174. Béla Szász 1963, 15.

175. Preisich 1998b, 123–124.

176. The following is a list of some of the government offices and ministries that occupied buildings in the area: Ministry of Defense, District 5, 7–11 Balaton Street (the ministry took over the wing on Falk Miksa Street in 1949 and the wing on Balaton Street and Honvéd Street in 1952); Ministry of Construction and Urban Development, District 5, 2–4 Zoltán Street (tenement buildings were redesigned to serve the new function), 1950; Ministry of People's Welfare, District 5, 6–8 Arany János Street, 1968, National Planning Office, District 5, 7–8 Roosevelt Square, 1979. Preisich 1998b, 124.

177. *Magyar Nemzet*, November 27, 1956; cited in Potzner and Sinkó 2003, 51.

178. Preisich 1998b, 129.

179. Potzner and Sinkó 2003, 50–53. Plans for the redesign of the Sándor Palace: HNA XIX-D-6 ce (documents of Deputy Minister of Construction Lajos Szilágyi) 171. b. Designs of the Public Building Planning Institute.

180. The seat of the Ministry of the Interior, which later became home to the Central Committee of the Hungarian Socialist Workers' Party, was built in 1950 in District 5, 19 Széchenyi Wharf. Preisich 1998b, 126.

181. Váczi 1989, 45.

182. Rózsa 2008, 11.

183. Dávid 1971; György 2005, 21–31. Péter György described the secco as "an authentic and true self-portrait of the Kádár system." Endre T. Rózsa, in contrast, saw irony and derision in it. Rózsa 2008, 10–11.

184. Bányai György: Képzavar, "A munkásállam mecénásai" [The Maecenases of the workers' state]. In *168 Óra*, June 3, 2004, 24–27.

SIX

STAIN ON THE BLUE SOFA
Luxury and the Elite

THE CREATIVE METHOD OF THE historian is somewhat similar to that of the psychoanalyst. In the process of uncovering various layers of time and meaning, the analyst searches for a point of understanding and recognition where she can finally grasp the essence. By no means can she approach the past without raising questions or encountering problems, so the essence of reflexivity lies precisely in the discovery and even construction of this personal relationship (and not just in the analyst's relationship to language as a social phenomenon). In this inquiry, I present the lives of the communist elite as a negative point of comparison in an attempt to further a more critical and nuanced approach to and understanding of the society of the system that existed at the time and the social injustices and inequalities of this system. The question of how the leaders of the socialist regime perceived themselves, however, is not simple. Did they see themselves as a community, and did any larger sense of belonging evolve among them? Did the meanings that were ascribed to their group by their contemporaries actually apply to them, or were they merely cultural, social, and political metaphors for attitudes toward power? In this last chapter, I offer selections from the few scattered recollections and memoirs that provide insights into the ways in which the elite saw itself and its own identity as a group (if indeed there was one), and its social role and position in comparison with other social groups.

When analyzing the inner dynamic of the Soviet elite, Fitzpatrick describes the top party functionaries as a "team."[1] In the organization of this group, informal links and one's personal relationship with the general secretary were more important than official positions. Personal relationships also influenced political acts in the Hungarian party leadership. Human behavior, experiences, and emotions (fears and desires) determined political careers and fates and gave rise to conflicts and friendships—that is, different groups—within the elite. In general, the everyday life experiences of the party leaders created a common lifestyle and the common (consumer) identity of this group, and this lifestyle influenced consumer habits in Hungary.

When the regime was first formed, members of the new elite were connected to one another through informal relationships. Friends and families often got together for informal dinners.[2] All the party leaders were men, and in general, the men had central roles in the everyday life of this group. Their hobbies were perceived as symbols of masculinity—hunting, for example—and determined how these families spent their spare time. Even after shared family dinners, the men usually played chess and cards separately from their family members. As I have pointed out with regard to hunting, communism also meant the revival of hegemonic masculinity within the circles of the Hungarian elite.

Mátyás Rákosi also aspired to play a kind of loosely defined role as patriarch. For example, he invited children to join him for hot chocolate, and he gladly showed them his collections of relics. The contemporary trend established by Rákosi to collect souvenirs can be regarded as the continuation of a middle-class Biedermeier custom. Pál Ignotus, a writer with a bourgeois background, wrote of Rákosi, "I detest his snobbery, which is a rather common feature among both communists and revolutionaries.

As the son of a wealthy provincial merchant, he must have suffered a lot of injustices for his social background, which was neither high enough nor low enough to be proud of."[3] Klára Szakasits Schiffer, the daughter of the former president, recalled the following typical incident in her memoir: "About 10:00 o'clock at night, in one of the dormitories of the Rákosi Children's Home, where between 10 and 12 children share a room. Irén Ganzel [director of the former Rákosi Children's Home; only children of top party leaders and their relatives could attend the kindergarten] turned on the light and said: Our good pal Rákosi came for a visit! Then, ignoring all the other children, she went directly to Palkó's bed. She stopped at his bed: 'Now, little Schiffer, you should be proud,' she told the child, 'your grandfather will be the president of the people's republic.'"[4]

László Nánási, a member of the National Peasant Party, offered the following description of Rákosi: "Of the so-called 'foursome' (Rákosi, Gerő, Farkas, and Révai), I held Mátyás Rákosi in the highest regard. I especially liked him at the end of the 1940s. Unlike Gerő, he was not 'a dry man,' and the 'air did not freeze in his presence,' like it did when Mihály Farkas or Révai were around. In smaller groups, he could jovially argue or even joke around. He used to call me 'my colleague Nánási.'"[5]

Initially, Rákosi held the ruling elite together as an exclusive circle of friends and acquaintances, but by that time, fault lines had already emerged within the group. In the first years, the most important difference was between the leaders who had returned from the Soviet Union and those who had remained in Hungary. The tension sprang from the excessive influence of the former. Later, during the Kádár era, this conflict was presented as an antagonism between politicians who had stayed in Hungary and those who had returned to Hungary at the end of the Second World War and who blindly followed the Soviet leadership. This distinction allowed the system to highlight the differences between the Rákosi and Kádár regimes as part of an attempt to make the latter more acceptable. The real difference, however, had been in their share of access to power.

In the 1950s, the sense of terror and intimidation became omnipresent not only for Hungarian society in general but also among the elite. The "foursome" used this terror to obtain an absolute hold on power.[6] Despite their luxurious lifestyles, members of the ruling elite might still have felt exposed to constant threat due to the activities of the state security and the show trials. The tragedy of Sándor Zöld and his family offers a revealing example. On April 19, 1951, Rákosi summoned Sándor Zöld, minister of the interior, to meet with him. He then announced Zöld's resignation at the meeting of the Political Committee. State security kept Zöld under observation. Following the incident, Zöld took a walk in the city park, where he had a long conversation (until dawn) with his wife. At the time, Zöld and his family lived near the park in a villa in Benczúr Street. The next day, he submitted his resignation at a sitting of the Council of Ministers. He then went home and shot and killed his wife, mother, two children, and, finally, himself. In his suicide note, he wrote the following: "My dear Comrades! I know what awaits me and my family. Why should I wait for this to be my fate after a long period of torment? I prefer to meet my end like this, with my family. This was not how I imagined the leadership of the communist party. I was not given criticism, but death."[7] The text breaks off here. State security officers wrapped the bodies found in the villa in Persian rugs and buried them on the outskirts of Budapest in an unmarked grave.[8] Due to the atmosphere of increasing terror and the constant sense of threat, many of Zöld's fellow party members believed that his family had been killed by the state security forces.[9]

In an interview, András Hegedüs claimed that there were only three escape routes available for the cadres: "certified insanity, alcoholism, or suicide."[10] On the thirtieth anniversary of László Rajk's rehabilitation, Antal Apró recalled,

> In the old days, initially, we were all a fairly friendly group, those of us who had remained in Hungary during the war, and we got together at the home of one family or another. We used these occasions to discuss daily politics, the issues on the agenda with which we struggled. We also talked about information we had heard, and we asked about one another's families. And during the Rajk trial all of these friendships, some of which were years old and some of which were decades old, ended. Distrust and an atmosphere of fear prevailed.... One day, one friend was arrested, the next day another.[11]

In contrast, the members of the party who had returned to Hungary from the Soviet Union after the war—the so-called muscovite leaders—included Mátyás Rákosi. Everyone continued to expect Rákosi to offer the solutions to the problems. As the paterfamilias, Rákosi was considered just and merciful by some, while others regarded him as unjust and merciless. The events that came in the wake of the tragedy of Sándor Zöld, as recalled by Hegedüs, were typical of the time:

> I spent almost the whole day in the Ministry of Agriculture, where the minister, Ferenc Erdei, held some ministerial meeting. It must have been early afternoon when his secretary called him out. Within a few minutes, he asked to see me in his office, where he informed me that his wife, Joci, had called because she had heard shots from the Zöld family's apartment, and now, when she wanted to go down to the garden, she had seen that something resembling blood was trickling from underneath the front door. Erdei was at a loss and asked me what he should do. Suspecting that a tragedy had taken place, I suggested that he call Rákosi. This he did, in my presence. According to him, Rákosi had not yet known anything of what had happened. At least that is what he told Erdei.[12]

Cadres sought answers to almost all their questions directly from Rákosi.

Within the small circle of the elite, the general secretary retained his role of patriarch—a role that stemmed essentially from the monolithic nature of the power structure—throughout his reign, though factions did emerge among the communist politicians, who came from diverse social and cultural backgrounds. In general, there was no ideology or social identity that would or could have strengthened the sense of belonging to an elite and privileged community for party leaders. The ideology of the regime and the fact that the elite was the representative of the "workers' state" may have given rise to a sort of working-class consciousness and identity among the party functionaries, but this served more as a reference point than a cohesive force.[13] Indeed, within the elite, fissures emerged along the fault lines of the old, traditional identities. For instance, in Imre Nagy's notes written during his post-1956 imprisonment in Snagov (where he and other exiled communists lived in villas built next to the Snagov Lake, about thirty kilometers from Bucharest), the martyred prime minister who was executed as part of the retaliatory and oppressive measures following the 1956 revolution, distinguished himself from other communist leaders on the basis of their positions on the so-called national question, and he mentioned the Jewish ancestry of his adversaries.[14] His reasoning is testament to how, within the communist identity, components of the traditional social identities persisted.

Party leaders had few doubts concerning the persistence of the traditional prejudices of Hungarian society. In a 1990 interview, Károly Grósz, the last general secretary of the Hungarian Socialist Workers' Party, brushed off the accusation of antisemitism by claiming that he had been accused of the opposite by the party: "One time, Kádár said, 'Tell me honestly, but really honestly, are you a Jew or are you not?' I replied, 'Look, Comrade Kádár, you have the necessary means to check, so why are you asking me.' Then I was a bit rude because I told him I could produce physical evidence in the matter, but I would prefer not to. Let them check!" Allegedly, Kádár's response to Grósz's question as to why the issue had been brought up at all was the following: "Well, because of your name. Don't you think you should change it?" Most

Hungarian Jews had names of German origin. The name Grósz is a Hungarian spelling of the German word for "gross," or "big." In fact, as Grósz recalled, "[István] Szirmai once said that with a name like mine, one could not work in the party in Hungary."[15] According to György Aczél, Kádár "introduced this strange argot according to which 'one's ethnic background should determine whether he is the right candidate for a ministerial position.' ... He drew a distinction in his thinking between institutionalized antisemitism and pragmatic acceptance of the fact that antisemitism existed among the people and the people should not be provoked."[16] As was typical of the time, the propaganda machine fashioned an image of Rákosi, who was from a petty bourgeois Jewish family, as someone from the lesser nobility.[17] Similarly, it was said of minister of defense Mihály Farkas, who was an illegitimate child, that his father had been a commanding officer in the Austro-Hungarian imperial army.[18]

Shared lifestyles and customs, however, did serve as a cohesive force that formed a unified community of the representatives of various trends within the party, even though the members of the party came from diverse backgrounds. Certain attitudes and ways of life were equally characteristic of Mátyás Rákosi, János Kádár, and Imre Nagy. The shared nature of these traditions can be interpreted as a manifestation of a formally undeclared identity (unacknowledged but evidently real), and this identity helped them adapt more quickly and easily to their new roles as statesmen, their new social standing, and the community of the contemporary ruling elite to which they belonged.

In an interesting illustration of the symbolic importance of lifestyle, one key issue in the debates surrounding the post-1956 deportation of Imre Nagy and his associates to Romania concerned accommodation and provisions for the exiled politicians.[19] In addition to betraying the pettiness of the party leadership of the Kádár era, the significance ascribed to this question even under comparatively extreme circumstances reveals that the party leadership in Hungary thought the lifestyle that the members of the exiled group were permitted to lead in Romania constituted a symbolic expression of their elite political standing. In other words, it indicated whether they had been permanently removed from the party leadership. The exiled politicians themselves may have interpreted this in very much the same way.

In an early October 1956 article in *Irodalmi Újság* titled "Why I Don't Like Them?" writer and literary translator Gyula Háy published a vicious attack against the uneducated, die-hard functionaries. Háy mocked the cadres, who rigidly clung to their privileges. Earlier, Háy himself had enjoyed the benefits reserved for those who were close to the circles of power. His article, however, is worth quoting here, not simply because he had firsthand experience of these privileges but also because, apparently, the functionaries he offended were never able or willing to forgive him. This partly explains why he remained ostracized throughout the Kádár regime.[20] Háy's fictional "Comrade Kucsera" character has the personality traits of the party functionaries, who were universally detested at the time: "Kucsera: a parvenu. And the parvenus, the nouveau riche, preening in their nouveau richness and their newly acquired power, are always disgusting. I don't think world history has born witness to a proliferation of parvenuship as extensive and widespread as that of the Kucseras."[21] This statement and Háy's indignation indicate that the party-state elite not only controlled the redistribution of nationalized resources but, in stark contrast with the ideology of the age, they benefited considerably from their access to these resources.

The following story also testifies to the virtually unbreakable unity of the ruling elite's lifestyle. As noted above, after the 1956 revolution, the party leadership under Kádár expatriated Imre Nagy, the prime minister of the revolution, and several of his close colleagues and their families to Snagov, Romania. In November 1956, one of the children, who was looking for cats that had gone astray on the shore of Lake Snagov, allegedly asked

Zoltán Szántó, a minister without portfolio in the revolutionary government and a veteran of the communist movement, "Mr. Kucsera, did you see my cats?" The child's parents called Szántó Kucsera behind his back. Zoltán Szántó was upset by this, and he resented the fact that his fellow prisoners secretly referred to him as a parvenu of the regime.[22]

From the perspective of the historian today, what does this word *parvenu*—or *parvenuship*, the phenomenon for which Háy coined such an awkward word (the Hungarian word is as awkward as the English translation)—actually mean? It may have referred to an individual's affiliation with or dissociation from a given group, expressed through the observance or violation of certain behavioral rules. One could paraphrase Oscar Wilde, who claimed that the true mystery of life is hidden not in the invisible but in the visible. Cadres found the pre–Second World War world to which they had access through their positions and the perpetuation of protocol much more comprehensible than the utopia of communism. To continue the opening metaphor of this book, the gate was opened and all the secrets of the manor house were revealed to them. In the spaces and times representing power, cadres saw a world that captured them in its tow like a whirlpool. The culture of the Hungarian ruling elite had always contained an element of the occult, as the sense of belonging to the select group was reinforced by rituals such as obsolete dress codes and anachronistic patterns of behavior. The elite was transformed into an exclusive, mysterious community by the rituals of initiation and the adherence to tradition.

The behavioral patterns displayed by individual members of the elite were of key importance. While customs associated with the elite during the 1950s indicated the position someone had reached and the power she or he had acquired, later they became a cohesive force and a kind of common law. Naturally, members of the elite formulated their own style, each according to his or her own personality and the role consciously taken within the group. György Marosán, a communist politician who originally had worked as a baker's man and who liked to pose as a representative of the working class in the party leadership (although he spent most of his career as a functionary and lived a professional life of privilege), allegedly started his speech in 1957 at the Győr theater by addressing the crowd as, "pimps, whores, ladies and gentlemen, and comrades! I hope I did not leave anybody out and did not offend anyone!"[23] Marosán made particular efforts to ensure that his speeches would be remembered for their informal simplicity, which he considered characteristic of working-class discourse but which, in fact, was rooted in his own style and lifestyle.

In contrast, Zoltán Vas, a party leader under the Rákosi regime, was widely known as a man about town. He frequented cafés and apparently was drawn to the world that was described as bourgeois but populated by party functionaries. Even as the head of the National Planning Office, Vas was liberal with finances. He allocated millions of forints by scribbling notes on scraps of paper, and he acted as if he were handing out money from his own purse. According to Sándor Gáspár, in the course of a labor council meeting during the 1956 revolution, Vas was invited to begin his speech by saying, "I have all my life been and continue to be a middle-class man." He was still shouted down: "Boo, communist, down with him."[24] Ede Horváth later offered the following remarks about the aging Vas: "The last time I saw him was in Váci Street. Two young women were hooked on his right arm and his left. 'Are you still in Győr?' he asked. 'Of course,' I said, 'and how are you, Comrade Vas?' He laughed out loud. 'Look at me, could I be doing any better than this?'"[25]

Everyone had to adopt some kind of attitude or approach to tradition, but among the party leaders, Kádár alone created a style to be followed. He led the colorful multitude of working-class-minded functionaries, bon vivants, and patrons of the arts. As had been the case in the Rákosi era, under Kádár, the essential feature of the cult of personality was the carefully constructed and staged appearances of the figure who was the center of attention. During the three decades of his reign, Kádár always avoided shows of luxury. He presented himself to the public as a puritanical man. He played this part not only when on the public stage but also when among the elite. As a consequence, his more reserved behavior and restrained conduct set the boundaries. As Miklós Horthy himself had done in the interwar period, Kádár presented himself as the veritable trustee of consolidation, both in his appearances before the wider public and when among the ruling elite.

If perhaps with shifting meanings and to different extents, the forms of conduct and behavior that are prescribed by society characterize the ruling groups and power elites of different eras, and it sometimes can seem as if they are intertwined in ways that depend neither on time nor on place. Elements of behavior that are passed on as tradition do not simply determine and hold together social groups; they also re-create these social groups as time passes. The ruling elite of the socialist era took form in a collision zone (a symbolic space) on the borders of opposing cultures and eras. With its mere existence, this borderland, in addition to being a symbolic battleground, created a link between the two eras and dissolved some of the tension. In their creation of traditions that passed to subsequent generations, the party leaders played a role as a kind of lifestyle intermediary. Like a dry sponge, they absorbed everything they could of the old traditions and thus became both trustees and even representatives of the traditions of the Horthy era. Beginning in the 1970s, members of increasingly affluent social groups—who, in terms of their wealth, were closing in on the elite—began to adopt the customs and lifestyles of the ruling elite.

Jacques Lacan has offered an allegory, by now familiar to many, concerning the potentials for recognition. Two siblings, a boy and a girl, are sitting in a train compartment, face to face. As the train arrives in the station, they both see a small building next to the platform and they both realize at the same time that they have arrived somewhere. "We're at Ladies," says the boy to the girl, to which the girl replies, "No, we're at Gentlemen." Looking from different perspectives, they see different images. The allegory touches on the relationship between the signifier and the signified. There are always several perspectives from which to confront any phenomenon, never merely the single perspective of one individual. If we wish to see a scene in its entirety, we cannot describe the spectacle with images that have been flipped over. There are common perspectives from which the spectacle can be described in its entirety. In examining society in socialist Hungary, the existence of the ruling elite symbolized both socialist power and the presence of the dictatorship, but through the privileges this ruling elite enjoyed, it also became a distinctive group with a distinctive lifestyle. It thus became a community separate from other groups in the larger society and therefore acquired clear social boundaries. The lifestyle of this elite constituted a distinctive point of comparison and orientation for the other groups of socialist society—and not only in terms of the relationship to power but also in the sphere of consumer habits. The ruling elite focused less on protecting the system and using force to ensure its own access to power and more on maintaining control of consumption and defending its own consumer interests. Gradually, its alleged identity as an agent and embodiment of "revolution" began to fray. Beneath the veil of socialist ideology, the members of the elite strove increasingly to maintain oversight over consumer habits and to shape these habits to meet their demands. And in the meantime, they, too, adapted.

This study of the lifestyles and consumer cultures in socialist Hungary dispels the pervasive myth of the grayness of everyday life under socialism. The Hungarian society of the era constructed and accommodated various forms of consumption, and competition among and within social groups continued during socialism. There was no abrupt rift between the lifestyles of the social classes and the elite under socialism on the one hand and the customs of the prewar period and consumer cultures of the West on the other. The self-identification of the different social groups was linked to consumer habits, lifestyles, and—through these—often to the trends and tendencies of the nonsocialist world. The communist ruling elite was not hostile to the consumer world of capitalism, and it attempted to enjoy the advantages of a form of capitalism in daily life. In many cases, the legal rules of the system were modified in accordance with this goal.[26] The ruling elite either followed its own individual or collective aims or sought to assert the legitimacy of its reign in everyday life.

The storms of history left clearly discernible marks on the legacy that the elite represented and passed on. Fülöp Merán's memoir, which I cited in the opening passages of this book, describes the front that passed through Csákberény in 1944. On one occasion, Merán went snipe hunting with his sibling. When they went into the parlor to show their parents the game they had bagged, they found three German air force officers on the sofa. One of them was a passionate hunter, and he eagerly examined the kill: "In the meantime, blood was dripping onto the blue sofa. No one noticed, and the blood was absorbed by the blue fabric, leaving a lasting stain, since no one washed it out. We noticed the blood stain on 11 December 1944, after our last lunch, when we had our last Csákberény coffee in the parlor. That afternoon we left the village of our birth for good."[27] In the 1970s, after having gone boar hunting in the Vértes Hills, an old guest at the Csákberényi hunting lodge noticed the blue sofa in a corner of the dining room of the newly furnished lodge. It had been thoroughly cleaned, but there was stubborn spot on the blue fabric.[28]

The blue sofa, an adornment in the parlor of the Csákberény mansion, was preserved by history—or rather by all the people who had taken care of it and stood (or stood guard) at the gate. They had kept watch over the road to the manor house, the people passing through its gate, and the rituals of initiation as it changed hands. The notion of the gatekeeper became part of the terminology in the social sciences through the example offered by Kurt Lewin of the housewife. According to traditional gender roles and stereotypes, the attentive mother and wife is the person who decides who and what will be allowed into the household.[29] She strolls down the aisles of the store and puts the things she has selected from the shelves (for the most part, according to her tastes) into the basket. She makes decisions that affect the health and well-being of the family. Thus, she stands (guard) at the gate. Only someone who can exert some degree of supervision over the group can be a gatekeeper.

The cadres of the socialist era in Hungary were both guards and conservators, for they first scrutinized traditions and then adopted them and passed them on. And though they had prepared to play roles as gatekeepers (and had indeed kept watch over the transformation of consumer habits), in the end they became the people who opened the gate in an era in which ideology and the political power system had erected a wall between the past and the present, and also walls between the various social groups. To extend the metaphor of the gatekeeper, the walls of the occupied manor house—in other words, the new order, consumer socialism—may have seemed sturdy, but after a while, no one was guarding the gates.

NOTES

1. Fitzpatrick 2015.
2. Schiffer 1985, 228.
3. Ignotus 1993, 62.
4. Schiffer 1985, 261–262.
5. Nánási 1983, 229.
6. András Hegedüs offers the following recollections: "When I became a member of the secretaryship, this was when I discovered that there was a high secretaryship with the Hungarian Workers' Party, to which Rákosi,

Gerő, Révai, and sometimes Farkas belonged. This high secretaryship called itself the oversight committee for the party secretaryship (it had some kind of awful name like this)." *Hegedüs András visszaemlékezése 1945 utáni tevékenységéről* (András Hegedüs' recollections of his activities after 1945), 25. Vera and Donald Blinken Open Society Archives (hereafter cited as OSA), fond 361, 0-4, box 29.

7. Report on the death of Sándor Zöld, March 29, 1962, Állambiztonsági Szolgálatok Történeti Levéltára (Historical Archives of the Hungarian State Security, hereafter cited as HAHSS), fond 2.1, IX/27, 2–4; László Varga 2001, 199.

8. Report on the death of Sándor Zöld. March 29, 1962, HAHSS, fond 2.1., IX/27. 2–4; László Varga 2001, 200.

9. In his book *Intelmek túlélőknek* (Admonitions to survivors), András Hegedüs cites poet Dezső Szabó: "Often, the sin of omission is greater than all the sins of commission." Dezső Szabó 1990, 51.

"This is the story of my entire life. I do not have a guilty conscience for what I have done so much as for what I failed to do. One clear example of this is the Zöld affair. I was silent about how I experienced the drama of Sándor Zöld, and how the pang of conscience has been awake in me ever since for not having found out the truth. I resigned myself to the fact that in all the publications the tragedy would be presented as if Zöld had massacred his family and then killed himself. I resigned myself to the fact that the so-called oversight committee for the party secretaryship, the "foursome," would sweep the whole thing under the rug, although it is almost certain that Sándor Zöld and his family were killed by the state security. This kind of Zöld case came up more than once in my life." Hegedüs 1999, 21.

In his memoir published in 1988, Hegedüs writes the following on the tragedy: "According to the official account, the inquiry led by the state security confirmed that Zöld had massacred his family in a hysterical fit and then killed himself. In contrast, a version of the events persists to this day according to which they had wanted to arrest Sándor Zöld, he had tried to defend himself, and his family had been killed in the firefight. My knowledge of the case suggests that the first version is more likely." Hegedüs 1988, 150.

10. "A nagy Mezei András-interjú I" (Interview with Andras Mezei), OSA, fond 361, 0-13, box 2.

11. Interview with Antal Apró, National Széchényi Library, Collection of Historical Interviews, 283.

12. Hegedüs 1988, 150–151. He tells the same story with minor changes in Hegedüs 1985, 125; Hegedüs András visszaemlékezése 1945 utáni tevékenységéről (András Hegedüs' recollections of his activities after 1945), 26. OSA, fond 361, 0-4, box 29.

13. It is worth citing Sheila Fitzpatrick, according to whom the socialist system naturally did not realize the vision of a state in which the working class was in power, though the individuals whom the system gave opportunities for social advancement did in fact see it, from their perspectives, as such a state. Fitzpatrick 1979a, 1979b, 1984.

14. Imre Nagy 2006, 93.

15. Interview with Károly Grósz, National Széchényi Library, Collection of Historical Interviews, 383.

16. György Aczél 1999, 119.

17. Lányi 1994, 37–38.

18. "A nagy Mezei András-interjú" (Interview with András Mezei), I. OSA, fond 361, 0-13, box 2, 4.

19. Initially, the Romanian party provided Imre Nagy and his wife with "accommodation and provisions" appropriate for the normal customs of hospitality. Beginning in January, however, when the political future of the group became increasingly hopeless, this changed and the conditions worsened. Nagy and his wife were then given the same treatment as the rest of the group: "They were no longer given chocolate, bonbons, jam, salami, cookies, raisin bread (Turkish bread), brioche, salted rolls, white bread, milk, cream, coco, poultry, apples, oranges or fruit, mineral water, wine, beer, cognac, vermouth, etc." Vida 2006, 14–15. At a sitting of the Temporary Executive Committee of the Hungarian Socialist Workers' Party, Gyula Kállai claimed that "the group is being treated like princes. No one in Romania or even Hungary lives like they are being treated.... The princely treatment should be brought down to middle class treatment." Baráth and Sipos 2006, 411.

20. Gyula Háy, "Why I Don't Like Them?" *Irodalmi Újság*, October 6, 1956. According to Háy, "Kucsera has no place in the class system, because the class society in which he would fit cannot come into being." In contrast, in an essay written in 1989, Iván Szelényi offered the following characterization of the Kádár bureaucracy: "The Hungarian Kádár bureaucracy has neither the power nor really the desire to reestablish the system. It too has become too 'embourgeoised.' They have built themselves villas, furnished their homes with antique furniture, and sent their children to English-language schools.... On the basis of this, I think that the specter

of communism, the danger of a return to a monolithic state economy and a corresponding social and political structure does not really threaten Hungary." Szelényi 1991, 205. The essay was based on one written for the Conference on Embourgeoisement of the Village Sociology Section of the Hungarian Sociological Society. It was published in 1989, in the sixteenth issue of *Hitel* (Credit).

21. Standeisky 1996, 320–326. For a collection of documents presenting the privileges and support provided for writers during the Kádár era, see Gyula Tóth 1992.

22. The story is recounted in Murányi 2006, 75–77.

23. Ede Horváth 1990, 58.

24. Interview with Sándor Gáspár, Országos Széchényi Könyvtár (National Széchényi Library), Történeti Interjúk Tára (Collection of Historical Interviews), 149; Zoltán Vas 1990, 276.

25. Ede Horváth 1990, 56.

26. Miklóssy 2014, 185.

27. Merán 2006, 62. Merán writes about the smaller stains on the fabric as well: "Antatelle, for instance, sat down on a sandwich, the young teacher couldn't hold his whiskey... and the violence of the war also left its marks on it." Ibid., 61–65.

28. Ibid., 65.

29. See Kurt Lewin's classic and frequently cited work on customs concerning food: Lewin 1943. See also David Manning White 1950.

AFTERWORD

THE HISTORIAN STANDS AT THE gate when she decides which stories to pass on from the past to the present and future, and how to write, structure, and edit these stories. The writing of history is a personal genre, but there are visible rules, as in the case of source criticism, as well as invisible arcs and lines, as in the case of the zeitgeist. The historian is a participant in and product of her own era and culture. She treats events as facts, but only the events that she herself thinks of as real or true. She searches for the form that best suits her narrative needs, and naturally this form is, at least to some extent, part of the content of the narrative. In her text, the historian creates the interconnections between the events of the narrated past and the information found in the sources.

This book is about communist party leaders who knew and who nurtured traditions and the customs of the elite of the Horthy era and who passed on everything that they were able to preserve of this heritage. The so-called K line, which I have suggested runs metaphorically like a thread through this historical process, has led us to a metaphorical manor house. I envisioned (and sketched in my narrative) the walls of the manor house surrounding this group, the cadres, so that we would be able to see them all standing together in one place at one time. In one of the tales in *One Thousand and One Nights*, Aladdin asks the genie to build a palace fit for the princess: "Build me a palace of the finest marble, set with jasper, agate, and other precious stones. In the middle, you shall build me a large hall with a dome, its four walls of massy gold and silver, each side having six windows, whose lattices, all except one, which is to be left unfinished, must be set with diamonds and rubies."[1]

I have finished this narrative, and the story ends here. An author might be tempted, now, to straighten up the books and photocopies on the table and offer a summary. Perhaps some readers will find fault with me for neglecting to do so, for failing to offer a clearly linear narrative that swells from a slow accumulation of details into long, carefully composed sentences and then ambitious generalizations, like a river flowing into the sea—or a story flowing into history. In my view, one reads in much the same manner as one writes, and the reverse is also true. Narrative is a constituent part of every history, and the manner and structure of the narrative matters. I have an aversion to resolute assertions, which can only be understood in a single, authoritative (authorial) way and which therefore are condescending, at best, to the reader.

And someday someone else will reexamine the themes and issues explored in this narrative from a new perspective, and that process will yield new and (for me) surprising insights.

NOTE

1. "Aladdin and the Wonderful Lamp," 2005, 305–306.

BIBLIOGRAPHY

Aczél, György. 1999. "Egy Kádár-portré töredékei" [The fragments of a Kádár portrait]. *Beszélő* [Speaker], no. 10, 101–129.

Aczél, Tamás, and Tibor Méray. 1982. *Tisztító vihar* [Cleansing storm]. Munich: Griff Kiadó.

Adorno, Theodor W. 2003. "Der Essay als Form" [The essay as form]. In *Gesammelte Schriften*, vol. 11, 9–33. Frankfurt: Suhrkamp.

"Aladdin and the Wonderful Lamp." 2005. In *The Arabian Nights Entertainments*, edited by Andrew Lang, 295–315. New York: Dover.

Alliluyeva, Svetlana. 1967. *Twenty Letters to a Friend*. Translated by Priscilla Johnson. New York: Harper and Row.

———. 1969: *Only One Year*. Translated by Paul Chavchavadze. New York: Harper and Row.

Almár, György, et al. 1961. *A dolgozó nő otthon* [The working woman at home]. Launched and with editing by Blanka Simon. Budapest: Táncsics.

Apor, Péter. 2002. "Immortalis imperator: A Munkásmozgalmi Panteon születése" [The birth of the pantheon of the workers' movement]. *Aetas*, no. 2–3, 179–205.

Asturias, Miguel Ángel, and Pablo Neruda. 1968. *Megkóstoltuk Magyarországot* [We sampled Hungary]. Budapest: Corvina.

Augustin, Andreas. 2002. *Grand Hotel Royal Budapest*. With the collaboration of Noémi Saly; translated by Tamás Nemes. The Most Famous Hotels in the World series. Vienna: n.p.

Bakó, Endre, Imre Hajdú, and Sándor Marik. 2005. *Általuk híres e föld: Kilencvenkilenc interjú három megyéből* [This soil is famous because of them: Ninety-nine interviews from three counties], edited by Sándor Ésik. Nyíregyháza, Hungary: In-Forma Kiadó.

Bán, István. 1996. "A vadászat általános etikai normái" [The general ethical norms of hunting]. In *Vadászetika I* [Hunting ethics 1], edited by István Bán, 29–44. Budapest: Lipták Kiadó.

Bányai, Tamás. 2005. "A kommunista hatalmi elit életmódja" [The lifestyle of the communist power elite]. Master's thesis, Eötvös Loránd Tudományegyetem [Eötvös Loránd University], Department of Sociology.

Baráth, Magdolna. 2007. "Kis októberi forradalom: Hruscsov leváltása és a magyar pártvezetés" [The small October Revolution: The replacement of Khrushchev and the Hungarian party leadership]. *Múltunk* [Our past], no. 4, 170–212.

Baráth, Magdolna, and Levente Sipos, eds. 2006. *A snagovi foglyok: Nagy Imre és társai Romániában. Iratok* [The Snagov prisoners: Imre Nagy and his associates in Romania. Documents]. Budapest: Napvilág; Hungarian National Archives.

Barthes, Roland. 1990. *The Fashion System*. Translated by Matthew Ward and Richard Howard. Berkeley: University of California Press.

Bartlett, Djurdja. 2010. *Fashion East: The Spectre That Haunted Socialism*. Cambridge, MA: MIT Press.

Beetham, David. 1991. *The Legitimation of Power*. New York: Palgrave.

Berecz, János. 2003. *Vállalom* [I take it upon myself]. Budapest: Budapest-Print.

Beretz, Katalin. 2001. *Puskák, pajzsok, fohászok* [Rifles, shields, petitions]. Budapest: Zeusz.

Berta, Erzsébet. 1994. "Egy új építészet felől" [From the perspective of a new architecture]. *Magyar Építőművészet* [Hungarian architecture], no. 3–4, 2–6.

Bibó, István. 1986. "Elit és szociális érzék" [Elite and social sense]. In *Válogatott tanulmányok* [Selected essays]. Vol. 1, *1935–1944*, 221–241. Budapest: Magvető.

Bódy, Zsombor. 2008. "A vásárlás és a történészek: A fogyasztás története a politikatörténet, a gazdaságtörténet és a társadalom/kultúrtörténet metszéspontján a német nyelvű történetírásban" [Shopping and historians: The history of consumption at the intersection of political history, economic history, and social/cultural history in German-language historiography]. *Múltunk* [Our past], no. 3, 17–39.

Bojár, Iván András. 1998. "Az öregember mögött: A Hilton Szálló építése (1969–1976)" [Behind the old man: The construction of Hilton Hotel]. *Beszélő* [Speaker] 3 (7–8): 149–153.
Borenich, Péter. 1995. "A Kádár-villa titka" [The secret of the Kádár villa]. In *A Kádár-villa titka* [The secret of the Kádár villa], 175–194. Budapest: Mécs László Lap- és Könyvkiadó. (Based on a radio broadcast, November 11, 1993, Kossuth Rádió, 17:05.)
Böröcz, József, and Ákos Róna-Tas. 1995. "Small Leap Forward: The Emergence of New Economic Elites." *Theory and Society*, no. 24, 754–781.
Bottomore, Tom. 1993. *Elites and Societies*. 2nd ed. London: Routledge.
Bren, Paulina. 2010. *The Greengrocer and His TV: The Culture of Communism after the 1968 Prague Spring*. Ithaca, NY: Cornell University Press.
Bren, Paulina, and Mary Neuburger, eds. 2012. *Communism Unwrapped: Consumption in Cold War Eastern Europe*. Oxford: Oxford University Press.
Brutyó, János. 1983. *A választott úton* [On the chosen path]. Budapest: Népszava.
Burant, Stephen R. 1987. "The Influence of Russian Tradition on the Political Style of the Soviet Elite." *Political Science Quarterly* 102, no. 2 (Summer): 273–293.
Butrym, Alexander J., ed. 1989. *Essays on the Essay: Redefining the Genre*. Athens: University of Georgia Press.
Campbell, Colin. 1987. *The Romantic Ethic and the Spirit of Modern Consumerism*. Oxford: Basil Blackwell.
Canetti, Elias. 1984. *Crowds and Power*. Translated by Carol Steward. New York: Farrar, Straus, and Giroux.
Carnap, Rudolf. 1931. "Überwindung der Metaphysik durch logische Analyse der Sprache" [Metaphysical elimination through linguistic logical analysis]. *Erkenntnis*, no. 2, 219–241. https://doi.org/10.1007/BF02028153.
Cavender, Mary. 2014. "Provincial Nobles, Elite History, and the Imagination of Everyday Life." In *Everyday Life in Russia: Past and Present*, edited by Choi Chatterjee, David L. Rancel, Mary Cavender, and Karen Petrone, 35–51. Bloomington: Indiana University Press.
Connell, R. W. 1987. *Gender and Power: Society, the Person, and Sexual Politics*. Stanford, CA: Stanford University Press.
Connell, R. W., and James W. Messerschmidt. 2005. "Hegemonic Masculinity: Rethinking the Concept." *Gender Society*, no. 19, 829–859.
Crowley, David, and Susan E. Reid, eds. 2012. *Pleasures in Socialism: Leisure and Luxury in the Eastern Bloc*. Evanston, IL: Northwestern University Press.

Csapó, Katalin. 1996. "A százéves irodalmi kávéház, a 'Newyork'" [The one-hundred-year-old coffee house, the "New York"]. *Budapesti Negyed* [Budapest quarterly], no. 2–3, 177–198.

Czibor, Zoltán. 1998. "A forradalomban" [In the revolution]. Text made available by György Szöllősi; with foreword and footnotes by József N. Pál. *Kortárs* [Contemporary], no. 10, 34–40.

Dékán, István, and Éva D. Kardos. 1975. *Utak és ösvények* [Roads and paths]. Budapest: Magvető.

Déri, Károly. 1952. *Hogyan teljesítette Pióker Ignác ötéves tervét 23 hónap alatt* [How did Ignác Pióker finish his five-year plan in 23 months]. Budapest: n.p.

Djilas, Milovan. 1966. *The New Class: An Analysis of the Communist System.* London: Unwin.

Dózsa, Katalin F. 2003. "Jó reggelt, búbánat! Állami Áruház" [Good morning woe! The state department store]. In *Párizs és Budapest a divat tükrében, 1750–2003: Kiállítás a Budapest Történeti Múzeumban* [Paris and Budapest in the mirror of fashion, 1750–2003: Exhibition in the Budapest History Museum], edited by Katalin F. Dózsa and Erzsébet Déri Hegyi, 109–112. Budapest: Budapest History Museum.

Dózsa, Katalin F., and Erzsébet Déri Hegyi, eds. 2003. *Párizs és Budapest a divat tükrében, 1750–2003: Kiállítás a Budapest Történeti Múzeumban* [Paris and Budapest in the mirror of fashion, 1750–2003: Exhibition in the Budapest History Museum]. Budapest: Budapest History Museum.

Dusza, András. 2003. *A birodalom végnapjai: Így láttam Horváth Edét* [The last days of the empire: How I saw Ede Horváth]. Győr, Hungary: X-Meditor Kft.

Easter, Gerald. 2000. *Reconstructing the State: Personal Networks and Elite Identity in Soviet Russia.* Cambridge: Cambridge University Press.

Elias, Norbert. 2005. *Az udvari társadalom* [Court society]. Budapest: Napvilág.

Ember, Mária. 2001. "A kis magyar 'focialista forradalom'" [The little Hungarian "socc(ialist)er revolution"]. *Eső* [Rain], no. 1, 40–45.

Epstein, Mikhail. 1999. "Essayism: An Essay on the Essay." In *Russian Postmodernism: New Perspectives on Post-Soviet Culture*, edited by Mikhail Epstein, Alexander Genis, and Slobodanka Vladiv-Glover, 152–157. New York: Berghahn Books. First published 1982.

Erki, Edit. 1996. *Pest-Budától Budapestig: Képek egy város életéből* [From Pest-Buda to Budapest: Pictures from the life of a city]. Budapest: Officina.

Faludy, György. 1989. *Pokolbéli víg napjaim* [My happy days in hell]. Budapest: Magyar Világ.
Fehérváry, Krisztina. 2009. "Goods and States: The Political Logic of State Socialist Material Culture." *Comparative Studies in Society and History*, no. 51, 426–459.
———. 2013. *Politics in Color and Concrete: Socialist Materialities and the Middle Class in Hungary*. Bloomington: Indiana University Press.
Fekete, Judit. 2006. "Divatot a dolgozó nőnek! Zamuskin elvtárs és az ötvenes-hatvanas évek divatja" [Fashion for the working woman! Comrade Zamushkin and the fashion of the 1950s and 1960s]. *Magyar Iparművészet* [Hungarian applied arts], no. 2, 8–10.
Fitzpatrick, Sheila. 1979a. *Education and Social Mobility in the Soviet Union, 1921–1934*. Cambridge: Cambridge University Press.
———. 1979b. "Stalin and the Making of a New Elite, 1928–1939." *Slavic Review* 38, no. 3 (September): 377–402.
———. 1984. "The Russian Revolution and Social Mobility: A Reexamination of the Question of Social Support for the Soviet Regime in the 1920s and 1930s." *Politics and Society* 13 (2): 119–141.
———. 1999. *Everyday Stalinism: Ordinary Life in Extraordinary Times; Soviet Russia in the 1930s*. New York: Oxford University Press.
———. 2005. *Tear Off the Masks! Identity and Imposture in Twentieth-Century Russia*. Princeton, NJ: Princeton University Press.
———. 2014. Afterword in *Everyday Life in Russia: Past and Present*, by Choi Chatterjee, David L. Rancel, Mary Cavender, and Karen Petrone, 390–415. Bloomington: Indiana University Press.
———. 2015. *On Stalin's Team: The Years of Living Dangerously in Soviet Politics*. Princeton, NJ: Princeton University Press.
Földes, László. 1984. *A második vonalban* [On the second line]. Budapest: Kossuth.
———. n.d. *Hobo Sapiens*. Budapest: Hírlapkiadó Vállalat.
Fóris, Zoltán, László Kozári, Mihály Németh, Tibor Tóth, and György Zohna, eds. 1964. *100 éves a Budapesti Bútorgyár (1864–1964)* [The Budapest furniture factory is 100 years old (1864–1964)]. Budapest: n.p.
Gábor, Eszter. 1997. *Budapesti villák a kiegyezéstől a második világháborúig* [Budapest villas from the compromise to the Second World War]. Budapest: Municipal Government, Office of the Mayor.
Gál, Éva. 2001. "A Hegyvidék betelepülése a török kiűzésétől a XIX. század közepéig" [The settlement of the hilly neighborhoods of Buda since the expulsion of the Ottoman Turks]. In *Hegytörténet: Hegytörténeti*

konferencia [Hill history: Hill history conference], edited by Ferenc Noéh, 19–27. Budapest: XII District Local Government; Tarsoly Kiadó.

———. 2009. "Lakás vagy nyaraló" [Apartment or summer home]. *Budapesti Negyed* [Budapest quarterly], no. 63 (Spring): 35–64.

Gál, László. 2005. *"Csak a szépre…" Budapesti életképek az 1950–60-as évekből* ["Only to the beautiful…" Pictures of Budapest from the 1950s and 1960s]. Budapest: Fekete Sas.

Gáspár, Ferenc, and Klára Szabó. 1985. "Adalékok a főváros lakóinak 1955: évi hangulatáról" [Data on the mood of the people of the capital in 1955]. *Budapest Főváros Levéltára Közleményei '84* [Publications of the Budapest municipal archive from '84], 351–383.

Getty, John Archibald. 1985. *Origin of the Great Purges: The Soviet Communist Party Reconsidered, 1933–1938*. Cambridge: Cambridge University Press.

———. 1999. "The Road to Terror and Samokritika Rituals in the Stalinist Central Committee, 1933–1938." *Russian Review* 58 (1): 49–70.

———. 2013. *Practicing Stalinism*. New Haven, CT: Yale University Press.

Gill, Graeme. 1988. *The Origins of the Stalinist Political System and the Rules of the Communist Party of the Soviet Union*. Basingstoke, UK: Macmillan.

Giustino, Cathleen M., Catherine J. Plum, and Alexander Vari, eds. 2013. *Socialist Escapes: Breaking Away from Ideology and Everyday Routine in Eastern Europe, 1945–1989*. New York: Berghahn Books.

Gorlizki, Yoram, and Oleg V. Khlevniuk. 2004. *Cold Peace: Stalin and the Soviet Ruling Circle, 1945–1953*. Oxford: Oxford University Press.

Gronow, Jukka. 2003. *Caviar with Champagne: Common Luxury and the Ideals of the Good Life in Stalin's Russia*. Oxford: Berg.

Gundel, Imre, and Judit Harmath. 1979. *A vendéglátás emlékei* [Memories of the hospitality business]. Budapest: Közgazdasági és Jogi.

Gyáni, Gábor. 1992. "Polgári otthon és enteriőr Budapesten" [Middle-class homes and interiors in Budapest]. In *Polgári lakáskultúra a századfordulón* [Middle-class interior design culture at the turn of the century], edited and with an introduction by Péter Hanák, 27–59. Budapest: MTA (Magyar Tudományos Akadémia) Történettudományi Intézet [HAS (Hungarian Academy of Sciences) Institute of History].

Gyarmati, György. 2009. "Hatalmi elit Magyarországon a 20: század második felében, 1945–1989" [The power elite in Hungary in the first half of the twentieth century, 1945–1989]. *Korunk* [Our time] 20, no. 3 (March): 75–88.

György, Péter. 2005. *Kádár köpönyege* [Kádár's cloak]. Budapest: Magvető.

György, Péter, and Zsolt Durkó Jr. 1993. *Utánzatok városa—Budapest* [City of imitations—Budapest]. Budapest: Cserépfalvi.
Habermas, Jürgen. 2011. *The Structural Transformation of the Public Sphere: An Inquiry into a Category of Bourgeois Society*. Translated by Burger Thomas with Lawrence Frederick. Cambridge: Polity. First published 1962.
Hadas, Miklós. 2003. "A vadászattól a lóversenyig" [From hunting to horse racing]. In *A modern férfi születése* [The birth of the modern man], 109–134. Budapest: Helikon.
Hadas, Miklós, and Viktor Karády. 1995. "Futball és társadalmi identitás: Adalékok a magyar futball társadalmi jelentéstartalmainak történelmi vizsgálatához" [Soccer and social identity: Data for a historical study of the social meanings of Hungarian soccer]. *Replika* [Replica], no. 17–18, 89–121.
Hajdú, Tibor. 1983. "Kérdőjelek R. M. hiányzó portréjához" [Question marks for the missing portrait of M. R.]. *Élet és Irodalom* [Life and literature], no. 6, 5.
Hajduska, István. 1988. *Tollforgató forgószélben* [Writer in a whirlwind]. Budapest: Tömegkommunikációs Kutatóközpont.
Hámori, Tibor. 1982: *Puskás: Legenda és valóság* [Puskás: Legend and truth]. 2nd ed. Budapest: Sportpropaganda.
Havadi, Gergő. 2006. "Az új 'népi szórakozóhely': A 'hosszú' ötvenes évek Budapestjének életvilága a szocialista vendéglátásban" [The new "people's amusement spot": Budapest life in the socialist hospitality industry during the "long" 1950s]. *FONS: Forráskutatás és Történeti Segédtudományok* [Source research and historical auxiliary sciences], no. 3, 315–354.
———. 2008. "Állambiztonság és a vendéglátás szigorúan ellenőrzött terei a szocializmusban: A 'Koccintós'-csoport leleplezése" [State security and the rigorously watched spaces of the hospitality industry during socialism: The discovery of the "toast-drinking" group]. In *Mindennapok Rákosi és Kádár korában* [Everyday life in the era of Rákosi and Kádár], edited by Sándor Horváth, 172–186. Budapest: Nyitott Könyvműhely.
Hegedüs, András. 1985. *Élet egy eszme árnyékában* [Life in the shadow of an idea]. Interview with Zoltán Zsille. Vienna.
———. 1988: *A történelem és a hatalom igézetében* [In the thrall of history and power]. Budapest: Kossuth.
———. 1999: *Intelmek túlélőknek* [Warnings to the survivors]. Budapest: Munkásakadémia Alapítvány.

Hoch, Róbert, Ilona Kovács, and Miklós Ördög. 1982. *Fogyasztás és jövedelem: Tervezés, elemzés, módszerek* [Consumption and income: Planning, analysis, methods]. Budapest: Közgazdasági és Jogi.
Hoffmann, David Lloyd. 2003. *Stalinist Values: The Cultural Norms of Soviet Modernity, 1917–1941.* Ithaca, NY: Cornell University Press.
Hollander, Paul. 1988. *The Many Faces of Socialism.* New Brunswick, NJ: Transaction.
Honvári, János. 2006. A hatalmi "elit" jövedelme az 50-es években [The income of the power "elite" in the 1950s]. Archivnet, 6, no. 1. Accessed June 15, 2007. https://archivnet.hu/gazdasag/a_hatalmi_elit_jovedelme _az_50es_evekben.html.
Horányi, Éva. 2006. *Kozma Lajos modern épületei* [The modern buildings of Lajos Kozma]. Budapest: Terc.
Horváth, Ede. 1990. *Én volnék a vörös báró?* [So I am the red baron?]. Edited by Imre Cserhalmi. Pécs, Hungary: Idegenforgalmi Propaganda és Kiadó Vállalat.
Horváth, Sándor. 2002. "Der Ungarische Stachanow: Imre Muszka" [The Hungarian Stakhanovite: Imre Muszka] In *Sozialistische Helden: Eine Kulturgeschichte von Propagandafiguren in Osteuropa und der DDR* [Socialist heroes: A cultural history of propaganda characters in East Europe and in the GDR], edited by Rainer Gries and Silke Satjukow, 214–219. Berlin: Links.
———. 2007: "A lakás és a fürdő: a munkás- és szociálpolitika prototípusai az ötvenes években" [Apartment and the bath: The prototypes of work politics and social politics in the 1950s]. *Múltunk* [Our past] 2: 31–49.
———. 2017. *Stalinism Reloaded: Everyday Life in Stalin-City.* Translated by Thomas Cooper. Bloomington: Indiana University Press.
Horváth, Sándor, György Majtényi, and Eszter ZsófiaTóth. 1997. "Élmunkások és sztahanovisták" [Outstanding workers and Stakhanovites]. Unpublished manuscript, Budapest.
———. 1998: "Élmunkások és sztahanovisták" [Outstanding workers and Stakhanovites]. *História* 8: 29–32.
Huszár, Tibor, ed. 2002. *Kedves, jó Kádár elvtárs! Válogatás Kádár János levelezéséből 1954–1989* [Dear, good comrade Kádár! A selection from the correspondence of János Kádár, 1954–1989]. Budapest: Osiris.
———. 2005. "A Kádár-rendszer intézményesített káderpolitikája és az erőszakszervezetek (1957–1989)" [The institutionalized cadre politics of the Kádár system and the trade unions (1957–1989)]. In *Nómenklatúra Magyarországon (1957–1989)* [The nomenclature in Hungary (1957–1989)], 5–90. Budapest: Elte Társadalomtudományi Kar.

———. 2006. *Kádár: A hatalom évei, 1956–1989* [Kádár: The years of power, 1956–1989]. Budapest: Corvina.

———. 2007. *Az elittől a nómenklatúráig: Az intézményesített káderpolitika kialakulása Magyarországon (1945–1989)* [From the elite to the nomenclature: The development of institutionalized cadre politics in Hungary (1945–1989)]. Budapest: Corvina.

Ignotus, Pál. 1993. *Fogságban* [In captivity]. Budapest: Cserépfalvi.

Jávor, Kata. 2000. *Életmód és életmód-stratégiák a pécsi Zsolnay család történetében* [Lifestyle and lifestyle strategies in the history of the Zsolnay family]. Budapest: Akadémiai Kiadó.

Kádár, János. 1968. *Hazafiság és internacionalizmus* [Patriotism and internationalism]. Budapest: Kossuth.

Kádár Jánosné hagyatékának árverése [The auction of the bequest of Mrs. János Kádár]. 1993. Budapest: Műgyűjtők Galériája, auction house.

Kállai, Gyula. 1984. *Két világ határán*. Budapest: Kossuth.

Kántor, László. 1950. *A nagy műszak: Ifj. Horváth Ede útja a Kossuth-díjig* [The big shift: Ede Horváth Jr.'s path to the Kossuth prize]. Budapest: Hungária.

Kardos, Éva D. 2004: *Vörös alkony* [Red dusk]. Budapest: Papirusz Book.

Karinthy, Ferenc. 1950. *Kőművesek* [Masons]. Budapest: Athenaeum.

———. 1954: *Hazai tudósítások* [Domestic reports]. Budapest: n.p.

Karkovány, Judit Z. 2007. "A balatonarácsi Brázay-villa" [The Brázay villa in Balatonarács]. *Füredi História* [The history of Füred] 7, no. 2 (December): 2–7.

Kasza, Peter. 2004. *Amikor a futball történelmet ír: A berni csoda* [When soccer writes history: The miracle of Bern]. Budapest: Alexandra.

Katona, András. 2002. *Magyar Autóklub* [Hungarian automobile club]. 2nd rev. ed. Budapest: Magyar Autóklub.

Keller, Suzanne. 1963. *Beyond the Ruling Class*. New York: Random House.

Khrushchev, Nikita. 1970. *Khrushchev Remembers*. Translated and edited by Strobe Talbott. Boston: Little, Brown.

———. 1974. *Khrushchev Remembers: The Last Testament*. Translated and edited by Strobe Talbott. Boston: Little, Brown.

King, Charles W. 1963. "Fashion Adoption: A Rebuttal to the 'Trickle-Down' Theory." In *Toward Scientific Marketing*, edited by Stephen A. Greyser, 108–125. Chicago: American Marketing Association.

Kis-Kapin, Róbert. 2007. *"Úgy éltem itt, mint a bugyborék a vizen..." Péter Gábor börtönben írt feljegyzései, 1954, május-augusztus* ["I lived like a bubble on the water": Notes written in prison by Gábor Péter, May–August 1954]. *Betekintő* [Insight]. Accessed June 15, 2007.

https://betekinto.hu/sites/default/files/betekinto-szamok/2007_2
_kis_kapin.pdf.
Kiss, Tibor. 2006. "Talált tárgyak országa, avagy az 'Öreg kocsija'" [The country of found objects, or "the old man's car"]. *Szoc.reál.* [*Soc.Real*], no. 8. Accessed June 15, 2007. www.szocreal.hu.
Klaus, Carl H., and Ned Stuckey-French, eds. 2012: *Essayists on the Essay: Montaigne to Our Time.* Iowa City: University of Iowa Press.
Kő, András. 1997. *Szemétből mentett dicsőségünk: Volt egyszer egy aranycsapat* [Our honor saved from the trash: Once there was a Golden Team]. Budapest: Magyar Könyvklub.
Kő, András, and Lambert J. Nagy. 2002. *Levelek Rákosihoz* [Letters to Rákosi]. Budapest: Maecenas.
Kocka, Jürgen. 1994. "Eine durchherrsche Gesellschaft." In *Eine Sozialgeschichte der DDR*, edited by Hartmut Kaelble, Jürgen Kocka, and Helmut Zwahr, 547–553. Stuttgart: Klett-Cotta.
Kókay, György. 2001. "Dokumentumok a volt Királyi Palota háborús veszteségeiről és újjáépítésének előzményeiről" [Documents on the wartime losses to the royal palace and the antecedents to its reconstruction]. In *A Budavári Királyi Palota évszázadai: Tanulmányok Budapest múltjából* [The centuries-long history of the royal palace of the Buda castle: Essays on the history of Budapest]. Vol. 29, edited by Katalin F. Dózsa and Gabriella Szvoboda Dománszky, 293–342. Budapest: Budapest History Museum.
Komiszár, Dénes. 2007. "Mezőgazdaság és protokoll—Losonczi Pál kitüntetései a sajtó tükrében" [Agriculture and protocol—Pál Losonczi's distinctions in the mirror of the press]. *Somogyi Múzeumok Közleményei* [Papers of Somogy Museums], 2006, 91–108.
Koós, Judith. 1959. *A művészet otthon kezdődik* [Art begins at home]. Budapest: Magyar Nők Országos Tanácsa.
———. 1960: *Modern otthon* [Modern home]. Budapest: Képzőművészeti Alap Kiadóvállalata.
Kopa, János. 1999. *Magyar vadászati szó- és szokásgyűjtemény* [Hungarian hunting dictionary of terms and customs]. Budapest: Mezőgazdasági Kiadó.
Kornai, János. 2005. *A gondolat erejével: Rendhagyó önéletrajz* [By force of thought: Irregular memoirs of an intellectual journey]. Budapest: Osiris.
———. 1999. "Hatalom és ideológia" [Power and ideology]. In *Magyarország társadalomtörténete (1945–1989)* [A social history of Hungary]. Vol. 1, edited by Nikosz Fokasz and Antal Örkény, 76–96. Budapest: Új Mandátum.

Kotkin, Stephen. 2009. *Uncivil Society: 1989 and the Implosion of the Communist Establishment.* With a contribution by Jan T. Gross. New York: Modern Library.

Kovács, Gábor. 2005. "Elitek és társadalmak: A globalizáció és az információs forradalom korában" [Elites and societies: In the era of globalization and the information revolution]. In *Túl az iskolafilozófián. A 21: század bölcseleti élménye* [Beyond schoolyard philosophy: The philosophical experience of the twenty-first century], edited by Nyíri Kristóf and Palló Gábor, 355–371. Budapest: Áron Kiadó.

Kovács, Péter. 2008. "Szilánkok felnőtté válásom történetéből" [Shards from the history of my growth into an adult]. *Holmi* [Assorted things] 20, no. 11 (November): 1469–1490.

Kovács, Zsuzsa. 1968. *A lakásberendezés ábécéje* [An ABC of interior design]. Budapest: Kossuth.

Kövér, György. 1998. *Losonczy Géza, 1917–1957* [Géza Losonczy, 1917–1957]. Budapest: 1956 Institute.

Kövér, György, and Gábor Gyáni. 1998. *Magyarország társadalomtörténete a reformkortól a második világháborúig* [A social history of Hungary from the Reform Era to the Second World War]. Budapest: Osiris.

Kozák, Gyula, and Adrienne Molnár, eds. 1993. *"Szuronyok hegyén nem lehet dolgozni!" Válogatás 1956-os munkástanács-vezetők visszaemlékezéseiből* ["You can't work at the tip of a bayonet!" Selection from the recollections of the 1956 Workers' Council leaders]. Budapest: Századvég Kiadó; 1956 Institute.

Kryshtanovskaya, Olga, and Stephen White. 1996. "From Soviet Nomenklatura to Russian Elite." *Europe-Asia Studies* 48 (5): 711–733.

Kurecskó, Mihály. 2001. *Diplomaták cilinderben* [Diplomats in top hats]. Archivnet, 1, no. 2. Accessed June 15, 2007. https://archivnet.hu/diplomacia/diplomatak_cilinderben.html.

A lakosság jövedelme és fogyasztása, 1960–1978 [The income and consumption patterns of the population, 1960–1978]. 1980. Budapest: Központi Statisztikai Hivatal [Central Statistical Office].

Lányi, Gusztáv. 1994. "Rákosi Mátyás politikai antiszemitizmusa: Pszichohistóriai és történelmi szociálpszichológiai elemzés" [The political antisemitism of Mátyás Rákosi: An analysis in psycho-history and historical social psychology]. *Világosság* [Lucidity], 35 (10): 21–47.

Lasswell, Harold D. 1934. *World Politics and Personal Insecurity.* Chicago: McGraw-Hill.

———. 1948: *Power and Personality.* New York: W. W. Norton.

de Laveleye, Emile. 1891. *Luxury.* 2nd ed. London: Swan Sonnenshein.

Lewin, Kurt. 1943. "Forces behind Food Habits and Methods of Change." *Bulletin of the National Research Council* 108: 35–65.

Lindenberger, Thomas. 1999a. "Die Diktatur der Grenzen: Zur Einleitung" [The dictatorship of borders: To the introduction]. In *Herrschaft und Eigensinn in der Diktatur: Studien zur Gesellschaftsgeschichte der DDR* [Rule and Eigensinn in dictatorship: Studies on social history of the GDR], edited by Thomas Lindenberger, 13–44. Cologne: Böhlau.

———, ed. 1999b. *Herrschaft und Eigen-Sinn in der Diktatur: Studien zur Gesellschaftsgeschichte der DDR* [Rule and Eigensinn in dictatorship: Studies on social history of GDR]. Cologne: Böhlau.

———. 2011. "Die DDR, nachdem das Tor zum Westen geschlossen war" [The GDR after the door to the West was closed]. In *50 Jahre Mauerbau: Vorgeschichte und Folgen* [50 years of building the wall: History and consequences], edited by Hans-Joachim Veen and Franz-Josef Schlichting, 37–51. Erfurt, Germany: Stiftung Ettersberg.

Losonczy, Géza. 1948. *Kommunista erkölcs* [Communist ethics]. Szemináriumi füzetek [Seminar notes]. Budapest: Szikra.

Lovell, Stephen. 2002. "The Making of the Stalin-Era Dacha." *Journal of Modern History*, 74 (June): 253–288.

Lüdtke, Alf, ed. 1991. *Herrschaft als soziale Praxis: Historische und sozialanthropologische Studien* [Rule as social practice: Historical and social anthropological studies]. Göttingen, Germany: Vandenhoeck and Ruprecht.

Lukács, György. 2010. "On the Nature and the Form of the Essay." In *Soul and Form*, translated by Anna Bostock, edited by John T. Sanders and Katie Terezakis, 1–18. New York: Columbia University Press. First published 1911.

Magyari, Péter. 2005. *Losonczi: TSZ-elnök az Azték Sas Szalagrendjével* [Losonczi: Agricultural cooperative president with the Order of the Aztec Eagle with collar]. Accessed March 10, 2008. https://www.origo.hu/itthon/20050329losonczi.html.

Majtényi, György. 2000. "Életstílus és szubkultúra: Az autózás története (1920–1960)" [Lifestyle and subculture: History of the automobile, 1920–1960]. *Korall* 1 (1): 101–118.

———. 2006. "'Nem mehet akárki vadásznak': Az elit és a vadászat a második világháború után ["Not everyone can be a hunter": The elite and hunting after the Second World War]. *FONS: Forráskutatás és Történeti Segédtudományok* [Source research and historical auxiliary sciences] 13 (1): 3–20.

———. 2007a. "Folt a kék díványon: Az uralmi elit életformája Magyarországon az 1950-es, 1960-as években, I" [A stain on the blue couch: Lifestyles of the dominant elite in Hungary in the 1950s and 1960s, I]. *Beszélő* [Speaker] 12 (9): 68–85.

———. 2007b. "Folt a kék díványon: Az uralmi elit életformája Magyarországon az 1950-es, 1960-as években, II" [A stain on the blue couch: Lifestyles of the dominant elite in Hungary in the 1950s and 1960s, II]. *Beszélő* [Speaker] 12 (10): 60–70.

———. 2008. "Az elit és a vadászat—újjáépítés és rendszerváltás között" [The elite and hunting—Between reconstruction and regime change]. In *Rendszerváltás és Kádár-korszak* [Regime change and the Kádár era], edited by György Majtényi and Csaba Szabó, 489–508. Budapest: Állambiztonsági Szolgálatok Történeti Levéltára, Kossuth Kiadó.

———. 2009. "K-vonal: Uralmi elit és luxus a szocializmusban" [Cadre-line: The ruling elite and luxury under socialism]. Budapest: Nyitott Könyvműhely.

———. 2012. *Vezércsel: Kádár János mindennapjai*. Budapest: Libr— Magyar Nemzeti Levéltár [Hungarian National Archives].

———. 2013. "Mi kezdjünk a Kádár-korral?" [How shall we deal with the Kádár era?]. *Élet és Irodalom* [Life and literature] 57, no. 18 (April 26): 11–12.

———. 2016. "Between Tradition and Change: Hunting as Metaphor and Symbol in State Socialist Hungary." *Cultural and Social History: Journal of the Social History Society* 13 (2): 231–248. https://doi.org/10.1080/14780038.2016.1166409.

Marger, Martin N. 1981. *Elites and Masses: An Introduction to Political Sociology*. New York: Van Nostrand.

Marosán, György. 1989: *A tanúk még élnek* [The witnesses are still alive]. Budapest: Hírlapkiadó.

Mateju, Petr, and Nelson Lim. 1995. "Who Has Gotten Ahead after the Fall of Communism? The Case of the Czech Republic." *Czech Sociological Review* 3, 117–137.

Merán, Fülöp. 2000. *A vadászat megmaradt* [Hunting remained]. Budapest: Nimród Alapítvány.

———. 2006. *Az emlékek nem hazudnak* [Memories do not lie]. Budapest: Nimród.

Merkel, Ina. 1996. "Der aufhaltsame Aufbruch in die Konsumgesellschaft" [The road leading to consumer society]. In *Wunderwirtschaft: DDR-Konsumkultur in den 60er Jahren* [Wonder economy: GDR's consumer culture in the 60s years], edited by Neue Gesellschaft für Bildende Kunst e.V. (Hrsg.), 8–20. Cologne: Böhlau.

Meuschel, Sigrid. 1992. *Legitimation und Parteiherrschaft in der DDR: Zum Paradox von Stabilität und Revolution in der DDR 1945–1989* [Legitimation and party rule in the GDR: On the paradox of stability and revolution in the GDR 1945–1989]. Frankfurt am Main: Suhrkamp.

Miklóssy, Katalin. 2014. "Concluding Remarks: Typology and Consequences of Competition." In *Competition in Socialist Society*, edited by Katalin Miklóssy and Melanie Ilic, 176–188. London: Routledge.

Montefiore, Simon Sebag. 2004. *The Court of the Red Tsar*. New York: Alfred A. Knopf.

Mosca, Gaetano. 1939. *The Ruling Class*. New York: McGraw-Hill.

Moszkva–Budapest: Hegedüs András levelezése [Moscow–Budapest: The correspondence of András Hegedüs]. 2009. "Sokszor vágytam az elméleti kérdésekkel való foglalkozásra..." [I often longed to deal with theoretical questions...]. Published by Béla Révész and Miklós Tamási, *Élet és Irodalom* [Life and literature] 53, no. 7 (February 13): 9–10.

Mravik, László. 2003. "'Hercegek, grófok, naplopók, burzsoák...' Száz év magyar képgyűjtése" ["Princes, counts, layabouts, bourgeoisie..." One hundred years of Hungarian painting]. In *Modern magyar festészet, 1892–1919* [Modern Hungarian painting, 1892–1919], 10–33. Budapest: Tamás Kieselbach.

Murányi, Gábor. 2006. "Kucseráék Snagovban—Akik cserbenhagyták Nagy Imrét" [The Kucseras in Snagov—The people who let down Imre Nagy]. *HVG*, no. 24 (June 17): 75–77.

Musil, Robert. 1995 (1914). "On the Essay." In *Precision and Soul: Essays and Addresses*, edited and translated by Burton Pike and David S. Luft, 48–51. Chicago: University of Chicago Press.

———. 1995. *Precision and Soul: Essays and Addresses*. Revised edition. Edited and translated by Burton Pike and David S. Luft. Chicago: University of Chicago Press.

———. 1996. *The Man without Qualities*. Vol. 2. New York: Vintage Books.

Nagy, Béla. 1987. *Ki kicsoda a Ferencvárosi Torna Club történetében?* [Who's who in the history of the Ferencváros sports club?]. Budapest: Ferencvárosi Torna Klub [Ferencvárosi Torna Club].

Nagy, Imre. 2006. *Snagovi jegyzetek: Gondolatok, emlékezések, 1956–1957* [Notes from Snagov: Thoughts, memories, 1956–1957], edited by László Szántó and István Vida. Budapest: Gondolat Kiadó; Nagy Imre Alapítvány [Imre NagyFoundation].

Nánási, László. 1983. *Emlékezetből* [From memory]. Budapest: Kossuth Kiadó.

Németh, Miklós. 1989. "A miniszterelnöknek is megvan a véleménye: Gyárfás Tamás interjúja Németh Miklóssal" [The prime minister also has his opinion: Interview with Miklós Németh by Tamás Gyárfás]. *Sport Plusz* 1, no. 1 (January 1): 5.

Nógrádi, Sándor. 1970. *Történelmi lecke* [Historical lesson]. Budapest: Kossuth.

Odescalchi, Eugénie. 1987. *Egy hercegnő emlékezik* [A princess remembers]. Budapest: Gondolat.

Osokina, Elena. 2001. *Our Daily Bread: Socialist Distribution and the Art of Survival in Stalin's Russia, 1927–1941*. Armonk, NY: M. E. Sharpe.

Pap, Zsolt, and József Pruzsinszky, 2000–2003. *Száz meg tizenöt év: A budapest-józsefvárosi Tisztviselőtelep 115 éves története* [One hundred and fifteen years: The 115-year history of the Budapest-Józsefváros functionary neighborhood]. Vol. 1, *1886–1920*; Vol. 2, *1921–1945*; Vol. 3, *1945–1990*; Vol. 4, *1990–2001*. Budapest: Széchenyista Öregdiákok Baráti Társasága.

Pápai, Gábor, ed. 2003. *Gyökerek és Lombok* [Roots and boughs]. Vol. 3. Budapest: Országos Erdészeti Egyesület.

Papp, Barbara. 2006. "'Az a drága Nagy Imre,' és 'az Erzsi lány rémséges ruhája': A történeti interjú lehetőségei" ["That dear Imre Nagy" and "that Liza girl's dreadful dress": The potentials of the historical interview]. *Sic itur ad astra*, no. 1–2, 209–236.

Pareto, Vilfredo. 1991. *The Rise and Fall of Elites: An Application of Theoretical Sociology*. New Brunswick, NJ: Transaction.

Parmer, György. 2001. *Magyar építészet a két világháború között* [Hungarian architecture between the two world wars]. 2nd expanded ed. Budapest: Terc.

Péteri, György. 2009: "Az autós a ludas: Az automobilizmus magyarországi recepciójának történetéhez az 1960-as években" [The automobile is to blame: On the history of the reception of the automobile in Hungary in the 1960s]. In *A felhalmozás míve: Történeti tanulmányok Kövér György tiszteletére* [The art of accumulation: Historical essays in honor of György Kövér], 302–315. Budapest: Századvég.

Piţurcă, Aurel. 2012. "Communism and Political Elites." *Revista de Ştiinţe Politice: Revue des Sciences Politiques*, no. 33–34, 8–13.

Poenaru, Florin. 2013. "Power at Play: Soccer Stadiums and Popular Culture in 1980s Romania." In *Socialist Escapes: Breaking Away from Ideology and Everyday Routine in Eastern Europe, 1945–1989*, edited by

Cathleen M. Giustino, Catherine J. Plum, and Alexander Vari, 232–251. New York: Berghahn Books.

Potzner, Ferenc, and Katalin Sinkó. 2003. "Előzmények" [Antecedents]. In *A Sándor-palota írásban és képben* [The Sándor palace in writing and image], edited by Katalin Sinkó, 50–53. Budapest: Akadémiai Kiadó.

Prakfalvi, Endre. 2001. "Adatok a budavári palotaegyüttes 1945 utáni építéstörténetéhez" [Data on the construction history of the palace ensemble of the Buda castle after 1945]. In *A Budavári Királyi Palota évszázadai: Tanulmányok Budapest múltjából, 29* [The centuries-long history of the royal palace of the Buda castle: Essays on the history of Budapest], edited by Katalin F. Dózsa and Gabriella Szvoboda Dománszky, 343–359. Budapest: Budapest History Museum.

———. 2009. "Lehel (Élmunkás) tér 2. A., B., C., D." [Lehel (outstanding worker) square 2. A., B., C., D.]. *Budapesti Negyed* [Budapest quarterly], no. 63 (Spring): 123–138.

Preisich, Gábor. 1998a. "A lakásépítés és a lakásállomány változása" [Changes in apartment construction and the available stock of apartments]. In *Budapest városépítésének története, 1945–1990: Tanulmányok* [The history of the construction of the city of Budapest, 1945–1990: Essays], edited by Gábor Preisich, 67–120. Budapest: Műszaki Könyvkiadó.

———. 1998b. "Intézmények, középületek" [Institutions, public buildings]. In *Budapest városépítésének története, 1945–1990: Tanulmányok* [The history of the construction of the city of Budapest, 1945–1990: Essays], edited by Gábor Preisich, 121–156. Budapest: Műszaki Könyvkiadó.

Pünkösti, Árpád. 1977. "A munkásosztály a Hiltonba megy" [The working class goes to the Hilton]. *Új Tükör* [New mirror] 14, no. 41 (October 9): 6–8.

———. 1979. "Márványaink" [Our marbles]. *Filmvilág* [Film world], no. 12, 20–22.

———. 1992. *Rákosi a hatalomért, 1945–1948* [Rákosi for power, 1945–1948]. Budapest: Európa.

———. 1996. *Rákosi a csúcson, 1948–1953* [Rákosi at his peak, 1948–1953]. Budapest: Európa.

———. 2001. *Rákosi bukása, száműzetése és halála, 1953–1971* [The fall, exile, and death of Rákosi, 1953–1971]. Budapest: Európa.

Rainer, M. János. 1996. *Nagy Imre: Politikai életrajz, 1896–1953* [Imre Nagy: Political biography, 1896–1953]. Vol. 1. Budapest: 1956 Institute.

Rákosi, Mátyás. 1997. *Visszaemlékezések, 1940–1956* [Memoirs, 1940–1956]. Vol. 2. Budapest: Napvilág.

Réczey, Ferenc, Dagmar Pekáry, and Ferenc Gondi. 1961. *Etikett—társasélet—protokoll: A hazai és a nemzetközi érintkezés szabályai egykor és ma* [Etiquette, married life, protocol: The rules of touch in Hungary and internationally in times of yore and today]. 2nd ed. Budapest: Minerva.

Révész, Sándor. 1997. *Aczél és korunk* [Aczél and our era]. Budapest: Sík Kiadó.

———. 2008. "A Homo Stalinicus halála" [The death of the homo stalinicus]. *Beszélő* [Speaker] 13, no. 5 (May): 68–78.

Ritoók, Pál. 2000. "Aki villát épít, Budára megy, Rózsadomb, Pasarét, ez van divatban" [Anyone building a villa goes to Buda, Rózsadomb, Pasarét, that is the fashion]. *Intérieur* 2 (3): 37–40. First published as *Pesti Futár* [Pest courier], 1935.

Róna-Tas, Ákos. 1994. "The First Shall Be Last? Entrepreneurship and Communist Cadres in the Transition from Socialism." *American Journal of Sociology* 100 (1): 40–69.

Rostás, Péter. 2001a. "Egy helyiség helye: A Budavári Palota Hunyadi Mátyás-termének története" [The place of a chamber: The history of the Mátyás Hunyadi room in the Buda castle palace]. In *A Budavári Királyi Palota évszázadai: Tanulmányok Budapest múltjából*, 29 [The centuries-long history of the royal palace of the Buda castle: Essays on the history of Budapest], edited by Katalin F. Dózsa and Gabriella Szvoboda Dománszky, 487–538. Budapest: Budapest History Museum.

———. 2001b. "Schmidt Miksa hagyatéka" [The bequest of Miksa Schmidt]. In *Egy közép-európai vállalkozó Budapesten: Schmidt Miksa bútorgyáros tevékenysége és hagyatéka* [A Central European entrepreneur in Budapest: The activity and bequest of Miksa Schmidt], 11–83. Budapest: Budapest History Museum.

Rózsa, T. Endre. 2008. "Nagy Imre, Kádár, Bernáth Aurél" [Imre Nagy, Kádár, Aurél Bernáth]. *Balkon* [Balcony], no. 3, 10–11.

Rózsahegyi, György. 1962. *Szállodai ismeretek* [Hotel skills]. Budapest: Közgazdasági és Jogi.

Rozsnyai, József. 2009. "A pesti Esterházy-palota és lakói" [The Esterházy palace in Pest and its dwellers]. *Budapesti Negyed* [Budapest quarterly], no. 63 (Spring): 5–34.

Ruffy, Péter. 1965. "Húsz év históriája" [The history of twenty years]. In *A New Yorktól a Hungáriáig* [From the New York to the Hungaria], edited by Konrádyné Gálos Magda, 226–227. Budapest: Minerva.

Saly, Noémi. 2005. *Törzskávéházamból zenés kávéházba: Séta a budapesti körutakon* [From my regular café to my music café: A stroll on the boulevards of Budapest]. Budapest: Osiris.

Sármány-Parsons, Ilona. 1992. "Villa és családi ház" [Villa and single-family home]. In *Polgári lakáskultúra a századfordulón* [Middle-class interior design culture at the turn of the century], edited and with an introduction by Péter Hanák, 179–223. Budapest: MTA (Magyar Tudományos Akadémia) Történettudományi Intézet [HAS (Hungarian Academy of Sciences) Institute of History].

Schiffer, Klára Szakasits. 1985. *Fent és lent, 1945–1950* [Up and down. 1945–1950]. Budapest: Magvető.

Schnitta, Sámuel. 1965. *Felszolgálói ismeretek* [Hospitality industry skills]. 2nd ed. Budapest: Közgazdasági és Jogi. First published 1962.

Sebes, Gusztáv. 1981. *Örömök és csalódások: Egy sportvezető emlékei* [Joys and disappointments: The memories of a sports leader]. Budapest: Gondolat.

Sennett, Richard. 2002. *The Fall of the Public Man*. London: Penguin. First published 1977.

Siegelbaum, Lewis H. 1988. *Stakhanovism and the Politics of Productivity in the USSR, 1935–1941*. Soviet and East European Studies series. Cambridge: Cambridge University Press.

———, ed. 2011. *The Socialist Car: Automobility in the Eastern Bloc*. Ithaca, NY: Cornell University Press.

Sík, Endre. 1966. *Egy diplomata feljegyzései* [A diplomat's notes]. Budapest: Kossuth.

———. 1970: *Bem rakparti évek* [The years of Bem wharf]. Budapest: Kossuth.

Simmel, Georg. 1904. "Fashion." *International Quarterly* 10, no. 1 (October): 130–155. (Republished in *American Journal of Sociology*, 1957, 62, no. 6 (May): 541–558.)

Simon, Blanka. 1957. *Házi* [Domestic polymath]. Budapest: Bibliotheca Kiadó.

Simonovics, Ildikó. 2008. "Az államosított divat célja: felöltöztetni az országot; A Ruhaipari Tervező Vállalattól Rotschild Klára szalonjáig" [The goal of nationalized fashion: To clothe the country; From the clothing industry planning enterprise to the salon of Klára Rotschild]. In *Mindennapok Rákosi és Kádár korában* [Everyday life in the era of Rákosi and Kádár], edited by Sándor Horváth, 187–213. Budapest: Nyitott Könyvműhely.

———. 2019. *Rotschild Klára: A vörös divatdiktátor* [Klára Rotschild: The red fashion dictator]. Budapest: Jaffa.

Sombart, Werner. 1998. "A luxus kibontakozása" [Luxury and capitalism]. Translated by Bognár Bulcsu. *Symposion* (March–April): 30–45.

Spencer, Herbert. 1982. "A divat" [Fashion]. In *Divatszociológia* [Fashion sociology], edited by Gábor Klaniczay and Katalin S. Nagy, 33–37. Budapest: Tömegkommunikációs Kutatóközpont.
Standeisky, Éva. 1996. *Az írók és a hatalom, 1956–1963* [The writers and the regime, 1956–1963]. Budapest: 1956 Institute.
Staniszkis, Jadwiga. 1991a. *The Dynamics of Breakthrough in Eastern Europe.* Berkeley: University of California Press.
———. 1991b. ""Political Capitalism" in Poland." *East European Politics and Society* 5, no 1 (Winter): 127–141. https://doi.org/10.1177/0888325491 005001008.
Suny, Ronald Grigor. 1998. *The Soviet Experiment: Russia, the USSR, and the Successor States.* New York: Oxford University Press.
Szabó, Csaba. 2006. "Gigászok harca Győr-Sopron megyében (1965)" [Battle of the titans in Győr-Sopron County (1965)]. In *Tanulmányok az 50 éves Bana Jocó tiszteletére* [Essays in honor of the fiftieth birthday of Jocó Bana], edited by Csaba Katona, 129–134. Győr, Hungary: Palatia Nyomda és Kiadó.
Szabó, Dezső. 1990. *A magyar káosz: Pamfletek* [Hungarian chaos: Pamphlets]. Budapest: Szépirodalmi.
Szántó, Miklós. 2001. "Hegedüs András emlékezete" [In memory of András Hegedüs]. In *Búcsú Hegedüs Andrástól, 1922–1999* [Farewell to András Hegedüs, 1922–1999], edited by Tamás Rozgonyi and Zoltán Zsille, 266–270. Budapest: Osiris.
Szász, Béla (Vincent Savarius). 1963. *Minden kényszer nélkül* [Without any compulsion]. Brussels: Imre Nagy Institute.
Szász, Imre. 1984. *Ez elment vadászni ... Magyarország felfedezése* [And this little piggy went hunting ... discovering Hungary]. Budapest: Szépirodalmi.
Szelényi, Iván. 1991. "A magyar polgárosodás esélyei" [The chances of emerging Hungarian civil life]. *Századvég* [End-of-century], no. 2–3, 202–211. (The text that served as the basis for the article was also published in *Hitel* [Credit], 1989, no. 16.)
Szendrői, Jenő, Lajos Arnóth, József Finta, Ferenc Merényi, and Elemér Nagy. 1972. *Magyar építészet, 1945–1970* [Hungarian architecture, 1945–1970]. Budapest: Corvina.
Szentgyörgyi, József N. 2005. "Megkóstolták Magyarországot" [They sampled Hungary]. *Az irodalom visszavág* [Literature strikes back], no. 3–4, 76–82.
Szigeti, Péter. 2002. "A szexualitás nyilvánossága a századforduló Budapestjén" [Sex and the public sphere in Budapest at the turn of the

century]. *Médiakutató* [Media research], no. 6 (Spring): 85–101. http://epa.oszk.hu/03000/03056/00006/EPA03056_mediakutato_2002_tavasz_07.html.

Szöllősi, György. 1997. *Czibor: dribli az égig* [Czibor, dribble to the skies]. Sárbogárd, Hungary: Print City.

Szűts, László. 1965. *A kormányzó úr medvéi* [The regent's bears]. Budapest: Kossuth.

Szvoboda Dománszky, Gabriella. 2001. "Az újkori Budavári Palota belső díszítése" [The interior decoration of the early modern palace of the Buda castle]. In *A Budavári Királyi Palota évszázadai: Tanulmányok Budapest múltjából, 29* [The centuries-long history of the royal palace of the Buda castle: Essays on the history of Budapest], edited by Katalin F. Dózsa and Gabriella Szvoboda Dománszky, 411–456. Budapest: Budapest History Museum.

Tabajdi, Gábor, and Krisztián Ungváry. 2008. *Elhallgatott múlt: A pártállam és a belügy: A politikai rendőrség működése Magyarországon, 1956–1990* [Silenced past. The party state and domestic affairs. The political police in Hungary, 1956–1990]. Budapest: 1956 Institute; Corvina.

Takács, Károly. 1998. "Az elit szociológiai fogalmáról" [On the sociological concept of the elite]. *Szociológiai Szemle* [Sociological review], no. 1, 139–148.

Takács, Tibor. 2008. *Döntéshozók: Városi elit és városi önkormányzat Nyíregyházán a XX. század első felében* [Decision makers: Urban elite and municipal government in Nyíregyháza in the first half of the twentieth century]. Budapest: L'Harmattan.

Tamás, Ervin. 1997. "A gebin története" [The history of the "Gebin"]. *História*, no. 9–10, 50–53.

Tarde, Gabriel. 1903. *The Laws of Imitation*. New York: Henry Holt.

de Tinguy, Anne, ed. 1997. *The Fall of the Soviet Empire*. New York: Columbia University Press, 1997.

Tischler, János. 2004. "Az Onódy-ügy, 1964." In *"Hatvanas évek" Magyarországon: Tanulmányok* [The "1960s" in Hungary: Essays], edited by János M. Rainer, 239–271. Budapest: 1956 Institute.

Tokár, Péter. 1951. *Muszka Imre munkamódszere és újításai* [The working method and innovations of Imre Muszka]. Budapest: n.p.

Tomka, Béla. 2020: *Austerities and Aspirations: A Comparative History of Growth, Consumption, and Quality of Life in East Central Europe since 1945*. New York: CEU Press.

Tóth, Eszter Zsófia. 1999. "A Csepel Vas- és Fémművek munkástanácsainak története" [The history of the workers' councils of the Csepel Iron and Steel Works]. *Múltunk* [Our past], no. 4, 162–199.

———. 2005: "Munkásság és oral history" [The working class and oral history]. *Múltunk* [Our past], no. 4, 78–99.

———. 2007. *"Puszi Kádár Jánosnak": Munkásnők élete a Kádárkorszakban mikrotörténeti megközelítésben* ["A kiss for János Kádár": The lives of working women in the Kádár era]. Budapest: Napvilág.

Tóth, Ferenc. 2002. *Magyar ejtőernyős partizánok: A repüléstörténeti konferencia közleményei* [Hungarian paratrooper partisans: Publications of the conference on the history of air flight]. Budapest: Magyar Repüléstörténeti Társaság.

Tóth, Gyula, ed. 1992. *Írók pórázon: A Kiadói Főigazgatóság irataiból, 1961– 1970* [Writers on the leash: From the documents of the publishing house directorate, 1961–1970]. Selection of Documents. Budapest: Hungarian Academy of Sciences, Institute of Literary Studies.

Tóth, Sándor. 2005. *A hírnév kötelez: Vadgazdálkodás és vadászat Magyarországon* [Bound by reputation: Animal management and hunting in Hungary]. 2nd expanded ed. Budapest: Nimród.

———. 2007. *Nyitány a hírnévhez: Vadászat és vadgazdálkodás Magyarországon, 1945–1951* [Overture to the reputation: Hunting and animal management in Hungary, 1945–1951]. Budapest: Nimród.

———. 2009. "Vadászat történelmi váltógazdálkodással" [Hunting with historically alternating management]. Unpublished manuscript.

Tóth, Vilmos. 1999a. "A Kerepesi úti temető másfél évszázada" [150 years of the Kerepesi Avenue cemetery]. *Budapesti Negyed* [Budapest quarterly] 7, no. 2 (Summer): 3–126.

———. 1999b. "A Kerepesi úti temető 1999-ben" [The Kerepesi Avenue cemetery in 1999]. *Budapesti Negyed* [Budapest quarterly] 7, no. 3 (Autumn): 174–472.

———. 2009. "Újratemetések Magyarországon a 19–20. században" [Reburials in Hungary in the nineteenth and twentieth centuries]. *Rubicon*, no. 3, 24–33.

Trotsky, Leon. 1972. *The Revolution Betrayed*. New York: Pathfinder.

Váczi, Tamás. 1989. *Újra a reformok élén: A beszélgetőtárs: Nyers Rezső* [Again at the vanguard of reforms: Conversation partner: Rezső Nyers]. Kecskemét, Hungary: Bács-Kiskun Megyei Lapkiadó Vállalat.

Vadas, Ferenc. 1996. "Belsőépítészet és térhasználat a New Yorkban" [Interior design and use of space in the New York Café]. *Budapesti Negyed* [Budapest quarterly], no. 2–3, 199–214.

Vadas József. 1977: "Formatervezés a Hiltonban" [Design in the Hilton]. *Élet és Irodalom* [Life and literature] 21 (29): 5.

Vadas, József. n.d. *A magyar bútor 100 éve* [One hundred years of Hungarian furniture]. Budapest: Fortuna.

Valuch, Tibor. 2001. *Magyarország társadalomtörténete a XX. század második felében* [A social history of Hungary in the second half of the twentieth century]. Budapest: Osiris.

———. 2004. *A lódentől a miniszoknyáig: A XX. század második felének magyarországi öltözködéstörténete* [From the loden coat to the miniskirt: The history of clothing in Hungary in the second half of the twentieth century]. Budapest: Corvina Kiadó; 1956 Institute.

———. 2006. *Hétköznapi élet Kádár János korában* [Everyday life in the János Kádár era]. Budapest: Corvina.

———. 2009. "A városi öltözködés változásai Magyarországon 1948–2000" [Changes in urban dress fashion in Hungary, 1948–2000]. In *Öltöztessük fel az országot! Divat és öltözködés a szocializmusban* [Let's clothe the country! Fashion and dress under socialism], edited by Simonovics Ildikó and Valuch Tibor, 99–129. Budapest: Argumentum; Budapesti Történeti Múzeum [Budapest History Museum]; 1956-os Intézet [1956 Institute].

———. 2018. *The Paradox of Consumer Objects and Modern Living in Hungary*. In *Promote, Tolerate, Ban: Art and Culture in Cold War Hungary*, edited by Cristina Cuevas-Wolf and Isotta Poggi, 71–83. Los Angeles: Getty Publications.

Varga, Balázs. 2009. "Az 1945–1956 közötti győri politikai és közigazgatási vezetőréteg társadalmi összetétele és életútjai" [The social composition and careers of the leading political and administrative stratum of Győr, 1945–1956]. Doctoral dissertation, Eötvös Loránd Tudományegyetem [Eötvös Loránd University].

Varga, György T. 1998. "Adalékok és szempontok a Magyar Dolgozók Pártja hatalmi helyzetéhez" [Data and perspectives on the power position of the Hungarian Workers' Party]. *Múltunk* [Our past], no. 2, 175–182.

Varga, György T., and István Szakadát. 1992. "Íme, a nómenklatúrák! Az MDP és a volt MSZMP hatásköri listái" [Lo, the nomenclature! The sphere of influence lists of the Hungarian Workers' Party and the Former Hungarian Socialist Workers' Party]. *Társadalmi Szemle* [Social review], no. 3, 73–95.

Varga, László, ed. 2001. *Kádár János a bírái előtt: Egyszer fent, egyszer lent, 1949–1956* [János Kádár before his judges: Now up, now down, 1949–1956]. Budapest: Osiris; Budapest Főváros Levéltára.

Vas, István. 1935. "Levél egy szocialistához" [Letter to a socialist]. *Válasz* [Reply] 2 (7–8): 442–448.

Vas, Zoltán. 1990. *Betiltott könyvem: Életem, III* [My forbidden book: My life, 3]. Budapest: Szabad Tér.
Vas, Mrs. Zoltán. 1990. "Rendhagyó utószó" [An unusual afterword], excerpt from an interview conducted by Gyula Kozák. In *Betiltott könyvem: Életem, III* [My forbidden book: My life, 3], by Zoltán Vas, 365–415. Budapest: Szabad Tér.
Veblen, Thorstein. 1994. *The Theory of the Leisure Class*. New York: Dover Publications. First published 1899.
Vida, István. 2006. Introduction. In *Snagovi jegyzetek: Gondolatok, emlékezések, 1956–1957* [Notes from Snagov: Thoughts, memories, 1956–1957], by Imre Nagy; edited by László Szántó and István Vida, 7–47. Budapest: Gondolat Kiadó; Nagy Imre Foundation.
Voslensky, Michael. 1984. *Nomenklatura: The Soviet Ruling Class*. New York: Doubleday.
Weber, Max. 1978. *Economy and Society: An Outline of Interpretive Sociology*. Translated and edited by Günther Roth and Claus Wittich. Berkeley: University of California Press. First published 1922.
———. 1992. *The Protestant Ethic and the Spirit of Capitalism*. Translated by Talcott Parsons. London: Routledge. First published 1930.
White, David Manning. 1950. "The 'Gatekeeper': A Case Study in the Selection of News." *Journalism Quarterly* 27 (4): 383–391.
White, Hayden. 1973. *Metahistory: The Historical Imagination in Nineteenth-Century Europe*. Baltimore: Johns Hopkins University Press.
Zbarski, Ilya, and Samuel Hutchinson. 1998. *Lenin's Embalmers*. London: Harvill.
Zeidler, Miklós. 2006. "A modern sport a nemzet szolgálatában a 19. századi Magyarországon" [Modern sports in the service of the nation in nineteenth-century Hungary]. *Századvég* [End-of-century], no. 4, 71–104.
Zelei, Miklós. 2003. "Tamás bácsi?" [Uncle Thomas?]. *Korunk* [Our time], no. 5 (May): 59–62.
Zolnay, Vilmos. 1951. *Pióker Ignác, az ország legjobb gyalusa* [Ignác Pióker, the country's best planer]. Budapest: n.p.
Zoltán, János. 1996. *Legenda és valóság* [Legend and truth]. Budapest: Dénes Natúr Műhely.

INDEX

1958 Brussels World Exhibition, 236
Ajtósi Dürer Street (Ajtósi Dürer sor), Budapest, 51
Akadémia Street (Akadémia utca), Budapest, 269
Alabárdos restaurant, Budapest, 228–232
Aliga, Hungary. *See* Balatonaliga
Amusement Park (Vidámpark), Budapest
Andrássy Avenue (Andrássy út), Budapest, 31–32, 34, 51, 55, 57, 64, 225, 227, 274n10
Andrássy Palace (Andrássy Palota), Budapest, 270
Angyalföld, Budapest, 196
Apostol Street (Apostol utca), Budapest, 31
Aquincum, Budapest, 51
architecture, 36, 49–50, 98n28, 239–240, 268, 271
aristocrat, aristocratic, 22, 25, 37, 62, 114, 129, 131, 141, 173, 227, 266
Árpád Street (Árpád utca), Budapest, 259
ARTEX (ARTEX Külkereskedelmi Vállalat), 56

Astoria Café (Astoria Kávéház), Budapest, 223
Astoria Hotel (Astoria Szálló), Budapest, 233, 256
Australia, 179, 182
Austria, 27, 79, 86, 176, 232, 239–240, 270
Auto Club (Autóklub), 63, 64
Automobile Club of the Hungarian People's Republic (Magyar Népköztársaság Automobil Klubja). *See* Auto Club
Automobile Club of the Hungarian Republic (Köztársasági Magyar Automobil Club, or KMAC). *See* Auto Club
Automobile Supervision (Autófelügyelet), 72
Avenue of the People's Republic, Budapest. *See* Andrássy Avenue

Bács-Kiskun County (Bács-Kiskun megye), Hungary, 132
Bagdad Café (Bagdad Kávéház), Budapest, 221, 223, 274n10
Bajina Bašta (Bajnabástya), Serbia, 201
Balatonakarattya, Hungary, 145

INDEX

Balatonaliga, Hungary, 49–53, 87, 158
Balatonarács, Hungary, 50–53
Balatonföldvár, Hungary, 51, 53
Balatonfüred, Hungary, 54
Balatonőszöd, Hungary, 49–50, 87
Balatonszemes, Hungary, 50, 87
"Baltika" ship, 81
bar, 185, 220–221, 223, 230, 232, 235, 237–238, 241–245, 277n78
Barcs, Hungary, 82
Baroque, 44, 98n31, 261, 285n165
Beauty Boutique, Budapest, 254
Béke Hotel (Béke Szálló), Budapest. *See* Britannia Hotel
Béke Square (Peace Square), Budapest, 196
Békés County (Békés megye), Hungary, 99n44
Béla király Avenue (Béla király út), Budapest, 2, 35, 87, 97n21, 224
Belgrade, Serbia, 101n55, 201, 255
Belle Boutique, Budapest, 254
Benetton store, Budapest, 254
Biedermeier, 261, 277n68, 282n144, 288
Bilbao, Spain, 186
BMW cars, 66
Bódvaszilas, Hungary, 114, 148n7
Bolgár Street (Bolgár utca), Budapest, 74
Borsod, Hungary. *See* Borsod-Abaúj-Zemplén
Borsod-Abaúj-Zemplén county, Hungary, 114, 143–144
bourgeois, 14, 75, 90, 204, 220, 251, 256, 265, 279n95, 288, 293, 296
Bozsik Boutique (Bozsik butik), Budapest, 188
Bristol Hotel (Bristol Szálló), Budapest, 233
Britannia Hotel (Britannia Szálló), Budapest, 233
Buda Castle (Budai Vár, Budavári Palota), Budapest, 31, 239, 269, 271

Buda, Budapest, 2, 30–35, 48–49, 55–56, 74, 77, 94n1, 108n145, 131, 132, 137, 147, 177, 183, 224, 228, 231, 238, 241, 243, 265, 267
Budaörs, Hungary, 63
Budapest Army Sport Association (Budapesti Honvéd Sportegyesület), 184
Budapest Army Team (Budapesti Honvéd), soccer team, 186, 211n53
Budapest Fashion Salon (Budapest Divatszalon), 250
Budapest Football Club of the Hungarian Athletes' Circle (Magyar Testgyakorlók Köre Budapest Futball Klub, or MTK), 181, 189
Budapest Furniture Industry Company (Budapesti Bútoripari Vállalat), 261
Budapest Hilton Hotel (Budapest Hilton Szálló), 238–242, 276n66
Budapest History Museum (Budapest Történeti Múzeum), 271
Budapest Hotel (Budapest Szálló), 254
Budapest Metropolitan Council
Budapest, Hungary, 25, 30–32, 37, 47, 51, 57, 65, 67, 69, 71, 78, 92, 108n145, 135, 174, 178–179, 191, 195, 200, 220, 222–223, 227, 232–236, 238–239, 245, 250, 253–254, 257, 258, 263, 270, 290
Buick cars, 61
Bulgaria, 176, 182, 214n90
bureaucracy, 18, 49, 52, 302n20

cadre (káder), cadre class, 24, 32–33, 37, 39–40, 46–49, 51–52, 57–58, 60, 64, 72–73, 78–79, 84, 86–87, 96n15, 114, 192–193, 224, 229, 244, 248, 290–291, 294–295, 300, 305
cadre competence list, 104n92
cadre line, K line (K vonal), 77–79, 122, 305

Cadre Ridge (Káderdűlő), 30–49, 73
café, 220–224, 296
cars, 2, 13, 34, 39, 58, 61–74, 75, 77, 108n147, 108n153, 108n155, 109n165, 137–140, 159, 179, 183, 185–186, 188, 204, 206, 230, 238, 250, 256, 280n99
Central Board of Inquiry (Központi Ellenőrző Bizottság), 39–40, 106n120, 206
Central Committee (Központi Bizottság), 2, 17, 44, 47–48, 51–52, 57–58, 60, 72, 78, 85, 86–87, 103n77, 109n166, 120–124, 135, 141, 151n48, 158, 204–205, 207, 219n128, 225, 272, 286n180
Central Hungarian Automobile Club (Központi Magyar Automobil Club, or KMAC). *See* Auto Club
Central Party School (Központi Pártiskola, Pártfőiskola), 51
Central State Hospital, Budapest. *See* Kútvölgyi Hospital
Chaika cars, 70
Czechoslovakia, 79, 148n5, 148n8, 185, 218n121, 240
Chevi. *See* Chevrolet cars
Chevrolet cars, 61, 66–67, 107n138, 159
China, 80
Chrysler cars, 61
circus, 115, 191, 230
Citadella Restaurant (Citadella Étterem), Budapest, 238
Citroën cars, 256
City Park (Városliget), Budapest, 32, 227
Clara Salon (Clara Szalon), Budapest, 224, 250, 255, 280n102
Classical period, 11n9
Classicist, 36, 98n29
Clothing Store Company (Ruházati Bolt Vállalat), 253
Cold War, 187, 229, 231
colonial-style furniture, 45, 269

Concord Hunting Society (Egyetértés Vadásztársaság), 97n16, 119–127, 130–134, 137, 139–142, 144–146, 162, 165–166
Continental Hotel (Continental Szálló), Budapest, 233
Corinthia Hotel (Corinthia Szálló), Budapest, 36, 98n29
Corvin Department Store (Corvin Áruház), Budapest, 243
Council of Ministers, government (Minisztertanács), 50, 65–66, 80, 85–87, 92, 108n155, 114, 120–121, 123, 141, 145, 148n8, 151n48, 154n94, 161, 225, 227, 270, 290
Council of Trade Unions (Szaktanács). *See* National Council of Trade Unions
Cuba, 164, 169
Csákberény, Hungary, 13–14, 25, 299
Csárdás dance, 265
Csepel Machine Tools Factory (Csepeli Szerszámgépgyár), 201
Cserje Street (Cserje utca), Budapest, 41, 43, 100n53, 100–101n54, 101n55

Damjanich Street (Damjanich utca), Budapest, 57
Danube (Duna) River, 25, 30–31, 51, 61, 132, 152n65, 232, 238, 270
Danubius Hospitality and Medicinal Bath Company (Danubius Vendéglátó és Gyógyfürdő Vállalat), 232, 276n64
Delta Electronic and Mechanical Ltd. (Delta Elektromos és Mechanikai Ktsz), 35
Dembinszky Street (Dembinszky utca), Budapest, 57
Derenk, Hungary, 115, 147–148n3, 148n5
Diána hunting society (Diána Vadásztársaság), 226
Dobogókő, Hungary, 51–53

Dohány Street (Dohány utca), Budapest, 55, 102n59
doric style, 36, 98n29
Dózsa György Street (Dózsa György út), Budapest, 57
Dreher Haggenmacher Brewery (Dreher Haggenmacheró Sörgyár), 233
Duna Hotel (Duna Szálló), Budapest. *See* Bristol Hotel
Duna Intercontinental Hotel (Duna Intercontinental Szálló), Budapest, 238–239, 254

East Central European, 19, 24, 41
Economic Division of the Hungarian Communist Party (Magyar Kommunista Párt Gazdasági Osztálya), 249
elite, 2, 5–9, 13–25, 27–28n38, 28–29n44, 52, 287–300, 305
Élmunkás Square (Élmunkás tér), Budapest. *See* Lehel Square
Élysée Palace (Élysée Palota), Budapest, 37
Empire style, 261, 269
Eötvös Loránd University (Eötvös Loránd Tudományegyetem), Budapest, 51
Erzsébet-Csepel Railway Bridge (Pesterzsébet-csepeli összekötő vasúti híd), Budapest, 200
etiquette, 260
everyday life, 6, 20–21, 23, 27n34, 43–44, 227, 231, 252, 288, 298–299
Executive Committee of the Budapest City Council (Fővárosi Tanács Végrehajtó Bizottsága), 238
Ezredes Street (Ezredes utca), Budapest, 183

Farkasrét Cemetery (Farkasréti temető), Budapest, 92–94

fashion, 10, 13, 20, 22, 27n26, 247–248, 250–256, 260, 278n87, 278n91, 280n114
Fashion Salon of the Capital Council of Made-to-Measure Tailors (Fővárosi Tanács Mértékutáni Szabóságainak Divatszalonja), Budapest. *See* Budapest Fashion Salon
Federation of Hungarian Stamp Collectors (Magyar Bélyeggyűjtők Szövetsége), 59
Ferencváros Sports Club (Ferencvárosi Torna Club, FTC), 176, 189–190, 211n53
Ferencváros, Budapest, 200
Fészek Artists' Club (Fészek Művészklub), Budapest, 185
Fiumei Avenue Cemetery (Fiumei Úti Sírkert), Budapest. *See* Kerepesi Cemetery
Ford cars, 68
Fórum Hotel (Fórum Szálló), Budapest, 232, 238–239
"foursome" (négyesfogat), 35, 118, 225, 289, 290, 301n9
Földvár, Hungary. *See* Balatonföldvár
"Fradi." *See* Ferencváros Sports Club
Franciscans' Square (Ferenciek tere), Budapest. *See* Liberation Square
Freedom Hill (Szabadsághegy), Budapest, 2, 35, 97n25
Freedom Hill (Szabadság-hegy), Budapest. *See* Swabian Hil
Friendship Hunting Society (Barátság Vadásztársaság), 124, 142, 146
functionary, functionary class, functionary elite, 33, 52, 54, 56–57, 72, 88, 120, 193, 197–198, 205, 214n78, 296
furnitures, 33, 37, 42–45, 54–55, 57, 59, 75, 102n63, 104n96, 104n102, 194, 234, 240, 246, 257, 260–262, 265, 268–269, 282n144, 302n20

INDEX

Galgamácsa, Hungary, 116, 146
Galyatető, Hungary, 191–192, 199, 215–216n94
Ganz Electric Works (Ganz Elektromos Művek). See Ganz factory
Ganz factory (Ganz-gyár), 71, 168
gatekeeper, 300
"gebines," 211n48
Gellért Hill (Gellérthegy), Budapest, 31, 238, 283n148
Gellért Hotel (Gellért Szálló), Budapest, 69, 168, 231–235, 245
Gemenc, Hungary, 116, 131–132, 147, 152n65, 152n66, 154n89
Gemenc Hunting Society (Gemenci Vadásztársaság), 115
Gödöllő, Hungary, 65, 125, 131, 140, 152n65
"golden team," 67, 173, 177–178, 180–181, 183, 187, 189
Golf Hotel (Golf Szálló), Budapest. See Red Star Hotel
government guard. See government militia
government militia (kormányőrség), 70, 136
Grand Hotel of Margaret Island (Margitszigeti Nagszálló), Budapest, 233, 238
Greater Budapest Party Committee (Nagybudapesti Pártbizottság), 193, 263
Gundel restaurant (Gundel étterem), Budapest, 135, 223, 227–232
guns, 59, 125–126, 141, 179, 183, 197, 201
Gyarmatpuszta, Hungary, 131, 140, 146, 152n65, 154n85
Győr, Hungary, 71, 284n150, 296
Gyorskocsi Street (Gyorskocsi utca), Budapest, 57
Gyula Meinl Ltd (Meinl Gyula Rt.), 64
Gyulaj, Hungary, 116, 125–126, 131, 139, 147, 151n47, 152n65

Habsburg monarchy, 257
Habsburg rulers, 90, 133, 266
Hankóczy Street (Hankóczy utca), Budapest, 36
Hármashatár Hill (Hármashatárhegy), Budapest, 68, 108n145
Hármashatárhegy Restaurant (Hármashatárhegy Étterem), Budapest, 228
Heimatstil, 36
Herend porcelain, 75
Heroes' Square (Hősök tere), Budapest, 34, 193
Hilton Hotel (Hilton Szálló), Budapest. See Budapest Hilton Hotel
Hilton Hotel, Las Vegas, 147
"Honey Bear" restaurant (Mézes Mackó Étterem), Budapest, 226
Horch cars, 66
Hudson cars, 61
HungarHotels, 228, 231, 239, 276n64
Hungária Café (Hungária Kávéház), Budapest. See New York Café
Hungária Hotel and Restaurant Company (Hungária Szálloda és Éttermi Vállalat). See Hungarhotels
Hungarian Academy of Sciences (Magyar Tudományos Akadémia), 76, 271
Hungarian Communist Party (Magyar Kommunista Párt, or MKP), 204, 249, 269
Hungarian Industrial Association (Magyar Iparszövetség). See National Association of Small Tradesmen
Hungarian Fashion Studio (Magyar Divatstúdió), 253
Hungarian folk music, 225, 258
Hungarian fruit brandy (pálinka), 44
Hungarian National Assembly (Magyar Országgyűlés), 35, 48, 60, 87, 100n53, 145, 225, 258, 270

Hungarian National Automobile
    Factory (Magyar Országos Gépkocsi
    Üzem Rt., or MOGÜRT), 68
Hungarian National Gallery (Magyar
    Nemzeti Galéria), Budapest, 271
Hungarian National Museum (Magyar
    Nemzeti Múzeum), Budapest, 125,
    284n156
Hungarian People's Army (Magyar
    Néphadsereg), 38, 59, 251
Hungarian Radio (Magyar Rádió),
Hungarian Radio and Television
    (Magyar Rádió és Televízió),
    121, 266
Hungarian round (Körmagyar),
    dance, 265
Hungarian Socialist Workers' Party
    (Magyar Szocialista Munkáspárt,
    or MSZMP), 2, 7, 47–48, 51, 57, 72,
    84–87, 103n77, 151n48, 160, 205–206,
    272, 286n180, 292, 302n19
Hungarian State Railways (Magyar
    Államvasutak, or MÁV), 235
Hungarian Train Car and Machine
    Tool Factory (Magyar Vagon- és
    Gépgyár), 203
Hungarian Workers' Party (also
    translated as Hungarian Working
    People's Party, Magyar Dolgozók
    Pártja, or MDP), 7, 33, 97n25, 101n55,
    157, 181, 210n28, 212n55, 217n114, 249,
    263, 267, 300
Hungarian Young Communist League
    (Magyar Kommunista Ifjúsági
    Szövetség, KISZ), 53, 85, 142, 205,
    235, 252, 266, 280n111
Hunguest Hotels, 135
hunting, 13, 33, 40, 45, 59, 77, 79, 88,
    96–97n16, 114–147, 162–166, 173, 204,
    226–227, 244, 247, 288, 299
Hunting Federation
    (Vadászszövetség). *See* National
    Hungarian Hunting Federation

Independent Hungarian Democratic
    Party (Független Magyar
    Demokrata Párt), 41, 100n53
Independent Smallholders' Party
    (Független Kisgazda Párt).
    See Smallholders' Party
Independent Smallholders', Agrarian
    Workers' and Civic Party (Független
    Kisgazda Földmunkás és Polgári
    Párt). *See* Smallholders' Party
India, 83
Institute for Party History
    (Párttörténeti Intézet), 269
intelligence. *See* State Security
intelligence agency. *See* State Security
intelligence agent, 87, 177, 184, 188,
    202, 243
intelligence services. *See* State Security
interior, 22, 43–45, 54–55, 61, 96n15,
    102n63, 102n64, 104n97, 104n102,
    109n160, 195, 223, 234, 237, 240,
    260–261, 265–266, 268–269, 271,
    277n68, 282n144
ionic style, 36, 98n29
Iron and Metal Workers' Trade
    Union (Vas- és Fémipari Dolgozók
    Szakszervezete), 48
Iron Curtain, 67, 178, 186, 252
Israel, 83
Istenhegyi Street (Istenhegyi út),
    Budapest, 31

Jászai Mari Square (Jászai Mari tér),
    Budapest, 272
József hill (Józsefhegy), Budapest, 41

Kalocsa, Hungary, 53, 131
Kalocsa folk art (kalocsai
    népművészet), 53
Karlovy Vary, Czech Republic, 79
Károly Boulevard (Károly körút),
    Budapest. *See* Tanács Boulevard
Kaszó(puszta), Hungary, 129, 154n91

INDEX

Katona József Street (Katona József utca), Budapest, 57
Kékestető, Hungary, 78
Kerepesi Avenue (Kerepesi út), Budapest, 89
Kerepesi Cemetery (Kerepesi temető), Budapest, 78, 89–94
Kígyó Street (Kígyó utca), Budapest, 188, 226
Komárom, Hungary, 186
Konsumex foreign trade company (Kosumex Külkereskedelmi Vállalat), 68
Kossuth Lajos Square (Kossuth Lajos tér), Budapest, 37, 79
Kossuth Prize (Kossuth-díj), 201–203, 215–216n94, 216n102, 264
Kossuth Publishing House (Kossuth Kiadó), 79
Kremlin, Moscow, 24, 267
Kútvölgy, Budapest, 77
Kútvölgyi Avenue State Hospital, Budapest. See Kútvölgyi Hospital, 112n214
Kútvölgyi Hospital, Budapest, 77–78, 84–89
Kútvölgyi State Hospital, Budapest. See Kútvölgyi Hospital

Lada cars. See Zhiguli cars
Lake Balaton (Balaton), Hungary, 49–51, 53–54, 158, 188, 205–206
Leányfalu, Hungary, 37, 51–52, 54, 226
Lehel Square (Lehel tér), Budapest, 195
Lenes, Hungary, 128, 139, 142, 154n89, 167
Liberation Square (Felszabadulás tér), Budapest, 253
Liberty Square (Szabadság tér), Budapest, 283
lifestyle, 2, 6, 8–9, 14–16, 20–24, 30, 32–33, 37, 39, 49, 58, 62, 67, 77, 114–115, 122, 128, 136, 181, 193–195,

221, 224, 234, 237, 265, 268, 288, 290, 293–294, 296–299
Lóránt Street (Lóránt utca), Budapest, 34, 56, 99n42
Louis Seize style, 269
Lovasberény, Hungary, 131
Luxury department store (Luxus Áruház), Budapest, 254
luxury, 2, 6, 21–23, 27n30, 27–28n38, 32, 35, 39, 54, 63, 66, 70, 83, 93, 102n64, 108n160, 136, 188, 193, 226–227, 231–234, 236–238, 240, 252, 254, 297

Mackó (Bear Cub) Hunting Society (Mackó Vadásztársaság), 226
Malév, the Hungarian airline (Magyar Légiközlekedési Vállalat, or MALÉV), 235
manor house, 15, 25, 37, 265, 267, 295, 299–300, 305
Margaret Bridge (Margit híd), Budapest, 272
Margaret Island (Margit-sziget), Budapest, 233, 238
Margaret Wharf (Margit rakpart), Budapest. See Mónus Illás Wharf
Mártonhegyi Street (Mártonhegyi út), Budapest, 57, 96n14
Marx Square (Marx tér), Budapest, 254
Mattie the Pheasant Boy (Fácán Matyi), 134, 153n68, 165
Mátyás király Street (Mátyás király út), Budapest, 87
Ménesi Avenue (Ménesi út), Budapest, 188
Mercedes-Benz cars, 68, 70–71, 73, 108n155, 140, 159, 179
Merci. See Mercedes-Benz cars
Merkur state automobile commercial enterprise (Merkur állami autókereskedelmi vállalat), 68, 73
Metropol Hotel (Metropol Szálló), Budapest, 233

Metropolitan Council (Fővárosi Tanács), 47
Mexico, 83
Mexikói Street (Mexikói út), Budapest, 57
Mezőföld, Hungary, 131
middle class, lower class, upper middle class, 27n25, 30–32, 37, 41, 49–50, 55–56, 59–60, 62, 116, 194, 195, 218n21, 245–246, 288, 296, 302n19
militia (munkásőrség), 133, 200, 216n100
ministerial line, or M Line (minisztériumi vonal, or M vonal), 78
Ministry of Agriculture (Földművelésügyi Minisztérium), 40, 120, 122, 148n6, 148–149n10, 291
Ministry of Agriculture and Food (Mezőgazdasági és Élelmezésügyi Minisztérium), 123, 131, 138–139, 146, 154n94, 211n53
Ministry of Defense (Honvédelmi Minisztérium), 182–183, 211n53, 285n176
Ministry of Domestic Trade (Belkereskedelmi Minisztérium), 232
Ministry of Foreign Affairs (Külügyminisztérium), 67, 183, 227, 256, 259, 263
Ministry of Foreign Trade (Külkereskedelmi Minisztérium), 70, 101n55
Ministry of Internal Affairs (Belügyminisztérium), 47, 53, 63, 71, 75, 87, 107n139, 184, 186, 211n53, 228–230, 243, 245, 270, 272, 277n72, 277n78, 286n180
Ministry of the Interior (Belügyminisztérium). *See* Ministry of Internal Affairs

Ministry of Transportation (Közlekedésügyi Minisztérium), 63
Ministry of Transportation and Postal Affairs (Közlekedés- és Postaügyi Minisztérium), 108n153
Mirthful Stage (Vidám Színpad), Budapest, 261
Model House (Modellház), Budapest, 253
Modern Architecture Club (Új Építészet Köre), 36
Módi boutique (Módi butik), 254
Mónus Illés Wharf (Mónus Illés rakpart), Budapest, 196, 213n76
Moscow, Russia, 75–76, 101n54, 118, 193, 244, 252, 280n114
Moskvitch cars, 68, 108n147
Munkácsy Mihály Street (Munkácsy Mihály utca), Budapest, 51, 225–226
Munkácsy Street (Munkácsy utca), Budapest. *See* Munkácsy Mihály Street
Munkásállam (Workers' state), 171, 272–273
Museum Café (Múzeum Kávéház), Budapest, 223
Museum of Applied Arts (Iparművészeti Múzeum), Budapest, 280n114
Museum of Hungarian Agriculture (Magyar Mezőgazdasági Múzeum), Budapest, 126, 151n47
Museum of the Hungarian Workers' Movement (Magyar Munkásmozgalmi Múzeum), Budapest, 272

Nádor Street (Nádor utca), Budapest, 269
Nagymező Street (Nagymező utca), Budapest, 64
Nap Hill (Naphegy), Budapest, 31
narcissism, 22–23

INDEX 339

National Association of Small
  Tradesmen (Országos Kisiparosok
  Szövetsége, or OKISZ), 254
National Casino (Nemzeti Kaszinó),
  119
National Commandership of the Board
  of Customs and Excise (Vám- és
  Pénzügyőrség), 70
National Commandership of the
  Workers' Militia (Munkásőrség
  Országos Parancsnoksága), 87
National Committee for Physical
  Education and Sports (Országos
  Testnevelési és Sportbizottság), 182,
  209n15, 210n28, 210n29
National Council of
  Agricultural Cooperatives
  (Termelőszövetkezetek Országos
  Tanácsa, or TOT), 145
National Council of Trade Unions
  (Szakszervezetek Országos Tanácsa,
  or SZOT), 151n48, 198, 212n62,
  214n86
National Hotel (Nemzeti Szálló),
  Budapest, 233
National Hotel Enterprise
  (Szállodaipari Nemzeti Vállalat), 233
National Hungarian Hunting
  Federation (Magyar Vadászok
  Országos Szövetsége, or MAVOSZ),
  154n95, 145
National Official Health Service
  Foundation (Országos Társadalom
  Biztosítási Tisztviselő Alap, or
  OTBA), 84
National Planning Office (Országos
  Tervhivatal), 35–36, 285n176, 296
National Savings Bank (Országos
  Takarékpénztár), 48, 139
National Society of Hungarian
  Gentlewomen (Magyar
  Úriasszonyok Nemzeti Szövetsége),
  119

National Theater (Nemzeti Színház),
  Budapest, 40
National Tourist Hotel and Restaurant
  Company (Országos Idegenforgalmi
  Szálloda és Éttermi Vállalat), 228
Nazi, 7, 31
Németvölgyi Street (Németvölgyi út),
  Budapest, 31
neo-baroque, 43–45, 55, 98n31, 133, 261,
  264–268
neo-classical, 268
Nepal, 83
nepman (nepper), 181
Newspaper Publishing Company
  (Lapkiadó Vállalat), 222
New York Café (New York Kávéház),
  221–223
New York, 242
"Nimród women," 124, 165
Nimród Youth Hunting Society,
  124, 147
nobility, 37, 114, 133, 265, 293
nomenclature (nómenklatúra), 24,
  26n11, 28n41, 122, 176, 204, 245, 250
nomenclature law, 52
Nomenclaturia. See nomenclature
Novi Kneževac (Törökkanizsa), Serbia
Nyugati Square (Nyugati tér),
  Budapest. See Marx Square

object (objektum), 10, 38, 229–230
Officers' Club of the People's Army
  (Néphadsereg Tiszti Klub),
  Budapest. See Officers' House of the
  People's Army
Officers' House of the People's
  Army (Néphadsereg Tiszti Háza),
  Budapest, 133, 251
Old Buda (Óbuda), Budapest, 30, 44,
  155n96
Olympic Games, 34, 182, 210n29
opera, Opera House (opera,
  Operaház), Budapest, 191, 263

Operetta Theater (Operettszínház),
    Budapest, 184–185
Orsó Street (Orsó utca), Budapest, 36,
    98n34
Országos Parancsnoksága), 70
Őszöd, Hungary. See Balatonőszöd

P70 model. See Trabant cars
pálinka. See Hungarian fruit brandy
Pannónia Restaurant and Buffet
    Company (Pannónia Éttermi és
    Büfé Vállalat). See Restaurant and
    Buffet Company
Panoráma Hotel (Panoráma Szálló),
    Budapest. See Red Star
Pantheon of the Workers' Movement
    (Munkásmozgalmi Pantheon),
    Budapest, 89–90, 93–94
paprika potato (paprikáskrumpli), 46
PARCOL-American Skinfood, 249
Park Hotel (Park Szálló), Budapest, 233
Party College (Pártfőiskola), 87
party garage (pártgarázs), 73
Pasha Meadow (Pasarét), Budapest,
    30–32, 37, 195
Pécs, Hungary, 154n85, 235, 284n150
Persian rugs, 43, 55, 177, 234, 257, 290
Pest, Budapest, 30, 232
Peugeot cars, 68
Pheasant Garden (Fácánoskert),
    Budapest, 31
Pierre Cardin, 254
Pobeda, 66, 241
Politburo (Politbüro, Politikai
    Bizottság). See Political Commitee
Political Committee (Politikai
    Bizottság), 17, 70, 120–122, 135,
    138–140, 144–145, 151n48, 153n82,
    154n94, 176, 204–207, 209n9,
    219n128, 225–226, 249, 272, 290
Political Main Group Directorate
    (Politikai Főcsoportfőnökség), 182
power, 4, 6–7, 15–17, 19–20, 23–25

Presidential Council (Elnöki Tanács),
    60, 82, 86, 92, 121, 123, 126, 132, 203,
    227, 241, 270, 283n148, 284n151
prostitute, 78, 202, 241–244
protocol, 54, 65–66, 70–72, 80–81, 120,
    137, 140, 146, 153n79, 159, 180,
    227–229, 231–232, 258, 260, 262, 295
Public Building Planning Institute
    (Középülettervező Intézet), 267,
    276n66, 286n179
pufajkás, 200–201, 216n100
puritanical, 43, 136, 297
Pusztaszer, Hungary, 127

Rába factory (Rába-gyár), 71
Radetzky March (Radetzky-induló), 25
Rajkó Orchestra of the Young
    Communist League Cultural
    Ensemble (KISZ Művész Együttes
    Rajkó Zenekara), 53
Rákóczi Avenue (Rákóczi út),
    Budapest, 254
Red Flag (Vörös Lobogó).
    See Budapest Football Club of the
    Hungarian Athletes' Circle
Red Shirt Ensemble (Red Shirt
    Együttes), 69
Red Star Hotel (Vörös Csillag Szálló),
    Budapest, 233
Renault cars, 68
Representative Hospitality Industry
    Company (Reprezentatív
    Vendéglátóipari Vállalat), 221
resorts, 49–54, 57, 87, 95n13, 97n25, 158,
    201, 224–225
Restaurant and Buffet Company
    (Éttermi és Büfé Vállalat), 226, 229
Rolls Royce cars, 62
Röltex network (Rövidáru és
    Lakástextil Kiskereskedelmi
    Vállalat, or Röltex, or), 253
Római-part (Roman shore), Budapest,
    51

INDEX   341

Romania, 114, 175, 293–294
romantic, romanticist, 5, 36, 55, 98n29, 264
Rose Hill (Rózsadomb), Budapest, 30–32, 36, 41–43, 96n15, 195
Royal Hotel (Royal Szálló), Budapest, 233, 235–237, 241–242, 245, 276n56, 277n75
Royal Hungarian Automobile Club (Királyi Magyar Automobil Club, or KMAC). See Auto Club
Royal palace (Királyi Palota, Budavári Palota), Budapest, 265, 267–271
Rózsa Street (Rózsa utca), Budapest, 57
Rózsadomb Restaurant (Rózsadomb Étterem), 228
rule, 19–20, 23
ruling class, 15–16, 218n21
ruling elite. See elite

Safari Club International, 147, 156
sailing, 53
Sándor Palace (Sándor-palota), Budapest, 270, 272, 286n179, 251
Sarolta Street (Sarolta utca), Budapest, 76, 111n184
Savaria Grand Hotel (Savaria Nagyszálló), Szombathely, 264
Savaria Orchestra (Savaria Tánczenekar), 265
secret police. See State Security
secret service. See State Security
show trial, 40, 58, 92, 290
"silver arrow" (Ezüstnyíl), special train, 171
Skála Budapest Grand Department Store (Skála Budapest Nagyáruház), 254
Skála Metro Department Store (Skála Metro Áruház), 254
Škoda cars, 66, 68, 108n147
Slovakia, 218n121, 243

Smallholders' Party (Kisgazda Párt), 62, 115, 117
S-Modell (S-Modell chain, S-Modell Studio), 254
snack bar, 51, 64
Snagov, Romania, 292, 294
soccer, 67, 119, 139, 167, 173–178, 180–182, 185–190, 210n29, 211n53, 250
social class, 15–16, 20–22, 25n2, 28–29n44, 30–32, 61–62, 122, 133, 173, 195, 197, 211n54, 299, 302n20
social status, 21, 31, 255
Sole Mio bar, 243
South America, 183, 186
Soviet elite, soviet nomenclature, soviet leadership, 24, 28n41, 288, 289, 291
Soviet Union, 24, 66, 79, 101n54, 101n55, 106n128, 112n227, 132, 160, 174, 182, 209n6, 215n91, 253, 261, 289
Spain, 104n96186
Specialty Women's Clothing Salon (Különlegességi Női Ruhaszalon). See Clara Salon
Spokane, Washington, 83
Sports Club of Iron and Metal Workers (Vas- és Fémmunkások Sport Clubja, or Vasas), 189–190
spy, 245
stadium, 174–175, 190
Stalin Street/Avenue. See Andrássy Avenue
State Casino (Országos Kaszinó), 119
State Commission for Unclaimed Property (Elhagyott Javak Kormánybiztossága), 32, 95n10
State Forestry and Wildlife Reserve (Állami Erdő- és Vadgazdaság), 131, 137, 152n65, 154n89
State Forestry Works (Magyar Állami Erdőgazdasági Üzemek, or MÁLLERD), 116, 148n6, 149n15

State Office for Church Affairs (Állami Egyházügyi Hivatal), 66
State Security (Államvédelmi Osztály, or ÁVO, Államvédelmi Hatóság, or ÁVH, later Állambiztonság), 32–34, 36, 38–40, 47, 55, 57–58, 64–65, 69, 74–75, 86–87, 95n13, 99n42, 99n44, 104n102, 112n214, 118, 120, 132, 175, 177, 184–186, 196, 200–201, 210n38, 214n78, 229–231, 236, 242–244, 246, 248, 250–251, 263, 276n56, 277n78, 278n88, 279n95, 283n148, 290, 301n9
Stefánia Palace (Stefánia Palota), Budapest, 133
Street of Flavors (Ízek Utcája) restaurant, Budapest, 241
Swabian Hill (Svábhegy), Budapest, 2, 32, 35, 177
swimming pool, 40–42, 51, 61, 74
Switzerland, 86
Sylvanus Hunting Society (Sylvanus Vadásztársaság), 146
Symphonia cigarettes, 43
Symphonic Orchestra of the Ministry of the Interior Cultural Ensemble (BM Művész Együttes Szimfonikus Zenekara), 53
Szabolcs County (Szabolcs megye), Hungary. *See* Szabolcs-Szatmár-Bereg County
Szabolcs-Szatmár-Bereg County (Szabolcs-Szatmár-Bereg megye), Hungary, 143
Szabó Hotel, Budapest, 233
Szabó József Street (Szabó József utca), Budapest, 34–35, 56
Széchenyi Street (Széchenyi utca), Budapest, 57
Szelce (Selci Đakovački), Croatia, 201
Személynök Street (Személynök utca), 57
Szemlőhegy Street (Szemlőhegy utca), Budapest, 48

Szemlő Hill (Szemlőhegy), Budapest, 76
Szilágyi Erzsébet Avenue (Szilágyi Erzsébet fasor), Budapest, 238
Szinpetri, Hungary, 115
Szögliget, Hungary, 114, 148n7
Szombathely, Hungary, 264, 284n153, 217n112
"Swiss-style," 36, 98n28, 98n29

Tanács Boulevard (Tanács körút), Budapest, 254
Tapolcsányi Street (Tapolcsányi utca), Budapest, 262
Tatra cars, 185
taxi, 72, 109n165, 241
Telki, Hungary, 131–132, 136, 152n65, 162, 164, 166
Temporary Executive Committee (Ideiglenes Intéző Bizottság), 79, 302n19
Tihany, Hungary, 51, 206–207
Tököl, Hungary, 75
Trabant cars, 68
Transportation and Technical Enterprise of the Party Administration and Management Division (Pártgazdasági és Ügykezelési Osztály Közlekedési és Műszaki Vállalata), 2, 72
Transylvania, Romania, 114
travel abroad, 79–84, 177, 251
Treaty of Trianon, 114, 148n5
Tretyakov Gallery, 252, 280n114
Trombita street (Trombita utca), Budapest, 48
trophies, 77, 126–128, 140–141, 150n46, 151n47, 179

Újpesti Dózsa soccer team, 211n53
Újpest Wharf (Újpest rakpart), Budapest, 57
United States of America, 28n38, 83, 86, 182, 201, 249, 257

vacation homes, 30–31, 35, 49–54, 61, 110–111n184, 188
Váci Avenue (Váci út), Budapest, 196
Váci Street (Váci utca), Budapest, 248, 250, 280n102, 296
Vadcoop Hunting Society (Vadcoop Vadásztársaság), 147
Veránka, Hungary, 132
Verseny Department Store (Verseny Áruház), Budapest, 254
Vértes Hills (Vértes hegység), Hungary, 79, 299
Victory sailing boat (Győzelem vitorláshajó), 53
Vienna, Austria, 25, 67, 69–70, 107n139, 178, 186, 188, 200, 249
Vienna Circle, 200
villa, 2, 13, 30–56, 61, 74–75, 77, 90, 95n13, 96n15, 97n25, 97, 27, 97n28, 97n29, 98n34, 98n53, 98n54, 104n96, 104–105n102, 110n184, 133, 152n65, 157–158, 188, 194, 224, 246–247, 290, 292, 302n20
Visegrád, Hungary, 131
Visegrád hills (Visegrádi hegység), Hungary, 51
Volkswagen cars, 62
Vörösmarty patisserie (Vörösmarty cukrászda), Budapest, 229
Vörösmarty Square (Vörösmarty tér), Budapest, 254

wages, 59–60, 65, 96n15, 105n117, 198
Warsaw, Poland, 71
Wartburg cars, 68, 108n147
Washington, DC, 257
Wekerle Estate (Wekerle telep), Budapest, 195, 213n73
Western Train Station (Nyugati Pályaudvar), Budapest, 254
Wildlife Management Supervisory Main Department (Vadgazdaság-felügyeleti Főosztály), 139
working class, 89, 108n143, 116, 148n10, 174–175, 190–192, 194, 196–198, 204–205, 207–208, 208n1, 213n67, 213n70, 234, 238, 258, 264, 281n124, 292, 296, 302n13

Yugoslavia, 132, 151n47, 182, 201, 255

Zakopane, Poland, 79
Zánka Pioneer Orchestra (Zánkai Úttörőzenekar), 53
Zeppelin cars, 62
ZIM cars, 66
ZIS cars, 66
Zhiguli cars, 68, 73, 144
zoo, 140, 154n85, 230
Zsolnay Manufacture (Zsolnay-gyár), 91
Zsolnay porcelain, 237
Zugliget, Budapest, 32, 37
Zugló, Budapest, 34, 55

INDEX OF NAMES

Aczél, György (1917–1991), politician, 44–46, 83, 93, 102n64, 124–125, 293
Aczél, Tamás (1921–1994), poet, writer, and journalist, 181
Ady, Endre (1877–1919), poet and writer, 222
Alpár, Ignác (1855–1928), architect, 32
Altai Emil, hunter, 116
Apró, Antal (1913–1994), politician, 48, 93, 120, 126, 192–193, 290
Arató, Mrs. Ferenc, manager of fashion salon, 250
Archduke Joseph August Viktor Klemens Maria of Austria (1872–1962), military officer and politician, 262
Asturias, Miguel Ángel (1899–1974), Guatemalan writer, 223–224, 274n13

"Babik," fictional literary character, 199–200, 216n95
Bácsi, József (1926–2015), organized workers' leader, 216n98
Balassa, Gyula (1903–1974), lawyer, politician, 120, 283n148
Balázs, Béla (1884–1949), writer and poet, 92

"Balikó Mária," state security code name, 243
Balogh, István (1894–1976), Roman Catholic priest, 41, 56, 100n53
Bata, István (1910–1982), politician and officer, 42, 100–101n54, 101n55, 110n84, 182, 210n28
Batthyány, Lajos (1807–1849), politician and statesman, 90
Bedny, Demyan (1883–1945), Soviet poet, 199, 215n91
Beér, János (1905–1966), lawyer, 284n150
Benkei, András (1923–), politician, 71, 120
Benkő, Imre (1943–), photographer, 203
Benkő, Mátyás, Viennese merchant, 188
Berda, Ernő (1914–1961), painter and graphic artist, 196
Berecz, János (1930–), politician, 42, 102n59
Berek, János, hunter, 132, 152–153n66, 154n89
Berényi, Mrs. Kálmán, caretaker of hunting lodge, 10, 136

INDEX OF NAMES

Bernáth, Aurél (1895–1982), painter, 171, 272–273
Bibó, István (1911–1979), lawyer, civil servant, politician, and political theorist, 24
Biszku, Béla (1921–), politician, 44, 71, 121, 125, 126, 135, 226
Boda, György, Mátyás Rákosi's bodyguard, 65
Bokassa, Jean-Bédel (1921–1996), African politician, 82
Bokros Birman, Dezső (1889–1965), painter and sculptor, 196
Bolz, Lothar (1903–1986), East German politician, 259
Bordás, András (1921–1956), lathe operator, Stakhanovite, 200
Bozsik, József (1925–1978), soccer player, trainer, 177, 181–182, 187–188
Brázay, Zoltán (1875–1951), tycoon, 50
Brezhnev, Leonid Ilyich (1906–1982), Soviet politician, First Secretary, 71
Brutyó, János (1911–1987), politician, 106n120
Budisavljević, Nada, Jovanka Tito's younger sister, 255
Budyonny, Semyon Mikhailovich (1883–1973), Soviet marshal, 258
Bukharin, Nikolai Ivanovich (1888–1938), Soviet politician and political theorist, 17

Canetti, Elias, 180
Castro Ruz, Fidel (1926–), Cuban politician, First Secretary, head of government, and head of state, 164
Charles I, Karl Franz Joseph Ludwig Hubert Georg Otto Maria (1887–1922), Emperor of Austria, King of Hungary, 270
Che Guevara de la Serna, Ernesto Rafael (1928–1967), Argentine-born, Cuban revolutionary, politician, physician, 169
Churchill, Sir Winston Leonard Spencer (1874–1965), British politician, prime minister, 78
Csányi, Sándor (1953–), financial expert, 139
Csapó, Andor (1901–?), state security officer, 33, 40, 55, 95n13, 96n14, 97–98n27, 104n101
Csémi, Károly (1922–1992), politician and military officer, 150n46, 88
Csergő, János (1920–1980), politician, 204
Cservenka, Mrs. Ferenc, born Ilona Székely (1918–2010), politician, 53
Cseterki, Lajos (1921–1983), politician, 121, 126, 150n46
Czapik, Gyula (1887–1956), Roman Catholic priest, Archbishop of Eger, 26n4
Czibor, Zoltán (1929–1997), soccer player (left-winger), 183–186, 209n15, 210n38
Czinege, Lajos (1924–1998), politician and military officer, 93, 121, 129, 150n46, 154n91
Czóbel, Béla (1883–1976), painter, 43
Czottner, Sándor (1903–1980), politician, 92, 97–98n27

Dapsi Károly (1917–2001), politician, 264
Darvas, József (1912–1973), writer, politician, 53, 185, 263–264
Dékán, István (1919–1975), state security officer, 243–244, 248, 278n81
Dénes, István (1914–?), state security officer, hunter, 40
Dénes, István (1923–2005), politician, 42, 101n55, 152–153
Derkovits, Gyula (1894–1934), painter and graphic artist, 43

INDEX OF NAMES

Dési Huber, István (1895–1944), painter and graphic artist, 92
Dinnyés, Lajos (1901–1961), politician, prime minister, 62, 266
Djilas, Milovan (1911–1995), Yugoslav politician and writer, born in Montenegro, 78
Dobi, István (1898–1968), politician, head of government, and head of state, 63, 82, 92, 115, 117, 283n148, 284n151
Döbrentei, Mrs. Aranka Károly, born Aranka Némety (1913–1987), politician, 284n150
Donáth, Ferenc (1913–1986), politician, 118, 211n54
Drapcsik, István (1916–), chauffeur, 65
Dudinszki László, landowner, hunter, 116

Egri, Gyula (1923–1972), politician, 181, 210n28
Egry, József (1883–1951), painter, 43, 102n64
Eichmann, Adolf Otto (1906–1962), SS lieutenant general, 31
Elias, Norbert, 22
Erdei, Ferenc (1910–1971), sociologist, politician, 258, 291
Erdélyi, Jenő, officer, 184–187
Epstein, Mihail, 4
Esterházy family, nobility family, 265–266
Esterházy, László (1891–1966), landowner, politician, and hunter, 116–117

Falus, Elek (1884–1950), graphic artist and painter, 266
Farkas, István, translator, 237
Farkas, Mihály (1904–1965), politician, 26n4, 35, 38, 97n21, 112n227, 116, 118, 149n22, 174, 177, 183, 218n121, 225, 228, 283n148, 289, 293, 301n6

Fehér, Lajos (1917–1981), journalist, politician, 71, 117, 121, 125–126, 151n48
Feiszt, Ottó, hunter and hunting writer, 10, 125, 144
Fejti, György (1946–), politician, 145
Finta, József (1935–), architect, 238
Flach, János (1902–1965), interior designer, 268–269, 285n170
Fock, Jenő (1916–2001), politician, 71, 121, 124–125, 131, 150n46
Földes László (1914–2000), politician, 79, 83, 120–121, 126, 129, 150n46
Földes, László (Hobo) (1945–), performing artist, 10, 129
Földes, Mihály (1905–1984), writer and journalist, 284n150
Franz Joseph I (1830–1916), Emperor of Austria, King of Hungary, 90

Gábor, Andor (1884–1953), poet and writer, 66, 94
Ganzel, Irén, director of the Rákosi Children's Home, 289
Garamvölgyi, Ágoston (1928–2012), soccer player, goalkeeper, 186
Gáspár, Sándor (1917–2002), politician and trade union officer, 48, 296, 67, 121, 124, 125, 135, 150n46, 151n48, 154n89, 226
Gerő, Ernő (1898–1980), politician, First Secretary, 35, 63, 84, 97n21, 97–98n27, 112n227, 118–119, 149n22, 149n24, 176, 182, 194, 210n27, 212n64, 218n121, 283n148, 285n165, 289, 301n6
Gömbös, Gyula (1886–1936), politician, prime minister, 89
Göncz, Árpád (1922–2015), writer, translator of literary works, president of Hungary, 82
Gonda, György (1923–2000), politician, 264
Gosztonyi, János (1925–1985), politician, 264

INDEX OF NAMES 347

Grósz, Károly (1930–1996), politician, Secretary General, and head of government, 93, 143–145, 207, 219n128, 219n129, 272, 292–293
Groza, Petru (1884–1958), Romanian politician, head of government, 61
Gyarmati, György, historian, 205

Habermas, Jürgen, 22, 274n3
Hajduska, István, journalist, 180
Hašek, Jaroslav (1883–1923), Czech writer, 45
Hatvany, Ferenc (1881–1958), painter and art collector, 117
Háy, Gyula (1900–1975), writer and translator of literary works, 294–295, 302n20
Hazai Jenő (1921–1998), politician, 182, 210n28
Házi, Árpád (1908–1970), politician, 284n150
Hegedüs, András (1922–1999), politician, head of government, 35, 74–77, 80, 111n185, 114, 218n121, 247, 279n98, 290–291, 300n6, 301n9
Hegedüs, Mrs. András, born Zsuzsanna Hölzel (1922–1998), communist resistant during the war, András Hegedüs's wife, married in 1947, 75–76, 247
Hermann, György, carpenter, 240
Hess, Rudolf (1894–August 1987), Nazi politician, deputy Führer, 127, 150n46
Hetényi, Károly, headwaiter, 10, 222
Hofi, Géza (1936–2002), humorist, 134, 166
Homm, Pál (1907–1987), actor, 185
Horthy, István (1904–1942), deputy regent, regent Miklós Horthy's elder son, 31, 62
Horthy, Miklós (1868–1957), naval officer, politician, regent, 6, 62, 71, 82, 84, 116, 132, 266, 268, 278n92, 297

Horthy, Miklós Jr. (1907–1993), regent Miklós Horthy's younger son, 31
Horváth, Ede (1924–1998), company director, 71, 203–207, 218n116, 219n128, 296
Horváth, Géza, musician, 265
Horváth, Márton (1906–1987), politician and journalist, 116–118
Hungler, Géza, carpenter, 240
Huszár, Károly (1882–1941), politician, 89

Idi, Amin Dada (1925–2003), African politician, 82
Ignotus, Pál (1901–1978), publicist, editor, writer, and translator of literary works, 288
Ilku, Pál (1912–1973), politician, 92, 94, 264
Illyés, Gyula (1902–1983), Hungarian poet and writer, 42, 45

Janáky, István Sr. (1901–1966), architect, 267
Jászai, Mari (1850–1926), actress, 272
József, Attila (1905–1937), poet, 92, 94
Justus, Mrs. Pál, born Edith Wagner (1912–1989), activist, politician, 61
Justus, Pál (1905–1965), politician, poet, and translator of literary works, 61

Kádár, János (1912–1989), politician, General Secretary, and head of government, 7, 40–47, 50, 52, 59, 70–72, 80–84, 89, 93, 100–101n54, 101n55, 102n59, 102n61, 102n64, 102n67, 118–126, 130–139, 14–142, 144–145, 150n46, 152–153n66, 157, 160, 162, 165, 171, 189–191, 193, 196, 204, 211n54, 225–226, 239, 252, 266, 271–273, 283n148, 292–294, 296–297
Kádár, Mrs. János, Tamáska Mária (1912–1992), politician, 42–43, 45, 70, 81, 205

Kalinin, Mikhail Ivanovich (1875–1946), Soviet politician, head of state, 17
Kállai, Gyula (1910–1996), politician, 93, 211n54, 225, 227, 258, 302n19
Kalmár-Maron, György (1939–2018), chief doorman, 10, 235–236
Kálnoky, László (1912–1985), poet and translator of literary works, 54
Kamenev, Lev Borisovich (1883–1936), Soviet politician, 17
Karakas, László (1923–1989), politician, 47
Kardos, Dr. Éva (1923–), officer, translator, writer, 243–244, 248, 278n81
Karinthy, Ferenc (1921–1992), writer, 194, 198–199, 215 n94
Karinthy, Frigyes (1887–1938), writer and poet, 194, 222
Károlyi, Mihály (1875–1955), politician, prime minister, 90
Kása, Ferenc, Viennese automobile dealer, 67, 177
Katona, Éva, (1923–2005), István Dénes's wife, 42
Keresztury, Dezső (1904–1996), poet, politician, 45
Khrushchev, Nikita Sergeyevich (1894–1971), Soviet politician, First Secretary, and head of government, 71, 79, 81, 83
Khrushcheva, Nina Petrovna, Kukharchuk (1900–1984), second wife of Khrushchev, 70
Kim Il-sung (1912–1994), North Korean politician, General Secretary, head of state, and head of government, 76
Kisházi, Ödön (1900–1975), politician, 264
Kittenberger, Kálmán (1881–1958), traveller and hunter, 116

Köböl, József (1909–2000), politician, 47, 280n150
Koch, Hugó, technical director, 64
Kónya, Lajos (1914–1972), poet and writer, 34, 38–39
Körner, József (1907–1971), architect, 35, 90, 97n22
Kossa, István (1904–1965), politician, 92, 266
Kossuth, Lajos (1802–1894), politician and statesman, governor-president, 90
Kosztolányi, Dezső (1885–1936), writer and poet, 222
Kotkin, Stephen, 18
Kotsis, Iván (1889–1980), architect, 267
Kozma, Lajos (1884–1948), architect, industrial designer, and graphic artist, 36–37, 98n31
Krestinsky, Nikolay Nikolayevich (1883–1938), Soviet politician, 17
Kucsera, fictional literary character, 294–295, 302n20
Kuczka, Péter (1923–1999), writer and poet, 54, 199

Ladislaus I, Saint Ladislaus (1046–1095), king of Hungary, 258
Lacan, Jacques, 297
Lasswell, Harold, 15
Latabár, Kálmán (1902–1970), actor, 185
Lázár, György (1924–2014), politician, head of government, 141
Lelovich György (1913–1993), landowner, falconer, 116
Lenin, Vladimir Ilyich, Ulyanov (1870–1924), Soviet politician and ideologist, head of government, 17, 28n41, 40, 55
Lessing, Erich (1923–2018), Austrian photographer, 37

INDEX OF NAMES

Lipthay, Béla (1892–1974), landowner, Eugénie Odescalchi's husband, 127
Lombos, Ferenc (1923–2011), politician, 206, 207
Losonczi, Pál (1919–2005), politician. Head of state, 81–82, 121, 241
Losonczy, Géza (1917–1957), journalist, politician, 39, 225
Louis I, Louis the Great (1306–1382), king of Hungary, 258
Lukács, György (1885–1971), philosopher and aesthetician, 92

Madách, Imre (1823–1864), lawyer, writer, and poet, 55
Mádl, Ferenc (1931–2011), legal scholar, politician. President of Hungary, 82
Major, Tamás (1910–1986), actor, theater director, 40
Mándy, Iván (1918–1995), writer, 119
Marosán, György (1908–1992), politician, 44, 80, 93, 283n148, 296
Marton, Károly, expert in the hospitality industry, 10, 135
Mata Hari, Margaretha Geertruida Zelle (1876–1917), Dutch exotic dancer, executed as a spy, 242
Matthias I, Matthias Corvinus, Mátyás Hunyadi (1443–1490), king of Hungary, 268
Merán, Fülöp (1926–), hunting writer, 13–14, 25, 25n2, 299, 303n27
Méray Tibor (1924–2020), journalist and writer, 181
Meskál, Tibor (1943–), duty hotel manager, 10, 237
Meštrović, Ivan (1883–1962), Croatian sculptor and architect, 255
Mihályfi, Ernő (1898–1972), politician and journalist, 271
Minarik, Ede, fictional film character, 119

Mindszenty, József (1892–1975), Roman Catholic prelate, 14, 26n4, 257
Molnár, Erik (1894–1966), lawyer, historian, and politician, 92
Molnár, Imre (1928–?), lawyer, politician, 284n150
Münnich, Ferenc (1886–1967), politician. Head of government, 92, 161, 176
Muszka, Imre (1914–?), turner, Stakhanovite, 192–195, 198–203, 212n60, 213n70, 214n88, 215n94, 217n112

Nagy, Endre (1913–1994), hunter, 117–118, 149n20
Nagy, Imre (1896–1958), politician, head of government, 36–38, 93, 98n34, 100n53, 149n12, 225, 273, 278–279n92, 292–294, 302n19
Nánási, László (1906–1985), journalist, politician, 289
Németh, Károly (1922–2008), politician, head of state, 121, 135, 151n48
Németh, Miklós (1948–), politician, head of government, 190, 211n53
Neruda, Pablo, Neftali Ricardo Reyes Basoalto (1904–1973), Chilean poet, 223–224, 274n13
Neuschloss, Marcell (1853–1905), construction entrepreneur, 31
Neuschloss, Ödön (1851–1904), construction entrepreneur, 31
Nezvál, Ferenc (1909–1987), politician, 121, 158
Nimrod (Nimród), biblical figure, 134, 146
Nógrádi, Sándor (1894–1971), politician, 243, 283n148
Novotný, Antonin Josef (1904–1975), Czech politician, First Secretary, and head of state, 229

Odescalchi, Eugénie (1898–1985), memoir writer, 127
Olcsai-Kiss, Zoltán (1895–1981), sculptor, 90
Olt, Károly (1904–1985), politician, 94, 262, 284n150
Onódy, Lajos (1920–1996), hotel industry specialist, 226–227
Orbán, László (1912–1978), politician, 44
Orbán, Viktor (1963–), politician, prime minister, 139
Örkény, István (1912–1979), writer, 199, 200, 216n95
Ortutay, Gyula (1910–1978), ethnographer and politician, 263

Pallavicini, Alfonz (1807–1875), margrave, landowner, 127
Pap, Gyula (1899–1983), painter and industrial designer, 196
Pap, János (1925–1994), politician, 54, 121, 154n89, 238
Papp, László (1926–2003), boxer (middleweight and light middleweight), 34, 67
Pareto, Vilfredo Federico Damaso, 15
Peidl, Gyula (1873–1943), politician, 89
Péter, Gábor (1906–1993), politician and head of state security, 35, 39–41, 57–58, 96n14, 97n27, 99n44, 100n52, 243, 246, 283n148
Péter, György (1903–1969), economist, 249, 279n98
Péter, János (1910–1999), Presbyterian minister and politician, 259
Pióker, Ignác (1907–1988), worker, Stakhanovite, 202–203, 216n94, 218n115
Piros, László (1917–2006), politician, 110n184, 180, 212n64
Poenaru, Florin, 175

Pozsgay, Imre (1933–2016), politician, 125
Prieszol, József (1906–1965), politician, 284n150
Pünkösti, Árpád, journalist, sociographer, 42, 64, 240
Puskás, Ferenc (1927–2006), soccer player (striker), trainer, 174, 177, 179, 183, 186–190, 210n45

Rácz, Antal (1928–2016), forestry engineer, hunter, department head, 10, 130, 137, 152–153n66
Radnai, Mrs. Pál, state security accountant, 67
Rajk, László (1909–1949), politician, 92, 94, 118, 266, 290–291
Rajk, Mrs. Júlia László, born Júlia Földi (1914–1981), activist, politician, and archivist, 59
Rakeczky, Béla Jr., hunter 10, 125
Rákosi, Mátyás (1892–1971), politician, First Secretary, and head of government, 7, 14, 26n4, 34–35, 37–40, 47, 50, 54, 56, 59, 64–66, 84–85, 92–93, 97n21, 104n96, 112n227, 114, 116–119, 147n2, 152n65,15, 163, 170, 172, 182, 187, 193, 198, 204, 214n88, 218n121, 225–226, 243, 258, 267–269, 271, 288–291, 293, 296, 300n6
Ráth, Károly (1903–1985), journalist and diplomat, 256
Rejtő, Jenő (1905–1943), pulp fiction writer, 237
Révai, József (1898–1959), politician, publicist, 35, 92, 97, 112n227, 118, 149n22, 218n121, 289, 301n6
Ries, István (1885–1950), lawyer and politician, 284n150
Rippl-Rónai, József (1861–1927), painter, 43
Romhányi, József (1921–1983), poet and writer, 261

INDEX OF NAMES

Rónai, Sándor (1892–1965), politician, 92, 94
Rosenberger, Pál, hunter, 10, 130
Rostás, Péter, art historian, 10, 102, 268
Rotschild, Klára (1903–1976), fashion designer, 250–251, 255–256

Ságvári, Endre (1913–1944), leftist activist, 92
Salamon, Béla (1885–1965), actor, 261, 282n146
Sallai, Károly, musician, 265
Sándor, József (1911–1985), politician, 44
Sándor, László (1910–1988), politician, 284n150
Sándor, Móric (1805–1878), politician, landowner, 131
Sándor, Pál (1939–), film director, 119
Sárdy, János (1907–1969), singer and actor, 185
Schiffer, Mrs. Klára Pál, born Klára Szakasits (1918–), memoir writer, Árpád Szakasits's daughter and politician Pál Schiffer's wife, 61, 262, 289
Schiffer, Pál (1911–2001), politician, 289
Schmidt, Helmut Heinrich Waldemar (1918–2015), West German politician, chancellor, 126
Schmidt, Miksa (1861/1866–1935), art dealer and owner of a furniture factory, 265
Schnitta, Sámuel, expert in the hospitality industry, 234
Schwarz, smuggler, 181–186
Sebes, Gusztáv (1906–1986), soccer player, trainer, 179–180, 189, 209n15
Sebes, Sándor (1902–1999), politician, 249
Shvoy, Lajos (1879–1968), Roman Catholic priest and county bishop, 26n4

Sík, Endre (1891–1978), politician, 68, 92, 169, 257, 259, 281n124
Simmel, Georg, 20
Simon, Blanka (1878–1959), journalist 260–261
Sólyom, László (1942–), legal scholar. President of Hungary 82
Somlyó, György (1920–2006), poet, writer, and translator of literary works, 224
Somogyi, László, expert in the hospitality industry, 10, 228, 242
Spencer, Herbert, 20
Stakhanov, Alexey Grigoryevich (1906–1977), miner, Stakhanovite, 191, 199
Stalin, Joseph Vissarionovich (1879–1953), politician, General Secretary, and head of government, 17, 55, 79, 193, 212n55, 213n70, 215n91
Stephen I, Saint Stephen (975–1038), king of Hungary, 258
Strauss, Franz Joseph (1915–1988), West German politician, prime minister of Bavaria, 126
Strauss, Johann Jr. (1825–1899), Austrian composer, 25
Strauss, Johann (1804–1849), Austrian composer, 25
Sumet, Lajos, colonel, president of the Budapest army team, 185
Švejk, fictional literary figure, 45
Szabó, Anna, architect, 262
Szabó, István (1924–), business executive, 205
Szabó, Lőrinc (1900–1957), poet and translator of literary works, 178
Szakasits, Árpád (1888–1965), politician, 37, 61–62, 92, 94, 212n64, 262, 266, 283n148
Szántó, Zoltán (1893–1977), politician, 295
Szász, Béla (1910–1999), journalist, 269

INDEX OF NAMES

Szász, Imre (1927–2003), writer, 143
Széchenyi, Zsigmond (1898–1967), traveler and hunter, 45, 57, 116, 125, 130
Székely, Bertalan (1835–1910), painter, 263–264
Szentessy, Zoltán (1924–1982), actor, 185
Szepesi, György (1922–), journalist and sports correspondent, 177, 189
Szirmai, István (1906–1969), politician, 44, 284n150, 293
Szőnyi, István (1894–1960), painter, 43, 102n64
Szűcs, Ernő (1908–1950), state security officer, 58, 110n184
Szűcs, Ferenc (1922–1999), major general, 59, 121, 124–125, 135, 137, 154n89
Szűrös, Mátyás (1933–), politician, 259

Tábori, Kornél (1879–1944), journalist and writer, 50
Tarde, Gabriel, 20
Teleki, József (1900–1985), a certified forestry engineer, 116–117
Teleki, Pál (1879–1941), geographer and politician, 89
Tereshkova, Valentina Vladimirovna (1937–), cosmonaut, 128
Tichy, Lajos (1935–1999), soccer player, trainer, 188
Tildy Zoltán, Jr. (1917–1994), photographer, 117
Tildy, Zoltán (1889–1961), Calvinist minister, politician, 62–63, 115
Tito, Josip Broz (1892–1980), politician, president, head of state, and head of government, 83, 132, 255
Tito, Jovanka, Jovanka Budisavljević Broz (1924–2013), politician and lieutenant colonel, Josip Broz Tito's third wife, 255–256

Tollner, György (1930–2018), hunter, director of hunting reserve, 10, 137
Tömpe, István (1909–1988), politician, 75, 121
Tóth, Árpád (1886–1928), poet, 199
Tóth, Eszter (1920–2001), poet and writer, 199
Tóth, Mihály (1926–1990), soccer player (left-winger), 179, 209n15
Tóth, Sándor, forestry engineer, head of department, 10, 105n114, 120, 122, 135, 139, 141, 155n98
Tóth, Vilmos, historian, 93
Trotsky, Leon, Lev Davidovich Bronstein (1879–1840), Soviet politician and political theorist, 17
Tsedenbal, Yumjaagiin (1916–1991), Mongolian politician, First Secretary, 125–126
Tulgay, Mrs. Ahmed, born Margit Halász, Klára Rotschild's acquaintance, wife of a Turkish diplomat, 251

Urbán, Ernő (1918–1974), poet, writer, and journalist, 264

Vadnai, Tibor, expert in the hospitality industry, 236
Vályi, Péter (1919–1973), politician, 92, 151n48
Váncsa, Jenő (1928–), politician, 10, 134, 138, 145–146
Vándor, Ferenc, accountant for the state security forces, 57
Vas, István (1910–1991), poet and writer, 199
Vas, Mrs. Zoltán, Sára Vadas, doctor, politician, 50, 227
Vas, Zoltán (1903–1983), politician, head of the National Planning Committee, 33, 35–36, 83, 93, 95n13, 97n27, 118, 222, 227, 296

Vedres, Márk (1870–1961), sculptor, 196
Vértes István (1893–1959), politician, 100n53
Villányi, Miklós (1931–), politician, 146
Villon, François, 88
Voslensky, Michael, 17, 24

Weber, Max, 19, 22
Wessely, Erzsébet, milliner's shop manager in Paris, 251
White, Hayden, 5, 7
Wilde, Oscar, 295

Zamushkin, Alexander, director of the Tretyakov Gallery, 10, 252
Zinoviev, Grigory (1883–1936), Soviet politician, 17
Zöld, Sándor (1913–1951), politician, minister, 290–291, 301n9
Zoltán, János, doctor, hunter, 135, 153n68, 154n89
Zsigmond, László (1910–1969), veterinarian and politician, parliamentary representative, 264
Zsofinyecz, Mihály (1906–1986), politician. Minister, 283n148, 284n150
Zsolnay family, porcelain industrial dynasty, 14, 91, 237

GYÖRGY MAJTÉNYI is Social Historian and Professor at Károly Eszterházy University. Between 2000 and 2011, he was Department Head of the National Archives of Hungary.

www.ingramcontent.com/pod-product-compliance
Lightning Source LLC
Chambersburg PA
CBHW031753220426
43662CB00007B/383